STERN'S
Guide to the
GREATEST RESORTS
of the WORLD

Steven B. Stern

Stern's Travel Guides, Ltd.

STERN'S GUIDE TO THE
GREATEST RESORTS OF THE WORLD

2007/2008 Edition

STEVEN B. STERN

Stern's Travel Guides, Ltd.
Boca Raton, Florida 2006

Library of Congress Cataloging-in-Publication Data
Stern, Steven B.
Stern's Guide to the Greatest Resorts of the World / Steven B. Stern
2007/2008 edition

ISBN 0-9778608-0-9
ISBN 9780977860807

l. Resorts—Guidebooks 2. Hotels—Guidebooks 3. Travel—Guidebooks
Title: Greatest Resorts of the World.

Information in this guidebook is based on authoritative data available at the time of printing.
Prices and hours of operation of businesses listed are subject to change without notice.
Readers are asked to take this into account when consulting this guide.

Front cover photographs: *Background courtesy Four Seasons Resorts, Lanai*
Back cover photographs: *courtesy Four Seasons Resort at Troon North, Scottsdale, Arizona; Cap Juluca,*
Anguilla; Las Ventanas Al Paraiso, Cabo San Lucas; Mauna Kea Resort, Hawaii; Four Seasons Resort
at Jimbaran Bay, Bali; Hotel du Cap-Eden Roc, Cap d'Antibes, France; Santa Caterina, Almalfi, Italy;
Bora Bora Lagoon Resort, Tahiti.
Author photo: *courtesy Steven B. Stern*

Printed in Slovakia by Polygraf Print Ltd.

Published by Stern's Travel Guides, Ltd.
Boca Raton, Florida
e-mail: SBS3150@aol.com
Distributed by BookWorld Companies
1941 Whitfield Park Loop
Sarasota, Florida 34243

448 pages; 22 x 28 cm

CONTENTS

CONTENTS

Introduction

Steven B. Stern

Troughout my life, I have found all kinds of travel infectious, a malady of which I hope never to be cured.

Some travelers are ardent sightseers whose vacations would not be complete without visiting noteworthy museums and archeological digs, paying homage to famous churches and monuments, browsing through souvenir shops and flea markets, and exploring every street and byway.

There is a different breed of travelers who prefer to spend their holiday at one sunny haven, devoting their leisure days to swimming, golfing, fishing, playing tennis, jogging, gambling, eating, and drinking. For these non-locomotive hedonists, a deluxe resort is the only real vacation.

Too often, inertia causes these people to return to the same pleasure palace year after year without realizing that the same luxurious facilities can be found elsewhere with a little variety and different flavor thrown in.

This book is dedicated to describing what our civilized world has to offer my non-locomotive, hedonistic soul mates who seek the very best resort hotels that exist today. If I have missed some of your favorites, first forgive, and then drop me a note so that I can explore the possibility of covering them in future editions. In the meantime, I invite you, one and all, to sample my current favorites.

Let us establish our definition of a resort hotel. Often, there is a fine line between a large hotel with a number of facilities and activities and a resort. Where we draw the line is somewhat subjective. In making my selections for this book, I have limited the considerations to self-contained properties where guests come primarily to vacation for longer periods without intending to leave the immediate premises, as opposed to those hotels that cater to transient businessmen or sightseers selecting a base of operations. Also excluded are the large hotels or rental condominiums in resort communities.

In addition, I have concentrated on unique resorts that offer the most luxurious accommodations and atmosphere, and I have excluded the "Club Med" style of complex. Obviously, some of the places included succeed at fulfilling their promise of elegance, service, and so on better than others. High prices are not necessarily synonymous with high quality. I could find no reason other than entrepreneurial greed for the outrageous tariffs charged by some properties.

Many tropical islands and popular resort areas are not represented because they do not offer one single hotel that meets the criteria or standards that I have set to qualify them as one of the greatest resorts of the world. This should not imply that you would not enjoy exploring all the Greek Islands, meandering through seaside cities in Central and South America, or visiting many of the smaller atolls in the South Seas. It indicates only that you will not be able to find the same excellence and comfort that is provided by the establishments herein described.

During the past few years, numerous new luxury resorts have been developed, especially in the United States, the Caribbean, and the Far East. The elegance and expanded facilities provided by some of these newer properties have set new standards of excellence for the resort industry. Sadly, some older properties have not kept pace with the changes, and therefore, they have lost their position in this book to the "new kids on the block." These substitutions are in keeping with our commitment that each new edition of this book will feature what we consider to be the very best resorts in the world.

Steven B. Stern

PART ONE

BEFORE YOU GO

Four Seasons Resort at Jimbaran Bay, Bali

CHAPTER ONE

PLANNING AND BOOKING YOUR TRIP – AND WHAT TO TAKE ALONG

Four Seasons Resort, Maldives

Once you have made the decision to spend your vacation at a resort, the task remains to make a selection, coordinate your arrangements, book the trip, and get ready to go.

First, you must select a location. Do you prefer a lazy island in the Caribbean, a cosmopolitan resort area on the Mediterranean, an exotic retreat in the South Seas, or the more predictable comfort of a pleasure palace in Europe or the United States? The time of year should influence your decision because it will determine the price, as well as whether the climate is suitable. Avoid Europe and the Mediterranean except during the late spring, summer, and early fall; the southeastern United States and the Caribbean during the hurricane season from mid-July through October; and the Far East and South Pacific during the muggy, rainy season, which varies from one area to another. Remember that the seasons in countries south of the equator are the opposite of those in the United States. Nevertheless, budget-minded travelers may wish to consider visiting resorts in their off seasons to take advantage of substantial reductions in rates. If enjoyment of outdoor activities is a priority, however, it may prove to be a serious mistake to go to those locales where the weather is unreliable.

Having selected the general area to which you will travel, your next concern should be where you will stay. To assist you, there are numerous travel guides that concentrate on everything there is to do and see and everywhere there is to eat and reside. By and large, these are broken down into geographic areas so that one individual guide book may cover all of Europe, or South America, the Caribbean, Mexico, Southeast Asia, and so on.

Perusing one of the more popular travel guides will furnish you with a good general background and direction from which to expand your exploration.

At this point, you should have narrowed down your choice to several resorts that appear appealing in the area you have chosen. For each property you are considering, obtain the promotional brochures that describe the accommodations, prices, facilities, and activities of the resort and that contain photographs of the rooms and grounds; or go to the resorts website on the internet. Remember that these are prepared by the hotels for promotional purposes and will tend to make the properties appear more attractive and luxurious than they really are. Additional information can be obtained from your travel agent, and the opinions of friends with similar tastes should also prove helpful. In the following chapter are the specific factors I recommend that travelers consider when making selections and comparing alternatives.

Having selected a resort, you are now ready to make reservations, which must be coordinated with your transportation. Booking space on an airline during busy periods such as Christmas, Easter, and top-of-the-season summer flights to Europe must be done in advance and can be accomplished most expeditiously through a knowledgeable travel agent. At no extra cost to the customer, the travel agent will make the calls, write letters, obtain the tickets, and coordinate the entire trip. However, many employees of these agencies are not as conscientious as you would be, and it is prudent to double check on all the arrangements where practicable.

Should your agent inform you that a particular resort is unavailable during the period requested, consider contacting the resort's reservation department yourself and ask to be placed on their waiting list. The hotel may receive a cancellation and offer it to you directly. Even a resort that, traditionally, is completely booked often has last-minute cancellations. Thus, if you make arrangements at a property nearby and pay only a one-night deposit, it may be possible to switch to your first choice once you arrive. This is one of my favorite ploys, which has proven successful approximately 75 percent of the time. Of course, there is never any guarantee of success, and you must be prepared emotionally for potential disappointment.

Another possibility for those who wish to stay at the best but cannot afford the high tariffs is to make arrangements at a less expensive hotel near the resort of your choice and then spend your days using the facilities and grounds of the more expensive property. This technique may seem too tacky for some of you; however, for those who do not embarrass easily, the fact remains that it is highly unlikely that you ever would be caught because large resorts cannot keep track of all their guests.

When pricing out the various hotels, be aware that rates are lower in the off season. Most resorts in the southern United States, Mexico, Hawaii, and the Caribbean lower their prices significantly between April 15 and December 15 each year. Thus, if you were planning a trip in March, you might be able to save 50 percent by waiting one month. The price lists in appendix B of this book reflect high-season rates. Those traveling off season should obtain the latest prices from the resort. You also will want to compare rates for European Plan (EP), Modified American Plan (MAP), and Full American Plan (FAP). Your decision does not have to be made in advance (unless MAP or FAP is compulsory). When possible, it is advisable to wait until you arrive and have an opportunity to look over the restaurants at the resort and the alternatives in the general area before making your choice.

Having finished all the preliminaries and completed your bookings, it is now time to pack. The technique I prefer is to mentally conduct a dry run of your upcoming trip. Consider the number of days you will be away, how you will be spending your time, and what you will wear during the day, at the beach, for your athletic endeavors, during the evening, and if it rains. Decide how often you are willing to wear the same outfit and to what extent you can coordinate bulky items such as shoes, purses, and jackets with the remainder of your wardrobe so as to cut back on excessive baggage.

Generally, during a one-week trip to a warm-weather resort, you will need three or four dress outfits for the evenings (although more and more upscale resorts have switched to a "country-club" casual' dress code); sufficient undergarments, stockings, and nightwear; shoes, tops, bottoms, and other equipment for sport activities; informal slacks, shorts, shirts, and blouses for during the day; a raincoat, umbrella, and sweater for inclement or cooler weather; and the toiletries, sundries, pills, and medicines you normally require. Finally, don't forget your camera and a good book. When traveling to countries that have no radio or television channels in your native tongue, or to resorts that do not provide radio or television in the rooms, you may wish to bring your own portable radio/cassette/DVD player.If you are traveling to several places or taking numerous airplane flights, you will want to cut back to reduce your load. On transcontinental flights, most airlines limit the number of pieces of luggage you are allowed to check in or carry aboard. It is imperative to check on this with the airline before packing. Generally, men can coordinate several acceptable outfits with one sport jacket or suit in order to avoid the necessity of bringing more than one pair of shoes or of having complete wardrobes in several different colors. Similarly, women can stay with one or two color combinations to avoid bringing too many dress shoes and purses, which monopolize space in suitcases.

Deciding whether or not to take along expensive jewelry is difficult. There is always a chance of theft or disappearance. Hotels will not cover losses in your room — or even in their vaults — over a few hundred dollars. (You would be shocked if you were to read the fine print in the contract you sign when you lease a safe-deposit box.) However, if having an opportunity to display your fine jewelry is a major consideration in choosing a resort-orient-

ed vacation, then be sure you have obtained the proper insurance before leaving home. When deciding what to take along, a good rule of thumb is to make out a preliminary list and then cut it in half.

If you are traveling to several places or taking numerous airplane flights, you will want to cut back to reduce your load. On transcontinental flights, most airlines limit the number of pieces of luggage you are allowed to check in or carry aboard. It is imperative to check on this with the airline before packing. Generally, men can coordinate several acceptable outfits with one sport jacket or suit in order to avoid the necessity of bringing more than one pair of shoes or of having complete wardrobes in several different colors. Similarly, women can stay with one or two color combinations to avoid bringing too many dress shoes and purses, which monopolize space in suitcases.

Cap Juluca, Anguilla

CHAPTER TWO

SELECTING
A RESORT HOTEL

For most of us, vacation time is a precious interlude in our daily lives, from which we wish to get the maximum enjoyment. To avoid disappointments, we need to research the possibilities, investigate what each has to offer and what each will cost, as well as the advantages and disadvantages of each.

What factors, then, should we weigh in our comparison and analysis of resort hotels? I recommend considering the following criteria and suggest that an evaluation of the eight areas covered below will result in an intelligent and satisfying selection.

Location

The great resorts are located in diverse areas of the world, each with its unique, special flavor. If you could be assured of similar accommodations, facilities, price, and service, then the only difference would be the location, which would dictate atmosphere, fellow guests, and environs. North Americans who require that the atmosphere and environs be as close as possible to home will prefer a resort in the continental United States, while those who desire informality, natural beauty, and a more restful atmosphere will prefer the Caribbean, Hawaii, the South Seas, the Indian Ocean, the Far East, and Mexico. Resorts in Europe tend to be more formal and cosmopolitan, frequented by guests from all corners of the globe; on the other hand most resorts in the Middle East and many in the Far East are merely respites for travelers committed to more hectic itineraries.

It is important to check out the temperature and rainfall in each location for the month that you plan to travel. Although resorts in the tropics often boast warm weather through the year, they do have rainy seasons. Nothing can be duller and more frustrating than spending a week without sun and without being able to indulge in your favorite sport because of inclement weather.

Cities in southern Europe that border the Mediterranean and cities in the southern United States may have mild winters. However, weather conducive to swimming and other outdoor activities may be limited to specific seasons of the year. Thus, those seeking fun in the sun should visit the following areas at these times: June through August is a good time to go anywhere in the United States, the Caribbean, Hawaii, Mexico, or Europe; September through October is ideal in the southern Caribbean (except for an occasional hurricane), South America, Hawaii, Mexico, southern Europe, or certain areas in the Southern Hemisphere; November through March is good in the Caribbean, South America, Mexico, the South Seas, subtropical and tropical areas in the Far East, the Indian Ocean, and Australia and New Zealand (which are best in January and February); March through May is the time to go to the southern United States, the Caribbean, Mexico, Hawaii, the South Seas, and tropical areas in the Southern Hemisphere.

Accommodations

No matter how charming the environs, how beautiful the grounds, how posh the lobby and dining areas, or how complete the facilities, there is no getting away from the necessity of providing utilitarian comfortable accommodations. In reviewing resorts, I like to inspect the average and the minimum guest rooms. The fact that royalty enjoyed the presidential suite will be of small comfort if you are suffering in inadequate lodgings.

You will want to consider the following: the size of the room – is it large and roomy, or are you tripping over the furniture and your luggage; the closets and dressers – do you have sufficient space to unpack and hang up your clothing, or must you live out of a suitcase and place several pairs of pants on the same hanger; the bathrooms – are they roomy, with plenty of cabinet and counter space for toiletries, or do you stub your toe on the toilet attempting to climb into the shower; the decor – is it bright, fresh, and pleasant, or is it drab, musty, and depressing; the age of the furniture – is it new, clean, and in good condition, or is it old, seedy, and falling apart; and finally, cleanliness – is the room immaculate, with clean towels, fresh sheets, covered glasses, and fresh soaps, or does everything seem a bit clammy, dusty, and in need of a good once-over?

Unfortunately, compromise in the quality of the accommodations was the most common weakness of many of the resorts I reviewed, especially in the Caribbean and the South Seas. In spite of very high tariffs, the average guest rooms were a bit austere and in need of refurbishing. In many of the tropical areas, the resorts were unable to eliminate the damp, clammy feeling of the rooms. The humid climate is an unacceptable excuse, because many of the more modern hotels that did not qualify as resorts were able to avoid these pitfalls. Some well-known golf and full-facility sport-oriented resorts have been left out of this book because their average guest rooms were not of acceptable quality. Other resorts, formerly included, have been bumped by newly constructed properties because of their failure to conduct sufficient renovations to keep up with the competition.

To meet today's standards, rooms in deluxe resorts should be air conditioned and should include their own refrigerators stocked with soft drinks, liquor, and snacks; private safes; remote-control color televisions with cable; internet connections international, direct-dial telephones; sitting areas; luxurious bathrooms; patios or verandas; amenities such as fancy toiletries, fresh flowers, and bathrobes; and good-night sweets on the pillows.

For travelers seeking the ultimate in luxury, the quality of the higher-priced suites may be a consideration. All of the resorts included in this book offer large luxury suites or bungalows. Actually, for travelers with children, a suite could turn out to be the better bargain.

In appendix, I have rated the average guest room at each resort. If comfortable accommodations are a high priority on your list, take special note, because this is the area where I found the greatest discrepancy between properties. In those resorts with the lowest rankings, a possible solution is to opt for the more expensive rooms or suites because they are generally larger, roomier, and in better condition.

Grounds and Facilities Available

Few people check into a resort with the intention of not leaving their rooms. Therefore, the beauty of the public areas and outside grounds, as well as the completeness of the facilities, is important. Quite frankly, the uniqueness of the setting and architecture, the beauty of the exterior grounds, and the quantity and quality of the sporting and other facilities were some of the key ingredients in selecting the resorts included in this book. Today you will find comfortable, posh rooms in hotels in every major city in the world; however, only a limited number of these offer the exterior space, natural setting, and facilities to qualify as a resort.

The facilities at a resort are often a key to whether or not you enjoy yourself. Whether you are a golfer, tennis player, skier, scuba diver, gambler, equestrian, jogger, fisherman, swimmer, or sun worshipper, you should make certain that the resort you choose offers sufficient facilities to accommodate your needs. Vacations offer an opportunity to pamper yourself, and it would be foolish to settle for a resort that does not fulfill your recreational preferences. Almost every new resort that comes on line has devoted space to fitness and spa centers, and many older properties have added or expanded these facilities. (In Part Two, you will find a description of the key facilities found at each of the resorts included in this book.)

Food and Restaurants

Although dieting may be healthy and fashionable, the true hedonist is not looking for a fat farm. Therefore, a consideration of the dining facilities is important in making a selection. You may be willing (or anxious) to try out a restaurant in the surrounding area. By definition, however, a great resort is expected to fulfill your culinary needs on the premises.

A review of the resorts in this book will indicate that some provide only one or two restaurants, while others emphasize a number of alternatives. This is certainly a consideration for resorts requiring compulsory meal plans. Therefore, you should obtain information on the restaurants at each property. Are they formal or casual? Is there a diversity of food offerings? Is there a gourmet dining room? Is there an informal coffee shop? Can you dine alfresco? How expensive is the food? Can special dietary needs be satisfied? What alternatives exist in the nearby environs?

For those who consider gourmet quality very important on the whole, the Caribbean, Mexican, and South Sea resorts may prove somewhat disappointing. In spite of the variety of dining rooms, few are able to achieve the culinary excellence of the European hostelries. The quality of food served in the restaurants of the resorts of the United States, including Hawaii, ranges from adequate wholesome to gourmet imaginative. Most of the resorts covered have specialty gourmet rooms that serve dinner. Generally, the food and service are superior in these restaurants. The restaurant ratings in appendix A are based upon my most recent personal experiences. A change in chefs or managerial policy could make a world of difference. Therefore, this is an area subject to frequent change.

For those seeking the ultimate in an epicurean experience, I strongly recommend driving through France or Switzerland while visiting the resorts listed in chapter 3.

Service

Inasmuch as this is not an item emphasized in travel brochures, if you are an individual who requires pleasant, efficient, and accommodating service, beware! Some resorts excel in providing top service in the rooms, restaurants, and public areas. However, by and large, the service in the Caribbean, South America, the South Seas, and Mexico is quite another story. These people have a different attitude and dance to a different drummer. If inefficient, indifferent, or rude service will ruin your vacation, you may have to avoid these areas of the world. Certain well-known resorts lauded by other writers, with the physical facilities to qualify for inclusion in this book, have been excluded because of the horrendous attitude and ineptness of their service staff.

Generally, resorts in the United States, including Hawaii (but not Puerto Rico or the Virgin Islands), offer helpful, friendly, efficient service. In Europe and the Orient, service can reach the heights of elegance and genius. In the Caribbean, it is often rude; in the South Seas, it varies from inefficient to inadequate; and in Mexico, there are two paces – slow and stop! However, do not let this deter you

Kahala Mandarin Oriental, Hawaii

from visiting the magnificent resorts in these areas with their unparalleled beaches and natural beauty. Simply be prepared to make allowances.

Activities and Entertainment

Some people are satisfied if left alone to relax and leisurely pursue their own hobbies and interests. Others may prefer planned activities. Therefore, the policy of the resort regarding this may be important. Some of those included offer little more than sport facilities and restaurants, while others feature organized games, tournaments, children's programs, nightly entertainment, and theme nights – something for everyone and every age group. Few resorts offer the around-the-clock activities found at a "Club Med" or on a cruise ship. However, many provide a daily program of special events. Those who require a more active environment may also want to consider what is available in the surrounding area. Some properties, such as Hayman Island, Wakaya Club, Vatulele, Four Seasons Maldives, and several resorts in Bora Bora, are set on private islands, miles from civilization. Others, like Fairmont Acapulco Princess, Grand Quisisana, Oriental, Mar-

bella Club, and Hôtel du Cap-Eden Roc, are only a short drive from all the action.

You should determine whether you are seeking solitude or activity, and then weigh what the resorts you are considering have to offer.

Price

The substantial difference in price between resorts is a phenomenon I have never been quite able to comprehend.

It seems to bear no relationship to the quality of the accommodations, the beauty of the grounds, the availability of facilities, the quality of the restaurants, or the efficiency of the service. It just is what it is, and if you want to play, you have to pay – a rationale I have always found difficult to accept. In any event, the wide range in tariffs among the great resorts included in this book has no logical basis. You can make your own comparisons by reviewing appendix B. Remember – rates during the off season will be substantially lower.

There are differences in price within a resort, and it is here that the more price conscious of you can save money. Many hotels charge a great deal more for rooms that are high up or that overlook the water. If the size, decor, and amenities in the rooms are the same or similar, you will be able to save a considerable sum by giving up an ocean view or accepting accommodations on a lower floor.

Beware of the practice of selling you or your travel agent an expensive room, even though a cheaper one may be available. To avoid this, you can ask to see less expensive accommodations upon arrival and then check whether there really is a sufficient difference to justify paying the higher price.

Be sure to investigate hidden charges that may not have been mentioned in the brochures: for example, compulsory gratuities, government taxes, and extra charges to use the tennis courts, golf courses, saunas, or to park your car. Some of the resorts included charge considerably more to park your car than they do for children sharing your room.

Many establishments offer optional or compulsory meal plans (MAP – half pension – two meals a day, or FAP – full pension – three meals a day). Often, this represents a good bargain because it tends to cost more for food on vacations than originally planned. For example, if a room without meals (EP – European Plan) costs $250 per night, and you normally eat a full breakfast and gourmet dinner each evening, your total daily cost for two could easily exceed $400. If MAP were $50 per person, this would bring your total daily tariff to $300, a $100 savings. However, beware of MAP arrangements that may prove unsatisfactory. Some restaurants have a supplemental charge for steak, roast beef, lobster, shrimp, and other expensive dishes. Others do not allow you to substitute lunch for dinner. Finally, the variety and quality of the MAP offerings or facilities may not be up to your expectations or requirements.

When traveling with your children, investigate whether or not the resort follows a no-charge policy for children sharing a room with their parents. Also, determine at what age the policy changes. Sometimes a suite or room with a refrigerator is more desirable when traveling with family, and in the long run, it can result in significant savings, making it unnecessary to go to restaurants for breakfast or lunch. Another consideration is the availability of an inexpensive, coffee-shop-style alternative restaurant that offers child-friendly fare.

Finally, you will want to compare prices for high season and low season because prices can vary from 20 to 50 percent between summer and winter. A slight change in timing of your vacation could save you some big bucks.

Fellow Guests

To many, a vacation is enhanced by meeting other guests and making new friends; you may, therefore, want to consider the makeup of your fellow guests.

Let me point out that expensive luxury resorts like those covered in this book cater almost exclusively to couples. Singles who are not content to relax and be alone are advised to travel with a companion when visiting the more exclusive properties. Singles traveling alone seeking companionship might be better off considering less expensive hotels, activity-oriented "Club Med" style resorts, or short-duration cruises. Unfortunately, the quantity and variety of singles at the high-priced pleasure palaces are limited.

Many of the resorts in this book provide special facilities and organized activities for children. However, you will find few youngsters at these resorts except during midsummer and during Christmas and Easter vacations. Although the tariffs at first might deter you from considering a total family vacation, most of the resorts have favorable rates for children sharing a room with their parents. Whether or not to bring along the youngsters is, of course, a question of personal preference. My own experience is that children thoroughly enjoy these great resorts, provided their enjoyment is in sharing experiences with their parents rather than finding acceptable companions their own age.

Most of the resort hotels in the United States and the Caribbean will be visited almost exclusively by North Americans and Canadians. Most South Americans opt for the Spanish-speaking Caribbean islands, Mexico, and Miami. On the other hand, properties in Europe and the Far East attract people from all corners of the globe. Resorts in the South Seas and the Indian Ocean have an international clientele with a large number of Australians. The higher the prices of the accommodations, the wealthier the clientele. The larger the property, the more vacationers there are. The smaller resorts are more intimate, creating an easier atmosphere in which to meet people.

CHAPTER THREE

FANTASY ISLAND: PUTTING TOGETHER THE PERFECT RESORT AND THE BEST OF THE BEST

Prince Maurice, Mauritius

After reading the descriptions of the great resorts of the world, you may wonder why someone has not taken the best of each and created the perfect paradise. You may also find it odd that the major resort chains have not investigated their competition and incorporated some of the stronger points of other properties in their own establishments.

Because I don't possess the capital to finance such a venture, the best I can do is to engage in a little fantasy. Assuming a rich uncle gave me a blank check, a large competent organization, and the directive to take the best from each of the entries in this book in order to build one supreme resort, I would create the following:

First, I would select the best natural setting where there would be a mild year-round climate, tropical foliage, white-sand beaches, and warm blue waters. Although several of the resorts reviewed would qualify, my first choice for climate, beaches, warm seas, and tropical setting would have to be the beaches found on Praslin, Le Digue, and Mahe in the Seychelle Islands. The beaches at Amanpuri (Phuket), Caneel Bay on St. John, Virgin Islands, Peter Island, Little Dix Bay (Virgin Gorda), Cap Juluca and Malliouhana (Anguilla), and Mauna Kea (Hawaii) would be runners-up.

Without marring its natural beauty, I would doctor up portions of the grounds with foliage and tropical gardens from Manele Bay Hotel in Lanai, Hawaii; the Romanesque statues and flora from the classical staircase at the Villa d'Este in Lake Como, Italy; the park, walkway, and bubbling River Oos that sits behind Brenner's Park-Hotel, Baden-Baden, Germany; the lagoon at the Kahala Mandarin Oriental in Honolulu, Hawaii, stocked with dolphins, fish,

turtles, and penguins; and the ancient fishing ponds at Mauna Lani, Hawaii. I would then add the little islets found in the waters surrounding Bora Bora Lagoons, Amanpuri, and Shangri-La's Tanjung Aru Resort in Sabah; and I would build a hill leading down to the sea, adorning it with flowers, trees, and torch-lit paths like those leading down to the ocean at Mauna Kea on the big island of Hawaii and at Amanpuri. I would recreate the overall mountain-lake setting at Le Mirador above Lake Geneva, Switzerland, combined with mountains, streams, and chalets that surround the Palace Hotel at Gstaad, Switzerland, or the Suvretta House in St. Moritz. It is my sincere wish that all of my readers might someday experience some, or all, of the wonders described above.

Having created the general environment, the next task would be to design the hotel, accommodations, and facilities. The main building itself would be designed and furnished like the elegant Château d'Artigny near Tours in France or the Beau Rivage in Lausanne, Switzerland, with the moat that surrounds Château d'Esclimont near Versailles. When furnishing the main lobby and public areas, I would combine the antiques, period pieces, art, and tapestries from the Ritz-Carltons in Naples, Florida, and Laguna Niguel, California; the Villa d'Este; Chateau Domaine du St. Martin (Vence, France); and the Beau Rivage. Were I to choose a more contemporary design, I would go with a South Seas/Oriental decor, taking the best of the structure, gardens, and open-air lobbies from Mauna Kea, Mauna Lani, and the Hilton Waikoloa Village on the big island of Hawaii; Manele Bay on Lanai; and Amandari, Amanusa, and the Four Seasons in Bali. For interior design, I would combine

Sandy Lane, Barbados

the bright, airy, floral effect of the decor at the San Pietro in Positano, and the decor of the various Four Seasons' resorts.

The standard bedrooms and baths would have the spacious comfort of those found at the Kahala Mandarin Oriental; the Ritz-Carlton, Laguna Niguel; the Fairmont Scottsdale Princess and Boulders in Arizona; Las Ventanas in Cabo San Lucas; Rancho Valencia in California; and the Shangri-Las in Singapore and Bangkok. For my most special guests, I would recreate the incredible period suites found at many of the French, Swiss, and German resorts, adding private terraces and pools like those found at Amanpuri and Banyan Tree resorts in Phuket; Four Seasons Resorts in Bali; or Las Brisas in Acapulco. In addition, I would have some low-rise villas and apartments extending into the sea, like those at the Bora Bora Pearl Beach Resort, Hotel Bora Bora, Bora Bora Beachcomber Inter-continental Resort, and Bora Bora Lagoons in French Polynesia, Four Seasons Maldives, and Prince Maurice in Mauritius.

Next, I would add the imaginative pools, waterfalls, slides, swim-up bars, suspension bridges, and gardens found in the pool area at the Fairmont Acapulco Princess in Mexico, the Hilton Waikoloa Village in Hawaii, and Hyatt Regency Grand Cypress in Florida. Lying between the hotel and the surrounding mountains would be the incredibly scenic golf courses at Mauna Kea and Mauna Lani, Hawaii, with backup courses from The Lodge at Koele, Lanai; Pebble Beach in California; Four Seasons on Nevis; and the Doral Golf Resort and Spa in Miami, Florida.

For the tennis complex and program, I would imitate those offered at the Colony on Longboat Key; the Boca Raton Resort in Florida; and at La Costa in California. For horseback riding, I would choose the stable and paths around the Greenbrier in West Virginia; through the mountains at the Peaks in Telluride, Colorado; or up in the mountains at Formentor or La Bobadilla in Spain. For joggers, I would duplicate the paths running through the property at Caneel Bay; curving around the lake in St. Moritz below Badrutt's Palace; bordering the river behind Brenner's Park-Hotel; or those running through the forests at the Dolder Grand in Zurich, Switzerland.

Adjacent to the main hotel and connected to the pools would be either the magnificent health spas at Sandy Lane, Barbados, Fairmont Scottsdale Princess and Boulders in Scottsdale, Arizona, the Oriental in Bangkok; Banyan Tree and Amanpuri in Phuket, Thailand; Brenner's Park in Baden Baden, Germany or the Saturnia at the Doral Golf Resort and Spa in Miami, as well as Victoria Jungfrau and Le Mirador in Switzerland, and Westin Turnberry in Scotland.

Providing a variety of scenic, romantic restaurants with excellent food and service is a must for any resort. For breakfast, guests at my resort could choose between a Continental breakfast in the lovely outdoor gardens at the Marbella Club in Spain or Auberge des Templiers in France; a hearty breakfast at the gracious all-American main dining room at the Hyatt Regency Grand Cypress; room service on their lanai at Mauna Kea; or the breakfast buffet at the Villa d'Este or Brenner's Park, and at the outdoor terrace of the Cipriani overlooking the canals of Venice.

For an exquisitely served Continental lunch, I would select the magnificent Italian fare served at the restaurant by the pool at the Cipriani and Villa d'Este in Italy; French cuisine served overlooking the Mediterranean at Eden Roc Restaurant, Hôtel du

Boulders, Arizona

Cap-Eden Roc, or at Michael Rostang's semi-open-air restaurant overlooking the Caribbean at Malliouhana; and the international mélange offered for lunch at the Marbella Club in Spain or Hotel Cala de Volpe in Italy.

For dinner, there would be a variety of choices, including the incomparable country French dining room of Master Cuisiner Georges Blanc at Vonnas in France; the equally superb French dining experience at Auberge des Templiers, Château du Domaine St. Martin, Domaine des Hautes de Loire and Les Crayères; the magnificent restaurant overlooking the park and hills at The Lodge at Koele (Lanai, Hawaii); the incredibly romantic Normandy overlooking the river at the Oriental in Bangkok; the romantic outdoor terrace at San Pietro overlooking Positano; the informal Swiss chalet Chesa Veglia at Badrutt's Palace, St. Moritz, Switzerland; and on the terrace at the Beau Rivage Palace in Lausanne. I would have a complement of violin, guitar, and accordion players strolling the area to set the mood with appropriate local background music at each of the restaurants.

After dinner, there would be dancing under the stars on the patio of the Villa d'Este; a Mexican folklore show from La Brisas or the Fairmont Acapulco Princess; or romantic dancing at the Grill Rooms in the Ritz-Carltons.

No resort can succeed without a gracious, competent service staff. For the lobby and public areas, I would take the friendly, efficient employees at the Ritz-Carlton and Four Seasons' Resorts around the world, Hôtel du Cap-Eden Roc and Château du Domaine St. Martin in France; or the Oriental in Bangkok.

I would take the chambermaids from the seven resorts in Switzerland and the well-trained Continental waiters from the resorts in Italy, France, and Switzerland.

Finally, I would steal Frank Marenbach of Brenner's Park Hotel, and Leon and Nigel Roydon of Malliouhana to manage and reign over this paradise, knowing they would be watching their domain from early morning until late at night.

This is a description of what I would personally consider to be the perfect resort, combining the best of natural beauty, comfort, accommodations, facilities, cuisine, entertainment, and service. Although this ideal pleasure palace does not exist today, just imagine how much fun we could have continuing to seek it out!

The Best of the Best

Although none of the resorts reviewed are totally perfect, some accomplish creating a distinct flavor better than others do. For those readers most comfortable with categorizations, the following are my personal opinions as to which resorts best capture the feelings they seek to portray.

For those of you who prefer to "*go native*" with a quiet, casual atmosphere in unspoiled surroundings that blend into the environment far from the madding crowds, I recommend Amanpuri and Banyon Tree in Phuket, Thailand; Amandari, Amankila, and Amanusa, and Four Seasons Jimbaran Bay and Sayan in Bali; Caneel Bay, Little Dix Bay, and Peter Island in the Virgin Islands; Cap Juluca and Malliouhana in Anguilla; Rancho Valencia and the Boulders in the United States; Wakaya Club and Vatulele Island Resort in Fiji; Four Seasons Maldives at Kuda Huraa; Prince Maurice in Mauritius; and Hotel Bora Bora, Bora Bora Beachcomber Inter-continental Resort, Bora Bora Pearl Beach Resort, and Bora

Hotel Cipriani, Venice

Bora Lagoons in French Polynesia. All of these properties, though very expensive resorts, offer few frills and little activity. However, each is totally secluded, located on a beautiful pristine beach and scenic locale, with lush vegetation affording its guests privacy and a low-keyed environment, good food, and as much tropical beauty as nature has to offer.

On the opposite side of the spectrum are those who enjoy the ultimate in luxurious accommodations – formal, sophisticated surroundings and superb food and service. The following resorts best accomplish this feel: in the continental United States – Ritz-Carlton, Naples and Laguna Niguel, and Four Seasons Aviara; in Hawaii – the Kahala Mandarin Oriental, Manele Bay Hotel, and the Four Seasons Maui; in the Indian Ocean – Le Saint Géran in Mauritius; in the Far East – the Shangri-La in Singapore, the Ritz-Carlton in Bali, and the Shangri-La and the Oriental in Bangkok; in Europe – Chewton Glen in England; Auberge des Templiers, Château d'Artigny, Château d'Esclimont, Les Crayères, Château du Domaine St. Martin, and Hôtel du Cap-Eden Roc in France; Villa d'Este and Cipriani in Italy; Marbella Club, Puente Romano, and La Bobadilla in Spain; Brenner's Park-Hotel in Germany; and Suvretta House, Badrutt's Palace, Le Mirador, Victoria Jungfrau, Beau Rivage, and the Palace Hotel in Gstaad, Switzerland.

Honeymooners, lovers, and other romantics seeking charming properties in picturesque settings, where they can linger over candlelight dinners, watch sunsets, and take leisurely strolls in the moonlight, will enjoy the fourteen casual resorts described above as well as the following more sophisticated, yet romantic treasures: in the Caribbean – Cap Juluca and Malliouhana; in Hawaii – Mauna Kea, Mauna Lani, and Four Seasons Hualalai; in Mexico – Las Brisas and Las Ventanas; in the South Seas, the Indian Ocean, and Far East – either of the Four Seasons in Bali, Indonesia; Banyan Tree in Phuket, Thailand; Shangri-La's Tanjung-Aru Resort in Sabah, Malaysia, on the island of Borneo and Four Seasons in the Maldives; and in Europe-- Auberge des Templiers, Domaine du St. Martin, and Georges Blanc in France; Villa d'Este, Cipriani, Splendido, San Pietro, and Santa Caterina in Italy; Marbella Club in Marbella and La Bobadilla in Spain; Formentor on the island of Mallorca, Spain; and the Palace Hotel in Gstaad, and Le Mirador in Switzerland.

With the exception of the small châteaus and inns of France, all the other resorts described in this book are self-contained properties with ample acreage and a full range of services and facilities. However, a number of the larger establishments offer more sport facilities, a greater variety of restaurants, and a great deal more services and activities, and are therefore better suited for families and vacationers seeking excitement and entertainment. A list of these more complete resorts includes: in the continental United States – The Boulders, Hyatt Regency Scottsdale, Fairmont Scottsdale Princess, Phoenician, and Four Seasons at Troon North, Lodge at Pebble Beach, La Costa, Four Seasons Aviara, Doral Golf Resort and Spa, Grand Cypress Resort, Ritz Carlton Naples and Laguna Beach, The Broadmoor in Colorado and Greenbrier; in Hawaii – Mauna Kea Beach and Hapuna Beach, Mauna Lani, Hilton Waikoloa Village, Four Seasons Hualalai, Manele Bay and Lodge at Koele; in Mexico – Fairmont Acapulco Princess and Four Seasons Punta Mita; in the Caribbean and Bermuda – Casa de Campo in the Dominican Republic, El Conquistidor

Acapulco Princess, Acapulco

Resort and Golden Door Spa in Puerto Rico, Four Seasons in Nevis, and Fairmont Southampton Princess in Bermuda; in the South Seas – Westin Denarau Island Resort and Spa; and in Europe – Westin Turnberry, Villa d'Este, Astir Palace Vouliagmeni, Bürgenstock Hotels and Resort, and Suvretta House.

Finally, certain resorts will best meet the demands of travelers who pursue definite special interests. Golfers in the continental United States can choose among The Lodge at Pebble Beach, La Costa, Four Seasons Aviara, Four Seasons at Troon North, The Boulders, Hyatt Regency Scottsdale, Fairmont Scottsdale Princess, Doral Golf Resort and Spa, Boca Raton Resort, the Grand Cypress Resort, and Greenbrier; in the Caribbean – El Conquistador in Puerto Rico, Four Seasons in Nevis, and Casa de Campo in the Dominican Republic; in Mexico – Fairmont Acapulco Princess and Las Ventanas; in Hawaii – Manele Bay and The Lodge at Koele, JW Marriott Ihilani, Four Seasons on Maui and the Big Island, Mauna Kea Beach, Hapuna Beach, Hilton Waikoloa Village, and Mauna Lani; and in Europe – Westin Turnberry. Many of the other resorts have lovely golf courses; however, for purists these are considered the best.

Every resort in this book has decent tennis facilities; however, tennis players will find the best courts and tennis programs in the continental United States at the Colony, La Costa, Fairmont Scottsdale Princess, Boulders, and Rancho Valencia; in Hawaii at Four Seasons in Hualalai; Mauna Kea Beach, Hapuna Beach, Kahala Mandarin Oriental, and Mauna Lani; in the Caribbean at Casa de Campo, Four Seasons in Nevis, and Caneel Bay; in Mexico at the Fairmont Acapulco Princess; and in

Europe at Villa d'Este, Hôtel du Cap-Eden Roc, and Puente Romano.

Beach afficionados will agree that the best sand, water, and scenery for sunning, swimming, and watersports will be found at Caneel Bay, Little Dix Bay, Peter Island, Sandy Lane, Casa de Campo, Hyatt Regency Grand Cayman, Cap Juluca, and Malliouhana in the Caribbean; the beaches adjoining the Southampton Princess in Bermuda; at Mauna Kea Beach, Hapuna Beach, Kahala Mandarin Oriental, JW Marriott Ihilani, and Four Seasons Maui in Hawaii; Wakaya Club and Vatulele in the South Seas; Four Seasons Maldives and the resorts in the Seychelles and in Mauritius in the Indian Ocean; on the islands off the coast of the Shangri-La's Tanjung Aru Resort on Borneo; and at Amanpuri and Banyon Tree in Phuket.

Those seeking a completely equipped health spa together with full resort facilities will prefer the Oriental in Bangkok; Banyan Tree and Amanpuri in Phuket; Prince Maurice and Le Saint Géran in Mauritius; the two Four Seasons resorts in Bali; Doral Golf Resort and Spa in Florida; Four Seasons Aviara and La Costa in California; Malliouhana, Sandy Lane and El Conquistidor Resort and Golden Door Spa and Golden Door Spa Resort in the Carribean; Le Mirador and Victoria Jungfrau in Switzerland; Turnberry Spa in Scotland; and Brenner's Park-Hotel in Germany.

Skiers wishing to stay at one of the best ski resorts can choose among Suvretta House, Badrutt's Palace, Victoria Jungfrau, Le Mirador, and Palace Hotel Gstaad in Switzerland; and the Peaks Resort and Golden Door Spa in Telluride.

For my personal ratings on accommodations, dining, service, and sport facilities consult appendix.

Doral Golf Resort and Spa, Florida

PART TWO

THE RESORTS

O n the following pages are my choices for the greatest resorts in the world. Where two resort hotels have common ownership, are located near each other, and provide reciprocal privileges, they are described together. Current prices, a comparison of facilities, and my personal ratings of the specific criteria appear in the appendixes.

The description of each resort is divided into five sections in order to assist the reader in obtaining a clear, organized conception of what each has to offer. The opening paragraphs provide **General Information** on location, setting, and historical background. The section on **Accommodations** describes the guest rooms, suites, and convention facilities. The section on **Restaurants, Lounges, and Entertainment** provides a description of these facilities, explains where meals are served, and tells what music and entertainments are available. **Sport Facilities** lists and describes the recreational facilities – such as golf, tennis, swimming, water sports,

jogging, health spas, and horseback riding – that are available at or in the immediate vicinity of the resort. The last section, labeled **Miscellaneous and Environs**, covers shopping possibilities, nearby points of interest, and other miscellaneous features unique to each property.

In appendix, each resort is rated in eleven separate categories, including accommodations, grounds, dining, service, sport facilities, etc. Appendix sets forth the 2006 high-season prices for standard rooms and suites. (The prices in high season can be significantly higher than during the remainder of the year.)

In this edition, several new resorts have been added and several have been dropped in order to provide my readers with my current, updated evaluation of the best of the best. It is my sincere desire that my readers will find the details provided for each property helpful when planning their luxury resort vacations.

CHAPTER FOUR

THE CONTINENTAL UNITED STATES

ARIZONA
The Boulders Resort & Golden Door Spa
Fairmont Scottsdale Princess
Four Seasons Resort Scottsdale at Troon North
Hyatt Regency Scottsdale Resort and Spa at Gainey Ranch
The Phoenician

CALIFORNIA
Four Seasons Resort Aviara
La Costa Resort and Spa
The Lodge at Pebble Beach
Rancho Valencia
The Ritz-Carlton, Laguna Niguel

COLORADO
The Broadmoor
The Peaks Resort & Golden Door Spa (Telluride)

FLORIDA
The Breakers
Colony Beach and Tennis Resort
Doral Golf Resort and Spa
Grand Cypress Resort
(Hyatt Regency Grand Cypress and the Villas of Grand Cypress)
The Ritz-Carlton Resorts of Naples

WEST VIRGINIA
The Greenbrier

TOURING THE UNITED STATES

It is possible for visitors to the United States to tour the country, following a leisurely itinerary, while staying at many of the best resorts. My suggestions for a four-week tour would commence with a flight into New York for a two-night stay; followed by two more nights in Washington, D.C.; a week in Florida, with a few nights at Disney World; a week divided up between Colorado, Arizona, and Nevada; a week in California; and one or two nights in Chicago, where travelers can make good connections for the flight home.

For your two nights in New York City (Manhattan), you will prefer a location on or near Central Park. Visitors should realize that New York City is not typical U.S.A. any more than Tokyo is typical Japan or Paris is typical France. In New York City the pace is faster, prices are higher, accommodations are usually a poor value, and service tends to be abrupt. However, there is no other city quite like it in the world, and most travelers to North America include this teeming metropolis in their plans.

From New York, you have a short flight to Washington, D.C., the nation's capital and the location of its branches of government. Here, you can tour the White House (the residence of the president), the houses of Congress, the Lincoln Memorial, and numerous museums and historical sites.

Continuing south to the state of Florida, your next stop would be Orlando for a three- or four-night stay at the Grand Cypress Resort, which is only 10 minutes from Disney World. The Grand Cypress Resort is one of the most elegant and complete family resorts in the world, offering excellent accommodations, food, service, and a full range of sport facilities, including a magnificent and imaginative pool complex. This is a relaxing location from which to explore Disney World and Universal Studios, two of the major tourist attractions in the United States.

For the remainder of your week in Florida, you may wish to choose one or more of the other resorts described in this chapter. Each is located in a major Florida resort area. The Breakers is a complete resort complex with a more formal, traditional flavor in three of Florida's most posh east-coast communities. Golfers will prefer the Doral Golf Resort and Spa and the Ritz Carlton in Naples, with their world-famous courses, while tennis players and beach-goers will be most pleased with the tennis program and white-sand beach at the Colony Beach and Tennis Resort. The Ritz-Carlton Resorts, Naples, on Florida's west coast, are considered by many to be the most elegant resorts in the United States. Those wishing to spend more time in Florida could take in each resort by renting a car in Orlando and driving to Palm Beach (The Breakers), Miami (Doral Golf Resort and Spa), Naples (The Ritz-Carlton), and Longboat Key/Sarasota (The Colony Beach and Tennis Resort). Visitors to the Miami area will also wish to explore the colorful "South Beach" area with its art deco hotels, restaurants, cafes and shops.

Those with more time may next wish to visit New Orleans, a unique Southern city in Louisiana, or Denver, Colorado, in middle-America, where you can enjoy a night or two at the venerable Broadmoor resort in nearby Colorado Springs or at the Peaks Resort and Golden Door Spa in Telluride.

Heading west brings you to the Phoenix-Scottsdale area of Arizona, a charming Southwestern U.S. community. You will not go wrong staying at any of the resorts described herein; each offers excellent food, service, accommodations, and facilities.

For many, no trip to the United States would be complete without a visit to Nevada, a "gambler's paradise". Las Vegas boasts numerous mega-hotels that offer more gambling devices, shows, restaurants, and shops under one roof than can be found anywhere else in the world.

From Nevada, you can continue west to California. If you have seven days, you may wish to start with two days in San Francisco, one of the United States' most charming cities, and then drive south for a one-night sojourn at The Lodge at Pebble Beach in the middle of the scenic Monterey-Carmel area. This resort boasts one of the most famous and most photographed golf courses in the world. From

The Braekers, Florida

here, you will take the well-known, picturesque drive down Highway 1 to Los Angeles, where you may wish to see the United States at its most flamboyant by driving through Bel Aire and Beverly Hills to view the million-dollar homes, or strolling down Rodeo Drive, where a constant stream of Rolls Royces and Mercedes disgorge their well-heeled owners for an afternoon of shopping at some of the world's most exclusive shops.

From Los Angeles, you can take a detour to the Palm Springs area, where there are numerous fine resorts, and then continue on to southern California and spend the night at The Ritz-Carlton, Laguna Niguel, one of the most elegant, sophisticated, and complete resorts in North America. From there, you are within a few hours' drive of Los Angeles, Dis-

neyland, and San Diego. A little further south lies La Costa Resort and Spa, Rancho Valencia, and Four Seasons Resort Aviara.

Travelers wishing to return across the Atlantic can fly from California to Chicago, where they have a choice of numerous connections to Europe. From mid-May through mid-October, Chicago is a scenic city with a mild climate boasting top restaurants, good hotel facilities, and shops. However, the remaining months can be harsh, and visitors may wish to merely change planes at O'Hare Airport.

Of course, it is impossible to explore the entire United States in three or four weeks. However, the preceding itinerary will enable foreign visitors to sample different areas of the country while relaxing at its most comfortable resorts.

ARIZONA

THE BOULDERS RESORT & GOLDEN DOOR SPA

This unique 1,300-acre development is owned and managed by LXR Luxury Resorts, an affiliate of The Blackstone Group and is located 33 miles northeast of Phoenix in the foothills of the Sonoran Desert. In conjunction with Rock Resort's founder, Laurence Rockefeller, The Boulders was designed to provide the utmost in modern luxury while leaving undisturbed the delicate environment, in keeping with Mr. Rockefeller's earlier projects. The main lodge, pool area, and sprawling casitas blend into the unusual granite outcroppings that form the dramatic backdrop from which the resort takes its name.

Other Arizona hotels and resorts boast of having a desert setting; however, they are actually located in highly accessible areas, only minutes from shopping centers and residential developments. The Boulders is set in secluded Carefree, Arizona, surrounded by towering cacti, vivid wildflowers, sagebrush, and a vast expanse of untouched desert where jackrabbits and cottontails abound and the dramatic evening sunsets are embellished with the calls and sounds of wild birds and crickets.

Overall, the atmosphere is casual. The main lodge, which houses reception, restaurants, and lounges, though new and modern, is still decorated in a typical Southwestern design with original art, pottery, and Indian crafts.

This is an ideal setting for discerning travelers who enjoy a casual yet sophisticated atmosphere, cherish the comfort and privacy of impeccably decorated, spacious accommodations, and wish to spend a portion of their vacation time at a world class spa, on two excellent golf courses, playing tennis, horseback riding, hiking, rock climbing, or just lounging around a pool. This is less of a convention resort than many of its competitors, and, therefore, more appealing to vacationing couples.

LXR Luxury Resorts has indicated an intent to spend considerable sums for renovations in the future.

Accommodations

The 160 distinctively designed one-bedroom adobe casitas that sprawl around the resort and golf courses are among the most comfortable and tastefully decorated guest accommodations to be found at any resort in the world. The casitas are similar in décor and size, differing only as to location. The combination bedroom/sitting room is gigantic (by normal standards), done in earth tones, with either one king-size or two oversized beds built into the wall beneath a wood-beam ceiling and colorful art with a view of both the outdoor patio and the television. The sitting-room area has a modern, attractive wood-burning fireplace, a ceiling fan, a large color television with remote control and VCR, several lounge chairs, a sofa, a writing desk, and refrigerator/mini-bar fully stocked with snacks, soft drinks, liquors, wines, and beer. The patios overlook the golf course or desert and have comfortable lounges, as well as garden tables suitable for your morning Continental breakfast.

Probably the nicest feature of the casitas is the bathroom/closet/dressing-room complex, which includes two six-drawer dressers, plenty of closet space, a makeup mirror and dressing table, a double sink and vanity, a separate toilet closet, a bathtub and separate shower stall, and white terry-cloth

Restaurants, Lounges, and Entertainment

Modified American Plan is optional throughout the year. Breakfast is available through the resort's room service, in the Palo Verde restaurant, where the full American breakfast that is included in the MAP arrangements is served, at the Bakery Cafe, at El Pedregal Festival Market Place, or at The Boulders Club adjacent to the golf course, tennis courts, and fitness center.

Lunch is served at The Boulders Club, as well as at the Palo Verde Room, which is a bit more casual than the Latilla Room, and overlooks the golf course and casitas. Each restaurant has attractive outdoor tables with umbrellas ideal for enjoying the fresh, clean Arizona air and scenic surroundings while having breakfast, lunch, or a snack.

In addition, sandwiches and snacks are served at the main pool pavilion from 11:00 a.m. to 4:00 p.m. during busy periods.

Dinner is available at all four restaurants. The Latilla Room features a table d'hôtel menu of imaginative Continental and American regional offerings. Dinner at the Latilla Room is a special experience in which guests are rewarded with exceptional presentation, service, and cuisine. The Palo Verde Restaurant features innovative Southwestern cuisine with a colorful exhibition kitchen. The Boulders Club overlooking the golf course emphasizes meats, fish, and seafood in a casual environment, and the Cantina del Pedregal features inspired Mexican items on an outdoor patio. Appetizing spa cuisine is offered at the Golden Door Spa Cafe. After dinner, there is music presented by small groups for listening and dancing in the warm, homey main lounge.

Sport Facilities

The main sport-offering at this resort are the two scenic, 18-hole championship golf courses with manicured greens and fairways, well-kept sand traps – one of which contains a 300-year-old towering Saguaro cactus – and unusual desert setting.

robes and towels with The Boulders' logo for use during your visit. Flip on some music or the television, pour yourself a drink, and luxuriate in these sumptuous accommodations.

In addition to the casitas, guests can choose to stay in the resort's 34 two-bed and two-bath or 16 three-bed and three-bath Pueblo Villas. The villas are perfect for families or large groups and include a fully equipped kitchen, spacious dining area and living room, fireplace, private patio, and laundry facilities. Each villa is individually decorated and features all the same amenities and services as the casitas. A resort fee is added to all casita and villa rates entitling guests to a daily newspaper, valet parking, daily membership to the Golden Door Spa and all cash gratuities to the bell staff.

LXR Luxury Resorts has indicated an intent to spend considerable sums for renovations in the near future.

Built by Jay Morrish, they are considered two of the more challenging courses in the Southwest and certainly two of the most unusual and beautiful. There are golf clinics available, as well as a pro shop and teaching staff.

The golf pro shop is located at The Boulders Club, which includes a restaurant and outdoor patio, a swimming pool/lounge area, a tennis shop, and eight all-weather tennis courts. The tennis teaching pros will give lessons, run clinics, arrange matches, and help set up ball machines. In 2001, the resort added a 33,000-square-foot Golden Door Spa with all the services, amenities, and treatments Golden Door is famous for. There are 24 treatment rooms, fitness and wellness classes, a yoga studio, a full-service salon, and spa café serving Golden Door Spa cuisine. Also offered are "watsu" fluid massages in a pool and meditation sessions in a genuine tipi. You commence with a seven-path classic labyrinth walk followed by a ceremony led by a Native American Shaman who cleans your aura with white sage and passes a peace pipe. Hiking and rock climbing can also be arranged through the spa. The "Horse to Heart" experience allows guests to get up close and personal with a horse.

The main swimming pool is located on a ridge to the side of the main lodge and overlooks an impressive boulder formation and waterfall. Snacks, drinks, and posh lounges are available at the pool. Another pool is located at the Golden Door Spa.

There are several trails for jogging and hiking around the resort, and horseback riding is available at Carefree stables only five miles away.

Miscellaneous and Environs

A full complement of sport clothes and equipment is available at both the golf pro shop and the tennis pro shop. Interesting gift items and sundries are sold at the gift shop in the lodge, which offers everything from logo items and regional frocks to Southwestern arts and crafts. Additional shopping is available at the nearby El Pedregal, a marketplace of 40 boutiques, restaurants, and galleries, along with the Heard Museum North, an internationally known Native American museum. The Bakery Cafe and Cantina restaurants located here belong to the resort and are dining options for MAP guests. Serious shoppers may prefer to also visit the more fashionable malls found in Scottsdale, such as the Borgota, 15 miles away.

The concierge desk will arrange for hot-air balloon rides over the desert, picnic-horseback rides, jeep excursions to watch the Sonoran sunset, and sightseeing tours of the surrounding area.

The Boulders is about a 40- to 50-minute drive from the Phoenix Airport. Although prices are quite steep in high season, they drop by 60% in the summer. Special golf, tennis and spa packages are available offering a savings for those who wish to indulge in these pursuits. Located in the Phoenix-Scottsdale area, which is blessed with so many wonderful resorts, The Boulders had to be special to survive. Its outstanding accommodations, charming, rustic beauty, natural quiet, desert environ, top golf and spa facilities, fine service, and superb dining have enabled this resort to stand out as the premier destination for vacationing couples seeking the ultimate Arizona regional resort.

The Boulders Resort & Golden Door Spa
P.O. Box 2090
34631 North Tom Darlington Drive
Carefree, Arizona 85377
Tel. (480) 488-9009, (800) 553-1717
Fax (480) 488-4118
Web: www.theboulders.com

ARIZONA

FAIRMONT SCOTTSDALE PRINCESS

The Fairmont Scottsdale Princess, Princess Hotels International's first major resort in the United States, opened in December of 1987. In August 1998 the resort was acquired by Fairmont Hotels and Resorts, and that chain now owns and operates the property. Located approximately 35 minutes from the Phoenix Airport and 20 minutes from downtown Scottsdale, this 651-room gem sits on 450 acres of desert property framed by the McDowell Mountains, somewhat removed from the vast commercial and residential developments of the Phoenix-Scottsdale area. The uniquely designed, Mexican colonial-style, four-story hotel building with terra-cotta, peach, and rust tones to match the Arizona sunset, is surrounded by waterfalls, fountains, ponds, courtyards, flowers, palms, and gardens.

The exquisite interior public areas and rooms are furnished in Southwestern contemporary style with earth tones, weathered copper accents, flagstone floors, and colonial antiques. Those desiring more privacy will appreciate the 119 spacious casitas that have their own pool and look out at the golf course.

The resort boasts a full range of sport facilities, theme restaurants, lounges, and numerous shops. Although many of the guests come for business meetings and conventions, the resort is also ideal for couples and families. Children under 12 stay free when sharing a room with their parents and there is an abundance of facilities to accommodate family activities, including an extensive children's program, Kid's Club.

Accommodations

Each of the 507 oversized guest rooms in the main building is at least 525 square feet; the 68 villas measure 825 square feet and 119 casitas are a spacious 725 square feet. Casita suites are also available at 850 square feet.

All accommodations have private balcony-terraces, king-size or two double beds with fine linens and European duvets, sitting areas, wet bars, refrigerator/mini-bars, walk-in closets, work desks with high-speed internet access (for $14.95 a day), remote-control color televisions – which include cable and in-house movies – clock radios, irons and ironing boards, and oversized bathrooms with double sinks, private toilet compartments with telephones, separate tubs and showers, makeup areas, terry-cloth robes, and complimentary amenities. The guest accommodations are designed in Southwestern contemporary style with distressed pine furnishings and fabrics done in soft earth tones. The spaciousness and comfort of the rooms is impressive even for the competitive Phoenix-Scottsdale area. A welcome feature is the spectradyne system, permitting guests to review their room bill and arrange for checkout via their television set. Ice machines are located throughout the hotel and casitas.

The casitas are spacious, comfortable, lavish and include butler service. The bathroom walk-in closet area is even larger than in the hotel guest rooms, and the lounging area is very cozy, embellished by a gas-burning fireplace. The resort will start the fire going at whatever time you prescribe. The patios and balconies of the casitas are large, affording an

ideal spot to enjoy breakfast or to watch the colorful Arizona sunsets.

In addition, there are 2 elegantly appointed, 2,700-square-foot, Presidential suites, 16 spacious 1,275-square-foot Master suites, 4 Villa suites, and 5 Honeymoon suites.

The convention facilities impressively sprawl along the property. The 22,500-square-foot Grand Ballroom is one of the largest hotel ballrooms in the state of Arizona, and can accommodate 1,800 banquet-style, 3,000 in a theater arrangement, or can be subdivided into a multitude of combinations for smaller meetings. In addition, there are two 19,000-square-foot pre-function areas, six casita meeting rooms--each room is 700-square-feet – and a Southwestern-style hospitality suite.

Restaurants, Lounges, and Entertainment

Room service can be ordered around the clock. Breakfast is also served indoors and outside at LVBistro, the three-meal-a-day casual restaurant located by the South pool. Lunch and dinner items offered here include many American favorites.

La Hacienda, the upscale Mexican restaurant patterned after its sister at the Acapulco Princess, and one of the only AAA Four Diamond Mexican restaurants in North America, offers dinner each evening with mariachis. The adjoining patio area is frequently the site for group dinner festivities.

The Grill, located in the golf clubhouse, with inside and outside seating, serves all three meals and snacks, as well as steaks, fresh fish, and seafood in the evenings.

For a romantic evening, dine by candlelight at Marquesa, which features imaginative Mediterranean cuisine with Spanish, French, and Italian influences. The elegant decor includes Spanish and Mexican colonial antiques. Sixteenth-century art adorns the walls, and a wood-burning fireplace and a classical pianist complete the mood. During high season, a market-style champagne brunch is featured on the garden patio.

The casual Cazadores Bar is open daily for afternoon and evening cocktails, as well as tapas, except for in the summer months when a selected menu is served. On Saturday evenings during the summer family theme movies are exhibited outside

at the South Pool and evening barbeques and theater snacks are available poolside at Cabana Café.

Sport Facilities

Pool aficionados will be delighted with the bevy of choices at this resort. The South Pool, the main U-shaped swimming pool, looks out at the golf course and lagoons, has its own bar and outdoor Jacuzzi, and is adjacent to LV Bistro and several shops. The East Pool provides an area for water activities, including volleyball, basketball, and lap lanes. Sonoran Splash is the resort's family water-recreation area, with two water slides, private cabanas and shallow swimming areas for small children.

The tennis complex includes seven courts – six lit for night play – a fully stocked pro shop, ball machines, teaching pros, and a 6,200-seat stadium court, site of several classic tennis tournaments.

The two 18-hole Tournament Player's Club golf courses were designed by Jay Moorish and Tom Weiskopf and are managed by the PGA. The PGA-TPC Stadium course is the site of the annual PGA Tour, the FBR Open (formerly the Phoenix Open), and the 18th hole has standing room for 40,000 spectators. There is a full-service pro shop here and The Grill restaurant with both indoor and outdoor seating.

The 44,000-square-foot "Willow Stream Spa and Fitness Center" is one of the most imaginatively designed and exquisite facilities in the United States, and possibly the world. Atop the complex is an adults-only, roof-top infinity pool surrounded by cabanas and fireplaces. The pool has waterfalls that cascade down rock formations to the two lower levels which include a waterfall-treatment pool adjacent to steam, sauna, Swiss showers and a marble

therapy/whirlpool. There are 25 treatment rooms, a beauty salon and a fully-equipped, state-of-the-art fitness center. This is an extraordinary facility. Admittance to Willow Stream runs $49 per day for those not booking a treatment. However, the resort also offers an additional (no charge) fitness center with a full array of exercise equipment, aerobic classes, sauna, and steam room.

There are also throw-back fishing on the property, desert fitness walks, volleyball, badminton, croquet, bocce ball, putt-putt greens, skittles and a daily recreational program.

Miscellaneous and Environs

On the premises there is a gift shop, fashion boutique, Southwestern specialty shop, a resort-wear store, hair and beauty salon, and tennis, spa, and golf shops. There is even "The Hangout", a room for teens with a music room, cyber café and refreshment/snack area. Numerous fashionable shopping centers are located in Scottsdale and Phoenix.

The resort will assist you with transportation to the airport, desert jeep rides, horseback riding, hot-air balloon rides, and any sightseeing you may desire.

The Fairmont Scottsdale Princess is a full-facility, self-contained resort located further from the heart of Phoenix-Scottsdale than many of its competitors, offering greater seclusion in a picturesque, casually elegant setting. The full range of sport facilities, children's programs, the exceptional spa, the numerous shops, wide selection of romantic restaurants, fine service, and exceptionally spacious, comfortable accommodations make this an excellent choice for business meetings, as well as couples and families wishing to enjoy the Arizona climate.

The Fairmont Scottsdale Princess
7575 East Princess Drive
Scottsdale, Arizona 85258
Tel. (800) 344-9758, (480) 585-4848
Fax (480) 585-0091
www.fairmont.com/scottsdale

ARIZONA

FOUR SEASON'S RESORT SCOTTSDALE AT TROON NORTH

Nestled in 40 acres of secluded Sonoran desert landscape with panoramic views of Pinnacle Peak, only minutes away from the renowned Troon North Golf Club, Four Seasons Resort Scottsdale opened its doors in December of 1999. This Pueblo-style village is composed of one- and two-story casitas that blend into the desert environs, a two-story main building that houses restaurants, meeting spaces, a gift shop, an award-winning spa, and a central pool complex. Unlike many other Scottsdale properties, this resort is located in the desert with a true desert aura away from the commercialism springing up along Scottsdale Road.

Accommodations

210 luxurious accommodations spread over 26 one- and two-story casitas include 188, 500-square-foot standard rooms and 22 suites ranging from 950 square feet up to the 3,000 square-foot Pinnacle Suite. All have private balconies or terraces (some with magnificent desert views), king or double beds with Frette sheets and European duvets, sitting areas, televisions with cable and in-house movie, private bars, irons and ironing boards, personal safes, walk-in closets, coffee and tea facilities, blackout shutters, outlets for fax machines and computers with internet access ($12 per day), two-line speaker telephones, gas-burning fire places and bathrooms with double vanities, hair dryers, telephones, deep soaking tubs, separate glass-enclosed showers, toilet compartments, and luxury amenities. In addition the various categories of suites have some or all of the following: separate parlors, plunge

pools (18), outdoor garden showers, outdoor gas-burning fireplaces, telescopes for star gazing with nightly constellation charts and guest bathrooms.

The 24,000 square feet of interior function space and 12,000 square feet of outdoor function areas include two 5,000+ square-foot ballrooms and a selection of meeting and board rooms. The Residence Club villa community that abuts the resort is designed for long-term travelers who reside in 1,670 square-foot, two bedroom, 2½ bath villas with fully equipped kitchenettes and living rooms with separate dining areas.

Restaurants, Lounges and Entertainment

The three-meal-a-day Crescent Moon restaurant with inside and outdoor seating has a rustic bistro atmosphere with a central Kiva oven, open kitchen and wrap-around buffet. The California-style menu is embellished with international influences and includes salads, sandwiches, pizza, pasta and grilled fish and meats.

Acacia, a contemporary steakhouse is designed with a Southwestern flair and artifacts and also offers indoor and al fresco seating. Located in this restaurant is a private room with it's own outdoor patio where private gatherings of up to 12 people can be accommodated.

Saguaro Blossom is the casual, pool-side dining venue, offering salads, sandwiches, snacks, desserts and Southwestern and Mexican specialties. Health-conscious, vegetarian and alternative spa cuisines are available in all restaurants. Coffee, cigars, cocktails and snacks are served in the Lobby Lounge, al-

so the spot for nightly entertainment, fine wines and liquors while enjoying picturesque views of the surrounding mountains.

Sport Facilities

The centrally located lagoon-style pool cascades on two levels with underwater lighting. Located here is a whirlpool, a shallow children's pool and complementary cabanas available on a "first come-first serve" basis. Pool guests enjoy ice water, chilled towels, Evian spritz and food amenities gratis. There are four tennis courts.

The full-service spa features a complete range of skin and body treatments, scrubs, mud packs, facials and massages in 14 treatment rooms, as well as a hair and beauty salon. Also located here is the state-of-the-art fitness center with a full range of cardiovascular machines, an aerobics studio offering complementary daily classes, and men and women's changing rooms with sauna and steam.

One of the main attractions to this property is its proximity to the world-famous, Weiskopf & Morrish-designed Troon North Golf Club. Resort guests enjoy club privileges and priority tee times to both the 18-hole Monument and 18-hole Pinnacle championship golf courses, described by some as the best desert courses ever built with spectacular vistas. Golf Digest awards the courses 5 stars. The Academy at Troon North offers comprehensive teaching facilities and a club house with a restaurant, pro shop and locker rooms.

Children and teens are not neglected. The "Kids for all Seasons" program for children 5-12 includes welcome gifts, a supervised children's center open daily from 9-5, activities such as movies, swimming,

sports, arts and crafts, desert hikes, treasure hunts and supervised meals. A "kid's concierge" provides assistance with child-related needs.

On request, the resort will arrange horseback riding, mountain biking, hot-air ballooning, jeep and hummer tours, river rafting, canoeing, helicopter tours, hiking and rock climbing.

Miscellaneous and Environs

Visitors arriving by plane will have a 30-mile ride from the Phoenix Airport. You can take 24th Street north to Lincoln; Lincoln east to Scottsdale Road; and then head north on Scottsdale Road past Pinnacle Peak Road. You then turn right at Happy Valley Road. Take Happy Valley Road east to Alma School Parkway where you will take a right and follow the road until you reach Crescent Moon Drive. The resort will be on the left.

Also on the premises is a gift shop, a 24-hour business center and a guest laundry facility.

Although the least expensive room starts at $495 in high season, many services, activities and amenities are included in the room rate that cost extra at other properties. Rates drop over 50% during the summer and various packages are available throughout the year.

Since its inception, the resort has received numerous awards from rating services and travel magazines. Four Seasons Resort Scottsdale at Troon North offers guests a panoramic, tranquil desert setting with luxurious accommodations, fine cuisine, impeccable service and the area's finest golf courses. A sojourn here will appeal to romantic couples, families and golfers, as well as business groups.

Four Seasons Resort Scottsdale at Troon North
10600 East Crescent Moon Drive
Scottsdale Arizona 85262
Tel. 480- 515-5700
Fax. 480-513-5300
www.fourseasons.com/scottsdale

ARIZONA

Hyatt Regency Scottsdale Resort and Spa at Gainey Ranch

Located in the midst of the 560-acre Gainey Ranch development, looking out at the McDowell Mountains and Sonoran Desert, the 493-room Hyatt Regency Scottsdale Resort and Spa opened in December of 1986.

The main, Southwestern-styled building, inspired by the desert work of Frank Lloyd Wright, is designed in a double-H shape with five landscaped garden courtyards filled with plants, trees and Native American sculptures and four glass-enclosed atriums providing natural lighting during the day and decorative illumination at night. On either side of the main building are eight two- and four-bedroom free-standing casitas overlooking the lake that separates the 27 acres of the resort from the adjoining Gainey Ranch Golf Club and residential developments. The buildings, grounds, and 2 ½-acre "water playground" were imaginatively designed and are embellished with fountains, a lagoon pond, waterfalls, hundreds of palms, plants, flowers, manicured gardens, and an international art collection.

Inviting, unique features of Hyatt Regency Scottsdale Resort and Spa are the dozens of comfortable lounging areas spread throughout the lobby, courtyard, gardens, and pools. Although each is conveniently located and accessible for afternoon and evening cocktail service, you receive the feeling of intimacy as though you are having your own private party rather than being lined up next to crowds of other guests. Each lounge area, as well as all of the restaurants, overlooks lakes, ponds, or the unusual pool complex. This resort is a "happening property" offering more entertainment and activities than many of its competitors.

Accommodations

There are 405 standard (medium size) guest rooms, plus 25 larger suites, as well as 18 additional guest rooms located in the eight casitas. Fifteen rooms are designed for the handicapped.

Every guest room is characteristic of the Southwest with furnishings that are rich in texture and natural in color. Each room has a king or two grand beds, a patio or balcony, a remote-control color television with cable and in-house movies, a clock radio, private safe, kimono robes for use during your stay, stocked mini-bar and newspapers daily, and small bathrooms with single vanities, hair dryers, scales, and various amenities. Ice machines are conveniently located in every hallway.

Each of the 12 petite suites has a separate sitting area and alcove with a king-size bed and two televisions.

The Fountain Court and VIP suites are larger, with additional features and more expensive furnishings.

Room rates in high season start at $430. Rates drop by over 50% in the summer and year-around golf, spa and romantic packages offer significant savings. For an additional $100 per night, you can enjoy one of the 45 Regency Club rooms, have complimentary use of the fitness center, and enjoy a European-style breakfast, afternoon snacks, evening hors d'oeuvres, and concierge service in the private Regency Club Lounge.

The three bi-level four-bedroom and the five two-bedroom casitas are attractively decorated and include large wood-burning fireplaces, dining rooms, living rooms, stereos, outdoor Jacuzzi spas,

lovely patios, and large open roof areas, perfect for small parties under the stars.

There is no charge for children under 18 sharing a room with their parents. This, coupled with the organized Camp Hyatt Kachina children's program, as well as, the family activities' program makes this an excellent resort for the entire clan.

In addition, there are 35,395 square feet of indoor meeting space and 34,045 square feet of outdoor meeting space. The 14,280-square-foot Regency Ballroom can accommodate 1,550 persons theater style, 1,200 for banquets, and can be subdivided into seven separate conference rooms. The new Arizona Ballroom is divisible into eight sections and boasts a 2,700-square-foot Desert Garden and a 1,200-square-foot Arizona Patio. There are also two boardrooms, five additional meeting rooms, a 9,000-square-foot outdoor ballroom, and numerous areas in the garden that can be utilized for outdoor functions. A three-story, covered parking garage services guests visiting the aforementioned ballrooms, and there are also 820 outdoor parking spaces.

Restaurants, Lounges, and Entertainment

Breakfast is served in the casual Squash Blossom restaurant where you can enjoy early morning coffee indoors or at an umbrella-protected table overlooking the pools. In addition to the usual breakfast items, some specialty Southwestern dishes are featured. Lunch and dinner are served here.

Dinner is also served at the more upscale Vu and at Ristorante Sandolo, an Italian Trattoria where you have a choice of indoor or outdoor dining, and are entitled to a complimentary Sandola (gondola-style boat) ride along the lake that surrounds the property.

The menu at Ristorante Sandolo offers a variety of pastas, veal and chicken dishes, and a list of Italian and California wines. The talented waiters offer musical entertainment to accompany your meal.

The resort's fine-dining restaurant, Vu, features a contemporary steak, chop and seafood menu in the evenings. It is especially delightful dining outdoors while looking out at the picturesque lagoon.

All of the restaurants are casual and jackets are optional in the evenings.

In addition, there are two drink and snack bars, as well as the Waterfall Juice Bar at the pool complex and the Lobby Bar with live entertainment in the evening.

On Sundays, an impressive "Chef's Champagne Brunch" is served at the Squash Blossom.

Sport Facilities

Hyatt Regency Scottsdale Resort and Spa features a full range of sport facilities and activities for the entire family. There are four tennis courts, all of which are lighted for night play. Teaching pros are available for lessons, to set up games, and to arrange tournaments. The $25 per hour per court charge includes pitchers of ice water or iced tea.

Three nine-hole golf courses adjoin the property at the Gainey Ranch Golf Club, and the clubhouse has a restaurant and pro shop.

The new 21,000 square-foot Spa Avania,Spa/Fitness Center that was completed in 2005 includes a well-stocked fitness facility with free weights, state-of-the-art cardio-vascular machines with personal TVs, both men and women's dressing rooms with sauna and steam, and a modern, full-facility spa offering dozens of customized massage, therapy and beauty treatments, coordinated with the times of day they are offered. Guests will enjoy this secluded tranquil setting in both indoor and outdoor treatment and relaxation areas, overlooking the beauty of the resort's French Celtic mineral pool, and the majestic Camelback Mountain.

You can bicycle or jog down the numerous paths and trails in the surrounding area. Several horseback riding stables are located only a few miles from the resort.

The main sport attraction is the 2 ½-acre "water playground", which boasts 10 uniquely designed pools, 28 fountains, 47 waterfalls, a three-story water slide tucked inside a clock tower, a water temple with a large Jacuzzi-style spa and 4 cold-water pools, a thundering waterfall, an adult-only pool, and a children's area with a real sand beach and a sand-bottom wading pool. There are numerous separate lounge areas with comfortable chairs

day session or a full day's worth of interesting and informative activities, such as Native American dances, Southwestern sand art, cactus-scapes, and designing their own bolo tie. As mentioned earlier, this program makes the Hyatt Regency Scottsdale an excellent choice for families with younger children.

The Native American Learning Center is an ongoing collaboration with native artists and educators interpreting aspects of their cultures for resort guests, as well as the community.

Miscellaneous and Environs

On the premises are a sundry-gift shop, a men's and women's hair salon, an Enterprise Rent-A-Car office, and concierge service.

Only 5 to 15 minutes from the resort are the numerous shops, galleries, museums and restaurants off Scottsdale Road. The concierge can also arrange hot-air ballooning, desert four-wheel adventures, horse-back riding and tickets for cultural events.

The attentive service staff members throughout the resort are always cheerful and gracious, and add an extra dimension to your visit. Although the standard accommodations are not overly spacious or luxurious, the Hyatt Regency Scottsdale Resort and Spa is an excellent choice for couples and business groups, and the best selection for families with children seeking comfortable accommodations, excellent service, and a plethora of sport facilities in a private setting only a short drive from the fashionable Scottsdale-Phoenix area.

spread around the pools so that you never feel you are relaxing in the midst of crowds.

A special feature at the resort is Camp Hyatt Kachina for young resort guests, ages 3-5 and 6-12. Programs are designed to focus on four major elements of the destination: flora, fauna, geography, and history of the area. Campers can enjoy a half-

Hyatt Regency Scottsdale Resort and Spa
7500 East Doubletree Ranch Road
Scottsdale, Arizona 85258
Tel. (480) 991-3388
Fax. (480) 483-5550
Web: www.scottsdale.hyatt.com

ARIZONA

THE PHOENICIAN

Conveniently located on Camelback Road, only minutes from the restaurants and shopping centers along Scottsdale Road, nestled below the flanks of Camelback Mountain, sits The Phoenician on 250 acres of magnificently landscaped property. As you enter the main gate, you drive past the landmark Jokake Inn and the manicured lush green fairways and picturesque lagoons of the golf course. You wind around the adjoining guest casitas and pull up to the entrance of the main hotel building.

The lobby, public areas, and restaurants are elegantly furnished in soft tones with marble floors, exquisite chandeliers, and $12 million dollars' worth of tasteful art and sculpture; and they look out at double-level swimming pools, tiered plants, and colorful flowers. Behind the hotel at the foot of Camelback Mountain is an extraordinary two-acre cactus garden.

The resort opened in October of 1988. In 1994 ITT Sheraton assumed management of the resort. Today it is managed by Starwood Hotels and Resorts Worldwide, as part of the Luxury Collection of properties. Winner of numerous awards, The Phoenician can boast some of the highest caliber service, finest accommodations, and best convention and sport facilities of any resort in the world.

Accommodations

The resort encompasses 654 total guest accommodations, including 57 luxury suites, 4 gigantic, Presidential suites, 7 villas, and 119 casita rooms and suites along the lake.

Every guest accommodation has a large patio, is furbished in soft tones, and includes two separate closets, a writing desk, a sitting area, a 32-inch Sony flat-screen television with remote control or a 42-inch plasma, a mini-bar/refrigerator combination, a private wall safe, a clock-radio/CD player, hands-free two-line telephones, and an oversized, marble bathroom with a soaking tub, a separate shower stall, a toilet compartment with an extension telephone (and some with bidets), a double vanity, a hair dryer, a scale, terry-cloth robes, a makeup mirror, and numerous complimentary amenities. Internet connections are available at $26 per day.

The rooms in the casitas have walk-in closets and options for a connecting parlor.

The over-64,000 square feet of meeting space includes a 5,700-square-foot multimedia theater with the latest state-of-the-art facilities featuring a simultaneous translation system into eight different languages, a 22,000-square-foot grand ballroom, 23 breakout rooms, and 3 boardrooms with 16-foot marble table tops and high-back leather chairs.

Restaurants, Lounges, and Entertainment

Dining is one of the highlights of The Phoenician experience. A marble staircase descends to the warm, elegantly furnished The Terrace with its adjoining outdoor patio tables. The Terrace serves all three meals and a spectacular Sunday champagne buffet brunch, where guests can enjoy musical entertainment, unlimited beverages, fresh juices and fruits, cold fish and seafood delicacies, pâtés, waffles, blintzes, crêpes, do-it-yourself omelettes, pas-

ta bars, ice-cream sundae bars, meat, fish and fowl creations, and a heavenly sinful patisserie table. In the evening, the Terrace features contemporary American steak and seafood, a good international wine selection, and live piano accompaniment.

Breakfast is also available through room service on your patio and each Sunday at Windows on the Green, which sits on the second floor above the golf clubhouse, overlooking the golf course. Windows on the Green is also opened for dinner specializing in Southwestern grill cuisine. Breakfast, lunch and snacks are offered throughout the day at the Oasis restaurant by the pool and the 19th Hole Grill.

The signature restaurant of The Phoenician is Mary Elaine's, offering renowned chef Bradford Thompson's interpretation of modern French cuisine accompanied by fine wines from an impressive list in a romantic, elegant setting atop the main hotel with views of the mountains and glimmering lights of Phoenix-Scottsdale by night. This is per-

haps the finest dining experience in the Phoenix-Scottsdale area, and has received the AAA 5-Diamond award.

Guests can enjoy before-dinner cocktails and hors d'oeuvres, as well as, after-dinner beverages accompanied by piano music at the Thirsty Camel Lounge in the main lobby. High Tea is served daily at the Grand Tea Court.

Sport Facilities

The over-one-acre, exotic nine-pool swimming complex includes an edgeless oval pool, two whirlpool spas, a children's pool, a 165-foot water slide, tiered waterfalls, adjoining duck ponds, lovely landscaping, numerous lounge areas, cabanas, and a central, oval-shaped, mother-of-pearl swimming pool.

Golf enthusiasts will certainly appreciate the complete golf facility consisting of a fully stocked two-story clubhouse (the location of Windows on the Green restaurant), a driving range, practice putting and chipping greens, locker rooms, and 27 holes of challenging, picturesque golf.

After completing a lavish $2 million upgrade, glistening new sand and water features have been added to the course and fresh new landscaping is lush and abundant.

The Tennis Garden offers 12 lighted tennis courts, including an automated practice court, plus a Wimbledon grass court, a clubhouse, and teaching pros.

The Center for Well-Being sits beneath the swimming pools, and contains a fully equipped gym, aerobics rooms, 24 treatment rooms, a meditation atrium, a full-service beauty/barber salon, sauna, steam, whirlpools, a beverage bar, and a retail shop. (There is a $20 entrance fee for those not booking a spa treatment before 3:00p.m. and after 3:00p.m. it is $10). Also available on the premises are croquet, lawn bowling, and jogging trails. Bicycles can be rented at the Tennis Garden.

The Funicians Club for children offers a daily, supervised program of games, crafts, discovery, and recreation for children ages 5 through 12.

Miscellaneous and Environs

The shopping arcade has numerous gift shops and boutiques, an ice cream-pastry-coffee parlor, and a sundry shop. The department stores and magnificent shopping malls along Scottsdale Road are all less than five minutes away by car. Sky Harbor International Airport is only nine miles away.

During the winter and fall, room rates are quite high, even for a luxury resort. However, various golf, spa and other packages are available and rates drop significantly during the hot summer months.

Although located in the middle of one of the most desirable residential and commercial sections of Phoenix, Scottsdale, and Paradise Valley, the vast acreage of The Phoenician gives guests the feeling of being set apart at a giant self-contained resort.

The Phoenician is not only one of the most complete convention facilities in the world, but also a good choice for the affluent independent traveler who wishes to be pampered in sumptuous full-amenity accommodations with solicitous service and grand dining experiences.

The Phoenician
6000 E. Camelback Road
Scottsdale, Arizona 85251
Tel. (480) 941-8200
Fax (480) 947-4311
Web: www.thephoenician.com

FOUR SEASONS RESORT AVIARA

Situated atop a plateau overlooking Batiquitos Lagoon, wildlife preserves and the Pacific Ocean, 30 minutes north of San Diego on the Southern California coast, the 329-room Four Seasons Resort Aviara opened its doors in August 1997. Serving as the focal point of the ultra-luxurious 1,000-acre Aviara residential community, the resort exudes style, class and ambiance.

Every guest accommodation is sumptuous; the airy, public areas with their abundance of marble, expensive art, greenery, and panoramic vistas are extraordinary, yet comfortable; the outside grounds are beautifully landscaped and dotted with J. Seward Johnson, Jr. bronze lifelike statutes; the dining experiences are outstanding, and service does not get better.

Accommodations

Each of the 329 spacious, air-conditioned, beautifully appointed guest rooms and suites has private balconies or landscaped terraces, one king or two double beds, an armoire that houses a multi-channel television, a private refrigerator/mini-bar and coffee-maker, a large closet with an in-room safe, two multi-line telephones with computer/fax connection capability, high-speed internet access a writing desk, and an iron and ironing board.

The marble bathrooms feature glass-enclosed showers, deep soaking tubs, a separate toilet compartment with its own telephone, double vanities, illuminated makeup/shaving mirrors, plush terry robes, hair dryers, and Four Seasons toiletries.

The standard guest room measures 540 square feet, and the 25 Executive suites are 855 square feet.

In addition, there are 15 one-bedroom suites that include a parlor, two patios, a second bathroom and television, a walk-in closet, and a guest closet; 3 two-bedroom suites with giant living/dining rooms, a pantry, and extremely elegant furnishings; and the Presidential Suite, which includes a living room, a dining room, kitchen, two king-sized bedrooms, and a double bathroom. In 2005, all accommodations were redecorated.

Thirty thousand square feet of conference center facilities encompass a 12,000-square-foot Grand Ballroom, a 4,000-square-foot second ballroom, a 2,300-square-foot conference room, and eight meeting rooms, all with state-of-the-art technical equipment. From Monday through Friday, the Conference Services Office offers secretarial services and office equipment for business travelers, as well as free use of computers to recover your internet messages.

Restaurants, Lounges, and Entertainment

For breakfast, guests can choose among room service, the charming Argyle restaurant at the golf club, or California Bistro, an indoor restaurant with an outdoor terrace overlooking the gardens. Lunch is also served at both restaurants, as well as at the Ocean Bar and Grill at the pool. Breakfast and lunch at the California Bistro are offered on an à la carte menu, as well as buffet style. The pastries and rolls are outstanding. At lunch, Argyle features an eclectic menu of appetizers, salads, sandwiches, seafood, pastas, and pizza and is frequented by members of the Aviara community, as well as golfers and hotel guests.

Afternoon tea with finger sandwiches, scones, rose-petal jelly, lemon curd, Devonshire cream, delicate pastries, and petit fours is featured daily in the lobby lounge area Wednesday through Sunday from 2:00 until 4:00 p.m.

Alternative cuisine for the health conscious is offered in all restaurants, and room service is available around the clock.

The resort's signature dinner venue, Vivace, boasts exceptional, gourmet Northern Italian cuisine in a casually elegant setting with some tables around a fireplace, others looking out to the ocean, and some on an outdoor terrace. We found the imaginative antipastos, pastas, entrees, and desserts to be uniformly satisfying and far above the fare served at most hotel-Italian restaurants. Service here is impeccable, as it is at all of the restaurants and throughout the resort.

Sport Facilities

The free-form, family swimming pool with underwater lighting, two nearby whirlpools, and a children's wading pool is surrounded by a multi-leveled landscaped deck with comfortable chaise lounges, a bar and grill, and canvas cabanas that come with a telephone and can be rented for $20 per half day or $30 for a full day. There is also a tranquility pool with panoramic views of the lagoon and Pacific Ocean.

The Spa and Fitness Center, which was renovated in 2001, features up-scale cardio-vascular equipment, each with its own private television, free-weights, tasteful his- and her- locker rooms with sauna, steam, showers, and changing facilities, and 20 massage and treatment rooms, 5 outdoor treatment cabanas and a couples' suite.

The professionally supervised and complementary "Kids for All Seasons" children's program provides indoor and outdoor activities for children ages 4 through 12 with guest appearances by Avie the Frog.

About a quarter-mile down the hilly road leading to the golf course is the resort's tennis center offering six illuminated courts, two of which are clay and four hard-surface. The tournament court has abundant spectator seating, and tennis lessons are available.

About a quarter-of-a-mile further down the road from the hotel is the entrance to the golf clubhouse, which is elegantly furnished and houses a fully-stocked pro shop, locker rooms, and the Argyle Restaurant, serving breakfast, lunch, and snacks in an attractive setting. The 18-hole, Arnold Palmer designed, championship golf course affords views of Batiquitos Lagoon and the Pacific Ocean, as well as the adjacent residential communities. The golf complex also includes a driving range, pitch-and-putt practice greens, and the Aviara Golf Academy, a three- and four-day golf school.

The resort provides a jogging trail map; most of the trails, however, involve running up and down steep hills. For an easier three-mile run, I would suggest proceeding down the hill leading past the tennis courts to the golf club house where you have easy access to the Batiquitos Lagoon Trail that runs through a forest bordered by the lagoon and golf course and brings you back to Batiquitos Drive, where you can run toward the tennis courts and catch a shuttle to the hotel. For a short run, you can proceed in the opposite direction on the walks that lead from the hotel to the entrance on Aviara Parkway and then return (about one mile).

Miscellaneous and Environs

Four Seasons Resort Aviara is a 30-minute drive from the San Diego airport. Take Interstate Highway 5 North and exit at Poinsettia Drive turn right

on to Aviara Parkway and proceed to the hotel. Palomar Airport is only five minutes from the property.

Guests are best advised to rent a car at the airport since taxis are expensive, and it is advantageous to have your own car to get around the area, visit the various attractions found in southern California, or just have quick access to the golf course. The resort does provide shuttle service to the tennis complex and golf clubhouse and to the beach on request.

On premises are a men's and women's boutique, a children's' store, a sundry logo shop, a jewelry store, a golf and tennis pro shop, and a Jose Eber hair salon. For more extensive shopping, Del Mar Plaza and Carlsbad Village is only a 15-minute drive on Highway 5 and Carlsbad Premium Outlet Center is 5-minutes away.

Surrounding the resort is Four Seasons Residence Club, a 156-villa, time-share, vacation home community with the hotel and sport facilities as its focal point.

Seasoned travelers to California who enjoy a pleasant, casually elegant environment, excellent dining, faultless service, and a full range of sport facilities will certainly want to place Four Seasons Resort Aviara on the top of their list.

Four Seasons Resort Aviara
7100 Four Seasons Point
Carlsbad, California 92009
Tel. (760) 603-6800
Fax (760) 603-6878
Web: www.fourseasons.com/aviara

CALIFORNIA

LaCosta Resort and Spa

This 400-acre self-contained resort, popular since it opened its doors in 1965, is nestled in a valley between the Pacific and the sloping hills of Carlsbad, California. It is surrounded by its own golf courses and by luxury private homes and villas. Located only 30 miles north of San Diego in southern California, La Costa Resort and Spa enjoys sunny days year round, with temperatures varying from the mid-60s to the low 80s.

In 2001 the resort was purchased by KSL Resorts and a new multi-million dollar renovation took place between 2001 and 2005, adding a new spa, a new fitness center, upgrading the rooms and re-designing the reception-clubhouse area so as to create an attractive outdoor plaza surrounded by the club house, restaurants and shops. If you have not visited the resort since 2000 you are in for a surprise.

Actually, La Costa Resort and Spa is two resorts in one. Many guests come for the outstanding spa facilities that include special nutrition diet, fitness, and longevity programs. Others make use of the excellent tennis and golf complex and enjoy the restaurants and entertainment.

Accommodations

Presently, there are 474 rooms, which include 18 parlor suites, 77 La Costa suites, and 2 Presidential suites. All of the rooms in the main building and adjoining the spa have been totally renovated and attractively redecorated. The large spa rooms and the new golf and tennis rooms and suites are attractively designed in a Spanish-southern California style. Every room and suite includes flat-screen Plasma

TV's with in-house movies, a writing desk, a private safe, a clock radio, either two queen- or one king-size bed, marble bathrooms with samples of La Costa line of creams and shampoos, and a La Costa terry-cloth robe for use during your stay.

The recently refurbished 40,000-square-foot conference center includes 14 conference rooms, a 8,140 square-foot ballroom that seats 600 people, a 190-seat theater, and the 18,000 square-foot Costa Del Sol Ballroom which is divisible into smaller meeting rooms.

Restaurants, Lounges, and Entertainment

All meals are offered daily at Legends California Bistro and through room service. Light lunches and snacks are available at the pools. On Sundays, Legends features a delicious champagne brunch. The breakfast, lunch, and dinner menus at Legends are quite extensive and the food is exceptional for a casual resort three-meal-a-day dining room. Some items from the Legend's menu are also available at the Lobby Lounge.

The resorts newest restaurant, Blue Fire Grill opened in 2005 with a cozy bar area, two separate indoor dining rooms, an open display kitchen and outdoor seating overlooking the Plaza. The cuisine is described as "California Coastal".

The Market Place located off the main reception area features coffees, bagels, pastries and other snacks to consume on premises or take back to your room. Also located here are sundry and logo items and computers with e-mail access.

Sport Facilities

The 36 holes of golf surrounding the property have hosted numerous tournaments, including the PGA TOUR'S Mercedes Championships. The 17th hole is renowned as "the monster" because its 573 yards are swept by the prevailing ocean breezes. There are teaching pros for lessons at the La Costa Golf School, a driving range and practice bunkers and greens.

There are 17 hard-surfaced and clay tennis courts (7 illuminated for night play), and teaching pros available. Court time goes for $15 an hour. There is also a well-stocked tennis shop.

A new 8,000 square-foot, athletic club is located atop the Clubhouse overlooking the golf course. The cardio-vascular machines have personal TVs and there is a cycling room, yoga and aerobics room and pilates studio. Unfortunately there is no changing room, steam, shower or saunas connected to the fitness center.

The nearest public beach is two miles away and only accessible by automobile. However, there is a large pool surrounded by lounges, ponds, and waterfalls right at the clubhouse, a somewhat larger pool near the spa, and smaller pools in the spa.

Joggers will enjoy running along the one-fifth-mile jogging course or the paths along the golf course in the early morning.

The cornerstone of the resort's renovation is the new Spa that opened in 2003. It offers 28,000 square-feet of indoor space and a 15,000 square-foot outdoor courtyard with an outdoor lounging pool and café. The Spa boasts 42 treatment rooms including 2 private suites for couples. The full range of massages, wraps, facials, rubs and other treatments run from $145 to $205. Half- and full-day "Spa Journeys" run from $400 to $750. Full-day access to the spa is included with purchase of a service; however, resort guests not taking a treatment are charged $60 to use the facilities which include a changing room, small gym, sauna, steam room, whirlpool, and the aforementioned spa café and outdoor pool.

Attached to the Spa is a Yamaguchi Salon emphasizing the Feng Shui approach to beauty, offering hair, manicure, pedicure and makeup services.

In addition, the Chopra Center, founded by renowned author Dr Deepak Chopra, based on East Indian Ayurvedic principles offers leading-edge programs, services and products for those seeking mind/body healings.

Miscellaneous and Environs

La Costa Resort and Spa is centrally located 1½ hours from Los Angeles, 90 minutes from Disneyland, 30 minutes from San Diego, and 60 minutes from the Mexican border. You can take excursions to the Wild Animal Park, Sea World, the village of La Jolla, the San Diego Zoo, Legoland California, and the Del Mar Race Track. Those driving should exit Interstate 5 at the La Costa Avenue exit, proceed east to El Camino Real, then turn north and drive one-quarter mile to the resort's entrance.

There are numerous shops and boutiques surrounding the resort's village-like plaza. Other shopping options can be found in the large mall in Carlsbad, and at the quaint shopping/restaurant area in La Jolla and Del Mar.

The resort features Camp La Costa, which is a fully supervised day-care program offered daily for children ages 3 through 12, at a nominal cost. Night camp is also offered from 6:00 p.m. to 10 p.m.

Fridays and Saturdays, and babysitting services can be arranged through the concierge.

For over 30 years, La Costa Resort and Spa has offered quality spa and resort facilities to residents and visitors to southern California. All have come to depend on its comfortable accommodations, good food, excellent service, top sport facilities, and superior health spa, diet, and fitness programs.

With the ongoing multimillion-dollar improvement program, the resort has reached new heights of comfort, beauty, and excellence.

La Costa Resort and Spa
2100 Costa Del Mar Road
Carlsbad, California 92009
Tel. (760) 438-9111, (800) 854-5000
Fax (760) 930-7070
www.LaCosta.com

CALIFORNIA

THE LODGE AT PEBBLE BEACH

The Lodge at Pebble Beach, formerly known as Del Monte Lodge, is located on Monterey Peninsula in the heart of a 5,300-acre preserve. As you enter the Del Monte Forest and travel 17-Mile Drive, you pass towering pines, gnarled cypress trees, craggy rocks, pounding surf, lush gardens, and magnificent homes. Here, where the land meets the sea, amongst massive rock formations, white sand dunes, and picturesque golf courses, sits the sprawling Lodge.

The original Hotel Del Monte was built in 1880 by the "Big Four" Southern Pacific Railroad men: Charles Crocker, Leland Stanford, Collis P. Huntington, and Mark Hopkins. It was the most grand resort hotel on the Pacific Coast, setting standards of luxury and elegance that are maintained by The Lodge at Pebble Beach even today. Fires destroyed the first Hotel Del Monte in 1917, and demolished the rebuilt hotel again in 1926. Del Monte Properties Company, under the directorship of Samuel Morse, operated the Hotel Del Monte and The Lodge at Pebble Beach during the first half of the century. During World War II, the Hotel Del Monte was used as a preflight-training school by the United States Navy. Today, it is a United States Navy post-graduate school. In 1977, the Del Monte Lodge on 17-Mile Drive changed its name to The Lodge at Pebble Beach.

The Lodge at Pebble Beach is located 120 miles south of San Francisco and 330 miles north of Los Angeles off California Highway 1 and United States Highway 101. United, U.S. Air, American, Delta, Pacific Southwest Airlines, and several commuter airlines make regular flights to Monterey Peninsula Airport, which is 10 miles away.

Temperatures range from an average of 51 degrees in January up to 63 degrees in September. During the summer, temperatures sometimes reach the 70s. However, in summer, the days and evenings can be quite cool compared to other parts of the country at this time of the year.

Accommodations

The 161 guest rooms, including 11 suites, spread throughout a number of two- and three-story buildings, are decorated with tasteful furniture, expensive fabric, and paintings. They include balconies, spacious sitting areas, and dressing rooms, with refrigerators, robes, and other amenities. About two-thirds of the rooms have wood-burning fireplaces. There are six meeting rooms.

Restaurants, Lounges, and Entertainment

Stillwater Bar & Grill at The Lodge at Pebble Beach allows a superb view of Carmel Bay, the golf course, and the Coastal Mountains. It is open for all three meals. Overlooking the first tee at Pebble Beach Golf Links is the Gallery, offering breakfast and light lunches in a casual atmosphere. Breakfast is also available through room service. In addition to the Stillwater Bar and Grill, lunch can be enjoyed at the Tap Room, indoors and outdoors at the Beach Club (near the pool), and at Club XIX. Also, the hotel will arrange box lunches for picnics. The atmosphere at the Beach Club is especially bright and charming in the middle of the day. Dinner is

available at the Stillwater Bar & Grill, Club XIX, and the Tap Room.

The Tap Room is an informal English-style pub serving snacks and complete meals from mid-morning through late evening. During the day, elegant and intimate, Club XIX offers contemporary fine dining. Sweeping views of the 18th green of Pebble Beach Golf Links and Carmel Bay, as well as a cozy brick patio warmed by fireplaces enhance the experience. Quiet music in the Terrace Lounge accompanies before-dinner cocktails, and a dance combo plays from 8:00 p.m. until midnight on Friday and Saturday nights.

Sport Facilities

At the Beach and Tennis Club, about one-half mile from The Lodge at Pebble Beach, there is an almost Olympic-sized swimming pool and a children's wading pool, both of which are heated. Saunas and changing rooms are located adjacent to the pool and sunbathing terrace. Also near the beach, there are 10 hard-surface and 2 clay tennis courts. There is a resident pro, a teaching staff, ball machines, and an instant-replay video machine. The beach in front of the pool isn't very good, and you may prefer to drive to Carmel Beach, which is located about a mile from The Lodge at the edge of the Pebble Beach Golf Course. However, the water may be too cold for swimming.

The resort is a golfer's heaven, with four famous 18-hole courses, a par-3 Peter Hay course, the Pebble Beach Golf Academy, two driving ranges, four putting greens, a pro shop, and a staff of pros. Pebble Beach Golf Links, home of many tournaments, considered one of the five best courses in the world, charges $425 for green fees. The Spyglass Hill course, designed by Robert Trent Jones, Sr., charges $290, and Old Del Monte, the oldest golf course west of the Mississippi, charges $100. The 103-yard seventh hole at the Pebble Beach course, which rolls down a hill to a green surrounded by sand traps and pounding surf, is one of the most famous and most photographed holes in the world.

The resort offers horseback riding over 34 miles of scenic trails, riding lessons, several jogging and hiking paths, including a nine-mile trail along the sea, and sport fishing on charter boats from Monterey Marina.

Miscellaneous and Environs

The resort has gift shops, boutiques, a delicatessen and liquor store, a flower shop, a travel agency, an art gallery, a bank, a jewelry store, barber and beauty shops, and a real estate office. Most visitors enjoy exploring the charming village of Carmel, with its art galleries, shops, and boutiques, and Fisherman's Wharf and Cannery Row in historic Monterey. Scenic Carmel Valley, Big Sur, and the wineries of the central California coast are within a day's drive.

The Lodge at Pebble Beach combines quiet elegance, comfortable, tasteful accommodations, and extraordinary golf facilities with a picturesque setting, making it an excellent choice for golfers and others seeking out a peaceful resort on the west coast of the United States.

The Lodge at Pebble Beach
17-Mile Drive
Pebble Beach, California 93953
Tel. 800-654-9300; 831-647-7500
Fax 831-625-8598
www.pebblebeach.com

CALIFORNIA

RANCHO VALENCIA

Nestled in the verdant, sloping hills of Rancho Santa Fe above the canyons of Fairbanks Ranch and San Dieguto Valley, amidst eucalyptus, ficus, California pepper, and citrus trees, sits the serenely beautiful secluded 40-acres of the Rancho Valencia resort. A 30-minute drive from San Diego and within 10 minutes of Del Mar and La Jolla, the property was built by Harry Collins in 1989. Emanating in a three-quarter-mile circle from the main hotel building are 26 luxurious two-unit adobe casitas, each surrounded by gardens filled with bougainvillea, pansies, lilies, lantana, and citrus trees.

The courtyards, patios and public rooms of the main Southwestern/Mediterranean style resort are adorned with flowers and plants and include a small registration lobby, an all-purpose boutique, the restaurants, lounges, fitness center, and meeting rooms.

Accommodations

The 26 Spanish-design, adobe casitas with clay tile roofs that spread along the property house 850-square-foot Del Mar Suites and 1,250-square-foot, one-bedroom Rancho Santa Fe Suites. These suites can be combined to create two bedrooms plus a living room area for families or couples traveling together. There is also one three-bedroom, 5,000-square-foot adobe Hacienda with its own private pool and Jacuzzi that goes for $5,000 per night and is frequently used for wedding receptions.

Every suite includes cathedral, white-washed wood beamed ceilings with ceiling fans, earth-tone stucco walls and furnishings, ceramic tile floors and counters, Berber carpets, glazed tile, fire places, plantation shuttered windows, French doors leading to large private patios shaded by umbrellas with lounge chairs, dining tables and sprawling flowers, cable television, video cassette recorders DVDs, CDs, coffee makers, and a well-stocked wet bar and refrigerator. The giant bathroom-dressing room facilities encompass a glassed-in shower, a soaking tub, a private toilet stall, a double sink with wicker baskets for used towels and trash, a separate, mirrored, makeup vanity with a hair dryer and numerous amenities, a walk-in closet, storage area with private safe, iron and ironing board, terry robes and slippers, and an umbrella. The bathroom design is very similar to those found at The Boulders in Arizona.

The Rancho Santa Fe Suites have smaller bedrooms with large separate living rooms where the wet bar, lounging and dining area, and fireplace are located. Both rooms have televisions and access to the patio.

All accommodations are sumptuous and create a warm, homey environment, making it extremely comfortable to lounge around your suite.

The resort offers 20,000 square feet of indoor/outdoor meeting and banquet space that can accommodate groups from 10 to 500.

Restaurants, Dining, and Entertainment

Breakfast, lunch, dinner, and snacks are available through room service and can be enjoyed on your private patio or in the sitting area of your guest accommodations.

The main dining room exudes casual charm with numerous green plants, a fire place, and views out over the tennis courts and citrus groves. All three meals are served here; however, most guests prefer to take breakfast in the adjoining French country-style Sunrise Room which is warmly decorated with dark blue, yellow and white ceramic tiles, matching yellow daisies on the bleached wood tables, beamed ceilings with ceiling fans, and another fire place, green plants, and views out to the open air dining terrace where breakfast and lunch are also available under shaded umbrellas.

The dining experience at Rancho Valencia is the tour de force of the resort and among the very best of any resort in the United States. Guests will appreciate the impeccable service, imaginative presentation, interesting variety of selections, and gourmet preparation by the resort's culinary team.

In the mornings you can enjoy a pitcher of freshly squeezed orange juice and Starbucks coffee in your casitas before treating yourself to delectable breakfast items such as cinnamon-raisin-walnut French toast, freshly prepared corned beef hash with poached eggs and hollandaise, and smoked salmon-eggs benedict, as well as a variety of low-calorie, low-fat healthy items.

At dinner, you can choose from an impressive selection of California, French, and Italian wines, including vintage French Bourdeaux and Burgundies. Although all of the appetizers and entrees are inviting, we especially enjoyed the sautéed Ahi Tuna Roll wrapped in spinach, nori, enoki mushrooms, scallions, and oriental breadcrumbs; the seared Sonoma foie gras with port wine and balsamic vinegar, the Oysters Rockefeller in pernod and sabayon, and a tangy ginger sauce infused with lemon grass, and, the grilled marinated duck breast with Israeli couscous in natural juices and plum sauce. The crème brûlée or chocolate gâteau accompanied by a rich cappuccino with chocolate shavings is a perfect finale for your gourmet repas.

After dinner there is a lounge for cigars, brandies, and after dinner drinks; presently, however, there is no music or entertainment. Cable television, VCRs, and CD players are located in each guest room.

Sport Facilities

Originally conceived as a John Gardner tennis ranch, the resort boasts 18 Deco-turf hard courts spread in the valley immediately below the proper-

ty. The tennis facility includes a small pro shop with eight tennis pros who offer private lessons, instructional clinics, children's tennis clinics, and arrange round robin play and matches among the guests. Rancho Valencia was rated one of the top 10 tennis facilities in the United States by Tennis Magazine.

The small rectangular outdoor pool with adjoining heated Jacuzzis surrounded by lounge chairs is tucked into an area protected by dense bushes and trees.

Bicycles are available, and the resort offers bicycle excursions on the rolling hills of Rancho Santa Fe. Next to the reception area in the main building is a regulation croquet lawn.

The fitness center includes Cybex weight machines, Lifecycles, treadmills, Stairmasters, and free weights, as well as saunas and spa services offering massages, skincare, makeup, manicures, and pedicures.

The resort will arrange tee times at Del Mar, Rancho Santa Fe Farms, or Grand Del Mar golf courses, hot-air balloon rides, tickets for Del Mar Race Track, and hiking excursions at Torrey Pines Beach.

Miscellaneous and Environs

There is a small gift shop off the front lobby, but serious shoppers will prefer the quaint shopping centers in Del Mar.

Guests arriving by air will have a 30-minute drive from San Diego or 2-hour drive from Los Angeles. From San Diego airport take Interstate 5 to the Del Mar Heights Road exit. Proceed to El Camino Real and turn left. When you arrive at the stop light on San Dieguito Road, turn right, and turn right again at Rancho Diegueno Road. Immediately on your left is Rancho Valencia Road, which will take you to Rancho Valencia Drive, the entry to the resort. From Los Angeles take Interstate 5 south to Del Mar. Go east on Via Della Valle. Turn right at El Camino Real, then left at San Diegueno Road, and then proceed as described above.

Two-night spa, tennis, romantic, and golf packages are available from $1,425 per couple.

Romantic couples, families, and tennis buffs will especially appreciate this uniquely beautiful, serene property where they can relax in very comfortable, spacious private casitas, partake in exceptional dining, brush up on their tennis skills, or just bask in the lovely surroundings.

Rancho Valencia Resort
P.O. Box 9126
5921 Valencia Circle
Rancho Santa Fe, California 92076
Tel. (800) 548-3664, (858) 756-1123
Fax (858) 756-0165
info@ranchovalencia.com
www.ranchovalencia.com

CALIFORNIA

THE RITZ-CARLTON, LAGUNA NIGUEL

Spread out over 18 acres on a 150-foot bluff affording a spectacular view of the Pacific Ocean and a wide, two-mile strand of surfing beach, the first full-facility resort in The Ritz-Carlton chain opened its doors in August of 1984. This four-story structure with a Mediterranean-style exterior and a lavish, impeccably tasteful interior of marble floors with inlaid carpeting, expensive antique furnishings, and an extensive art collection, is unquestionably one of the most elegant resorts in the United States and as close as you will come to a European grand deluxe hotel (and even better).

"My pleasure" is the conditioned, yet genuine response to your thank you's to the members of the warm and gracious 900-person service staff. Seldom have I experienced a more dedicated, courteous, and efficient group of employees – truly a credit to management and the owners of this "one-of-a-kind" establishment.

Whether you are having lunch at a table adorned with fresh flowers in the ocean-view restaurant or at the imaginative free-form pool, having a cocktail in the Bar as you watch the sunset burst in a plethora of colors over the blue Pacific, or having a first cup of coffee on your private balcony as the day breaks, you will be immediately enthralled with the elegance and charm of this resort and totally overwhelmed with the creative genius that went into the planning and design of the property.

The outdoor areas, though not as vast as some resorts, are tastefully decorated with tropical flowers and trees and include paths for strolling, jogging, and cycling, as well as numerous sitting areas in which to relax and enjoy the magnificent views.

While I was visiting, I witnessed an outdoor wedding on the lawn by The Gazebo, which sits on a cliff overlooking the beach. This picturesque ceremony, followed by the exquisite food and service of a Ritz-Carlton-catered reception, and then a wedding night in one of the ocean suites, is a "not-too-tacky" way to start a marriage.

Accommodations

All of the 393 rooms, including 30 suites, are virtually identical, with a small balcony or patio that overlooks the ocean or one of the pools. Each room contains a king-size or two double beds, plush carpeting, elegant, traditional furnishings and art, crystal table lamps, a 42-inch plasma television, DVD player and a digital clock alarm radio, terry-cloth robes for your use, a refrigerator stocked with drinks and snacks, and full maid service twice daily. Overnight parking is $25.

The bathrooms are done in imported Italian marble and contain two sink-vanities with mirrors affording a 180-degree view of your favorite face, as well as an additional ladies' makeup area, an enclosed toilet, and a large bath and shower with clothesline and super-posh towels. The free accoutrements include soaps, shower caps, shampoo, conditioner, a shoehorn, talcum powder, nail files, laundry soap, a morning newspaper, and a chocolate on your pillow each evening.

If this is not enough, you can opt for a "club room" on the fourth floor. For an additional tariff, you receive personal concierge service, your choice of newspapers, a Continental breakfast, midday snacks, before-dinner hors d'oeuvres, free drinks

and desserts until 11 p.m., and a tad more exclusivity.

The resort also services the conference trade, especially during the week. There are 19 meeting rooms covering 24,000 square feet of space, including the ballroom at 9,207 square feet. All of the latest audiovisual systems are available, as well as the ultimate in support and catering services.

Restaurants, Lounges, and Entertainment

Restaurant 162' serves breakfast, lunch and dinner with a view of the Pacific Ocean. A very special Friday Seafood Buffet and Sunday Champagne Brunch, which includes an impressive array of pâtés, terrines, and desserts is also served in the restaurant. Although Restaurant 162' is not billed as the premier restaurant at the resort, the dinners include imaginative fare in a comfortable setting with impeccable service.

The Club Grill and Bar serves a variety of meat, fish, and poultry dishes. Here, in a sophisticated, yet very romantic comfortable English club setting, with oils and tapestries on the walls and expensive pine wood furnishings, you can enjoy an intimate dinner for two or a convivial evening with friends. From 9:00 p.m. until 1:30 a.m., the Club Grill offers live music for show dancing. I found the experience to be a delightful change from the raucous discos or glitzy show rooms at other hotels.

Drinks, sandwiches and snacks are offered at the pool bar and restaurant, and room service is available around the clock.

Sport Facilities

Although one's first impression of The Ritz-Carlton, Laguna Niguel, is of a luxurious, sophisticated hotel, don't sell it short. This is a full-service resort, with most of the sport facilities offered by other such establishments. The two swimming pools are

surrounded by comfortable lounge chairs adorned with large beach towels set out even before you sit down. Two heated, outdoor Jacuzzis are also in the area. The two-mile beach, though typical of California surfing beaches, affords a lovely expanse on which to take a reflective walk, jog, or sun.

There are four outdoor tennis courts, and lessons are available. A so-so 18-hole Robert Trent Jones II Links public golf course is located across the coastal highway and boasts two ocean-side holes.

The Ritz-Carlton Spa offers 11 treatment rooms for a variety of massages and other treatments along with men and women's locker rooms with saunas. The two-level fitness center is perched atop the bluff and features state-of-the-art cardiovascular and Icarian strength training equipment, as well as, free-weights. Much of the equipment has multi-media televisions. Special classes and services include T'ai Chi, Yoga and Pilates and personal training sessions.

The "mapped out" jogging trails encompass inclines too steep for my taste, and I would recommend limiting your jogging to the beach or the surrounding residential areas.

Miscellaneous and Environs

Guests can fly to the Los Angeles Airport (a 90-minute drive), the Long Beach Airport (a 1-hour drive), the Orange County Airport (a 30-minute drive), or the San Diego Airport (a 75-minute drive). Additional time must be allowed at rush hour.

On the premises, there is a gift and logo shop with men's, women's, and children's apparel. Most of the nearby towns such as Laguna Beach, Dana Point, and San Juan Capistrano have quaint shopping areas. Fishing charters can be arranged at the marinas at Dana Point. At Newport Beach, the Fashion Island outdoor mall attracts serious shoppers, and boat trips can be arranged to Catalina Island.

Disneyland, Knott's Berry Farm, the San Diego Zoo, South Coast Plaza, and numerous other attractions are all within an hour's drive.

Many resorts can boast more acreage and natural resources, a far more impressive history steeped in tradition, greater sport facilities, or better climate, but few can equal The Ritz-Carlton's enviable blend of impeccable, gracious service, outstandingly tasteful and comfortable accommodations, imaginative variety of culinary experiences, elegant public areas, full range of facilities and amenities, and its unrivaled "touch of class".

The Ritz-Carlton, Laguna Niguel is an absolute must for all serious resort aficionados.

The Ritz-Carlton, Laguna Niguel
One Ritz-Carlton Drive
Dana Point, California 92629
Tel. (949) 240-2000, (800) 241-3333
Fax (949) 240-0829 (Room Reservations)
www.ritzcarlton.com/resorts/laguna_niguel

COLORADO

THE BROADMOOR

Situated around a lovely man-made lake stocked with ducks, geese, and swans, with the snow-capped Rocky Mountains in the background, are the main buildings that compose this traditional, elegant resort. During the summer, guests enjoy tennis, swimming, exceptional golf courses, pleasant walks around the lake, trips up to Pikes Peak, and the moderate, dry Colorado climate. Then, with the approach of Jack Frost, The Broadmoor converts to a winter wonderland, where guests can enjoy Christmas celebrations and spend cozy evenings sipping cocktails, dancing, and enjoying outstanding gourmet dinners in romantic settings.

The property consists of five major buildings: the original Broadmoor Main was built in 1918; Broadmoor South was added in 1961; Broadmoor West opened its doors in 1976, West Tower in 1995, and the Lakeside Suites in 2001. These buildings are connected by a circular path, studded with pines and elms that encircle a picturesque lake. The Rockies rise to the west, and many guest rooms, as well as most public rooms, look out on this magnificent scenery. You would have to travel to Switzerland to find a resort with a comparable setting. The Broadmoor was developed by Spencer Penrose, who came to Colorado after the turn of the century and made his millions in gold and copper mining. An admirer of the grand hotels of Europe, Penrose and his wife, Julie, embarked on a lifetime dream of building an elegant European-style resort in Colorado Springs. They purchased the land and lake from a Prussian count, constructed Broadmoor Main, commissioned golf architect Donald Ross to design the first golf course, and imported priceless

antiques and artwork from Europe and the Far East to decorate the public areas. After Mrs. Penrose passed away in 1961, the resort was owned and operated by El Pomar Foundation, a charitable organization established by the Penroses. In 1989 the resort was sold to the Oklahoma Publishing Company. This organization has expended millions of dollars renovating the property.

The daytime temperatures average 40 to 45 degrees during the winter, while summer temperatures range from 75 to 85 degrees. Travelers to The Broadmoor can fly directly into the airport at Colorado Springs, eight miles from the property, or they can fly into Denver, rent a car or limousine, and take a 60-mile drive to the resort on good highways.

Accommodations

Spread out among the five buildings are 700 guest rooms and luxury suites. In addition, there are three elegant executive suites for the rich and famous who can afford beaucoup bucks ($1,630-$3,195). All accommodations have air-conditioning, heating, color televisions, high speed internet access, wall safes, mini-bars, CD/clock radios, and ample closet and dresser space.

The regular guest rooms in the original three buildings that comprise Broadmoor Main received a total renovation a few years ago that included upgrades to bedrooms and bath facilities.

The nine-story, high-rise Broadmoor South Tower underwent a major renovation to the rooms and Penrose Restaurant atop the Tower commencing in 2005. The newly redesigned rooms feature either

one king or two double beds; some rooms have gas fireplaces and many sport balconies with expansive views of the golf course, the lake and mountains.

The Broadmoor prides itself on being one of the leading convention resorts in the world, conventions and conferences making up 70 percent of its trade. In addition to the 58 meeting and banquet rooms in the three buildings, there is a new 60,000 square foot ballroom bringing the total meeting and banquet space up to 185,000 square feet.

Restaurants, Lounges, and Entertainment

The restaurants here are among the best at any United States resort, featuring a variety of choices with uniform quality.

Breakfast is available through room service, at the golf club, at Charles Court (West), or Lake Terrace Dining Room (Main) and features freshly squeezed juices, fresh fruits, home-baked rolls and pastries, and hearty entrecés, served either off a menu or buffet style.

Lunch is offered at the Tavern (Main), the newly redesigned Golf Club Dining Room, at The Golden Bee, the indoor Spa Pool Café and seasonally at the outdoor Pool Café. The Tavern features excellent salads, sandwiches, and luncheon fare in an attrac-

tive setting, with its Toulouse Lautrec lithographs. Daily, lighter fare and ice-cream specialties are available through the early evening at Café Julie's (West) and Espresso (Main).

Dinner is served at the Golf Club Dining Room, the intimate pub-style Golden Bee (behind the International Center), the Penrose Room (South Tower), The Tavern (Main) and Charles Court (West), as well as, in the new Summit restaurant, located across the street from the hotel adjacent to Broadmoor Hall.

The romantic Penrose Room, located atop Broadmoor South on the ninth floor, features French cuisine and table-side service under the direction of Executive Chef Bouquin, formerly of Maisonette. Evening dancing adds to the continental atmosphere, and picturesque views. During my most recent visit, this proved to be the outstanding dining experience at the resort.

Charles Court, at lobby level in Broadmoor West overlooking the lake, features indoor and outdoor dining, with a menu described as Contemporary Colorado cuisine with an imaginative variety of offerings, including their specialty Colorado Rack of Lamb and Filet Mignon of buffalo. Charles Court also features an exclusive Chef's Table for parties of 4 to 12. A special menu is prepared in an intimate setting just off the kitchen, where five courses are

presented by the chef and matched with wines from the restaurant's 3,000-bottle collection.

The new Summit restaurant features American Brasserie fare with a diverse menu of seasonal items that changes every other week to reflect the freshest of ingredients from around the country.

All of the restaurants feature an unusually complete wine list with an excellent choice of French Burgundies and Bordeaux at not-too-outrageous prices.

The redesigned Hotel Bar is reminiscent of the 1920's with amber Tiffany light fixtures, comfortable leather chairs and richly upholstered sofas, floor-to-ceiling window walls that open to the lake and an outdoor fireplace when weather permits. Located here are three large plasma screen televisions for watching sporting events.

The sing-along and rag-time piano at the Golden Bee has guests waiting in line to get a seat at this authentic English-style pub. First-run movies are offered each evening in the large theater at Broadmoor Main.

Sport Facilities

The three championship golf courses are all highly rated among golf authorities. The East course was built in 1918 by Donald Ross. In 1958 Robert Trent Jones Sr.reconfigured the course to form the now historic East Course where Jack Nicklaus won his first major championship. The East Course will play host to the 2008 US Senior Open.

In 1976 Jones added the remaining nine holes to form the West course and in 2006 Nicklaus Design unveiled the totally redesigned Mountain Course offering spectacular views.

There are seven tennis courts with Plexi-play surfaces in the Golf and Tennis Club at the south end of the resort, two of which are surrounded by a heated bubble during the colder months. There are two swimming pools, and the newly constructed pool at Main looks as if it is part of the lake. Guests can rent paddleboats and bikes during the summer.

Joggers will enjoy the scenic three-quarter-mile path around the lake.

The full-service spa sports 43 treatment rooms and offers more than 100 services adding to The Broadmoor's year-round appeal. With 43,000 square feet of space, it includes an indoor pool, fitness center, hair and nail salon and a relaxation room.

Miscellaneous and Environs

The 21 shops scattered around the premises include designer men's and women's boutiques, a jewelry store, a children's shop, a florist, a resort shop, beauty shop, sportswear stores, gift shops, and a large sundry store where you can purchase logo items, soft drinks, espresso and most typical drugstore items.

The concierge will arrange tours to the Cheyenne Mountain Zoo, and the Will Rogers Shrine of the Sun, up the famous Cog Railway to Pikes Peak, and to other scenic points of interest in the area. Don't miss a visit to the picturesque Garden of the Gods, ten minutes from the resort, or Seven Falls, only one and one-half miles away.

There is an organized children's program for ages 4-12 during the summer and holidays.

The service in the hotels and restaurants is very friendly, efficient, and gauged to please the most discriminating travelers. For conventioneers and vacationers seeking a traditional, elegant resort with many facilities, and excellent food and service in an incredibly picturesque setting, The Broadmoor fits the bill.

The Broadmoor
P.O. Box 1439
Lake Avenue
Colorado Springs, Colorado 80906
Tel. (800) 719-577-5775
Fax (800) 719-577-5738
Web: www.broadmoor.com

COLORADO

THE PEAKS RESORT AND GOLDEN DOOR SPA

In the midst of the panoramic San Juan mountain range of southwest Colorado, 755 feet from the historic town of Telluride, sits The Peaks Resort and Golden Door Spa, designed to blend into its natural surroundings with materials comprised of soft earth tones, sandstone, and natural oak. Doral Hotels and Resorts, in a joint venture with Japanese investors, spent $75 million to develop the luxury resort in this secluded, peaceful location with stunning mountain vistas offering year-round appeal to discerning ski, spa, golf, and outdoor sport enthusiasts. Today the resort is owned and operated by LXR Luxury Resorts.

Since its opening in May of 1992, the resort has quickly gained recognition as a full-facility, world-class destination where independent travelers, families, and business groups could luxuriate in a casual environment while pursuing exercise routines, a bevy of spa treatments, and sports ranging from skiing, golf, tennis, hiking, biking, and horseback riding to hunting, fishing, mountain climbing, whitewater rafting, and hang gliding.

The interiors of the four, six, and eight-story buildings that comprise the hotel are done in soft earth tones and light woods with tasteful art and other decorations, giving a homey, comfortable, yet elegant feel with picturesque views of the mountains from every public and private room. The entrance to the hotel opens into the Great Room, a large four-story lobby featuring a warm fireplace, evening piano music, and cocktail service. The front desk concierge, Simon Telluride Restaurant, conference room facilities, and entrance to the Golden Door Spa are all located on the same level. The two-meal-a-day, indoor/outdoor restaurant and Après Ski Dining are located on other levels.

Accommodations

The 174 very comfortable and tastefully furnished accommodations are composed of 145 spacious guest rooms, each of which includes two double beds or one king-size bed, refrigerator/mini-bar, private room safes, remote-control color television with VCR/DVD attachments for rentals from the movie library, coffee makers, and bathrooms with twin marble stalls and bathtubs, hair dryers, magnifying mirrors, and toilet compartments. The 29 suites are similarly equipped and also include a king-size bed, a couch that converts to a double bed, a second bathroom, and a full living room with its own television, refrigerator/mini-bar, lounge area, and dining table. Some suites have Jacuzzi tubs. Every guest room has a panoramic view of the surroundings and 60 percent have small balconies.

The resort is designed to offer a remote, peaceful site for business meetings. The 2,150-square-foot ballroom can seat 170 for banquets and 225 at meetings, whereas each of the two 520-square-foot conference rooms can accommodate 30 persons.

Room rates vary widely throughout the year. High season occurs from mid-December through mid-March; however guests can find discounted rates from May through November. Several four- and seven-night spa, ski, and fitness packages are offered at significant savings. Spa services, meals, taxes, and most of the sport activities are not included in the room rates. Tax and a resort tariff are added to the room rate.

Restaurants, Lounges, and Entertainment

In addition to 24-hour room service, there are three other dining options. The elegant Legends restaurant with an outdoor deck (when weather permits), offers breakfast and lunch daily, and features what the resort describes as Colorado Ranchlands cuisine. Lunch and dinner are served daily in Chef Kerry Simon's new Simon Telluride Restaurant, his first venture outside of his famed Simon's Kitchen and Bar located in the Hard Rock Hotel in Las Vegas. The casual Greatroom, off the main lobby, serves Kerry Simon light fare from 11:00 a.m. until 11:00 p.m. At each food outlet there is a large variety of spa cuisine with caloric and fat content indicated. Those visitors wishing to sample the variety of restaurants in Telluride can be transported to town.

Legends restaurant, immediately below the lobby, offers a traditional eclectic menu with some Southwestern specialties. The buffet presented at each meal includes a variety of low-calorie, low-fat spa items. Here imaginative presentations include a selection of hearty exotic game dishes, including buffalo, antelope, pheasant, and venison. Dress is casual in all eating outlets. There is entertainment in the evening in the Greatroom, off the main lobby, as well as, Legends Terrace during Après Ski.

Sport Facilities

In this category, The Peaks Resort and Spa has few equals; there is something for everyone, no matter how unusual your preference. There are six outdoor tennis courts, an indoor squash and racquetball court, an 18-hole Alpine golf course, an indoor/outdoor pool with a water slide, an indoor lap pool, four whirlpool spas, a rock-climbing wall, ski-in/ski-out facilities, cross-country and helicopter skiing, mountain biking, hiking, aerobic classes, cardiovascular machines, an indoor climbing wall, Cybex exercise equipment, and access to hunting, fishing, horseback riding, snowmobiling, ice skating, whitewater rafting, and hang gliding.

However, the trademark of The Peaks Resort and Spa is the emphasis on health and fitness with the 42,000-square-foot, four-level Golden Door Spa fa-

cility as the focal point. Guests check in at the main level and proceed to the men's or women's locker rooms, where they are provided with workout clothes, sandals, and terry-cloth robes, and they are invited to indulge in the Roman-style whirlpool, sauna, and steam rooms; to spruce up with complimentary toiletries; and to luxuriate with a choice of healthy beverages, recent newspapers, and television.

On the level above the locker rooms, for varying extra tariffs in no less than 44 treatment rooms, you can arrange for numerous types of massages, various hydrotherapy treatments, stress management services, facials, herbal wraps, and body rejuvenation therapy. There is a salon that provides his and hers hair styling, nail service, and waxing. Consultation options include makeup, total image, comprehensive health and fitness assessment, personal nutritional plans, and blood and cholesterol analysis. In addition, the menu includes dozens of other health/fitness-oriented treatments and services too numerous to describe.

Below the main entrance are located the 25-yard indoor lap pool, the Cybex weight room, the Pilate's and cycling room, the aerobic deck, the cardiovascular deck with exercycles, step machines, and treadmills looking out to the mountains, the indoor racquetball and squash courts, the climbing wall, Jacuzzis, and the children's pool and water slide.

Another feature that makes the resort an ideal family retreat is its "Base Camp" program. While

parents take advantage of the many pleasures of the breathtaking Rocky mountain setting, children 8 through 11 years can have just as much fun – with the guidance of a professional staff – exploring, learning and playing amidst the wonders of an alpine resort.

There are full-day and half-day child care services for children. Activities include songs, story time, swimming, aerobics, dancing, arts and crafts, horseback riding, tennis and games. Other favorites are outdoor excursions like panning for gold on the river, picnicking, and hiking the Boomerang Trail into town. To partake, reservations have to be made 24-hours in advance.

Miscellaneous and Environs

Daily air service to Telluride and nearby Montrose is provided by several carriers, including America West, American, Continental, Delta, Mesa, and United Airlines. There are daily nonstop flights to Telluride from Denver and Phoenix, and non-stop flights into Montrose from Chicago, Dallas, Denver, Houston, Los Angeles, Newark, and Phoenix.

The resort is located 10 minutes from the Telluride Airport, one and ¼ hours from the Montrose Airport, and two and ½ hours from the airports at Grand Junction, Durango, and Gunnison. Complimentary transportation from the Telluride Regional Airport is provided by the Wyndham Peaks Resort and Golden Door Spa. The resort also can arrange transportation from the Montrose, Gunnison, Grand Junction, and Durango Airports.

A gondola that leaves from Mountain village right outside the resort carries visitors over the mountain and drops them off in the heart of Telluride, a very small Colorado town steeped in history. Today, the retail area runs for six or seven blocks and is lined with souvenir shops, colorful pubs, a variety of restaurants, and other stores. A golf shop, gift shop, ski shop and spa boutique are located at the resort.

Guest services will arrange day horseback rides and overnight campouts, fly fishing in mountain lakes and streams, sleigh rides, snowmobile rides, cross-country skiing, scenic hikes to a waterfall, mountain bike rides, and jeep excursions throughout the area – including rides to gold and silver mines, a 19th-century mining camp, and places to pan for gold.

One of the highlights of my visit was the two-hour trail ride from the nearby Roudy Roudebush Stables. Roudy, a loquacious, animated Marlboro-man type, will personally lead guests through scenic mountain trails and dense aspen forests, where they will be treated to close-up views of deer and elk and unparalleled panoramic vistas. During the late summer and early fall, city slickers will be overwhelmed by the unbelievable beauty of yellow-leaved aspens set off by blue spruce and snow-clad mountain backdrops. Roudy's slogan is "Gentle horses for gentle people, fast horses for fast people, and for those who don't like to ride – horses that don't like to be rode".

LXR Luxury Resorts took over management in 2005 and the company has indicated that they intend to spend large sums for renovations in the near future.

The Peaks Resort and Golden Door Spa is one of the most complete luxury resorts in Colorado, offering its health conscious and sport-oriented visitors – as well as active families – some of the best ski, spa, and sports facilities in the United States, with a comfortable, luxurious, yet casual environment in a secluded, incredibly picturesque mountain setting.

The Peaks Resort and Golden Door Spa
P.O. Box 2702, 136 Country Club Drive
Telluride, Colorado 81435
Tel. (970) 728-6800, (800) 789-2220
Fax (970) 728-6567
www.thepeaksresort.com

FLORIDA

THE BREAKERS

Situated on 140 acres of beachfront property surrounded by lush, tropical flora and fauna, only six miles from the Palm Beach Airport, and a few minutes from the fashionable Worth Avenue shopping center, this venerable Italian Renaissance-style resort has catered to socialites, dignitaries, and the well-heeled since the turn of the century.

Henry Flagler – cofounder with Rockefeller of the Standard Oil Company – originally built the Palm Beach Inn on this site in 1896. In 1903, it was destroyed by fire and replaced by the larger Breakers. The hotel was again razed by a fire in 1925 and was rebuilt immediately by architect Leonard Schultze (of Waldorf-Astoria fame). The facade and twin towers were inspired by the Villa Medici in Rome. The decor of the public areas is done in the style of the Italian Renaissance, and there are nineteenth-century Flemish tapestries, vaulted, hand-painted ceilings, marble floors, and Mediterranean-style gardens and fountains.

Today, the resort is operated by Flagler Systems, Inc., a privately held corporation owned by heirs of Flagler's third wife, and boasts a friendly service-minded staff of over 1,700. A 10 percent sales tax is added to all rooms, and an 18-20 percent gratuity is added to all food and beverage checks.

A $225-million renovation and revitalization of the guest rooms, restaurants, public areas, golf course and landscaped grounds was commenced in 1990 and completed by 2000. The new Ocean Golf Clubhouse and ocean-front Beach Club and Spa were also added about the same time. However, this modernization has not changed the unique decor of The Breakers, which is a combination of Old World Italian Renaissance, circa 1920 Florida and present-day casual Palm Beach.

Accommodations

There are 560 renovated guest accommodations, including 57 suites. The more expensive rooms are very large and have separate dressing rooms, double closets, a separate tub and shower, and special seating areas. The junior suites, two Imperial suites, and two Royal Poinciana suites are even larger. All rooms are appointed with hardwood furniture, tasteful prints, plush carpeting, mini-bars, remote-control color televisions, AM/FM radios, hair dryers, irons and ironing boards, robes, makeup mirrors, fax modems, and private safes. Rooms feature garden, fairway, or ocean views.

The ambient Flagler Club, a concierge lounge with an extensive outdoor balcony area, is located on the sixth and seventh floors of the hotel offering enhanced amenities, including Continental breakfast, afternoon tea, and evening cocktails and cordials with hors d'oeuvres.

There are 10 cabanas for rent by the pool and 58 in the beach area, as well as 45,000 square feet of flexible meeting space in the main hotel which includes 21 meeting rooms that double as banquet facilities. Some have vaulted, hand-painted ceilings with valuable art and tapestries. Twelve hundred guests can be accommodated in the Venetian Ballroom. The relatively new 15,000-square-foot Ponce de Leon Ballroom is divisible into six sections. This resort is definitely equipped to cater to the high-end conference and convention trade, as well as the social guest.

Restaurants, Lounges, and Entertainment

Dining possibilities include the casual Circle Dining Room, an ocean-view restaurant with a 30-foot oval ceiling adorned with Renaissance-period murals, serving an impressive breakfast buffet daily, as well as à la carte items and an impressive Sunday brunch; the elegant L'Escalier at the the Florentine Room is the fine dining venue, featuring modern French cuisine, and fine wines from the resort's 6,000-bottle cellar; the "clubby" Flagler's Steakhouse at the Golf Clubhouse, highlighting prime meats, seafood and specialties both indoors and on its patio open for lunch and dinner; the casual Italian Restaurant at the Family Entertainment Center; and the French Riviera-inspired Beach Club Restaurant and Terrace offering imaginative soups, salads, sandwiches, light and spa cuisine.

In addition, guests can enjoy fresh fish, seafood, and chowder at the Seafood Bar; salads, sandwiches, and libations at the seaside Reef Bar; appetizers, cocktails, and wines at the Tapestry Bar next to L'Escalier; and pastry, salads, sandwiches, coffees and ice cream treats at "News and Gourmet" while browsing for eclectic gift items. Of course, room service is available around the clock.

Off site, only a few minutes from the main hotel, is Echo, a stylish destination for Asian cuisine that features culinary specialties from China, Japan, Thailand and Viet Nam. The resort will provide transportation if needed.

There is little nightly entertainment save a jazz trio in the Tapestry Bar Thursdays through Sundays during high season.

Sport Facilities

The half-mile, private beach runs behind the hotel, extending out to the Beach Club. On a calm day, the beach and swimming area are quite good by Florida standards, and the availability of chaise lounges, unlimited towels, bar service, and the adjacent pool, cabanas, and children's playground make this an ideal spot for sun and fun. The Mediterranean-style Beach Club and Spa has four pools including a new luxury relaxations pool, a new active family pools, a children's pool and a four-lane lap pool. Located at the beach are duplex and triple-plex beach bungalows with various amenities available for day-time rental.

The 20,000-square-foot, indoor/outdoor Spa includes the four-lane lap pool, 17 massage and treat-

ment rooms, one over-sized Jacuzzi, a fully-equipped fitness center, beauty salon, and his and her locker rooms with steam and sauna. Guests can choose from 12 different massage offerings, Guerlain skin-care services, numerous body treatments, spa-suite treatments, fitness classes, personalized fitness services, beauty services, as well as spa cuisine. For those not booking a treatment there is a $35 per day charge for use of the spa and fitness facilities and/or participation in fitness classes. An additional equipped fitness center is available for guests in the main hotel gratis.

Across the street from the main hotel entrance, a new Golf Clubhouse opened in 2000. At the pro-shop, you will find a bevy of golf and tennis attire and equipment, as well as, racquets and clubs for rent. The 18-hole Ocean course that emanates from the Clubhouse was renovated by Brian Silva in 1999, and guests can enjoy an additional 18 holes of championship golf at Breakers Rees Jones Course, which was reconstructed in 2004.

10 Hard Tru tennis courts (with lighting for night play) are adjacent and the tennis program includes teaching pros and clinics. Atop the Clubhouse is the aforementioned Flagler Steakhouse with a traditional Florida-style dining patio looking out over the golf course.

In addition, the resort offers putting greens, lawn bowling, croquet, table tennis, shuffleboard, bicycle rentals, snorkeling, sailing, and scuba diving. The Lake Worth jogging and bicycle trail is located about a quarter mile from the hotel, providing a paved path with Lake Worth and yacht slips to the west and lovely homes and gardens to the east.

Miscellaneous and Environs

Although there are several specialty boutiques, swim wear and children's shops, a Piaget jewelry and a fine crystal store, a hair salon and a sundry-gift shop in the main hotel, visitors may want to visit the famous Worth Avenue shopping center a mile from the resort, with its 200 shops, galleries, and restaurants.

The resort offers fabulous children's facilities with programs designed for tots, children and families. Throughout the year, youngsters can be enrolled for a half or full day in the supervised Coconut Crew Camp. The 6,100-foot Family Entertainment Center includes children's' and tots' play rooms equipped with computers, crafts and movie facilities, as well as, a game arcade with video and electronic games and an outdoor maze called "The Secret Garden". The casual, family-friendly Italian Restaurant is in this building across the hall from a children's play room affording an outlet for family members who get antsy during the meal. An additional playground is located on the beach.

Palm Beach is a rather formal resort area, and The Breakers, in keeping with the general aura of this posh Florida community, exudes a casually sophisticated atmosphere. The resort seems very comfortable with its elegant image. This is not a haven for swingers, bon vivants, or budget-minded vacationers; however, vacationing couples and families, and those on business meetings seeking understated elegance, very friendly, efficient service, outstanding sport and children's facilities, and diverse dining possibilities will find their visit to The Breakers highly rewarding.

The Breakers
South County Road
Palm Beach, Florida 33480
Tel. (561) 655-6611, (888) BREAKERS
Fax (561) 659-8403
www.thebreakers.com

FLORIDA

THE COLONY BEACH AND TENNIS RESORT

This is the tennis buff's dream resort. Located eight miles from Sarasota Airport on a large, lovely white-sand beach on Longboat Key, The Colony Beach and Tennis Resort offers the ultimate in spacious accommodations and semi-tropical atmosphere in an area boasting many sophisticated shops and restaurants. The unusually large guest units with kitchen facilities, the special children's program, and the excellent tennis instruction for youngsters make this an ideal family resort (especially for those involved in tennis).

The apartment-suites surround the tennis courts, in front of which are the 800-foot private beach, dining rooms, a freshwater pool, and the main six-story building.

Accommodations

The 235 one- and two-bedroom apartment-suites are located in 18 wood-frame buildings that are situated around the 21 tennis courts and the six-story main hotel building. There are individual parking spaces next to each building. Each guest unit has a large living/dining room area with live plants and fresh flowers, an enclosed balcony, twin hideaway beds, color television, and a kitchenette stocked with eating utensils, plates, glasses, pots, pans, dishwasher, toaster, refrigerator, ice maker, cabinets, soap, and everything needed to keep house. Maid service is included. The master bedroom area is also very large and tastefully appointed with dressers, two closets, a separate mirrored dressing room, and a master bathroom with a tub-shower unit that includes whirlpool and steam. Those who choose the

two-bedroom apartment-suites get everything that comes with the one-bedroom units, as well as a second-floor loft that contains another large bedroom, walk-in closet, and bathroom. Thus, a family with four children could be very comfortably accommodated. Washers and dryers are conveniently located in each building unit.

There are additional guest suites in the six-story main hotel building and luxury suites for couples directly on the beach. Three beach cottages are also available. Conference room facilities with over 8,000 square feet of meeting space can accommodate up to 250 people and include a full range of equipment and services.

Restaurants, Lounges, and Entertainment

The bright, airy restaurant overlooking the beach is tastefully decorated in soft tones with an elegant yet comfortable ambiance. The award-winning kitchen, which serves gourmet cuisine and fresh seafood, is considered one of the best in the Sarasota area. Our recent visit reaffirms our opinion that this is one of the top resort restaurants in the United States.

Lunch and dinner are served in The Colony Dining Room, including a buffet Sunday brunch that is a favorite with local residents, as well as guests. Less formal, The Monkey Room restaurant offers all three meals in its casual indoor and outdoor areas, both affording spectacular water views. The Monkey Room Patio near the outdoor pool patio serves cool, tropical drinks and is open daily. In the evening, there is live entertainment in The Monkey Room Bar (adjacent to The Monkey Room), as well

as a piano bar. A welcome facility on the property is Tastebuds, a gourmet wine and deli market. For the convenience of the guests, the store offers soft drinks, wines, liquors, bakery, and deli specialties, as well as a range of grocery items permitting guests to prepare breakfast, lunch, and snacks in their kitchenettes. Guests can preorder groceries from Tastebuds prior to their arrival and have them in their suite.

Sport Facilities

When the weather is ideal, the waters of Longboat Key are reminiscent of the clear, warm waters of the Caribbean; however, at other times of the year, they are colder and can be choppy. The beach is wide and lovely and you can take a walk or jog along the sand for miles in either direction. Sailboats,

kayaks, and windsurfing boards are available. There is also a freshwater pool right off the beach. The hotel provides complimentary chaise lounges and towels.

The men's and women's health spas offer sauna, steam, whirlpool, and a variety of massages, body treatments, facials and salon services. Guests of The Colony Beach and Tennis Resort enjoy privileges at several local championship golf courses. There are facilities for basketball and volleyball. The complimentary state-of-the-art fitness center includes free weights, cardiovascular equipment, and varied aerobic classes for guests. A children's playground is also available on the premises, and bicycles can be rented by the hour or day.

Never mind the spacious accommodations, excellent cuisine, and numerous facilities. Tennis, tennis, and more tennis is what this resort is all about.

There are 21 excellent all-weather courts, two of which are lighted for night play, and 10 of which are soft courts. Tennis is free, and the helpful staff of 10 USPTA pros will arrange games for you around the clock. In addition, there is a superb daily tennis instruction program, including tennis classes for all levels of play, as well as regular tournaments for the guests. A week at The Colony Beach and Tennis Resort will go a long way toward sharpening your tennis game.

Miscellaneous and Environs

The Colony Beach and Tennis Resort is a family resort and a daily children's recreational program, run by special counselors, is available at no charge. There are arts, crafts, shell collecting, games, scavenger hunts, fishing and movies.

There is also a pro shop and a designer boutique at the hotel; however, guests may want to explore the shops at St. Armand's Circle, only five minutes away by car.

Although you will not want to miss the marvelous gourmet restaurant at The Colony Beach and Tennis Resort, you will also have a choice of several French Continental, Spanish, Pacific Rim, and seafood restaurants scattered over Longboat Key and St. Armand's Circle.

The Colony Beach and Tennis Resort offers unusually spacious and workable accommodations for the entire family, a superb tennis program, one of the best Florida beaches, and truly exceptional dining in a lovely subtropical, unspoiled resort area. This may be one of the best bargains for a family vacation to an upscale resort in the United States.

The Colony Beach and Tennis Resort
1620 Gulf of Mexico Drive
Longboat Key, Florida 34228
Tel. (800) 237-9443 (United States and Canada),
    (941) 383-6464
Fax (941) 383-7549
E-mail: info@colonyfl.com
Web: www.colonybeachresort.com

DORAL GOLF RESORT AND SPA, A MARRIOTT RESORT

Only a short distance from the Miami International Airport, the Doral Golf Resort and Spa is located on a most attractive, spacious 650-acre property. Surrounded by beautiful gardens, waterfalls, and five championship golf courses, the recently renovated Doral Golf Resort and Spa offers a full complement of facilities.

In September 1987, the magnificent $78-million, 48-suite Spa at the Doral Golf Resort and Spa opened (originally called Doral Saturnia International Spa). Located a short walk from the main resort complex, surrounded by Italian-style walkways and floral gardens, the spa, with its clay-tiled rooftop, Roman arches, formal balustrades, gushing cascades, and 100-foot-high atrium, reflects the mood of Saturnia in the heart of Tuscany, Italy, the home of the foremost Italian spa, Terme di Saturnia. Spa guests have access to all the facilities of the golf resort. Those staying at the resort and wishing to visit the spa can enjoy half- or full-day use of all spa facilities, including several spa services, for a fee.

In 2005, Marriott took over management and the resort is scheduled to receive $40 million for renovations to the golf course and for a new 60,000 square-foot meeting and conference facility.

Accommodations

At the resort, there are ten three- and four-story lodges adjacent to the main building, containing 693 guest rooms, all of which have received various renovations over the years. The guest rooms are average in size, pleasantly decorated, and include a refrigerator, a mini-bar, an entertainment center, and a small balcony or patio. Room rates vary according to size and location, with a 17 percent gratuity added to all food and beverage charges. There is no charge for parking your own car, but valet parking costs $15 overnight. Currently there are 40 meeting rooms and 3 ballrooms, the largest of which accommodates up to 1,500 persons. With the new ballroom facility which will be completed by late 2006, as well as, the many other facilities, Doral is an ideal spot for large conventions and small executive conferences.

The exquisite Spa at Doral offers 48 spacious suites varying in size and lavishly designed by Sarah Tomerlin Lee. Most have living rooms, entertainment centers, and two European marble bathrooms with gold-plated fixtures, Jacuzzi bathtubs, oversized shower stalls, separate toilet compartments, and separate his and hers vanities, closets, and dressing areas. Several of these suites have two separate bedrooms. Six of the suites, known as Executive Suites, are smaller with single vanities, a sitting area rather than a living room, and a Jacuzzi tub with shower attachment.

Restaurants, Lounges, and Entertainment

There are five restaurants on property, all under the direction of world renowned chef Jean Claude Lanchais. Each location offers guests a unique menu and dining experience. The Terrazza Restaurant and Café, a casual venue with both inside and outside seating, serves a buffet breakfast and an à la carte lunch and dinner, specializing in a blend of American and Caribbean cuisines. For dinner, Windows affords dining in a romantic setting with a spectac-

ular view and superb cuisine and service, with emphasis on excellent quality meats, fresh fish, and seafood. Monday through Friday, Windows features a luncheon buffet renowned throughout the area. The Champions Sport Bar is open for sandwiches, snacks, and drinks until 2 a.m. Drinks and snacks are also served by the pool at Bungalou's Bar and Grill.

At the Spa, the bright, airy restaurant known as The Atrium soars four stories to a sky-lit cupola and features spa food (referred to as "clean cuisine") for all three meals. Lunch is also charmingly served outdoors on the patio overlooking the formal gardens and pool. The food could be described as gourmet spa cuisine with a Tuscan influence. The menu includes a "fat point system" for those on a health or diet plan. This imaginative spa menu makes dieting fun. After each item is listed the calorie count and fat point count. Though health oriented, the tasteful presentation and clever seasoning renders the dining experience very satisfying and

never boring. Although formal in appearance, the dress and ambiance is relaxed and casual.

Sport Facilities

The Doral Golf Resort and Spa is one of the largest self-contained golf facilities in the world, with five 18-hole golf courses, a driving range, and three practice putting greens. Discounted green fees are available for hotel guests on all the courses, including the famed Blue Monster, site of the PGA Tour's Ford Championship. The Doral Golf Resort and Spa offers golfers an extensive array of amenities, including a golf learning center, a driving range, three practice putting greens, a pro shop and boutique, and golf club rental, cleaning, and storage service.

There is a small exercise facility at The Doral Golf Resort, but guests will prefer the far superior facility at the Spa. The scenic jogging track – three miles round trip – winds around the golf courses. The Blue Lagoon swimming pool sits out in front of the main building and is surrounded by a large deck area with numerous lounge chairs, and Bun-

galou's Bar and Grill. For the youngsters, there is a basketball court and a fully equipped electronic game room. For fishing enthusiasts, 34 acres of well-stocked lakes meander around 140 acres of golf courses; fishing equipment is available for rent.

Camp Doral is located at the Blue Lagoon recreation area. Inside, there is 1,200 square feet of space for activities. Children ages 5 through 12 can enjoy tennis, golf, swimming, arts and crafts, and movies.

The Spa at the Doral Golf Resort and Spa offers 24 different aerobic, stretching, and strengthening exercises (including jogging, swimming, golf, tennis, rowing, riding, and cycling); lectures on diet, cooking, exercise, and stress management; three pools (two outdoor and one indoor); a state-of-the-art fitness center; an indoor jogging track located on the top floor; an outdoor exercourse; yoga, steam, saunas, massage, herbal wraps, hydromassage, mineral and plankton baths, facials, fangos, detoxification, and face and hair makeovers; and everything else you can imagine. The men's and women's spas are clean and inviting. Attendants are always on hand.

Miscellaneous and Environs

In addition to its friendly service, another of the Doral Golf Resort and Spa's pleasant features is its location – 15 minutes from Miami International Airport. This is the basis for the resort's promise to have you teeing off on one of its five courses within 20 minutes of arriving in Miami.

The Doral Golf Resort and Spa has several shops spread around the premises. The resort offers various golf, tennis, and spa packages that afford savings over the normal daily rates for guests wishing to take advantage of these facilities.

The magnificent Spa at the Doral Golf Resort and Spa is one of the most elegant, beautifully appointed, luxurious, and complete spa facilities in the United States. The Doral Golf Resort and Spa, for years, has been the best self-contained resort in the Miami area. Together, they combine to offer visitors to southern Florida an unusually wide range of sport and spa facilities, as well as a variety of dining possibilities, good service, and comfortable accommodations.

Doral Golf Resort and Spa, a Marriott Resort
4400 North West 87th Avenue
Miami, Florida 33178-2192
Tel. (305) 592-2000, (800) 71-DORAL
Spa (800) 331-7768
Fax (305) 591-9266
Web: www.doralresort.com

GRAND CYPRESS RESORT
HYATT REGENCY GRAND CYPRESS
THE VILLAS OF GRAND CYPRESS

The magnificent, world-class Grand Cypress Resort complex enjoys an enviable location near Disney Village, 18 miles from the Orlando airport, and only a 10- to 20-minute drive from Universal Studios, SeaWorld, the Magic Kingdom, Epcot, MGM, Animal Kingdom and numerous other Orlando attractions. Surrounded by 45 holes of Jack Nicklaus-designed, championship golf courses with impeccably manicured, verdant green fairways, the Grand Cypress Resort is unquestionably the most luxurious family golf resort on the United States mainland.

Rising 18 stories above the resort, the $110-million, 750-room, luxury Hyatt Regency Grand Cypress hotel opened its doors in February of 1984, and it soon became one of the top upscale family destinations in the United States. The hotel is owned by Grand Cypress Florida, Inc., but is managed by Hyatt. It exemplifies the taste, expertise, and friendly service that have come to be associated with Hyatt Corporation. The open 200-foot-high atrium lobby, with tropical plants, trees, fresh flowers, original artwork, and glassed-in scenic elevators, is breathtaking. The $1 million dollars' worth of artwork that is scattered throughout the resort includes Oriental jade, Thai sculptures, Italian marble carvings, bronze statues, and original tapestries.

Approximately a mile down the road from the Hyatt is the entrance to The Villas of Grand Cypress – cleverly designed, Mediterranean-style town homes offering 146 additional rooms in luxurious, spacious club suites or one-, two-, three-, and four-bedroom villas spread along the fairways and waterways of the golf course, all proximate to the golf clubhouse and an attractive pool area. This is an ideal choice for families traveling in grand style but requiring extra space and kitchen facilities.

In addition to the two properties on the Grand Cypress Resort acreage, guests can enjoy the Grand Cypress Golf Club, a comfortable golf clubhouse with restaurants, a pro shop, PGA-certified instructors, an award winning golf academy, and 45 holes of Jack Nicklaus-designed golf; the Grand Cypress Equestrian Center, featuring trail rides, clinics, horse shows, and professional trainers; the Grand Cypress Racquet Club, with 12 tennis courts and a clubhouse; a man-made lake for boating; a self-contained Executive Meeting Center; seven diverse restaurants; and a nature area and Audubon walk. This is one of the most complete full-facility resorts in the world.

Accommodations

The 750 newly renovated guest rooms at the Hyatt are done in airy tones, bright, vivid greens with natural wood and wicker chairs, ceiling fans, shutters, and balconies. In each room, there is a clock, color television with cable and closed circuit movies, available internet access either one king-size or two double beds, and complimentary soaps, lotions, colognes, and other amenities.

There are also 67 expensively furnished suites that are among the most lavish to be found anywhere in the world. The five super-deluxe, bi-level penthouse suites have two-story-high parlors, giant sun decks for entertaining, and come complete with sleeping lofts, marble bathrooms with Jacuzzi tubs and separate shower stalls, dining rooms, kitchens, and wet bars; three even have baby grand pianos.

In addition, the 42 Executive suites, 16 VIP suites, and 11 Hospitality suites are incredibly spacious, lavishly decorated, and exude that special touch of class.

There are 27 convention meeting rooms, totaling 65,000 square feet, including a 25,000-square-foot ballroom; 16,768 square feet of exhibition area, divisible into nine separate breakout rooms; and a complete inventory of audiovisual equipment. In addition, a new Executive Meeting Center for use by The Villas of Grand Cypress guests is adjacent to The Villas, offering 7,000 square feet of flexible meeting space in seven meeting rooms with terrace and lakeside setting, ideal for smaller groups and executive level conferences.

Regency Club guests are located on the 11th and 17th floors and receive special touches such as complimentary breakfast items, snacks and beverages, evening cocktails, and hors d'oeuvres, plus private concierge service, all for anl additional room charge.

There is no charge for children under 18 who share a room with their parents.

For those requiring even larger accommodations, or who prefer more seclusion, the spacious Mediterranean-style Villas of Grand Cypress, located along the waterways and fairways of the golf course would be the best choice. Here, there are 146 rooms spread among Club suites, or one-, two-, three-, and four-bedroom Villas, all with marble bathrooms with separate showers, hair dryers, and amenities; sitting areas; electronic safes; wireless high speed internet access; CD/cassette players; private patios or verandas; and choice of fireplaces,

whirlpools, full kitchens, and dining rooms. French doors, cathedral ceilings, soft fabrics, and natural bleached wood trim give these accommodations an airy, spacious feel. Guests staying at The Villas are provided transportation around the property and, like all guests visiting the Grand Cypress Resort, enjoy full privileges at the Hyatt, as well as all of the other resort facilities, restaurants, and amenities.

Restaurants, Lounges, and Entertainment

Cascade, the main dining room, with a 35-foot waterfall bathing a bronze mermaid, tropical greenery, comfortable chairs, and a panoramic view, serves breakfast, lunch, and dinner. It serves in place of the ordinary coffee shop found in most hotels. Dress is casual here. At breakfast, you are greeted by friendly service people who immediately pour you a tall glass of fresh Florida orange juice and a cup of coffee. All entrées are presented with fresh strawberries and other garnishes.

Hemingway's perched above the swimming pool, with a Key West atmosphere features fresh fish, seafood, steaks, and snacks in a casual atmosphere for dinner. Gourmets will prefer the more formal, elegant dining at La Coquina, where 120 guests can be treated to new world cuisine, fine wines, and music, all in a setting overlooking the lake. From the Fitz and Floyd china and gracious waiters to the rosette butters, complimentary Evian water, and imaginative presentation, you will feel pampered beyond expectation. Especially noteworthy is the Chef's champagne Sunday brunch, as well as, the "Chef's Table", where participants dine in the chef's kitchen for an epicurean orchestrated meal.

In the evening, the Western-style White Horse Sports Bar and Grill menu features steaks, chops, prime rib, and sea food specialties while patrons can watch their favorite sport event on large screen televisions.

The Golf Club is the location of the Black Swan Restaurant, featuring Continental cuisine in an intimate setting overlooking the golf course. A second, more casual, restaurant, The Club, offers breakfast, lunch, and dinner at the Golf Club along with high definition televisions for viewing sports events. An impressive display of golf memorabilia is also located here.

At the Hyatt buffeteria-style Palm Café, there are fast-service foods for the family from 6:30 a.m. until 9:30 p.m., ideal for informal meals with children. Adjacent to the Palm Café, the general store offers convenient one-stop shopping for all of your snack food cravings. Rolls, breads, and bakery items are outstanding throughout the resort.

Sport Facilities

A $13-per-room, per-night, resort fee affords guests complimentary use of bicycles, boats, a nine-hole Pitch 'n Putt course and driving range, court time at the racquet club, use of the health club, and shuttle transportation to Disney, Sea World and Universal theme parks.

The half-acre free-form pool, with 12 waterfalls, three whirlpools, a 45-foot water slide, grotto bar, suspension bridge, and tropical landscaping, is one of the most outstanding this side of the Acapulco Princess. Across from the pool is a 1,000-foot white-sand beach on Lake Windsong. (There is no swimming in the lake.) There is also a marina with sailboats, windsurfers, canoes, and paddleboats. A large, free-form pool, Jacuzzi, bar, and clubhouse with sauna and steam rooms are located at the Villas.

Adjacent to the pool at the Hyatt is a 9-hole, pitch-and-putt golf course; and proximate to the villas are the Grand Cypress Resort's golf courses, which include three 9-hole courses and the 18-hole "New Course" designed to resemble the world-famous "Old Course" at St. Andrew's, Scotland. All of the 45 holes are highly rated by Golf Digest and Golf Magazine. The golf facilities, designed by Jack Nicklaus, include a fully stocked pro shop, a driving range, a golf academy with "Model Golf Video" computer graphics and instruction programs, and teaching pros.

The Grand Cypress Racquet Club includes 12 tennis courts (8 clay and 4 Har-tru), 6 of which are lighted for night play, and two racquetball courts. There are ball machines, practice backboards, a clubhouse, shops, and tennis pros for lessons.

The health club by the pool at the Hyatt has exercise equipment, a steam room, sauna, and massage therapists. The club is free with the resort services program. Massage, therapy and boutique spa services are available at an additional charge.

There are 3.2- and 4.7-mile jogging trails, and bicycles are available at the pool hut.

Children will enjoy the above facilities and also a special playground, an electronic game room, volleyball, shuffleboard, and the Camp Hyatt Grand Cypress program. In addition, there is a child-care center staffed with qualified counselors right in the main hotel.

The Equestrian Center offers English and Western saddles, escorted trail rides, pony rides for youngsters, jumping rings, a tack and gift shop, full boarding for visiting horses, and horseback riding lessons for beginners, as well as advanced riders.

Miscellaneous and Environs

Although there are only a few shops at the resort, Downtown Disney is only a few minutes away, offering almost every form of retail shopping imaginable.

The Grand Cypress Resort provides a unique location for family vacationers in that it is only a few miles from the Magic Kingdom and Epcot Center, Animal Kingdom, MGM, and Universal Studios, and it is also near Pleasure Island, Circus World, Sea World, and Wet N' Wild, all well-known family entertainment areas. There is a complimentary shuttle to the major theme parks from the Hyatt at pre-arranged times.

Several vans transport guests around the resort, to the golf course, and to other resort facilities.

Hyatt and the investment group who created the Grand Cypress Resort have come up with a definite winner here, combining to offer the ultimate resort near the greatest family attraction of all time. Guests at The Villas of Grand Cypress and the Hyatt Regency Grand Cypress enjoy superior service and accommodations, truly exceptional dining, and a complete assortment of sport facilities in beautifully unique surroundings.

Hyatt Regency Grand Cypress
One Grand Cypress Boulevard
Orlando, Florida 32836
Tel. (800) 239-1234
Fax (407) 239-3800
Web: www.hyattgrandcypress.com

The Villas of Grand Cypress
One North Jacaranda
Orlando, Florida 32836
Tel. 800-835-7377
Fax (407) 239-7219
Web: www.grandcypress.com

THE RITZ-CARLTON RESORTS OF NAPLES
THE RITZ-CARLTON
THE RITZ-CARLTON GOLF RESORT

The second resort to be built by The Ritz-Carlton Hotel Company opened its doors to the public in December 1985. Located on 20 acres of prime beachfront property on the Gulf of Mexico at the north end of Pelican Bay, it is the only luxury resort of its kind on the southwest coast of Florida.

The facade of the 14-story hotel building is styled to look like a Mediterranean palace circa the early 1900s. However, the interior is traditional Ritz-Carlton grandeur with English antiques, expensive reproductions, 18th- and 19th-century art, lavish antique Oriental rugs, warm woods, high ceilings, and French doors overlooking landscaped courtyards and seaside gardens. The lobby, main dining room, and all guest room balconies afford panoramic views of a tropical waterway and white-sand beach fronting the calm Gulf waters.

Nestled in the 700-acre residential/golfing community of Tiburon, the 295-room Ritz-Carlton Golf Resort opened in 2002. Located three and a half miles to the east of the Beach Resort, guests can go back and forth by a shuttle service that operates every half hour from 6 a.m. until midnight and thereby enjoy reciprocal privileges at both properties. Although unquestionably "Ritz-Carlton" style, the decor is a bit less traditional with an Italian flare and Mediterranean accents.

The Ritz-Carlton Hotel Company, formed in 1983, has the rights to "The Ritz-Carlton" name and manages numerous Ritz-Carlton hotels throughout the United States, including the resorts in Orlando, Key Biscayne and Manalapan, Florida, and in Laguna Niguel, California. The company plans to open additional resorts and hotels in the United States and abroad in the next few years.

Accommodations

The 450 standard guest rooms at the Beach Resort are beautifully decorated, and all have small, French-doored balconies with views of the Gulf, as well as a remote-control color television, a writing desk, an entryway with a dressing table, a refrigerator and mini-bar, multi-line telephones with voice mail, computer and fax hookups, personal safes, plush terry-cloth robes for use while at the resort, a king-size or two double beds, and marble bathrooms with a separate toilet compartment complete with telephone, and premium bath essentials.

In addition, there are 25 junior suites that have all amenities of the regular guest rooms plus a parlor area with television, an extra sink in the dressing area, and an additional balcony.

The two Presidential suites are lavish with a large bedroom, two bathrooms, two televisions, a giant living room and dining room, a pantry, a wood-burning fireplace, two balconies, and exquisite furnishings.

The 295 guest rooms including 38 suites at the Golf Resort are similar, and each has a balcony overlooking the golf course and a bathroom with double vanities and separate shower stalls. The suites are divided into two separate rooms and include a guest bathroom. 54 of the rooms and suites are designated "Club" rooms with similar privileges as those at the Beach Resort.

For an additional $100-$250 per day, guests can enjoy a regular guest room on the Club floors, accessible only with a special elevator key. For the extra tariff, you receive special concierge service, newspapers, a magnificent Continental breakfast, a light lunch and snacks and alcoholic beverages throughout the day, at cocktail hour, and after dinner.

This Ritz-Carlton, Naples is very interested in wooing the convention and meeting trade which makes up from 50% to 60% of the clientele, and has devoted a good portion of the public areas to lavish meeting and conference facilities. Included in the over 35,000- square feet of facilities at the Beach Resort are 19 such rooms, the largest being 10,000 square feet, accommodating 600 people for meetings and up to 1,000 for receptions. The parking facilities will service 560 cars. At the Golf Resort there is an additional 15,000-square feet of meeting and conference space. The resort is recognized as one of the top meeting and incentive destinations by the travel industry.

Restaurants, Lounges, and Entertainment

The Beach Resort:
The Terrace, near the two pools, has both indoor and outdoor tables, is open from 6:30 a.m. until 10:00 p.m., and offers all three meals, as well as snacks and beverages, throughout the day.

The Dining Room done in traditional Florida decor looks out through French doors onto terraced gardens, with romantic banquettes for couples in addition to its larger tables. The epicurean menu is composed of regional dishes with European techniques. The more intimate Grill, next door, has its own bar and features prime beef, steaks, fish, and seafood in a romantic English-club setting.
Throughout the evening, pianists play in The Dining Room, The Grill, and in The Lobby Lounge. Afternoon tea and cocktails are served in The Lobby Lounge in the Ritz-Carlton tradition with Devonshire cream, finger sandwiches, pastries, and an assortment of teas served on Wedgwood bone china.

Gumbo Limbo, on the boardwalk overlooking the Gulf with umbrella-protected tables, provides specialties for lunch and dinner and sunset cocktails and drinks. Sandwiches, salads, snacks, and drinks are also available around the pool. After dinner, The Club features a live band and entertainment in an elegant, charming, bi-level room similar to the nightclub at Laguna Niguel. Cocktails are also served throughout the evening in The Lobby Lounge.

The Golf Resort:
All three meals are offered at Lemonia both indoors and on an outside terrace. Lunch and dinner feature imaginative creations from Tuscany and other regions of Italy. Lighter fare is available at the Poolside Grill and at the Lobby Lounge. At "eXpresso", guests can take out specialty coffees, homemade desserts and fruits. The Bar Room is a venue that encompasses a lounge bar, billiard tables and a card room. A piano player and vocalist perform nightly in the restaurant and lounge.

Sport Facilities

The Beach Resort:
Two swimming pools, one free form, the other for swimming laps are surrounded by comfortable lounge chairs and a service bar with solicitous waitresses and deck attendants, and are adjacent to The Terrace restaurant and tennis courts. The tennis courts can be illuminated for night play, and a professional instructor helps arrange games and is available for lessons.

The white-sand beach which fronts the resort is as good as one finds in Florida and will be especially enjoyed by joggers, power-walkers and shell collectors. Windsurfing, wave runners, and sailboats are available; and offshore fishing can be arranged through the concierge. There are 40 umbrella-style, beach cabanas, as well as a beachside restaurant that serves meals, snacks, and drinks, and has toilet facilities. Lounges are available on the beach, and attendants will set you up with towels.

Shuttle service to and from the two 18-hole Greg Norman-designed golf courses at the Golf Resort is available throughout the day.

In 2001, a magnificent, world-class, three-story spa and fitness center was incorporated into the main hotel building. The exercise facility is most impressive with numerous cardio-vascular machines (including treadmills with individual TV.'s) free-weights and Paramount equipment. Aerobic, yoga, Pilates, power-cycling and dozens of other classes are offered throughout the day. There is a $10 charge for a group class and private lessons and consultations are available from $45 to $75.

The luxurious men and women's changing rooms have private lockers, sauna, steam, therapy pools and many personal amenities. Guests not taking spa treatments are charged $35 for use of these facilities.

The spa includes over 30 treatment rooms featuring numerous massage therapies, body wraps and peels, facials, collagen infusions and other services that range in cost from $85-$430 per hour. A full service beauty salon is also located here.

The Golf Resort:

The two 18-hole, Greg Norman designed, championship courses are connected to the Rick Smith Golf Academy offering group and private instruction. Resort guests have access to the clubhouse with its lounge and locker rooms, equipment rentals, a driving range and pitch and putt facility. Also at the Golf Resort are four lighted tennis courts, a free-form heated pool with lap lanes and an outdoor Jacuzzi surrounded by lounge chairs and the Poolside Grill, a children's playground, a putting green, a small fitness center with massage and body treatments.

Miscellaneous and Environs

On the premises of the Beach Resort are men's and ladies' fashion boutiques, a sundry shop, and a full-service beauty salon. The Pavilion Shopping Center, with supermarket and other stores, is a mile up the road. Old Naples shopping area, six miles away, has fashionable boutiques, art, and curio stores, as well as cafés and restaurants. There is a Ritz-Carlton signature shop and a sundry shop at the Golf Resort.

For a fee, both resorts offer daily Ritz-Kids, a day camp for children, ages 5-12 with organized activities, crafts and computer games. A variety of other activities are offered each day for all guests ranging from cooking and etiquette classes to nature walks and art tours.

Visitors can fly into the new southwest Florida Regional Airport in Fort Myers and then drive south for 25 miles; or fly into Naples Airport, which is only 10 miles from the hotel; or take the two- to two-and-one-half-hour drive across Alligator Alley (Interstate 75) from the Miami or Fort Lauderdale airports.

The Ritz-Carlton Hotel Company has provided the answer for those seeking an elegant, exclusive, self-contained resort with a world-class spa, excellent food and impeccable service, with the option to be located on a beautiful white-sand beach on Florida's southwest coast or in a picturesque golf community.

The Ritz-Carlton Resorts of Naples
280 Vanderbilt Beach Road
Naples, Florida 34108
Tel. (239) 598-3300
Fax (239) 598-6690
www.ritzcarlton.com/resorts/naples_golf_resort

WEST VIRGINIA

THE GREENBRIER

This 6,500-acre resort located in the upland valley of the Allegheny Mountains, with 12 acres of formal gardens and walkways, a service staff of 1,800, and over 225 years of history, has been praised by many writers and has received a number of awards through the years.

The first hotel was completed in 1858, and the cottages were added in the early 1800s. The 250-room main structure that forms the center wing for the present hotel was built in 1910. This was enlarged to 600 rooms in 1930. In 1941 and 1942, the complex was used as an internment center for German and Japanese diplomats, and it was then turned into a hospital.

After World War II, the resort was renovated and redecorated by Dorothy Draper and her successor, Carlton Varney. The basic color used in the hotel is white sparked with splashes of red, pink, blue, green, and yellow with large floral prints. Although this may not be everyone's favorite color scheme, and some combinations of carpet and wall covering don't seem compatible, it does seem appropriate for The Greenbrier. It captures the traditional, Old South grand hotel flavor. The furniture is period Americana with numerous antiques thrown in.

The west wing was built in 1954, the West Virginia wing in 1962, and the conference complex in 1974. Many of the hotel's public rooms contain priceless works of art, antiques, and magnificent chandeliers. The Greenbrier is a wholly owned subsidiary of CSX Corporation, a conglomerate that owns railroads and natural gas resources.

Sixty percent of the clientele are repeaters who enjoy the unique low-key, traditional atmosphere and southern hospitality. At least 75 percent of the summer guests are golf-oriented and enjoy the three excellent golf courses, as well as the facilities that permit them to have lunch, cocktails and dinner. Sixty percent of all guests come for conventions, conferences, or meetings; and independent visitors must make allowances for this. The golf attracts enthusiasts of all ages. The year-round and holiday programs for children are especially appropriate for families, and the down-beat, homey, southern atmosphere and the diagnostic health clinic appeal to regulars who have frequented The Greenbrier for decades.

Accommodations

The 802 guest rooms include 221 rooms located in cottages spread around the gardens, 33 parlors that can be used in conjunction with a guest room, and 10 luxury suites. Although each guest room is different from the others, all contain large closets, a desk or vanity table, seating area, color cable television, and a choice of king-size or two double beds. The furniture is either mahogany or painted white with colored trim. The rooms, like the rest of the hotel, are white with large prints and florals. Many of the bathrooms have been updated recently.

My preference is for one of the charming one-, two-, three-, or four-bedroom cottages, some of which date back to the 1800s. They have been renovated frequently and contain large parlors, fireplaces, and full kitchens or wet-bar facilities. Top Notch and Valley View are ultra-deluxe estate homes that accommodate up to eight guests. They

have magnificently furnished living rooms, dining rooms, kitchens, bedrooms, porches, and dens.

There are 30 conference meeting rooms, the largest seating 2,000 auditorium style. In addition to the actual rooms, there are many halls, indoor and outdoor reception areas, and other facilities permitting the serving of food and beverages in a more refreshing atmosphere. The Greenbrier has received many awards for its conference facilities, and is considered a top convention resort.

Restaurants, Lounges, and Entertainment

A full-course, Southern-style breakfast is available in the Main Dining Room. Breakfast is also available through room service or in Draper's Café, (in

season) which also features luncheon specialties and desserts throughout the day.

From April through October, lunch is served at Sam Snead's at the Golf Club, where patrons can sit in an informal atmosphere overlooking the golf course, or at the Ryder Cup Snack Bar downstairs at the Golf Club. Snacks are also available at the indoor and outdoor pools.

In the Main Dining Room, an elegant dinner is offered each evening from a new menu printed daily, and it includes appetizers, soup, salad, a choice of seven entrées – fish, seafood, beef, fowl, veal, and so on – cheeses, and desserts. The cuisine is best described as American regional with Continental overtones. Don't expect French or gourmet cooking.

As alternatives, guests can dine informally at Sam Snead's at the Golf Club or in the more formal Tavern Room specialty restaurant for a surcharge. The Tavern Room is unquestionably the superior experience at The Greenbrier. There is music at dinnertime in all the restaurants. There is music for dancing at the Old White Club Lounge.

First-run movies are featured nightly at the theater.

An 18.5 percent service charge is added to all à la carte food and beverage bills.

Sport Facilities

Although landlocked, this resort offers one large, infinity-edge, outdoor, freshwater pool and one indoor pool. The outdoor pool is surrounded by comfortable lounges, a beach shop, and Tree Tops Café. The attentive staff is available to bring a snack or beverage to the deck chairs. The pillared indoor pool, built in 1912, is reminiscent of an old Roman bath. The spa facility, which opened in late 1987, received a 12,000-square-foot expansion and renovation in 2001 and includes saunas, steam rooms, mineral baths, whirlpools, masseuses, as well as aerobic and exercise classes and a salon offering hairstyling, manicures, pedicures, and facials. There is a significant charge to use these facilities.

Tennis players will enjoy 5 outdoor Har-Tru courts, 5 indoor dynaturf courts, and the spectator galleries. The tennis club, which houses the indoor courts and is next to the outdoor clay courts, contains a pro shop and will arrange for games, lessons, and clinics. Ball machines and video replays are also available.

Equestrians can ride along miles of beautiful bridle trails that wind along the golf course and through the hills. There is a nine-station Meditation Trail and a number of paths for hikers, golfers, and for those renting bicycles.

Of all the many sport facilities, the resort is best known for its three excellent 18-hole golf courses. The Greenbrier course, redesigned by Jack Nicklaus, is ranked highly by golf periodicals and combines a tough challenge with a scenic setting. In addition, there are the Old White Course, the Meadows Course, a driving range, a practice put-

ting green, teaching pros, Sam Snead's Golf Academy, and a fully stocked clubhouse with a cocktail lounge and restaurants.

If all this is not enough, the resort also offers an eight-lane bowling center, a Gun Club with trap, skeet and sporting clays, an off-road driving school, an exercise room, a game room, a falconry academy, and a hunting and fishing preserve with trout and bass fishing at nearby Howard's Creek.

Throughout the year, there is an organized program, The Adventure Zone, for children where counselors entertain and feed tots and preteens either for half the day or all day. In the evening, children can also eat with the counselors and be entertained until 10:00 p.m.

Miscellaneous and Environs

During the winter, temperatures range from zero to 40 degrees Fahrenheit. They climb up into the 70s and 80s during the late spring, summer, and early fall.

The resort is located 12 miles from Greenbrier Valley Airport in Lewisburg, West Virginia, which is serviced by US Airways and Delta Air Lines. It is also available for private crafts. Many visitors fly into Roanoke, Virginia, rent a car, and take the 80-mile drive. There is convenient Amtrak service from New York, Washington, Chicago, and Cincinnati.

The Greenbrier Clinic, a medical facility devoted to diagnostic and preventive medicine, is located on the premises, and many guests check into the hotel and take the complete two-day physical. The over 30 shops at the resort include men's, children's, and women's clothing stores, a sundry shop, a memorabilia shop, a gourmet shop, an imported gift shop, a jewelry store, beauty salon, a barber shop, and golf and tennis shops.

In spite of the endless variety of facilities and activities available at The Greenbrier, it is important that prospective visitors have a clear understanding of what the resort is and is not. The Greenbrier is very successful in maintaining the image of an understated Old South grand hotel; however, the accommodations are not ultramodern, like a Hyatt Regency, or Old World luxurious, like at a European grand hotel. The golf facilities are among the best at any resort, and the wide variety of other sport facilities is incredibly impressive. However, do not expect to find bikini-clad beauties lying out on a white-sand beach, juggling piña coladas to the beat of a calypso band. The dining rooms are stately and subdued, offering a wide variety of American fare with friendly down-home service; they are not gourmet French with Continental waiters. In the evenings, you will find quiet dancing, a good movie, and congenial conversation; you will not find luaus, folklore dancers, or Vegas-style variety shows.

The Greenbrier is a resort steeped in tradition. It has superior convention facilities, it is a golfer's and sportsman's dream, and it offers a chance for visitors to sample the quiet ambiance of the region.

The Greenbrier
300 West Main Street
White Sulphur Springs, West Virginia 24986
Tel. (800) 624-6070/(304)536-1110
Fax (304) 536-7854
E-mail: the_greenbrier@greenbrier.com
Web: www.greenbrier.com

CHAPTER FIVE

THE CARIBBEAN, BAHAMAS, AND BERMUDA

ANGUILLA
Cap Juluca
Malliouhana Hotel

ANTIGUA
Curtain Bluff

BAHAMAS
One & Only Ocean Club

BARBADOS
Sandy Lane

BERMUDA
Fairmont Southampton

DOMINICAN REPUBLIC
Casa de Campo (La Romana)

NEVIS
Four Seasons Resort, Nevis

PUERTO RICO
El Conquistador Resort & Golden Door Spa

ST. MARTIN
La Samanna

VIRGIN ISLANDS
Caneel Bay (St. John)
Little Dix Bay (Virgin Gorda, B.V.I.)
Peter Island Resort and Yacht Harbour (B.V.I.)
The Ritz-Carlton, St. Thomas

Four Seasons, Nevis

Some of the hotels not included in this chapter have fabulous settings and facilities that surpass many of the resorts in this book. However, those not included lack the service, food, or accommodations necessary to assure a pleasant, trouble-free experience. In general, attitude and service in the Caribbean Islands and the Bahamas fall far short of what you would find in the United States, the Orient, and Europe. However, for those seeking the best weather, beaches, and surroundings, this area is unparalleled.

The standards and the facilities of the hotels in South and Central America have caused me to rule out most of the establishments I visited.

ANGUILLA

CAP JULUCA

Designed in the style of a Moorish village, the gleaming white towers, cupolas, turrets, and arches of the villas and public areas of Cap Juluca stretch out over 179 acres along a magnificent one-mile of white-sand beach that lines the clear expanse of aqua waters of Maundays Bay at the west end of the British island of Anguilla. All guest rooms and suites have large, partially sheltered patios and terraces surrounded by tropical gardens filled with palms, bougainvillea, jasmine, and frangipani, and look out to the beach and sea. At night, the hypnotic sound of the waves lapping the shore can be heard through the louvered doors and windows as it gently lulls the privileged guests to sleep. Though luxurious and expensive, very casual dress is the order of the day, and it is this casual, very private, romantic setting that lures the resort's affluent clientele to tiny Anguilla for a very special respite away from the hustle and bustle of their everyday routine. Cap Juluca has a second long stretch of white sand beach at Cove Bay which is wild and uninhabited except for a beach bar and fishermen with their boats.

The resort presently owned by Dion Friedland, opened for business in the late 1980s. However, it did not complete all of its construction until December of 1991. After the hurricanes of 1995 and 1999, much of the resort and grounds underwent renovations. Over the years, the resort has received numerous top awards and is frequently the site for photo shoots and TV travel specials. This was the first overseas destination wedding for the NBC Today Show in 2004.

Accommodations

There are 98 guest accommodations in 18 individual Moorish-style villas abutting the beach and sea that can be sold in a variety of configurations. All of the rooms are a bit different in design, and range from what the resort calls a superior and luxury double (700-790 square feet) and several 1,100-square-foot junior suites to spacious one- to five-bedroom suites and villas, which boast private pools, as well as full-service kitchens, dining rooms, parlors, and numerous terraces. All guest accommodations are air-conditioned and have ceiling fans, king-size beds, refrigerator/mini-bars, telephones with Internet access, private room safes, large closets, terraces looking out to the beach, white tile floors, and louvered doors and windows to maximize the sea breezes. The bright, airy, palatial bathrooms include separate tubs and showers, hair dryers, makeup mirrors, terry-cloth robes, and slippers. Many have their own solariums. 30 junior suites all feature two-person travertine marble bathtubs complete with cushioned head rests. Some junior suites and luxury rooms have roof-top sun decks accessible by a private staircase. Every three villas have their own villa manager who micro manages the guest experience from arrival to departure including concierge duties, maintenance problems and similar areas.

The mini-bar is stocked with a complimentary bottle of rum and a complimentary supply of beer, water and soft drinks, and additional bottles of water are available in coolers along the beach. There is maid service throughout the day, with a maid's

galley stationed in each villa. It is possible to book an entire villa with three to five guest rooms, including the villas that have private pools and full kitchens, which come with the use of a golf cart to get around the resort. Every pool suite and villa comes with its own butler. This offers an interesting alternative for several families wishing to vacation together or for a small executive-level business meeting.

There are no radios, televisions, clocks, or pictures, simplicity and tranquility being the order of the day. A limited supply of radios and televisions can be rented from the front desk and are included in the living rooms of the pool suite villas. As mentioned previously, the rooms are all different, and space and amenities are somewhat proportionate to what you pay. The least expensive, however, are not cheap. During high season, per-night rates range from $750 for the least expensive room, up to $6,450 for a 5-guest room, pool villa, plus 10 percent service charge and 10 percent taxes. However,

rates reduce by approximately 35 percent during the balance of the year. Complementary amenities include a welcome rum punch, continental breakfast on your patio or full breakfast in the restaurant, complementary mini-bar set ups, all water sports, tennis, an aqua-golf driving range, a group Tai Chi Class for two, a NY Times Fax newspaper, morning coffee, afternoon tea and sorbet on the beach.

The library is available for meetings up to 50 people theater- style.

Restaurants, Lounges, and Entertainment

The main dining room at the resort is Pimms, serving lunch, dinner, and cocktails six nights a week in a lovely, white-washed, Moorish-designed cupola sitting directly on Maundays Bay and looking out through open-air arches to the vast expanse of beach and guest villas. The dining room offers an especially romantic setting at night. While you are

sitting six feet from the lighted waterfront you can see the lights which emanate from the villas meld into the twinkling of the stars. French/Asian/Caribe-style specialties are featured. Kemia, a tapas-style restaurant/bar, shares the same building and panoramic views with Pimms.

A complimentary Continental breakfast is efficiently served on your terrace when the maids from your villa spread out a white linen tablecloth, a thermos of freshly brewed coffee or tea, orange juice, a fruit plate presented in a Bento Box, and a basket of hot croissants, rolls, bagels, and muffins. Additional standard breakfast fare such as eggs, omelets, pancakes, bacon, etc., is available for a charge in your suite, but complimentary if served in the restaurant.

George's is an informal open-air bar/restaurant, located between the pool and beach, serving topical cuisine which includes grilled meats and fish, pizza from the oven, salads and sandwiches at lunch-time, and eclectic entrées for lunch and dinner. Breakfast and lunch are also offered at George's, and tropical beverages, ice creams, and sorbets are available at the adjoining bar. There are two special nights at George's – a West Indian night on Mondays, and on Fridays, the big beach BBQ when everyone dines on the beach and dances under the stars. Items at all restaurants are very expensive.

Lunch can also be served with a special menu on the beach if the guest does not wish to leave his or her lounge.

Dress is always very casual (jackets for men are neither required nor appropriate).

Special Caribbean-style dinners served in guest suites and picnic baskets for excursions to more remote beaches are possibilities. It is also possible to arrange a very romantic dinner for two on the beach surrounded by lighted flares with your own menu organized with the chef, along with your own private waiter.

You can enjoy after-dinner drinks and musical entertainment at George's or Kemia under the stars, or television and movies are available in the media room at the main house.

All in all, dining though quite pricey is quite good for the Caribbean.

Sport Facilities

In addition to swimming and quiet sunning on the lovely three-quarter-mile expanse of white-sand beach, guests can snorkel, windsurf, sail, water ski, or arrange for snorkel, scuba, and deep-sea fishing expeditions departing from the resort. During various seasons, the beach can be quite windy on the western end of the bay, especially as you get farther away from the main house and reception area.

There are three omni-turf surfaced tennis courts, two of which are lit for night play. The teaching pro gives lessons and will organize games or tournaments on request.

Located at the resort is an aqua-golf driving facility, a croquet lawn and bicycles for rent. Presently there is no golf on the island, so golfers will have to ferry over to St. Martin; however, in 2004 construction of an 18-hole golf course was commenced not far from the resort and it is expected to be completed by the end of 2006.

In 2006, a large spa/fitness center was completed with a fully stocked gym and cardio center, men and women's dressing areas with sauna and steam available to all guests free of charge; as well as, 6 new spa treatment rooms and a beauty salon. Numerous massage, therapy and beauty treatments are offered for varying tariffs. Yoga is available every morning, as well as a beach fitness class.

Joggers can run back and forth on the beach or along the quiet country roads leading from the hotel. Few cars will disturb you; the most you will hear is the occasional baa of a sheep or neigh of a goat – both of which abound on Anguilla.

Children, ages four to fourteen, have their own clubhouse and activity program from the middle of March to the end of April and from the 1st of July to the 31st of July.

The resort offers half-day boat tours to Shoal Bay and Sandy Island, and full-day tours to Prickly Pear Cay and Little Bay several times each week.

Miscellaneous and Environs

Visitors can fly into Anguilla from San Juan or take a 20-minute ferry ride from neighboring St. Martin. Ferry service extends from 7:30 a.m. to 7:00 p.m.

the resort. There is also a private motor launch transfer to the resort's Sea Shuttle for $65 each way available from the Lagoon opposite the airport in St. Maartin to Maundays Bay at Cap Juluca. This service also works in reverse. There is a small boutique and logo/sundry shop at the resort, as well as an art and antique store.

Although there are no compelling points of history or interest on Anguilla, there are some interesting possibilities for snorkelers and beach dwellers. On the island proper, Little Bay and Shoal Bay East are unusual and beautiful, and Sandy Island, Scilly Cay, and Prickly Pear Island are worthwhile half-day excursions. Accessible only by boat, Little Bay Cay, with its small private white-sand beach, fascinating snorkeling, and incredibly picturesque setting, is a must for connoisseurs. Horse back riding is also available at Cove Bay (next door to Cap Juluca) and at Blowing Point.

For those wishing to dine away from the hotel, Anguilla offers numerous excellent restaurants in charming settings, the most highly rated (outside the hotel) being the dining room at Malliouhana, Blanchards, and Mangos.

Cap Juluca provides its affluent clientele a totally restful, private, casual, yet upscale experience on a lovely beach with friendly service and romantic dining.

from Blow Point, Anguilla to Marigot, St.Martin; and, vacationers who wish to explore boutiques and shops may wish to spend a day on St. Martin since there are few shopping possibilities on Anguilla. There is executive arrival and departure service available to and from the airport in St. Maarten to Blowing Point. From here you must take a taxi to

Cap Juluca
P.O. Box 240
Maundays Bay
Anguilla B.V.I.
Tel. 1 (264)497-6779
Fax 1(264) 6617
From U.S. toll-free: 1-888-858-5822
info@capjuluca.com

ANGUILLA

MALLIOUHANA HOTEL

In 1980, Leon Roydon selected this spectacular location on the unspoiled island of Anguilla to build his dream resort, which opened its doors in 1984. Since that time, this lovely gem has caught the fancy of movie stars, noted politicians, and various personalities who have sought out secluded luxury in the Caribbean.

Many years ago, Leon Roydon lost out in the bidding to the late Jo Rostang when the highly rated La Bonne Auberge Restaurant in Antibes, France, was up for auction. The two remained friends and when Roydon opened Malliouhana Hotel, he was able to get the Rostangs to oversee the restaurant. As a result, this is the very finest French restaurant in the Caribbean. Today, the chefs are trained by world-renowned Michel Rostang, whose Paris restaurant has received two Michelin stars.

The resort consists of a main building composed of a semi-open-air lobby and dining terrace, with palms, banana trees, ginger, frangipani, hibiscus, and bougainvillea growing everywhere, and 20 guest rooms. Thirty-five additional guest rooms and suites are located in the villas and the new Terrace complex. The spa/fitness center that was added in 2002 is one of the finest facilities of its kind in the Caribbean.

The setting is tropical and elegant, with breathtaking views of the ocean and beaches everywhere. The floors are terra-cotta ceramic and the architecture is a mixture of woods, white plaster arches accented with Haitian paintings, and exquisite rattan furnishings. The pounding surf beating against the rocky cliffs below the hotel creates a hypnotic rhythm throughout the day, and lulls you to sleep at night.

Malliouhana has received many awards for excellence from prestigious rating services and periodicals and is one of my favorites in the world.

Accommodations

In the main house there are 20 guest rooms. In the 7 villas there are 7 suites with a separate parlor and 14 double rooms. The 4-unit Bougainvillea includes three junior suites each with their own private outdoor Jacuzzi, plus a pool suite that has a master bedroom, a parlor, a separate study or additional bedroom and a private swimming pool directly overlooking the sea.

The accommodations are completed by the terrace area, which consists of six luxury junior suites and two 2-bedroom suites, all overlooking Turtle Cove Beach. All junior suites and full suites have additional hideaway beds and are excellent choices for families. All 55 accommodations are air-conditioned, and have large balconies or patios, rattan furnishings, Haitian paintings, ceiling fans, telephones, ice makers and mini-bars, safety deposit boxes, dressing tables, and large marbled bathrooms with tubs, separate shower stalls, and make-up mirrors. There are no radios or televisions. By Caribbean standards, these rooms are gigantic, clean and modern, marvelously furnished, and the ultimate in comfort and privacy.

Although the European plan tariff in high season reaches $850 for an ocean-view double room and $1,240 to $3,030 for a suite, from May through August you can luxuriate in the same facilities from $385 for a double room and from $695 for a suite. A 10 percent service charge is added in lieu of gra-

tuities plus a 10 percent government room tax. Children can stay in the room with an extra daybed for an extra $100 in season and $25 in the summer. There are even more economical packages offered to off-season vacationers.

Restaurants, Lounges, and Entertainment

Leon and Nigel Roydon and the Rostang family have created the finest restaurant in the Caribbean. The setting is unequaled, overlooking the beach and aqua sea with trade winds cooling the warm air. French Chef Alain Laurent, under the direction of Michel Rostang, has created a menu reminiscent of the best restaurants on the Côte d'Azur. Restaurant manager, Jacques Borderon, formerly with La Bonne Auberge, graciously helps guests make the appropriate selections for their mood and the time of day.

Service is so incredible you forget you are on Anguilla, and not in Antibes.

Breakfast is available in your rooms or in the restaurant and runs the gamut from fresh fruits, juices, yummy croissants, and brioches to eggs, omelets, pancakes, cheeses, and breakfast meats.

Lunch and dinner are typical of a two- or three-star Michelin restaurant in France. For lunch, I started with an excellent gazpacho, followed by a fabulous salad of radicchio, warm crayfish, bacon, and leaf lettuce. Freshly baked warm rolls accompanied each course. The lobster crêpe was superbly prepared in a seafood bisque sauce and the lemon-chocolate soufflé melted in my mouth.

For dinner, you can start with lobster consommé en croute with French-style peas, followed by sautéed escargot with young vegetables in a potato shell and a vintage wine sauce, or perhaps a grilled foie gras crusted with spiced lemon grass-ginger sauce and stewed bok choy. Entrées include imaginatively prepared meats, fishes, sea-foods, and fowl. I enjoyed the fillet of snapper crisply grilled with a choice of soya dressing or saffron sauce, crayfish ensconced in a shell of zucchini and egg-plant with cêpe mushrooms and spinach, followed by slices of duck breast in a sweet and sour curry sauce. Next came an assortment of fine imported cheeses and a hazelnut meringue with dark chocolate surrounded by vanilla sauce or a freshly baked apple tart with your choice of ice cream – not too tacky for Anguilla! Culinary perfection does not come cheap, and a dinner for two without wine can cost from $110 to $160, depending on how much you can consume. Menus constantly change, and the items listed above may or may not be available throughout the year.

The wine list is one of the most extensive in the Western Hemisphere. There were over 42 varieties of champagnes, hundreds of French reds and whites, as well as Italians and Americans. You could purchase a 1985 Mouton Rothchild, a 1989 Château Margaux or Latour, a 1971 Château Ausone, a 1986 Romanée Conti, a Chevalier or Bâtard Montrachet, or Corton Charlemagne, as well as a simple Macon Village or Beaujolais. This is the only restaurant in the Caribbean to receive Wine Spectators magazine's grand award. For gourmets and connoisseurs who wish to vacation in the Caribbean, this is the logical choice.

An open-terrace bistro-lunch restaurant, with an adjoining swimming pool and sun terrace, is located on the beach. Here guests can enjoy lighter fare. Located near the children's aquatic playground, also offering a special children's menu, this is a good choice for a family lunch. There are several lounges and bars throughout the resort. Most evenings, there is live music at the bar but no entertainment. There are televisions and DVD movies in two rooms off the lobby.

Sport Facilities

The beach runs along the side of the hotel, and the clear aqua waters can be calm or quite wavy depending on the weather. The multi-tiered main pool is picturesque with a small waterfall, deck chairs, and an adjoining large outdoor Jacuzzi seating up to 10 persons. A second pool – surrounded by the bistro restaurant, children's playground and beach--offers an additional option. At the beach, water-skiing, catamarans, small boats, and wind surfing can be arranged. There are four tennis courts, all of which are illuminated for night play, and two of which have a plexi-cushion undersurface to be gentler on the knees, a pro shop, and a teaching pro who can also arrange matches for the guests, all of which is managed by a resident tennis professional. Joggers will enjoy running along the long strand of beach or along the country road.

In late 2002, a large state-of-the-art spa and fitness center opened. The spacious fitness facility features the latest Life-Fitness cardiovascular equipment (with personal TVs), Cybex weight machines and free weights. Personal trainers are available and aerobic, Chi Gung, power stretch, meditation and yoga classes can be arranged. The dozens of spa services include an assortment of therapeutic massage treatments, body polish and peels, body wraps, facials, hydrotherapy and bathing rituals. A full range of hair services, nail care and waxing and hair removal are also available. For a special treat, couples, families and small groups of friends can book one of the three luxurious spa suites choosing among half day and full day packages that range in price from $325 to $1,340. (Add $30 for every additional person sharing the package). The suites are composed of their own lounge areas, private balconies overlooking the sea, wet and dry treatment tables, hydro-therapy baths, multi-jet showers and bathrooms with fully-stocked vanities.

The fitness facilities, dressing rooms, steam, sauna, showers and large outdoor heated whirlpool and lounge area are available to all guests gratis whether or not they take a treatment.

The impressive children's playground adjoining the beach on Meads Bay includes a one-on-one basketball court, table tennis, two small paddling pools, a pirate ship with a water slide, and many other facilities; it is staffed from 9:00 a.m. to 5:30 p.m. This adds to the resort's appeal for family vacationers.

Miscellaneous and Environs

Malliouhana Hotel is accessible from San Juan and St. Martin by propeller planes or a 20-minute ferry ride; also there are daily flights from Antigua and St. Kitts.

On the premises are a beauty shop, a boutique, a sundry gift shop, and a tennis shop.

For a special treat, guests can arrange for the resort's 40-foot cruiser, the Dakota, to take them around Anguilla with stops at Little Bay and Sandy Island for swimming and snorkeling. Little Bay is a uniquely picturesque secluded cove accessible only by boat. Here you will find a tiny white-sand beach with turquoise, azure, and verdant green waters. This is a romantic spot for a private picnic lunch and offers good snorkeling possibilities. Sandy Island is a small isle surrounded by powder-fine white sand. There are good reefs for snorkeling just a few strokes away, and you can enjoy some barbecued ribs, chicken, or lobster with a cold beer or rum punch at the small snack facility. Another fine public beach on Anguilla is at Shoal Bay.

Although the Caribbean offers some of the best beaches and tropical scenery in the world, there are few sophisticated, elegant resorts. Malliouhana Hotel is possibly one of the outstanding exceptions located on an outstanding stretch of beach, offering spacious accommodations, picturesque surroundings, superior service, a most impressive fitness-spa facility and one of the best restaurants in the Caribbean.

Malliouhana Hotel
P.O. Box 173
Meads Bay, Anguilla B.W.I.
Tel. (264) 497-6111, (800) 835-0796
Fax (264) 497-6011
E-mail: malliouhana@anguillanet.com

ANTIGUA

CURTAIN BLUFF

Set on 20 tropical acres of a private peninsula on Antigua's south shore, between two beaches, is one of the Caribbean's class acts dating back to its birth in 1962. The country club atmosphere is set by its creators and owners Howard and Chelle Hulford, who preside over their splendid domain in an exquisite home atop the bluff. The suites and guest rooms descend down the bluff to a windy beach with picturesque cliffs and pounding surf. Most guests relax on the sandy strand that borders the calm lagoon on the other side of the property.

Room prices range from $555 per night for a standard room in low season, up to $2,520 for a two-bedroom Presidential Suite in high season. Included in the price of all accommodations are three meals; tea, before-dinner hors d'oeuvres, soft drinks, alcoholic beverages, and wine by the glass; all water sports; and mail/postage service. There is no tipping, but a 10 percent gratuity and 8.5% tax are added to your bill.

The grounds are lush with tropical flowers, shrubs, and trees. Service throughout the resort is helpful and friendly, with most of the staff having worked at the resort for many years.

Accommodations

The 73 guest accommodations include 18 described as deluxe rooms, 42 junior suites, 5 one-bedroom suites, 5 executive two-bedroom suites, 2 Presidential Suites with terrace spas, and the Terrace Room. The suites, which cascade in tiers down the bluff, were built in 1985. The two-bedroom suites can be divided and sold as one-bedroom suites and exec-

utive deluxe rooms. All accommodations are frequently renovated and redecorated.

Every guest room has a veranda overlooking the sea, and the executive suites also have a dining terrace ideal for room service meals and snacks.

The deluxe rooms are of average size with small bathrooms and include king-size beds, verandas, robes and wall safes. Although not luxurious, at $595 to $995 double occupancy depending on the season, including three gourmet meals, soft drinks, alcoholic beverages, and most water sports, Curtain Bluff offers an interesting bargain for vacationers wishing to experience an exclusive upscale Caribbean resort at prices not much higher than what it would cost at a more ordinary resort.

Those requiring a higher level of comfort and opulence will prefer the junior suites, or the one- and two-bedroom executive suites which are considerably larger and include marble bathrooms with separate toilet-bidet-shower compartments, double vanities, large tubs, his and hers separate closets, and abundant storage space. The one-bedroom executive suites offer not only refrigerators and the outdoor dining terrace, but also a protective terrace with a hammock, high cedar-trimmed ceilings in the living rooms and bedrooms, and the feeling of luxuriating in a rambling villa.

Rooms are ventilated with ceiling fans and strong ocean breezes; however, there is no air-conditioning and a breeze by any other name is still a breeze. Also, there are no televisions or radios in the guest rooms so as not to interfere with the sound of the waves breaking against the bluff and to maintain the "escape from the stresses of civilization" envi-

ronment. High speed internet access is available in all rooms and suites at an extra cost. There are two television rooms one located over the Pro Shop, and the other over the main reception area.

Restaurants, Lounges, and Entertainment

The main dining pavilion, which serves breakfast and dinner, encircles an open court with a sprawling tamarind tree behind the lobby, offering totally sheltered and semi-alfresco seating. In the evening, a small orchestra plays romantic music for dinner dancing, and honeymooners can reserve the private gazebo about 130 yards away.

A buffet and a la carte lunch is served at the bay beach; cocktails and hors d'oeuvres are featured nightly at the open-air patio adjacent to the lobby; and once each week there is a steel band and buffet at the beach.

Wine enthusiast-owner Howard Hulford boasts one of the most impressive wine cellars in the Caribbean, reputed to have 25,000 bottles, including most classified Bordeaux and Burgundies with vintages dating back to the 1970s.

Room service is available for refreshments and all meals, and as mentioned earlier, all victuals, soft drinks, and alcoholic beverages (other than bottles of wine) are included in the daily rate.

Once a week, owner Hulford and managing director Rob Sherman and their wives invite guests to a cocktail hour at their panoramic villa set atop Curtain Bluff with commanding sunset views of the resort and ocean below. This lends to the intimate, family-like aura the resort seeks to emit.

Sport Facilities

As one would expect, the focal points of the resort are the beaches. Most guests choose to relax at the calm bay beach with its numerous lounges, thatched umbrellas, hammocks strung between shady palm trees, water sport facilities, and bar and open-air restaurant, where lunch is served.

Water sports, which are furnished gratis to the guests, include windsurfing, sunfish, deep-sea fishing, scuba diving (for certified divers), water-skiing, snorkel gear, and aqua lungs. Dive trips to a reef for snorkeling and scuba are offered daily. The beach stretching beneath the guest rooms and bluff sometimes has heavy surf and may not be ideal for swimming. Both beaches have fine tan sand, but you will experience some small pebbles as you enter the water. A swimming pool was added in 1997.

Another favorite with guests is the tennis facility, which includes a squash court, four illuminated courts, a fully stocked pro shop, a resident pro, and young villagers aspiring to be tennis pros, who will pinch hit as a tennis partner when needed.

In addition, there is a fitness center where morning aerobic classes are held, and exercycles, a step machine, a treadmill, and free weights are available. There is a croquet lawn, as well as a putting green.

Guests can charter a sailboat by the day and half-day and the resort will arrange tee times at the Harbour Club's 18-hole golf course, fifteen minutes away, and at Cedar Valley's 18-hole golf course, one half-hour away.

Miscellaneous and Environs

There is a small boutique and a tennis/sportswear shop at the resort. Those wishing to engage in more extensive shopping can take the 35-minute taxi ride into St. John's. The taxi drive from the airport across the island also takes about 35 minutes and costs from $26 to $30.

The resort closes during the summer months. The large contingencies of repeat clientele who seek accommodations in prime season (late December through mid-March) book well in advance.

Curtain Bluff has a unique, intimate, sophisticated, and lovely setting with concerned service; many knowledgeable, seasoned travelers call it their favorite Caribbean retreat.

Curtain Bluff
P.O. Box 288
St. John's, Antigua, West Indies
Tel. (888) 289-9898, (268) 462-8400
Fax. (268) 462-8409
e-mail: curtainbluff@curtainbluff.com
www.curtainbluff.com

One&Only Ocean Club

Located amidst tropical gardens adorned with flowers and statuary abutting a gentle cliff that leads down to a white-sand beach and the azure ocean that surrounds Paradise Island, the elegant, colonial-style One&Only Ocean Club offers an exclusive retreat to its discriminating clientele. Under the same ownership as its neighbor, the massive Atlantis complex, Ocean Club guests have access to the bevy of restaurants, entertainments and facilities located at Atlantis while enjoying the privacy, pristine beauty and pampering of their own more refined resort.

Originally built as a private estate named Shangri-la, the property was purchased in 1962 by Huntington Hartford II, heir to the A&P food chain. He proceeded to build a 52-room hotel, a restaurant and an 18-hole golf course on the site and renamed it Ocean Club. Carrera marble and bronze statues were imported from Europe along with an Augustinian Cloister and placed in a magnificent, terraced, floral garden leading down to a swimming pool creating an uniquely beautiful setting that lends a special aura to the property. Kerzner International acquired the resort in 1994 and undertook a $100 million renovation and expansion in 2000. In 2003, the Ocean Club became a member of One&Only Resorts.

The main, colonial-style hotel building is lavishly furnished, houses the reception area, a library and indoor bar and lounge and leads out to a patio overlooking the ocean. The restaurants, swimming pools, tennis courts, spa, fitness facility and guest accommodations are disbursed throughout the lovely grounds. The golf course and Ocean Club Residences and Estates are located nearby, all within a comfortable distance from the Atlantis complex.

Accommodations

The majority of the 104 accommodations are spread between the two-story, classic colonial Hartford Wing and the more contemporary two-story Crescent Wing. In the Hartford Wing there are forty-seven 340-square-foot rooms and four 830-square-foot suites, all of which surround a garden pond. The forty 550-square-foot rooms and ten 1,100-square-foot suites in the Crescent Wing are set on a cliff and all overlook the beach. Three luxury villas are perched above the beach.

Each accommodation includes a king-size bed, a patio or balcony, a satellite television, a DVD and C/D player, a two-line telephone with voice mail, a high speed internet access port, a private safe, a service bar, complementary bottled water, champagne and strawberries in the afternoons and 24-hour butler service. The suites and villas also are furnished with lap-top computers with wireless internet access.

For the ultimate in hedonistic luxury, you can book one of the three- and four-bedroom, 4,400-square-foot villas which opened in 2004. This will set you back from $5,000 to 7,000 per night depending on the season; however, you can squeeze in seven to nine of your closest friends or relatives. Each enormous bedroom has a king or two queen beds, floor to ceiling sliding-glass doors, ocean or garden vistas and its own bathroom with indoor/outdoor showers that open on one side to a secluded sun deck. Gated villa entries lead into gar-

den courtyards with jet tubs and shaded dining patios. The elegant villa great rooms with their 25-foot wide louvered doors offer expansive views out to the villa's private infinity-edged pool and the ocean below. Included in each villa is a full-service kitchen staffed with a private chef and 24-hour butler service.

For small business meetings there is an executive board room that can accommodate up to 20 people. The facility has a pull-down plasma screen and video teleconferencing capabilities.

Restaurants, Lounges and Entertainment

All three meals are available daily at Dune, the main restaurant which overlooks the ocean, as well as, through room service. Lunch, drinks and snacks are served at the Pool Terrace Café.

The French-Asian cuisine at Dune is the creation of renowned chef Jean-George Vongerichten. The menu features signature dishes from the chef's New York restaurants with Bahamian influences. This 150-seat beachfront restaurant is an elegant eatery set literally in the dunes, offering spectacular panoramic views of the beach and ocean.

For variety, guests can visit the numerous restaurants located at the nearby Atlantis resort or in the town of Nassau. At Atlantis there are various entertainment venues, and a giant casino.

Sport Facilities

Numerous water sports are available at the resort's lovely white-sand beach, as well as, comfortable lounges and sun-beds. On the cliff overlooking the beach are two massage cabanas where guests can receive open-air massage treatments.

The freshwater swimming pool overlooks the famous terraced Versaille Gardens. Adjacent are seven Har-Tru tennis courts (four lit for night play), a 1000 square-foot fitness center with cardiovascular machines, steam rooms, showers and lockers and the Pool Terrace Café. In 2004, a family pool was opened complete with waterfalls and a jetted fountain. Bicycles are available for touring the island.

The Tom Weiskopf-designed, 18-hole Ocean Club Golf Course is only a few minutes from the property. The course offers seaside green and tee settings and alternating fairways, all with expansive views of the ocean.

Eight exquisite, Balinese-designed, air-conditioned, private spa villas offer a wide range of massage, therapeutic and beauty treatments. Each villa features a waterfall shower, a day bed and jetted bath in the gardens, a private bathroom and two teak massage tables. Massages are also available in your guest room or in the ocean-view cabanas described above.

Throughout the year there are supervised activities for children 6 to 12 known as the "Kids Only"

program. This 1,780 square-foot supervised facility is stocked with games, arts, crafts, computers and X-Boxes. Various group activities are offered including sports, cooking classes, educational endeavors, treasure hunts and dress-up parties. Both half- and full-day programs are available.

Miscellaneous and Environs

Guests can fly into Nassau from numerous cities around the world. From the airport, a 20-minute taxi ride traversing the bridge over to Paradise Island will take you to the resort.

Also located on Paradise Island, a comfortable distance from the resort, are Club Med, Atlantis, private homes, numerous shops and the One&Only Golf Course.

One&Only Resorts is a subsidiary of Kerzner International with other resort properties located in the Maldives, Mauritius, Los Cabos, Mexico and Dubai. On Paradise Island, the company also built the Ocean Club Estates, 121 luxury beachfront properties; and is in the process of completing 88 luxury condo homes near the golf course.

One&Only Ocean Club offers discriminating vacationers an elegant, colonial-style resort amidst lush grounds overlooking a lovely beach, while providing luxurious accommodations, fine dining, excellent service, an unique spa experience and a variety of sport activities.

One & Only Ocean Club
P.O. Box N-4777
Nassau, Bahamas
Tel. (242)363-2501
Fax. (242) 363-2424
U.S. (800)321-3000 or (954)809-2150
www.oneandonlyresorts.com

BARBADOS

SANDY LANE

Formerly a sugar plantation on the west coast of Barbados, this property was acquired in 1957 by Ronald Tree, a member of the British Parliament. The hotel was opened to the public in 1961, after the completion of the first nine holes of the golf course. Later in the 1960s, the Forte group purchased the 380-acre resort, intending to make the property its showcase in the Caribbean. The resort was renovated in 1991 and 1992, with major upgrading to the guest rooms and refurbishing of public areas. However, the decade of the nineties also brought some very strong competition to the luxury-resort market, and there was only so much that could be modernized in a structure built almost 40 years earlier. In order to maintain an eminence in that market, Sandy Lane closed its doors in June 1998 (after being sold to private investors) and commenced a total reconstruction and renovation at a cost estimated to exceed $400 million. In March 2001, the new Sandy Lane emerged with totally modernized, state-of-the-art, luxurious accommodations, public areas, and facilities; a new 18-hole, Tom Fazio-designed golf course; and a world-class spa. Improvements in the dining experience and an upgrading of service accompanied the new look. A second Fazio-designed, 18-hole course was recently opened.

The majority of guests are Europeans, Americans, and Canadians who can afford the exceptionally high tariffs. The cheapest double room at Christmastime (EP with breakfast) costs $2,700 per night, and the most expensive penthouse suites fetch $8,800. Rates reduce considerably in the summer months from $850 to $1200 for the standard rooms and $3,500 for the penthouse suites, but they are still among the highest in the Caribbean (or anywhere else for that matter).

The new Sandy Lane is the premier luxury resort in the Caribbean, offering the most luxurious accommodations, a high standard of service and the finest golf and spa facilities, seldom found in this part of the world.

Accommodations

The 112 air-conditioned guest rooms (which include 16 suites), elegantly furnished, average 900 square feet and each boasts a huge private veranda. Giant marble bathrooms include soaking tubs, separate shower stalls, double vanities, hair dryers, separate toilet compartments with phones, generous storage space, and upscale amenities. Every guest room includes a refrigerator and stocked mini-bar, private safe, dressing table, king-size bed, flat-screen plasma color television, in-room entertainment system, multifunction phones with Internet linkage, marble floors, his and hers closets, and personalized butler service.

In addition there are three conference facilities and a 7,300-square foot private villa that goes from $8,000 to $25,000 per night depending on the season. At Christmas time the resort requires a 14-night minimum stay (14 x $25,000 = $350,000). The price includes afternoon tea, alcoholic beverages and Champagne and tropical fruit on arrival. (What a deal?).

Restaurants, Lounges, and Entertainment

The two main restaurants overlook the sea – affording spectacular views. L'Acajou, located on the second floor, is the fine-dining spot, featuring New World cuisine with Asian influences along with an emphasis on local seafood and imported wines. Two course dinners cost $85 per person; add dessert and you are up to $95 per person. The wine list is extensive and includes numerous French vintages over $1,000 a bottle such as a 1995 Romanee Conte for $10,095. (Would it not be fun to send this one back after it is opened?) Bajan Blue, immediately below at terrace level, offers similar items plus lighter fare in a more relaxed ambience. Lunch buffets here are spectacular, but pricey. Meals are also available at the golf club-house overlooking the course. At the spa café, heart-healthy spa items are featured. The Monkey Bar is the venue for before-dinner cocktails and after-dinner liquors. Room service is available around the clock. English-style high tea is served each afternoon, and at the beach, attendants offer sun-bathing guests sorbet and fresh fruits.

Sport Facilities

The 1,000-foot expanse of beautiful white-sand beach is one of the chief attributes of the resort. Swimming is much calmer here, on the west coast of Barbados, than it is on the rougher east coast, on the Atlantic side. Guests can relax on the beach and enjoy the comfortable lounges and umbrellas, cold refresher towels, instant bar service at the wave of a flag, and complimentary sorbet and fruits. Most water sports are available, including water-skiing, windsurfing, kayaking, snorkeling, scuba diving, sailing, and deep-sea fishing.

In addition to the lovely beach, there is a 7,500-square-foot, two-level, meandering swimming pool, nine floodlit tennis courts and a tennis pavilion, the original nine-hole golf course, as well as the two new, Tom Fazio-designed, 18-hole courses. Horseback riders can be accommodated at a nearby stable, and joggers will enjoy romping along the miles of beach that extend in both directions from the resort.

The Treehouse Club is a facility accommodating children and teenagers, with Internet access, a children's playground and game room, a teenage recreation room, and fully trained childcare professionals.

The 4,700-square-foot Sandy Lane Spa, done in marble, with 14 treatment suites, is only available to registered guests. A multitude of spa services by trained professionals are available around the clock. Massage rooms include personal bathrooms, showers and outdoor garden-relaxation areas, and some have private spas. Personal and group exercise, yoga, pilates and Tai Chi classes are available. Also located here are a 2,500 square-foot fitness room with state-of-the-art equipment, an ice cave, hydrotherapy pool, a hair and nail salon, gift shop and spa café. This is possibly the most luxurious and most impressive spa facility in the Caribbean, and perhaps the world.

Miscellaneous and Environs

Sandy Lane sits seven miles from Bridgetown and about 19 miles from the airport. The area around the hotel is made up of nice homes, guest cottages, and other resort facilities. On the premises are a ladies' and a gentlemen's boutique, a duty-free import shop, a sundry shop, hairdresser, and golf and tennis shop. 112 private villas are in the process of being developed around the Green Monkey Golf Course.

Over the years, Sandy Lane has been considered one of the better resorts in the Caribbean, frequented by some of the wealthiest people in the world, as well as dignitaries and movie stars. However, you must be prepared to pay an extraordinary freight for the privilege of sharing the experience. Those that choose to do so, will be well rewarded with one of the class experiences in the Caribbean.

Sandy Lane
St. James, Barbados, West Indies
Tel. (246) 444-2000
Fax (246) 444-2222
E-mail: mail@sandylane.com
Web: www.sandylane.com

BERMUDA

FAIRMONT SOUTHAMPTON

Perched upon a hill overlooking the golf course and some of the most picturesque coves, inlets, and beaches in the world, the 100-acre Fairmont Southampton (formerly the Southampton Princess) offers Bermuda vacationers an endless variety of accommodations, sport facilities, restaurants, and shops. Built in 1972, the resort was acquired from Princess Hotels in 1998 by Fairmont Hotels and Resorts, which owns and operates 43 luxury resorts and city hotels in Canada, the continental United States, UK, Europe, Hawaii, Mexico, Barbados, and Bermuda. Since the purchase, the Fairmont Group has spent millions of dollars renovating, redecorating, and modernizing the accommodations, public areas, and facilities.

A regular shuttle service transports guests down the hill to the tennis courts, golf course, beach area, and the bay behind the hotel, where the Waterlot Inn Restaurant and the complimentary ferry service to its sister property, the Fairmont Hamilton Princess, are located.

Although Bermuda sits in the Atlantic and has a prime season that extends from April through November, it can best be described as a sophisticated Caribbean island with a British flavor but without the poverty, hostility, and indifference found in the Bahamas, Jamaica, and many of the other Caribbean islands. The weather is temperate; the people are polite and pleasant; the accommodations, shops, and restaurants are civilized; and the pink-sand beaches that surround the island are among the most beautiful in the world.

Accommodations

The hotel has 568 spacious accommodations, each with a balcony, plus 36 suites, including some duplex units with upstairs, loft bedrooms. All of the guest rooms are comfortable, tastefully appointed, recently renovated, and include remote-control, color cable television, direct-dial international telephones, private safes, walk-in closets, writing desks, hair dryers, mini-bars, and numerous amenities. Each room is identical in size and furnishings; those with the best locations, however, are more expensive than those with less desirable views. Those who opt for one of the 84 rooms or 8 suites on the sixth-floor, club level in high season pay an additional amount as part of the special concierge area, known as Fairmont Gold. Fairmont Gold guests enjoy additional room amenities, as well as complimentary food and an honor bar with a wide selection of beverages throughout the day.

There are 16 conference rooms and a full-service business center. The Poinciana Room accommodates 1,500 people in its 12,000 square feet and can seat nearly 1,000 banquet-style. The lavish Boardroom seats 14 at a rosewood conference table and 12 more on adjoining couches. It includes a built-in bar, hidden movie screens, and blackboards. The 7,400-square-foot Mid-Ocean Amphitheater – the largest multimedia amphitheater available in the resort market in North America, Hawaii, and the Caribbean – provides the ultimate meeting environment for groups up to 700 (theater) or 450 (schoolroom style).

Restaurants, Lounges, and Entertainment

In the morning, a buffet breakfast is served in Windows on the Sound, which has large glass windows affording a panoramic view of the sound. Breakfast is also served â la carte and buffet style in Wickets.

Lunch is available at Wickets and at the Cabana, a beautiful terrace overlooking the beach where snacks, sandwiches, salads, ice cream, and drinks are served.

For dinner, there are a number of possibilities. The casual indoor/outdoor Whaler Inn, on the beach, features a diverse menu of seafood and fish specialties. This is a good choice for an alfresco dinner. The Bacci Restaurant, near the golf course, places emphasis on Italian cuisine. For gourmet-style dining, guests can choose between the elegant, romantic, nautical-themed, AAA 5-Diamond award, Newport Room in the main hotel – with its Wedgwood china and crystal, impeccable service, and creative Continental cuisine – and the romantic Waterlot Inn on the bay, which boasts a fabulous wine cellar and is an excellent location to enjoy an incredible sunset accompanied by melodious piano music and flavorful Mediterranean fare. The cuisine in these latter two restaurants is imaginative and superb. The dining experience at the Newport Room is reminiscent of the finest restaurants in Europe. Some of the restaurants are seasonal, not operating at various times during the year.

In the evening, guests can enjoy cocktails at the Jasmine Lobby Lounge.

There are meal plans available where guests can choose among the various restaurants at the resort, as well as at its sister property, Fairmont Hamilton Princess, across the harbor near town. A 15 percent gratuity is added to all restaurant checks.

Sport Facilities

There are two pools attached to the main hotel – one outdoor and one indoor pool, part of the Willow Stream Spa. Each pool area has a Jacuzzi. The new 37,000-square-foot Willow Stream Spa opened in 2003. The facility has 15 treatment rooms, including special-treatment rooms for couples, a beauty

salon, a fully equipped workout center, sauna, steam, and Thalassotherapy rooms.

To the side of the hotel is an 18-hole, par-3 golf course that winds around the premises and adds to the picturesque setting. The course is highly rated by Golf Digest; however, serious golfers may prefer the regulation Robert Trent Jones 18-hole course 10 minutes away.

There are five tennis courts at Turtle Hill next to the hotel, and down by the hotel beach are six additional courts with a pro shop, lockers, showers, a snack bar, a drink bar, and a sundry/beachwear and Dolphin Quest souvenir shop.

To the left of the hotel's private beach sits the fabulous Horseshoe Beach, with its pink sand and intriguing private caves and coves. These beaches, running for about two miles to the left of the Fairmont Southampton, are among the world's loveliest. At the beach, you can arrange for snorkeling and scuba diving; and from the Waterlot pier, you can charter a boat for fishing, water-skiing, and other water-sport activities.

Miscellaneous and Environs

Eleven of the better downtown Bermuda shops have branches in the resort's shopping arcade. These shops feature British and Scottish woolens, Irish linens, china, crystal, and many European imports.

Over the years, Bermuda has been the choice of many newlyweds, and this resort offers a wedding planner for those who want to get married in Bermuda. There are also attractive packages which include meals that are designed for honeymooners, golfers, tennis buffs, and those who want to inter-

act with the dolphins. Family members ages 5-18 will enjoy the kids' Explorer's Camp, which is divided into four different age groups.

The airport is 12 miles away, and town can be reached in 40 minutes by bus, or in 30 minutes by taxi.

The Fairmont Southampton is the largest and only full facility resort in Bermuda, offering vacationers a wide range of excellent restaurants, shops, and sport facilities, as well as comfortable accommodations on one of the most friendly and beautiful islands in our hemisphere.

Fairmont Southampton
P.O. Box HM 1379
Hamilton, HMFX, Bermuda
Tel. (441) 238-8000 (direct)
Fax (441) 238-8968
www.fairmont.com/southampton

LA ROMANA

CASA DE CAMPO

Located near the town of La Romana on the southeastern coast of the Dominican Republic, 90 miles from Santo Domingo, this vast resort complex sprawls over 7,000 acres along the edge of the Caribbean with the Dominican countryside and mountains in the background.

Casa de Campo was built in 1974 by Gulf and Western, who operated the resort for 10 years. In 1984 it was purchased by the Central Romana Corporation, a Dominican corporation co-owned by the Fanjul family, Cubans who operate sugar plantations throughout Florida. Its original rooms were designed by William Cox and decorated by Oscar de la Renta. Over the years, additional accommodations and sport facilities have been added, making it the most complete sport resort in the Caribbean.

The central hotel area includes a lobby, a gift shop, a charming terrace lounge, the convention section, two restaurants, and the main pool complex consisting of two large pools, a swim-up bar, a children's wading pool, an imaginative thatched tree house above the pool, and a large lounge area, as well as a snack bar. The shrubbery, lawns, and flora throughout the complex are extremely well maintained and provide the floral beauty that adorns this resort.

Spread throughout the 7,000 acres is a vast vacation home development, which includes magnificent luxury estates, vacation homes, villas, and guest rooms. Many of the villas are available for rent through the hotel.

Ten minutes from the resort is the charming artist's village of Altos de Chavon. Built to look like a Mediterranean village, it features art galleries, an open-air concert stadium in the design of a Roman or Greek amphitheater, shops, and restaurants frequented by guests of the resort. The cobblestone paths, fountains, magnificent views, and quaint establishments make this one of the more picturesque, well-conceived commercial areas in the world. Many fashion magazines use this as a backdrop for their advertisements. In 2002, a charming new Marina opened, reminiscent of Portofino in Italy and Puerto Banus in Spain, adding additional upscale shops, boutiques, and restaurants to the area.

The majority of guests are from the U.S.; however, many are from Latin countries and Europe. This provides a rather international environment. Although the employees in key positions speak some English, some familiarity with Spanish is desirable.

Accommodations

There are 300 guest rooms located in one- and two-story red-roofed complexes set informally around the main area. All accommodations were renovated after 1998 and include a touring cart for each room. All guest rooms are air-conditioned and include king-size or two double beds, private safes, Bose Wave radios, hair dryers, iron and ironing boards, remote control television with cable, direct-dial telephones, mini-bars, and sitting areas. They are decorated with colorful fabrics, native woods, and tile.

There are also 150 two-, three-, and four-bedroom private villa homes, spread out near the ocean or around the golf courses and other areas that can be rented to resort guests. Every villa comes with the guests' breakfast prepared for them

each morning by a private maid, and the three- and four-bedroom villas also have butler service. Each of the bedrooms is air-conditioned and has its own bathroom, remote-control television, and hair dryer, and each villa has a living area, kitchen, and patio area. The two-bedroom villas feature a four-passenger touring cart, whereas, the three- and four-bedroom villas receive two touring carts for transportation around the resort. Each of the villas comes with a pool or whirlpool, and those in the Exclusive Excel category feature both. The villa accommodations are ideal for families, couples, or golf buddies traveling together, because they are a great deal more spacious than the standard guest rooms and everyone has their privacy.

Guests may also rent cars or additional golf carts and even bicycles to get around, or they can use the shuttle service that transports guests throughout the grounds and to Altos de Chavon.

Another option that can be added to any guest room or villa accommodation is the "Inclusive Supplement" which features all three meals in a resort restaurant, unlimited drinks in resort restaurants, bars and lounges, unlimited horseback riding, tennis, non-motorized water sports at Minitas Beach, one round of 25 shots of skeet/trap shooting (one time, per adult only per stay) and taxes and service charges on featured supplement items. Golfers can play the courses by the round or by purchasing a three-day or one-week golf supplement that includes green fees on alternating courses, shared cart while playing golf, unlimited practice balls, club storage and taxes.

There are two large conference centers, one with a room that can seat up to 500 theater-style and 320 banquet-style. There are seven additional meeting rooms.

Restaurants, Lounges, and Entertainment

On the immediate grounds are numerous restaurants. La Tropicana, the main dining room, with a lovely outdoor terrace overlooking the gardens and pool, is open in the evenings for dinner, featuring Angus beef and a good selection of seafood. The new Pot Bunker Sports Bar is the place to catch your favorite sports team while on vacation and is open from 11 a.m. until 1a.m. serving light meals and snacks in a casual, air-conditioned setting. Lago Grill, near the Golf Club, serves a hearty American breakfast and lunch buffet. There are snack bars at the main pool, tennis center, and at Minitas Beach, where the Pescador Restaurant offers seafood, salads and brick oven pizzas. Casual dress is acceptable by the day; however, resort-elegant attire (jackets optional) is required at some restaurants in the evenings. Breakfast buffet-style is especially enjoyable at Lago Grill.

At the nearby Altos de Chavon artist's village are a number of additional specialty restaurants. La Piazzetta is a romantic Italian restaurant with a strolling violinist and guitar player; El Sombrero is a quaint indoor/outdoor tapas restaurant and sports bar with a Mexican flair; and Café del Sol offers a large variety of pizzas, antipasti, salads, and ice cream creations. The service, though sometimes inexperienced, is unusually friendly for a Caribbean island. For lunch you can also swing by the Safari Club during the winter season at the Shooting Center. Lunch and dinner are also available at Chinois, the resort's Cantonese restaurant at the Marina.

There is live entertainment nightly at La Cana Bar in the main area of the hotel and a disco – Genesis – at Altos de Chavon. From November through mid-April, performances of Kandela are performed at the outdoor amphitheater featuring 50 dancers, two singers in an extravaganza of the sounds, rhythms and costumes of the Caribbean.

Dining at most resorts can become repetitive and boring after a few days. However, at Casa de Campo, dining is comparable to being in a cosmopolitan city with endless choices of ethnic restaurants, each with an entirely different kitchen and environment. Overall, the food is exceptional for the Caribbean.

Sport Facilities

Casa de Campo is one of the few Caribbean resorts that has it all – golf, tennis, water sports, horseback riding, trap and skeet shooting, jogging, bicycling, polo, river and deep-sea fishing, and more.

Las Minitas, a lovely white-sand beach, is only a five-minute drive from the main lobby. Here, guests can windsurf, snorkel, rent sailboats, or take the snorkel adventure to explore coral reef gardens and underwater trails. In addition, river fishing, river excursions, and a sunset catamaran sailing cruise can be arranged through the guest service desk. Those preferring a pool have the pool complex at the main hotel described earlier. Fourteen other pools are spread throughout the villas for use by the villa guests. In addition, there is a remote pool at Altos de Chavon adjacent to the Dye Fore golf course.

A small fitness center is equipped with free weights, Universal equipment, and exercycles. Massages from the Spa Treatment Center are available in your room, villa, or at the beach. Although a larger fitness center and/or spa may be added in the future, at present, these facilities are not available.

There are 13 clay courts at La Terraza, the tennis village five minutes away. Ten of the courts are illuminated for night play. At La Terraza, you will find a pro shop, teaching pros, a snack bar, a spectator deck, ball-boys, and a number of young, aspiring pros who will serve as your tennis partner for about $15.00 an hour.

There are three 18-hole Pete Dye golf courses, one recently completed. The famous "Teeth of the Dog" course has seven holes overlooking the Caribbean, and is rated among the best golf courses in the world by Golf Magazine. The course was renovated by Peter Dye in 2005. Peter Dye also created the new Dye Fore course with seven cliff-side holes at the Altos Chavon artist's village as well as the inland "Links" course. At the golf complex, there is also a driving range, a pro shop, a restaurant, and teaching pros.

Equestrians will appreciate the dude ranch and polo club. Both eastern and western saddles are available, and there are guided trail rides for all ages, as well as "Donkey Polo". This is one of the best equestrian centers to be found at any resort throughout the world. The shooting range, with skeet, trap, and the world's most extensive sport clay shooting facilities, is nearby and features shooting at night as well as during the day.

There are numerous paths for joggers, as well as bicycles for rent, and volleyball on the beach.

Children have not been overlooked. The award-winning family programs provide four separate agendas for children – "Toddlers" for ages 1 to 3, "Kidz'n Casa" for ages 4 to 7, "Casa Tweens" for ages 8-12 and "Bonche4teens" for ages 13-17with age-appropriate activities including swimming and horseback riding lessons, tennis, games, picnics, and movies. Also, there are separate club facilities for the exclusive use of teens. In addition, a full range of activities and facilities are offered for the entire family.

Almost all of the sport facilities (other than the beach and pool) exact an extra charge not included in your room rate, unless you participate in a special package arrangement.

Miscellaneous and Environs

In addition to the unisex beauty parlor and several shops on the premises, there are several interesting shops, restaurants, and art galleries at Altos de Chavon – the artist's village – 10 minutes from the resort, as well as additional upscale boutiques, shops, and restaurants at the new marina. Do not miss visiting these areas both during the day and in the evening.

The hotel concierge will arrange sightseeing and shopping tours to La Romana and to Santo Domingo. Shuttle buses take guests around the resort and to Altos de Chavon throughout the day and evening.

The weather varies only slightly from a mean in the range between 70 and 85 degrees. Visitors can fly to the international airport outside Santo Domingo by jet and take the 75-minute drive to the resort or fly into the La Romana-Casa de Campo International Airport, 8 minutes from the resort, on daily flights from Miami and San Juan. The resort will arrange transportation upon request.

Casa de Campo is one of the best-equipped full-facility resorts in the Caribbean, offering vacationers dependable, sunny, warm weather (except during the rainy months of August and September), comfortable accommodations, friendly service, a wide variety of excellent restaurants, exceptional sport facilities, and an opportunity to visit the Dominican Republic.

Casa de Campo
P.O. Box 140
La Romana, Dominican Republic
Tel. (800) 877-3643 (U.S.)
Fax (305) 858-4677
Tel. (809) 523-3333 (Dominican Republic)
Fax (809) 523-8548
E-mail: res@pwonline.com
Web: www.casadecampo.com.do

NEVIS

FOUR SEASONS RESORT

In February 1991, Four Seasons Hotel and Resorts opened its first resort in the Caribbean on the tiny tropical island of Nevis, which is located between St. Martin and Antigua. Sprawling over 350 lush tropical acres, the 12 two-story cottages and plantation-style Great House overlook a long strand of beach with the rolling, verdant hills of its championship golf course and the volcanic mountains of Nevis as a backdrop.

Four Seasons Hotel, Ltd. manages this magnificent property. This resort creates a new standard of luxury in the Caribbean, offering super-luxurious guest accommodations, gourmet dining, competent service and exceptional sport facilities.

Accommodations

The 196 spacious guest rooms and suites are located in 12 cottages, 10 facing the sea, and 2 located on the golf course with panoramic mountain views. The 179 standard rooms each measure 490-560 square feet inside, with 185-square-foot outside verandas. Every room includes a king-size bed or two doubles, a fully stocked mini-bar and refrigerator, private safes, remote-control color televisions with 54 cable stations, DVDs, umbrellas, elegant traditional furnishings done in colorful fabrics, and giant bathrooms with double sinks, makeup mirrors, hair dryers, separate shower and tub, private toilet compartment, scale, amenities, and signature terry-cloth robes. Every cottage unit has its own ice machine, washer, and dryer.

For families and those requiring additional space, the resort offers 10 "Four Season Suites" with attractive parlors, 5 one-bedroom ocean suites, and 2 luxury suites that can be booked with from one to three bedrooms. Thirty-six villas and estate homes are also available on the property.

The quality and comfort level of living accommodations you have come to expect from Four Seasons Hotels has not been compromised.

Business conferences and incentive groups are also welcome here, and the property contains 13,500 square feet of meeting facilities.

Restaurants, Lounges, and Entertainment

Dining at Four Seasons Resort, Nevis is among the best in the Caribbean. The chef and the food and beverage manager have combined their respective talents to create magnificent buffet breakfasts and delectable gourmet dinners with emphasis on Caribbean specialties with a traditional French finesse.

Breakfast and dinner are offered in the restaurant, Neve. The Pool Cabana offers traditional and regional cuisine. In the evening, guests especially appreciate candlelight dinners in the romantic Dining Room, with its rich wood-plank floors, high-raftered ceilings, stone fireplace, and elegant crystal and china table service.

Guests can enjoy cocktails on the Ocean Terrace or in the intimate Library Lounge and at Mango, a beach front dining venue featuring a casual, open-air concept with a menu of grilled specialties. Live bands are also featured on select evenings.

Although room rates do not include meals, Full American Plan (FAP) is available at the cost of $125

per person per day and Modified American Plan (MAP) at a cost of $100.

Sport Facilities

The sport facilities at the resort are exceptional. The Robert Trent Jones II, 18-hole golf course is the most scenic in the Caribbean, boasting rolling green hills sprinkled with palms, colorful flora, rain forests, and occasional goats and monkeys. Golf enthusiasts will have the opportunity to play a 663-yard hole requiring a 240-yard drive over a deep ravine. The highest tee on the course reaches 400 feet above sea level, affording a dynamic panorama that includes neighboring islands. The golf facilities include putting greens, practice areas, a fully stocked pro shop, and two teaching pros.

A beverage cart is driven around the golf course, offering beverages and wet towels. Similarly, hotel personnel offer ice water, chilled aromatherapy towels, and Evian spritzer sprays to sunbathers on the half-mile strand of beach that fronts the property, and at the three, attractive free-form swimming pools. Comfortable chairs – some of which offer protection from the sun – line the beach and a large array of water-sports are available, including snorkeling, scuba, diving, windsurfing, sailing and water-skiing. Resort guests enjoy complimentary use of all non-motorized equipment. The beach does not have white nor light-colored sand, and the water is not as clear as that which you may experience on other Caribbean beaches.

Peter Burwash International runs the tennis facility, which includes four clay and six, all-weather composition courts, three of which are illuminated for night play and stadium seating. Group clinics and individual lessons are offered by PBI professionals.

Located next to the golf and tennis pro shop is the health club facilities. The fully air-conditioned Sports Pavilion features a fitness room with state-of-the-art workout equipment, including cardiovascular machines and free weights. Adjacent to the health club facilities is the spa. The 12,000 -square -foot spa includes 12 treatment rooms offering a variety of massages and procedures. Also located here is a beauty salon and the men's and women's locker rooms.

There are three horseback riding stables on the island, offering both English and Western saddles. Arrangements can be made through the resort's concierge desk.

A special "Dive and Dine" experience hosted by the resort's executive chef, Cyrille Pannier, an expert diver and fisherman, is available for groups of two to six certified divers. Guests enjoy a two-tank dive to catch their own Caribbean spiny lobsters which are then prepared at a beach barbecue by chef Pannier.

Miscellaneous and Environs

On the premises are a gift-souvenir shop, a boutique, and a golf and tennis pro shop. Handicrafts can be purchased in nearby Charlestown, and the neighboring island of St. Kitts is well known for its batiks.

The resort features an all-day children's activity program known as Kids For All Seasons, which makes this property an excellent destination for families.

Guests traveling to the resort can fly directly to Nevis from San Juan, Antigua or St. Martin or into St. Kitts from San Juan. At St. Kitts, the Four Seasons' staff will greet you, escort you to their water launch, and transport you to the resort via a scenic 30-minute launch ride.

Visitors to the Caribbean need no longer settle for primitive accommodations, mediocre sport facilities, ho-hum dining, and indifferent service. Four Seasons Resort, Nevis rises above its traditional, expensive Caribbean competitors and attains a much higher standard of elegance and creature comforts. Affluent couples and families who wish to enjoy a typical Caribbean island while ensconcing themselves in the most luxurious accommodations and enjoying the finest dining, friendly service, and outstanding facilities will be well rewarded at Four Seasons Resort, Nevis.

Four Seasons Resort Nevis
P.O. Box 565
Charlestown, Nevis, West Indies
Tel. (869) 469-1111 or (800)-332-3442
Fax (869) 469-1085
www.fourseasons.com/nevis

PUERTO RICO

EL CONQUISTADOR RESORT AND GOLDEN DOOR SPA

After spending several decades in retirement, the El Conquistador Resort and Country Club received a several-hundred-million dollar facelift and emerged in the 1990's as a 918-room full-facility mega-resort dynamically spread along a cliff descending to the sea. Formerly a Wyndham International property, in August of 2005, LXR Luxury Resorts (a subsidiary of the Blackstone Group) purchased El Conquistador and Las Casitas along with numerous other former Wyndham resorts. Over 100 million dollars has been earmarked for renovations including all accommodations, many of the public areas and the construction of an additional funicular railway running from Las Casitas to the Marina.

The resort boasts a vast array of dining and entertainment facilities, around-the-clock activities for the entire family, and an impressive selection of accommodations. The attitude of the service staff in the restaurants and public areas is as good as it gets in the Caribbean and is quite an accomplishment for a rural Puerto Rican property.

The hotel lobby, which is set above the sprawling main swimming pool and lounge area, is the focal area for dining, entertainment and shopping. In the evening this area is alive with guests enjoying the restaurants, casino, lounges and entertainers.

Guest accommodations are divided into four somewhat distinct areas. Those wishing to be close to the action will prefer the Grand Hotel, which is divided into the Las Brisas and Las Vista wings. Those wishing for more seclusion and closeness to the sea will prefer Marina Village, where the units are attractively spread around the harbor, or Las Olas Village, which is built into the side of the cliff

between the Grand Hotel and Marina Village, has its own swimming pool, and is recommended for honeymooners. These two areas are accessible from the main hotel only by two cable cars that run down the cliff.

Discerning vacationers, families, or several couples traveling together seeking a more upscale, pampered experience can opt for the five-diamond, award-winning Las Casitas, a complex of one-, two-, and three-bedroom casitas set on a cliff adjacent to the Grand Hotel that are privately owned and leased out to hotel guests. The one-bedroom luxury villas, with living rooms, dining areas, kitchens, and large verandas, go for $909 to $1,519 per night during high season ($379 to $879 in the summer) and include 24-hour room service, a private butler, Continental breakfast, three private pool areas, luxury transportation to and from the airport, numerous special amenities, and a great deal of exclusivity. Two- and three-bedroom casitas are also available. Las Casitas is really a resort within a resort and considerably more luxurious than the main property.

Accommodations

Whichever residential area you reside in, you will find the guest rooms to be spacious, recently redecorated and renovated, many with balconies, king- or queen-size beds, multi-line telephones, cable television with movie channels and DVDs, an additional telephone in the bathroom, stereos with compact disc players, high speed internet access, mini-bars, in-room safes, irons and ironing boards,

coffee and coffee machines, hair dryers, and large bathrooms/dressing areas.

Forty-five rooms on the fifth floor of the Las Brisas wing are designated "The Club Conquistador", and guests opting for these more expensive accommodations enjoy special amenities, including a VIP Lounge offering Continental breakfasts, before-dinner hors d'oeuvres and cocktails, as well as after-dinner brandies, liquors, and coffees.

The new owners that took over the resort in 2005 will totally renovate all of the rooms rendering them far more attractive and upscale than they were previously.

Those who can handle the rates will love Las Casitas, and those who can't may prefer the newer rooms at the Marina Village. The area is less congested and permits walks along the sea. The disadvantage is the necessity of taking the funicular railroad ride up to the main hotel. Each residential area has its own pool.

The 70,000-square-foot conference and meeting facilities with 22 breakout rooms, including a 20,000-square-foot Grand Ballroom, can service groups from 10 to 2,500; the facility is described as the largest of its kind in the Caribbean. The layout of the resort and vast variety of facilities make this an excellent choice for business meetings and conventions.

Restaurants, Lounges, and Entertainment

Three of the main restaurants are located on the mezzanine above the lobby. Isabella's presently describes itself as an American steakhouse with a menu and presentation reminiscent of a stateside Morton's or Ruth's Chris. The wine list is impressive but expensive. Otello's is a more intimate, but noisy Italian restaurant featuring a good variety of antipasti, pastas, veal, and fish specialties. Blossom's is an upscale Chinese/Japanese restaurant offering gourmet Hunan and Szechwan delicacies, sushi, and tableside teppan yakki. Epicureans will appreciate the gastronomic indoor/outdoor restaurant, Le

Bistro, at Las Casitas, offering a very intimate dining experience with French/Continental cuisine. Café Caribe, across from the Casino, is a contemporary coffee shop and ice cream parlor open daily for lunch, dinner and late night snacks, featuring salads, sandwiches and traditional American favorites.

Breakfast is served buffet-style at Las Brisas Terrace overlooking the pool. A casual lunch is also served here. Café Bella Vista is an informal open-air café/pizzeria, overlooking the pool and offering a wide selection of pizzas, sandwiches, salads, tapas, and Mediterranean specialties for lunch and dinner. When occupancy is high, the lobby bar, Amigos, converts to Café Expresso, serving coffee and Danish pastries. Other smaller restaurants are located at the various residential villages and at the golf course. Stingray Café at Marina Village specializes in Caribbean-influenced seafood and Las Olas Cantina Bar and Grill offers Mexican-style cuisine and margaritas at Las Olas Village. Ballyhoo Bar and Grill at the Marina Village is an atmospheric outdoor, casual spot for drinks, shrimp, pizza and burgers.

Exclusively for Las Casitas guests there are two open-air restaurants offering breakfast and lunch with a view.

The dining choices are varied, service in the dining venues is attentive, quality of cuisine is quite good and prices are very high.

Instrumentalists entertain in different areas of the resort throughout the evening. The flamenco guitar Latin variety show at Amigos Lounge is enjoyable. The large, exciting casino offers blackjack, baccarat, craps, roulette, and slots. Drakes is a combination club bar and billiard lounge.

El Conquistador is an exciting place to spend the evening; guests enjoy the before-dinner cocktail hour, the selection of dining possibilities, the casino, and the after-dinner entertainment.

Sport Facilities

The resort is one of the most complete sport complexes in the Caribbean. All that it is missing is an attractive area in which to jog or take a long walk and a sauna and steam facility (other than the steam room at the Golden Door Spa, which is not available to resort guests except at an extra charge.

The 18-hole championship 6,700-yard golf course is spread over steep rolling hills and sits in front of the main entrance. There is a pro shop, lessons are available, and green fees range from $95 to $165, depending on the season. Below the front entrance is a seven-court tennis complex. Tennis lessons are also available and court time goes for $25 per hour.

The small, air-conditioned fitness center by the pool is complimentary and permits guests to watch television as they utilize the numerous exercise and cardiovascular machines.

Although each residential area has its own swimming pool, the large imaginative main pool and Jacuzzis are located right off the lobby and look out down the cliff across the sea. They are surrounded by bars, restaurants, and the fitness center. At Las Casitas there are three, more intimate pools, all of which are available exclusively for Las Casitas guests.

One of the most unique features is the resort's beach facility on Palomino Island, accessible by a 10-minute motor launch ride from the Marina. Here you will find clear waters, white sand, many comfortable lounge chairs, umbrellas, toilets, a bar, nature trails, and a bevy of water-sports, including windsurfers, kayaks, sunfish, Hoby cats, wave runners, parasailing, snorkeling, and scuba diving. Palomino Divers is a company offering beginning and advanced diving excursions to shallow reefs off Palomino Island or more advanced locations such as Cayo Diablo and Calebra Island.

For $45 per day youngsters between 3 and 13 can enjoy the Camp Coqui program between 9:00 a.m. and 4:00 p.m., which includes lunch and a T-shirt.

In December 1998, the famous Golden Door Spa opened a branch adjacent to Las Casitas. For $20 a day, resort guests can use the 26,000-square-foot facility, which includes a state-of-the-art fitness center, spa pool, locker rooms, steam rooms (but no saunas), and relaxation areas. For varying prices, including attractive packages, the spa features a bevy of massage, body and beauty treatments and therapies in 25 treatment rooms. Exercise, Tai Chi, and other classes are offered daily. A full-service beauty salon, a juice bar, and a boutique are also located at the complex. The spa facilities are also scheduled for renovation and improvements by the new owners.

Miscellaneous and Environs

El Conquistador is located in Las Croabas on the northeast coast of Puerto Rico, 31 miles from the airport in San Juan. The resort provides regular bus and limousine service to and from the airport. Most guests avail themselves of the comfortable, 36-passenger motor coach, which takes approximately one and one-quarter hours and costs $60 round trip. The friendly airport staff will assist you with loading your bags on the bus (which are ticketed and delivered to your room); provide a preliminary check-in; serve you a choice of beverages during the ride; and play a video introduction to the resort.

Located on the main level of the Grand Hotel are numerous shops, including jewelry stores, men's and women's boutiques, a signature shop, art galleries, and a sundry-commissary store where soft drinks and snacks can be purchased.

Popular excursions include a tour of the 28,000-acre El Yunque Rainforest, which encompasses 240 species of trees, 200 species of birds, tropical ferns, bamboo groves, tropical flowers, splashing waterfalls, and shaded pools; a two-hour horseback trail ride to the rainforest and Luquillo Beach; guided tours through old and new San Juan; and air excursions to St. Thomas.

The El Conquistador resort experience will hold special appeal to couples and families, as well as business meeting guests who appreciate a dynamic, unique setting, a large variety of sports, dining and entertainment facilities, polite, concerned service, comfortable accommodations, a full-scale gambling casino, and a pristine, private-island beach. Those seeking more exclusivity and pampering will wish to book the Las Casitas Villas and indulge in the Golden Door Spa programs.

El Conquistador Resort & Golden Door Spa
Las Croabas, Puerto Rico
Tel. (787) 863-1000
Fax (787) 863-6500
Mailing Address:
1000 El Conquistador Avenue
Las Croabas, Fajardo, Puerto Rico 00738
Web: www.wyndham.com

ST. MARTIN

LA SAMANNA

The white stucco Mediterranean-style hotel and villas sprawl along 55 acres of pristine beachfront property on the French side of St. Martin, only a 10-minute drive from Juliana International Airport and 15 miles from the French capital of Marigot. La Samanna was conceived and built in the early 1970s by its owner, James Frankel, who operated the property until his death in 1989. The resort was one of the first super-deluxe, super-expensive properties with a European flair built in the Caribbean.

In 1996, La Samanna was purchased by Orient Express Hotels, which also owns and operates the fabled Venice-Simplon Orient Express, as well as 34 upscale properties, including Cipriani in Venice, Splendido in Portofino, and Bora Bora Lagoons in French Polynesia. Extensive renovations have taken place during the last few years throughout the property, including renovating, redecorating and air-conditioning all guest rooms, adding balconies to many, redesigning and redecorating the restaurant and reception area, enlarging and restructuring the swimming pool and adjoining areas, construction of 28 new suites, a small European spa, enlarging the fitness center and considerable landscaping.

La Samanna brochures describe it as "a small, ultra-exclusive resort catering to an affluent clientele seeking privacy, sophistication and understated elegance". In the 1970s, many famous movie stars and dignitaries graced the resort's lovely grounds. During the 1980s several more modern and luxurious properties were constructed on neighboring Caribbean islands, borrowing the concept from La Samanna. Some of the more fickle of the rich and famous moved on to greener pastures; however, La Samanna still enjoys a high percentage of annual repeaters. About 30 percent of the clientele are European, and the balance comes from the United States, Canada, and South America.

The main hotel building consists of a small reception area connecting to a sheltered, open-air restaurant dramatically perched on a cliff overlooking the sea. At one side is an indoor/outdoor bar, lounge, and grill restaurant adjacent to the swimming pool. Other than the 11 rooms and suites atop the main hotel building, the accommodations are located in the numerous villas that stretch along the beach connected by floral paths and archways.

Prices in high season range from $765 to $4450 per night; and, there are minimum stay requirements on weekends and at various times during the year.

Accommodations

In total, there are 81 guest accommodations consisting of the 11 rooms and five specialty suites in the main hotel, as well as one-, two-, and three-bedroom suites that share the villas spread along the beach. The villas have small living rooms, private patios looking out to the sea, bedrooms with ceiling fans, and bathrooms done in colorful hand-painted ceramic tiles. All rooms are air-conditioned and feature kitchens or mini bars that can be stocked to the guest's personal needs, private safes, satellite televisions with VCRs or DVDs, signature bathrobes, hair dryers, and skincare amenities. The rooms have a Mediterranean flavor with white walls, terra-cotta tile or white marble floors, wicker

Restaurants, Entertainment, and Lounges

The picturesque, alfresco restaurant sitting atop the cliff, looking out to the sea, is the main dining room at La Samanna. An extensive breakfast buffet in included daily for all guests. Dinner features a broad selection of imaginative Fusion-style cuisine, as well as the opportunity to choose a bottle of French wine from its impressive 10,000-bottle wine cellar. Food and beverage prices have been reduced somewhat from prior years with the goal of keeping the guests dining more frequently at the hotel; however, food and wine is still quite pricey, and dinner and wine for two can easily run $150-$250. A meal plan is available at $140 per person and may be the best bet for those who enjoy numerous courses. The panoramic, open-air Rotisserie Grill is situated at the poolside, offering lunch and becoming a steak house during the evening for diners seeking a more relaxed atmosphere during their visit. The completely renovated Beach Bar now offers lunch and BBQ evenings under the stars. After a recent renovation, the renowned Wine Cellar now offers a truly gastronomical evening for private dinner parties, with advance reservations being required.

The bar and terrace that overlook the pool are the spot for before- and after-dinner cocktails.

Sport Facilities

La Samanna is located on a two-mile stretch of curving white-sand beach at Baie Longue abutting crystal-clear aqua blue waters. At times, the surf can be a bit strong, and during the summer, the tides obliterate a portion of the beach. Because most of the rooms open out to the beach, guests can reposition the lounge chairs from their patios to anywhere along the sand. Beach attendants provide towels, chairs, umbrellas, cold refresher cloths, water, and sorbet throughout the day. Bar service is available along the beach whenever guests hoist their blue flags.

Snorkeling, sailing, and kayaking are available gratis. The mid-size freshwater pool is located directly off the lobby and lounge, and guests can en-

and bamboo furnishing accents, and vivid fabrics of tropical prints in sea-blue, green, and yellow color schemes. All rooms offer a balcony or terrace with ocean views.

If you book far enough in advance, you can reserve exclusive use of the property for a group or meeting.

On our last inspection we found the tile floors, furnishings, window treatments, hardware, size of the bathrooms, and the plumbing in about half of the units still reflect the style of the hotel rooms built in the 1970s. However, management advises that much of these items have been recently modernized.

joy a drink or cocktail here during the day or evening. The new exercise facility includes Stair-Master stair climbers, treadmills, aerodyne bicycles, free weights, and other equipment. Complementary Yoga and tennis classes are offered twice each week. The spa, which includes nine massage rooms, several of which open up to a beautiful garden with waterfalls, offers numerous beauty, massage, and therapy treatments.

The three all-weather tennis courts (two omni-surfaced) are busy throughout the day, illuminated for night play, and a tennis pro is available for lessons. The resort will arrange fishing trips and golf at nearby Mullet Bay.

Miscellaneous and Environs

The resort is a 10 minutes from Juliana International Airport, 35 minutes from Philipsburg (the capital of the Dutch side of the island), and 10 minutes from Marigot (capital of the French side).The resort now offers all guests the option to book a fast-track service at the airport, where you are met as you deplane and are whisked through immigration to a waiting luxury vehicle. The return trip to the airport, also allows guests to wait in the VIP lounge. The return trip is priced at $60 per person.

There is a small sundry shop and signature item boutique in the main hotel, and three other boutiques on the property offering fine jewelry and apparel; but guests may prefer to shop in Philipsburg, in Marigot or at the shopping centers at the nearby Mahoe Bay hotel.

There are casinos at hotels on the Dutch side of the island. The resort is closed from Labor Day through October 31, which is also the rainy season. During the rest of the year, the weather is generally pleasant, with temperatures ranging from the mid-70s to the mid-80s.

Overall, La Samanna continues to offer a casually elegant, sophisticated, comfortable, and romantic experience with fine dining to its wealthy American and European clientele at one of the choice beachfront locations in St. Martin.

La Samanna
P.O. Box 4077
97064 St. Martin
French West Indies
Tel. (590) 876400
(800) 854-2252 (United States)
Fax (590) 878786
Fax (212)575-7039 (United States)
Web: www.orient-express.com
E-mail: reservations@lasamanna.com

CANEEL BAY, A ROSEWOOD RESORT

Caneel Bay, a Rosewood Resort is a unique, informal tropical beach resort, located on a 170-acre estate on St. John, one of the loveliest spots in the Caribbean. The resort's seven crescent-shaped beaches are among the most beautiful and pristine in the world. This is an incomparable property, with lush green hills, endless paths of tropical flora, exotic white-sand beaches, and secluded lodgings, most of which abut the sea. A retreat for movie stars, politicians, honeymooners, and well-heeled travelers from around the world, this low-key unspoiled resort was built by Laurence Rockefeller in 1956 as part of an environmental preserve that included nearby Cinnamon Bay campground and the 5,000-acre Virgin Islands National Park.

In 1993, management was taken over by Rosewood Hotels and Resorts, Inc. Subsequently the guest rooms and public areas have been air-conditioned.

Accommodations

166 air-conditioned guest rooms are spread out in low buildings scattered throughout the grounds, with 131 rooms overlooking one of the seven crescent-shaped private beaches. Although adequate, the accommodations seem a bit worn and cannot be described as deluxe, even though the prices might indicate that such is the case. But then, one does not vacation at Caneel Bay to be ensconced in material luxuries. The charm and wonder of this resort lies in the natural beauty of the surroundings, the incomparable beaches, and the acres of lush vegetation. To encourage guests to totally disconnect from their harried daily lives, there are no radios, telephones, or televisions; however, each room includes a refrigerator/mini-bar, an ice bucket filled daily, complimentary bottles of rum and bottled water, an iron and ironing board, a private room safe, hair dryer, cotton robes, and umbrellas. Renovations of all bathrooms were completed in 2005.

There is only one small meeting room because conventions are not encouraged, but small executive-level programs are welcome in the off-season. It is the belief of the owners that this is a special place where guests should be left to savor the beauty and tranquility without the clamor of large groups.

Restaurants, Lounges, and Entertainment

The main dining room at the indoor/outdoor Caneel Beach Terrace--with its open-line kitchen with wood-burning stove, Mediterranean grill, and rotisserie--serves a buffet breakfast and lunch, as well as a grand buffet on Monday evenings. The more formal Turtle Bay Estate House Dining Room, at the northern tip of the property, offers dinner each evening and breakfast and lunch from mid-December through March. Informal dinners are served at Equator Restaurant perched atop an 18th-century sugar mill on a lovely hill and affording a picturesque view of the environs. Grilled meats, poultry, and seafood are featured here, accented with the executive chef's signature Asian flair.

The breakfast buffet is quite extensive and includes a variety of freshly squeezed juices, fresh

fruits, and freshly baked croissants and pastries, as well as smoked salmon, breakfast meats, French toast, and made-to-order omelets.

Light lunches, snacks, and beverages are served during the day at the Beach Bar and English-style high tea is offered in the afternoon at Turtle Bay.

Dinner at the picturesque Turtle Bay Restaurant is a multi-course meal with numerous seafood and fish offerings, as well as a variety of meat and fowl preparations. The cuisine could be described as Continental with West Indian flair. The wine list offers numerous selections, and on clear evenings, guests can opt to dine alfresco. The terrace here is a charming place to have afternoon tea or before-dinner cocktails.

The Sunset Terrace, located above the Beach Bar, is a pleasant location to enjoy drinks, a light lunch, or supper, overlooking the cove.

There is music and dancing nightly in the lounge of the main building and sunset cruises twice each week, as well as, evening movies.

Guests are offered the options of European, Modified, or Full American Plan at all restaurants. This may be a good choice, since food prices are very steep.

Sport Facilities

Although there is a swimming pool, most guests wouldn't dream of using a man-made pool when they are surrounded by seven of the most perfect beaches in the world. Lying out on a secluded crescent-shaped strand, shaded by palms and sea-grape trees that border the clear, warm turquoise water is the real sport here. Tiny tropical fish brush by your ankles, and you are as close to paradise as you can imagine.

There is no golf course, but there are 11 above-average tennis courts with complimentary court time. Caneel Bay's tennis program is under the direction of Peter Burwash International, with a resident professional on-site year round. Facilities are available for scuba diving, sailing, snorkeling, windsurfing, and bicycling. The numerous paths throughout the property are a jogger's dream.

Other guest facilities include a small fitness center with stationary bicycles, steppers, treadmills, free weights, a fully equipped children's center with counselors and a "mind/body program", which includes yoga, meditation, relaxation therapy, and massage.

Miscellaneous and Environs

To reach Caneel Bay, you fly to St. Thomas. At the St. Thomas airport, there is an air-conditioned airport lounge. After checking in at the lounge, arriving guests are directed to a jitney for a short trip to the Ferry Dock. From the dock, guests are transported directly to the resort on a Caneel Bay ferry-boat – a 35-minute trip.

The resort offers daily ferry service to St. Thomas so guests can enjoy a day of shopping on the neighboring island. Every Monday, Wednesday, and Friday there are excursions on the Caneel Bay ferry to the sister resort at Little Dix Bay, Virgin Gorda. Cruz Bay is a quaint little Caribbean town 10 minutes from the resort that offers numerous shops and several restaurants. Visitors may also enjoy exploring USVI National Park and snorkeling at Trunk Bay.

This is not a vacation spot for golfers or for those seeking luxurious facilities, amenities, or many activities. However, for those seeking the ultimate in beauty and tranquility, Caneel Bay has few equals.

Caneel Bay
P.O. Box 120
Cruz Bay, St. John
United States Virgin Islands 00830
Tel. (340) 776-6111
Fax (340) 693-8280
E-Mail: caneelres@rosewoodhotels.com
www.caneelbay.com

VIRGIN ISLANDS

LITTLE DIX BAY

This uniquely beautiful, boutique resort consists of one- and two-story ocean-view cottages, spread out over 240 acres overlooking one of the Caribbean's most beautiful half-mile crescent-shaped white-sand beaches on the island of Virgin Gorda in the British Virgin Islands. Little Dix Bay is the second such resort to be developed in the Virgin Islands by Laurence S. Rockefeller's Rockresorts, Inc., and is in keeping with Rockefeller's concept of promoting conservation while providing understated style and comfort in naturally beautiful surroundings.

In June of 1993, management was transferred from Rockresorts to Rosewood Hotels and Resorts, Inc., which also manages Caneel Bay on St. John. Major refurbishments have been made throughout the years including the addition of a Cliffside Spa and Beachfront swimming pool.

The resort opened its doors in 1964 with 50 rooms. Fifty additional units have been added. The resort actually owns 540 acres on Virgin Gorda, including a yacht harbor-marina opened in 1971, which accommodates 120 yachts, an adjoining shopping center, and boatyard.

Although reminiscent of its sister resort, Caneel Bay on St. John, Little Dix Bay has a character all its own and is considered by many of its repeat clientele as more intimate. Rather than being spread out along numerous small beaches, the buildings all overlook one large crescent beach. The similarities in food, service, accommodations, facilities, and activities between the two properties are certainly present, and preference is really a matter of personal taste.

Accommodations

The 100 beachfront rooms, including four 1-bedroom suites, one 2-bedroom villa and one 3-bedroom villa, are located in one- and two-story accommodations spread out over the resort, nestled among sea grape trees and bougainvillea, not visible from the water. Some rooms have a rectangular design, while others are hexagonal, but the furnishings and decorations are very similar. Some of the hexagonal rooms are ground level, and others are on stilts, giving a tree-house effect.

Rooms include two twin beds or a king-size bed, large closets, Bose wave radio/CD players, a ceiling fan, and a private patio or terrace (some with hammocks). There are no locks on the doors and no televisions. All guest rooms are air-conditioned and have patios and porches, phones, mini-bars, wall safes, robes, hair dryers, irons, and umbrellas.

In 2005, the rooms were refurbished with all new soft goods and furniture.

The standard rooms are ample, but not luxurious. Management maintains that the accommodations are what their guests prefer and seek out when vacationing at Little Dix Bay.

Little Dix Bay can accommodate small meetings and groups. The resort welcomes families with children and provides special children's activities, in a 2,000 square-foot "Children's Grove."

Restaurants, Lounges, and Entertainment

There are three restaurants: the open-air Pavilion Dining Room, the adjoining Sugar Mill Restaurant,

and the Beach Grill at the boat dock. All three offer panoramic views of the resort's magnificent beach and surrounding vegetation.

Full breakfasts are offered in the Pavilion, and lunch is served buffet-style daily, including tempting cold meats, salads, and desserts, together with hot offerings. Sandwiches, salads, and other items are available at lunchtime at the Beach Grill or Ocean Bar.

In the evenings, an international menu is featured at the Pavilion, and Caribbean bistro cuisine at the Sugar Mill. The Beach Grill also serves a casual dinner in season. In addition to a manager's cocktail party on Monday evenings, there are beach picnics and other special events.

Complimentary tea is served daily. On some evenings, there is music and dancing to combos and other local entertainers.

The variety and quality of the very pricey offerings are adequate but could not be described as gourmet or outstanding. The open-air breakfasts with fresh juices and pastries are especially pleasant.

Full room service is available from 7:00 a.m. until 10:00 p.m.

Sport Facilities

Little Dix Bay is a beach-oriented haven, and most guests spend their days lazing in lounges on the beautiful crescent-shaped, beige-sand beach lined with sea-grape trees and coconut palms that front the resort. This is possibly the most picturesque hotel beach in the Caribbean. For variety, motor launches called Boston Whalers will transport you, together with a picnic lunch, to one of the seven less populated beaches around Virgin Gorda. Here you can enjoy complete privacy and serenity, a total escape from the maddening world.

Sailing excursions, snorkeling and scuba tours, water-skiing, fishing, and kayaking can be arranged.

There are seven asphalt tennis courts, two of which are flood lit, and a teaching pro, who will arrange games and lessons. The tennis program is under the direction of Peter Burwash International. There is no golf course at the resort; however, off-property golf excursions can be arranged.

The personnel will assist you in finding suitable trails for nature hikes. Joggers will enjoy romping around the beach or the scenic acreage, exploring their own paths at will. There is also a small, well-equipped fitness center.

Miscellaneous and Environs

Virgin Gorda is located in the midst of the British Virgin Islands, which include Tortola, Peter Island, Norman Island, Jost Van Dyke, Salt Island, Scrub Island, Great Camanoe, and the Dogs. Motor yacht or sailboat excursions to these neighboring islands can be arranged through the resort.

Visitors to Little Dix Bay can fly into Beef Island/Tortola from San Juan in 40 minutes or from St. Thomas in 20 minutes. Those arriving by air will be met at the Beef Island airport, and representatives from the hotel will take your luggage and check you in while you are transported directly from the airport to the resort in 20 minutes aboard a private catamaran for a charge of $85 round trip.

On the premises, there are personnel who can provide massages, facials, pedicures, and manicures, but there is no sauna, steam or spa. There is one gift shop with souvenirs, clothes, Little Dix Bay specialty items, and sundries, as well as a tennis shop. At the Virgin Gorda Yacht Harbor, 10 minutes away, is a shopping center, which includes an Eng-lish Pub, ice-cream parlor, wine shop, drug store, supermarket, bank, launderette, a ship's commissary store, and several craft shops and boutiques.

Visitors may enjoy exploring Coppermine Point, the site of an old abandoned coppermine; Spring Bay, an unusual beach with a pool enclosed by gigantic boulders; and "The Baths", another beach where boulders form natural pools and seaside caverns that are fun to climb and bathe in. The resort holds its Thursday picnics at Spring Bay.

A Modified American and Full American meal plan are also available. Considering the high prices of food items, this may be your best choice. You may wish to take advantage of a special arrangement where you can divide your vacation between a stay at Little Dix Bay and Caneel Bay, the sister resort on St. John.

Little Dix Bay offers well-heeled vacationers (not too fussy about service), a unique opportunity to experience an exclusive, tranquil resort in a dependable tropical climate with a casual, low-key atmosphere amidst some of the most beautiful beaches and scenery that exist in the Caribbean.

Little Dix Bay
P.O. Box 70, Virgin Gorda
British Virgin Islands
Tel. (284) 495-5555
Fax (284) 495-5661
idreservatons@rosewoodhotels.com
www.littledixbay.com

VIRGIN ISLANDS

PETER ISLAND RESORT

Peter Island Resort and Spa is located on Peter Island, a 1,800-acre private Caribbean island paradise. Surrounded by deep turquoise waters and bathed in perpetual sunshine, Peter Island is one of the 50 islands comprising the British Virgins. Sitting 90 miles east of Puerto Rico, 4 miles east of St. John, and 4 miles southeast of Tortola, the island is accessible by motor launch, ferries, and helicopters that can transport you from neighboring islands. The property was built in 1971 by a Norwegian shipping company and acquired by Amway Corp. in 1978. In 1999, the founder of Amway, Van Andel, purchased the island and the resort. Considerable sums are spent annually refurbishing and maintaining this tropical paradise.

Guests arrive at the picturesque yacht harbor via the resort's private yacht, only a few steps from the reception lobby. Thirty-two of the guest rooms are located in the villas adjacent to the reception area and overlook the freshwater pool, main dining room, and Sprat Bay. Twenty additional beachfront accommodations are a quarter-mile away on Deadman's Beach, near the Beach Bar and Grill, watersport center, gym and tennis courts.

The atmosphere is casual, quiet, laid-back, and ideal for couples wishing "to get away from it all" in a romantic setting.

Accommodations

Thirty-two ocean-view guest rooms are located in eight villas on Sprat Bay, and 20 beach-front junior suites are located in four villas on Deadman's Beach. The beach-front rooms are larger, with walk-in closets and more luxurious bathrooms, and are the most desirable.

All of the guest accommodations are air-conditioned, have ceiling fans, direct-dial telephones, refrigerators, CD/clock radios, fresh flowers, hair dryers, private safes, coffee makers, irons and ironing boards, and patios with sea views, but no televisions.

Two luxury villas, the four-bedroom Crow's Nest and the three-bedroom Hawk's Nest, are located atop of hills and can be rented from $5,150 to $9,700 per night in high season. Rates drop somewhat during the summer months and early fall.

There is one air-conditioned meeting room that can accommodate up to 60 guests for a small meeting.

Restaurants, Lounges, and Entertainment

A three-meal-a-day, FAP (Full American Plan) is included in the room rates.

The main dining room is called Tradewinds Restaurant. It is opened for breakfast and dinner and is located near the pool and reception area. Lunch, cocktails, soft drinks, coffees and dinner are offered at Deadman's Beach Bar and Grill, which features grilled fish, chicken, and meats by the beach. A Continental breakfast is available through room service, which will be delivered to guest's verandas or terraces for those opting not to eat in the restaurant.

On Monday evenings, there is a manager's cocktail party followed by a barbecue at the beach restaurant; and on Saturday evenings, the resort offers a lavish buffet dinner featuring fresh fish, seafood, and roast beef.

Entertainment in the evenings alternates between groups playing steel drums, folk guitarists, and calypso bands. Complimentary hot hors d'oeuvres are served before dinner at the lounge area adjacent to the dining room.

Each season, the chef crafts a seven-day rotating menu with a combination of his own signature dishes, local favorites and international staples.

Sport Facilities

Although there is a small pool right off the bay villas, most guests prefer to lounge and swim at one of the lovely white-sand crescent beaches, where the water is calm, warm, and crystal clear. Deadman's Bay, the most popular strand, runs for a quarter of a mile in front of the beach villas and beach restaurant. Here, there are numerous comfortable lounges and several thatched shelters offering some respite from the bright Caribbean sun. Water-sports, including board sailing, Sunfish and Squib sailboats, and ocean kayaks are available at the recreation area on this beach. Four laykold tennis courts are also located here, two being illuminated for night play.

Guests wishing more seclusion can choose from the beaches known as Little Deadman's Bay, Honeymoon Beach, Reef Bay, and White Bay. White Bay is on the other side of the island and the resort will arrange transportation and deliver a complimentary picnic lunch complete with fine linens, china, and flatware.

At the fitness center located on Deadman's Bay Beach guests can look out at the beach while exercising with free weights, stair-masters, and stationary bikes. A 10,000 square-foot spa overlooking its own beach was competed in 2004 offering 10 indoor treatment rooms and two outdoor seaside "bohios", a beauty salon, steam rooms, a swimming pool and meditation and relaxation areas.

Bicycles are available at most locations, and guests enjoy cycling, jogging, and walking along the roads and paths of this private island.

The resort's classic sports-fishing boat can be rented and scuba diving excursions can be arranged with the on-site dive center to over 36 dive sites, including the Wreck of the Rhone, a 19-century British mail ship (the underwater location for the filming of the movie The Deep). In addition, the resort offers complimentary Sunfish, windsurfers, motorboats, sailboats, and snorkeling.

Miscellaneous and Environs

Shops at the resort carry sundries and beach and casual wear, as well as snorkel and dive equipment.

Newspapers are complimentary to the guests. Arrangements can be made to spend the day at St. Thomas for those wishing to indulge in more serious shopping. Excursions can also be arranged to neighboring Tortola and Virgin Gorda.

Visitors generally fly to San Juan, Puerto Rico, or St. Thomas and catch a small aircraft to Beef Island airport, which connects with Tortola by a bridge. The resort then provides transportation by private motor launch. As an alternative, the resort will provide for a motor launch and taxi direct to the airport in St. Thomas. Arrangements can be made in advance to take a helicopter from St. Thomas airport directly to Peter Island. In addition, the yacht harbor at the resort can accommodate private yachts and sailboats.

There is regular ferry service between Peter Island and Road Town, Tortola, and there are several flights each week that connect Tortola with Antigua, St. Kitts, St. Martin, St. Croix, and St. Thomas.

Although most facilities and accommodations at the resort are within walking distance, there is a regular transport service to all areas around the island.

Peter Island Resort is possibly a bit more laid-back than some of its competitors in the luxury Caribbean resort market. It offers its guests from all over the world (many of whom are annual repeaters) very comfortable accommodations, friendly service, quality dining, and extraordinary watersports in a relaxed, quiet, casual, private island environment.

Peter Island Resort
P.O. Box 9409
St. Thomas, USVI 00801
Tel. (284) 495-2000
Fax (284) 495-2500
In U.S.: Tel. 770-476-9988 or 800-346-4451
Fax. 770-476-4979
www.peterisland.com
E-mail: reservatons@peterisland.com

VIRGIN ISLANDS

THE RITZ-CARLTON, ST. THOMAS

The incredibly beautiful low-rise, Mediterranean-style buildings of St. Thomas' premier, luxury resort stretch along a semi-circular hill that descends through lush tropical gardens to turquoise seas on a secluded, 30-acre private estate located on the eastern tip of the island. This grand European-influenced property with peach-colored stucco walls, coppertone roofs, and breezeways covered with bougainvillea was built in the early 1990s as the Grand Palazzo and taken over by The Ritz-Carlton in 1996 after a $2.5 million enhancement. Reminiscent of palatial villas one would find in Cap Ferrat, Cap Antibes, Lake Como, or on the Amalfi coast, guests are treated to a little bit of European style on a tropical Caribbean island with The Ritz-Carlton brand of service.

Public areas are absolutely awesome, combining lavish marble, Mediterranean designs, and exotic plants. The restaurants, public areas, and guest rooms all command magnificent panoramic views. Wherever you turn, you have the feeling of being totally ensconced in ultimate luxury.

Accommodations

The 152, identical, 450-square-foot rooms, all with 125-foot balconies and the 4 one-bedroom suites are located in three buildings arranged in a semicircle overlooking the sea connected by walk-ways and gardens filled with lush tropical plants and flowers. Every room is elegant in decor with a private terrace or balcony, a sitting area, a writing desk, an étagère housing a remote control television and mini-bar/refrigerator, an international direct-dial telephone, a walk-in closet with private safe, iron and ironing boards, and marble bathrooms with two sinks, a shower/tub combination, a ladies makeup area, robes, and a hair dryer.

The one-bedroom suites are twice the size of the other rooms with separate showers and tubs, king beds, an additional bathroom, and a parlor with a wet bar. Conference facilities include over 10,000 square feet of meeting space with indoor and outdoor function rooms. Wedding and honeymoon packages and an on-site wedding coordinator are available.

Restaurants, Dining & Entertainment

In addition to 24-hour room service there are four dining venues. The outdoor Iguana's and Coconut Cove Beach Bar and Grill, located midway between the pools and beaches, offer snacks and meals throughout the day, including an assortment of sandwiches, salads, pizzas, seafood, and tropical libations. The charming, casually elegant open-air Café with an outside terrace features impressive â la carte and buffet breakfast offerings and an eclectic dinner menu where diners are entertained nightly by a harpist or guitarist.

In The Ritz-Carlton tradition, the more elegant air-conditioned dinner restaurant, The Great Bay Grill, overlooking the sea, features Mediterranean-inspired cuisine and a premium wine collection. A classical pianist performs at the adjoining formal bar area.

Sport Facilities

The focal point of the outside grounds is the pool/beach area where guests can laze around a free-form, fresh-water pool located immediately above two separate quarter-mile strands of white sand beach. Equipment for wind surfing, Hobie Kats, kayaks, snorkel, scuba gear, and floating mats can be rented from the full-service aquatic center, and the resort can arrange parasailing, water-skiing, and deep-sea fishing. A full service dive operation exclusively for hotel guests is also offered. The 53-foot Lady Lynsey Catamaran offers day time and not-to-be-missed sunset cruises, both favorites with guests.

In addition, on property are two tennis courts that are illuminated for night play, and there is a teaching pro available. The new spa/fitness center offers a nice range of cardio and exercise equipment, aerobic classes, and a variety of massage therapies, body treatments, facials, hair and nail care services, as well as, make-up artistry. Golfers are transported to Mahogany Run with pre-arranged tee times.

Families will appreciate the year-around Ritz Kid program where counselors entertain youngsters, from 4 through 12, with special activities.

Miscellaneous and Environs

The property is a 20-minute drive from Charlotte Amalie and a 30-minute drive from the airport. The Ritz-Carlton, St. Thomas has made arrangements with special taxis to transport its guests.

On property are men and women's boutiques, a logo and sundry shop, a jewelry store, and a full-service beauty salon. Of course, visitors to St. Thomas should spend at least a few hours in town checking out the incomparable bargains in duty-free goods, including liquors, perfumes, watches, fine jewelry, and imported china and crystal.

Adjacent to the resort is a new 81-residence mid-rise building complex offering two- and three- bedroom apartments where owners purchase fractional interests. One of the pools and beaches at the resort, and the Coconut Cove Beach Bar and Grill

is located in front of these buildings. All facilities are mutually available to resort guests and residence owners.

Day trips to neighboring Virgin Islands can be arranged, St. John being an excellent choice to experience some of the world's most pristine beach-

es and beautiful scenery. (See sections on Caneel Bay, Little Dix Bay, and Peter Island Resort and Spa).

St. Thomas is the world's busiest cruise destination and The Ritz-Carlton, St. Thomas is an excellent venue to spend a few days or weeks before of after cruising in this area. Sophisticated travelers who appreciate European-style decor and elegance in an idyllic Caribbean climate will find The Ritz-Carlton, St. Thomas without a peer.

The Ritz-Carlton St. Thomas
6900 Great Bay
St. Thomas, U.S. Virgin Islands
Tel. (340) 775-3333
Fax (340) 775-4444
www.ritzcarlton.com/resorts/st_thomas

CHAPTER SIX

MEXICO

ACAPULCO
Acapulco Princess
Las Brisas

CABO SAN LUCAS
Las Ventanas Al Paraiso

CANCUN
The Ritz-Carlton, Cancun

PUERTO VALLARTA
Four Seasons Resort Punta Mita

Acapulco Princess

The design, architecture, pools, gardens, and shrubberies of the Mexican hotels are the most lavish in the world. However, the service and commercialism are so distressing that few can qualify as great resorts. The four selected are the most outstanding and unusual properties in the country.

For those on a budget, there are a number of acceptable hotels with a resort atmosphere in Acapulco, Puerto Vallarta, Cancun, and Ixtapa.

ACAPULCO

FAIRMONT ACAPULCO PRINCESS

About 20 minutes from the center of Acapulco and 10 minutes from the Acapulco Airport is situated one of the largest resort complexes in Mexico. Rising from the sea in the shape of an Aztec pyramid, the Fairmont Acapulco Princess is located in the center of 480 magnificent acres of landscaped lawns, palm-lined lagoons, tropical foliage, scenic golf courses, and 1,500 feet of golden beach. In contrast to the high-rise opulence of the Princess, its sister hotel, the Fairmont Pierre Marques, located one-half mile down the beach toward town, is composed of more casual low-rise buildings and casitas spread amidst coconut palms, monkey pod trees, hibiscus, and bougainvillea. The Fairmont Pierre Marques is open only from November through March. There is reciprocity between these two properties and the restaurants and other facilities can be enjoyed by guests at either hotel. In August 1998 both properties were acquired from Princess Hotels International by Fairmont Hotels and Resorts.

The vast open-air atrium lobby of the Fairmont Acapulco Princess is incredibly beautiful, the view from the interior corridors in front of the guest rooms is breathtaking, and the positioning of the many tropical gardens, the imaginative pools, and the outdoor landscaping is certainly among the most creative in the world. However, the Fairmont Acapulco Princess is a busy hotel, with crowds, activities, and tumult.

Accommodations

The 1,017 guest rooms in the Fairmont Acapulco Princess are located in three high-rise buildings. The rooms are a little larger than average, with modern Mexican furnishings, private safes, radios, televisions, balconies, and large bathrooms with private toilet compartments and hair dryers.

The resort boasts excellent fully equipped convention facilities, including 11 convention meeting rooms, a Presidential suite, a boardroom that seats 14 people comfortably at its conference table, and a state-of-the-art amphitheater that can seat 450 theater-style and 300 schoolroom. The Fairmont Acapulco Princess plays host to many conventions and business meetings each year.

Modified American Plan is recommended in high season; the wide variety of restaurants, however, makes this a pleasant experience. Rates go down by almost a third in the off-season. There is a 15 percent government tax and a 2 percent lodging tax added to all bills. Children under 12 who stay with parents are only charged for meals.

Restaurants, Lounges, and Entertainment

At the Fairmont Acapulco Princess, numerous restaurants serve a variety of meals ranging from casual buffets to haute cuisine. La Hacienda, my personal favorite, offers barbecued meats and Mexican gourmet fare complemented with romantic music. The open-air Chula Vista serves a buffet-style breakfast and dinner and a la carte lunches. The dinner buffet includes a vast array of foods ranging from giant prawns, roast beef, and grilled meats to Mexican specialties, imaginative appetizers, salads, fruits, and pastries. La Posadita serves breakfast,

lunch, and dinner and emphasizes seafood specialties. The Veranda Restaurant features an array of Italian specialties, while diners look out to the sea. The Beach Club Restaurant and adjoining bar offers seafood specialties, veggies, meat, and poultry with a Caribbean touch and musical accompaniment. Specialty coffees, pastries, and light snacks are served at Café Los Angeles.

Casual dress is acceptable in all of the restaurants. Dinners at La Hacienda are not included in MAP, nor are lunches at any of the restaurants. Some of the restaurants close during the less crowded seasons.

There are a number of picturesque bars and lounges located both indoors and around the pools and gardens. The famous La Palapa swim-up bar allows you the option of swimming up for a drink.

In the evening, there are strolling mariachis at the Laguna Bar off the lobby and at most of the restaurants. Other options include the nightclub, Yuca, featuring salsa music.

Sport Facilities

The long stretch of beach fronting the Fairmont Acapulco Princess is superior to the other beaches in Acapulco, and swimming is somewhat better, although there is a perpetual surf. The travel agency located in the hotel will help arrange for scuba diving, water-skiing, sailing, and deep-sea fishing. Equestrians can ride the many beat-up nags right on the beach. The resort offers nine outdoor tennis courts (all are lit for night play) and two that are indoors and air-conditioned.

There are two scenic championship 18-hole golf courses, one at the Fairmont Acapulco Princess and the other at the Fairmont Pierre Marques, as well as a two-mile jogging path, which starts in front of the golf clubhouse at the Fairmont Acapulco Princess.

Possibly the most unique feature of the resort is its numerous pools, which make swimming an adventure. While enjoying the awesome beauty of the pools, you can massage your back under a waterfall, shimmy down a water slide, swim up to a bar for a "coco loco", or just float around on a raft and soak up the sun. There is a small gymnasium and

for young children there is a special pool and a playground.

Massage and spa services are available at the resort's 14,000-square-foot Willow Stream Spa. Offering 17 treatment rooms and two couples' massage suites, the spa embodies the unique landscape and history of Acapulco, featuring a striking palapa-thatched roof. Specialized treatments range from the Bougainvillea Aromatherapy Facial to the Mexican Aloe Body Wrap.

Miscellaneous and Environs

The Fairmont Acapulco Princess offers a large array of shops, featuring a selection of items that range from gold, silver, fine jewelry and designer sportswear to Mexican arts and crafts, sundries, and T-shirts. A barber shop and beauty shop are located on premises.

Although these hostelries are somewhat removed from the hustle and bustle of the town, a 20-minute taxi ride will put you among the boutiques, discos, fast-food franchises, specialty restaurants, and street vendors on hotel row. Also, the travel agency at the hotel will arrange nightclub tours, sightseeing glass-bottom boat rides, yacht cruises, transportation to the bullfights, and to La Quebrada, one of the city's most famous sites where cliff divers dive from the top of 100-foot high cliffs.

Whatever your pleasure, this resort complex is designed to provide it. You will be delighted with the natural beauty of the surroundings, the vast facilities, and the diverse services, restaurants, and entertainment.

Fairmont Acapulco Princess
P.O. Box 1351
Acapulco, Mexico
Tel. 011-52-74-69-1000
(800) 441-1414
Fax 011-52-74-69-1016
Web: www.Fairmont.com

ACAPULCO

LAS BRISAS

Las Brisas is a unique resort-complex composed of pink and white casitas with private and semi-private swimming pools. It is spread over 40 acres on a hillside, high above the sea, overlooking the panorama of Acapulco Bay. The property was opened in 1957, operated by Hilton until 1964, and then run independently by its Mexican owners until 1976. In July 1976, Western International Hotels, now Westin, assumed management. There have been many additions and renovations through the years.

The gentle Pacific breezes that give Las Brisas its name also provide a climate several degrees cooler than Acapulco at sea level, and render sitting out on the private terraces of the casitas especially enjoyable. The hotel provides transportation and shuttle service on the premises and down to La Concha Beach Club on the sea.

Accommodations

The 263 air-conditioned casitas, including 21 junior suites, 3 Jacuzzi suites, and 2 master suites, share 210 freshwater pools (164 accommodations have private pools and 92 share a pool). Unlike most hotels, each casita offers the ultimate privacy. Each is an independent structure with its own terrace, private or semi-private swimming pool, beautifully landscaped gardens, pink flowers, private safes, and refrigerators and well-stocked mini-bars, radios and televisions. Large fluffy white beach towels are left on the chairs of the terraces each day. Casitas with private pools and those located at higher elevations fetch higher tariffs. The size of the bedrooms and bathroom is about the same, except for the larger

suites. The terraces and grounds are maintained immaculately, and the absence of bugs and insects demonstrates masterful extermination.

Continental breakfast and a fresh basket of fruit, which are delivered daily to the casitas, are included in the room rate. A 15 percent government tax, 2 percent room tax and $20 service charge (in lieu of tipping) will be added to your bill. The hotel's pink and white Jeeps are available for $80 per day, including gas, insurance and unlimited mileage.

Recently, the resort has added two salons, each accommodating up to 30 people and the Pink & White Lady Salon that accommodates up to 60 people, overlooking the bay. For larger conferences, the partition between the salons can be removed, and the Mezzanine at Bella Vista Restaurant is ideal for meetings or cocktail parties of up to 80 people. Banquets and theme parties at La Concha Beach Club also can be arranged, accommodating up to 600 people.

Restaurants, Lounges, and Entertainment

As mentioned above, Continental breakfast and a basket of fresh fruit are delivered to the room each day for those wishing to lounge on their terraces and look out over the bay. Full breakfasts are available in the semi-open-air Bella Vista Restaurant, the hotel's main dining room.

Lunch is served buffet-style on weekends and à la carte daily from 12:30 p.m. to 5:30 p.m. at the restaurant by the pool at La Concha Beach Club, located on the shore of the bay and accessible by shuttle van from the lobby. The restaurant is sur-

rounded by bougainvillea and attractive flora and looks out over the expanse of Acapulco Bay.

For a breathtaking view of Acapulco Bay at night, in a romantic setting, you will be enchanted by excellent gourmet cuisine at Bella Vista Restaurant, specializing in imaginative fresh fish, seafood, and Continental offerings. Soft piano music accompanies the meal.

Friday night is Mexican Fiesta Night; guests can enjoy a 17-course Mexican buffet, mariachi music, folk dancing, cockfights, a piñata, and fireworks.

The perfect location for libations watching the sunset over Acapulco Bay is the Sunset Bar, below the tennis courts.

Las Brisas is located only a few miles away from the numerous fine restaurants and colorful discotheques that line the main road into town.

Sport Facilities

Guests who wish to venture out from the privacy of their own pools and terraces have membership privileges at the private La Concha Beach Club, located seaside at the foot of Las Brisas bluff. In addition to the scenic view and imaginative freshwater pool, there is also a seawater pool, which is really an extension of Acapulco Bay in a protected area, with a raft in the middle and calm, warmer waters. In addition, snorkeling, scuba diving, water-skiing, sailing, parasailing, and deep-sea fishing are available. Snorkelers can view some interesting tropical fish here without venturing out to the rougher ocean. Also at La Concha are numerous comfortable lounges spread around the pools and sea, some with white Moroccan tents for protection from the sun, as well as a swim-up bar and a terrace restaurant.

There is a tennis club with five laykold, illuminated courts, a resident pro, and a shop. Horseback riding and golf courses are only 10 minutes away. There is also a spa and fitness center.

Miscellaneous and Environs

Among the shops located on the premises are an art gallery, several boutiques, a sundry shop, an international cigar store, silver and jewelry stores, and a deli.

Many fine restaurants, discos, shops, and points of interest are only a few miles away in town, and guests may want to consider renting one of the pink and white Jeeps to have maximum mobility both to town and around the resort itself. Las Brisas is located halfway between the airport and the main part of town, with a 15- to 20-minute drive to reach either destination. (For a more information on points of interest in Acapulco, see the discussion in the chapter for the Fairmont Acapulco Princess.)

The views across Acapulco Bay, especially from the terraces of the casitas, during the day, at sunset, and during the evening are the most breathtaking in Acapulco. It is the beauty, comfort, and privacy of the terraces and the outstanding panorama that makes Las Brisas so special. This is a lovely semi-secluded yet conveniently accessible resort. It appeals to those who seek privacy in comfortable, relaxed surroundings, Mexican flavor, and picturesque views. It is not ideal for children, golfers, or those seeking more activities.

Las Brisas
P.O. Box 281, 39868
Acapulco, Mexico
Tel. (744) 4696900
Fax (744) 4465328
Tel. (866) 427-2799 (United States)
      (866) 716-5862 (Canada)

LAS VENTANAS AL PARAISO, A ROSEWOOD RESORT

During the summer of 1997, Rosewood Hotels and Resorts, Inc. opened its first Mexican property in Los Cabos at the tip of Mexico's Baja Peninsula, mid-way between Cabo San Lucas and San Jose del Cabo, along the Sea of Cortez where it meets the Pacific Ocean.

Atypical of other Mexican resorts, Las Ventanas al Paraiso (windows to paradise) is a quiet, refined, low-rise enclave with modern white stucco and sandstone suites dramatically embellished with desert vegetation, artistic masonry, winding waterways that meander down to infinity-edged swimming pools, and a pristine strand of light-sand beach, all surrounded by verdant green fairways.

The semi-open-air reception area where guests receive personal check-in looks down over the various buildings, cacti, lantana, flowers and serpentine network of pools to the aqua blue waters of the Sea of Cortez. The restaurants and lounges are located by the pools and beach, creating a very casual, pleasant environment in which to enjoy meals and beverages.

The clientele, primarily well-heeled couples from the United States, Canada and Europe, come to enjoy the extremely lavish accommodations, the picturesque surroundings, golf, lovely spa facilities, and special exclusivity of Mexico's most upscale resort.

Accommodations

Seven white stucco, two-story buildings house 56 spacious 960-square-foot Mexican motif, junior suites, each with a separate entry way, raised bed platforms with either a king or two queen beds, conchuela floors with inlaid pebble work, beamed latia-wood ceilings with fans, charming wood-burning fireplaces, telescopes, fully stocked bars and refrigerators, in-room safes, television with cable and VCR/DVD connections, high-speed internet access, direct-dial telephones, expensive Mexican style objets d'art and lavish bathroom/dressing areas with two vanities, giant soaking tubs, glassed-in showers and separate toilet compartments, waffle robes, and expensive toiletries.

The ground-level units have lounging terraces and Jacuzzi bathroom tubs. The second-floor units have both a patio with a heated outdoor Jacuzzi and built-in seating area, and a roof-top terrace with lounges, which is ideal for watching sunrises and sunsets.

In addition, there are four ultra-deluxe, one-bedroom, superior suites located in the two most exterior casitas, each with a formal entry way, a large living room, a giant bathroom which includes an indoor/outdoor shower, a walk-in closet and Jacuzzi tub, a kitchenette with optional butler service, and a cozy outdoor patio garden on the ocean with plunge pool, service bar, stone dining table, lounges, and torches illuminated in the evenings.

For $5,000 a night, in season, guests can reserve the three-bedroom, three-bathroom suite with its own swimming pool, ideal for families, several couples traveling together, or a top-level executive meeting.

The resort can accommodate small, high-level corporate groups in its conference center with multiple room configurations for meetings, banquets, and group events, and it is possible to reserve blocked accommodations off season.

Restaurants, Lounges, and Entertainment

The bright, airy, three-meal-a-day main dining room has floor-to-ceiling glass doors that open to the sea, an adjoining outdoor patio area, and an intimate enclosed wine-room that can accommodate up to 16 guests for a private 5-course degustation dinner with appropriate wines for $180 a head. The dining room with modern-Mexican-style decor looks out to the imaginative pool complex and sea. There is musical entertainment in the evenings.

The type of cuisine offered is referred to as Baja Mediterranean, with numerous unusual and innovative offerings at each meal. The wine list is impressive.

The casual Sea Grill, open for lunch and dinner, consists of several outdoor tables located between the pool bar and beach with an open-air kitchen specializing in grilled fish, seafood, chicken, meats, salads, wraps and contemporary Mexican cuisine.

All meals are offered through suite service and guests frequently opt to dine on their comfortable patios and terraces.

Near the lobby is a tequila and ceviche bar, and the semi-open-air lounge adjacent to the main dining room features a variety of live entertainment for your listening pleasure while enjoying before- or after-dinner beverages.

Those wishing to partake in the wild night-life scene can be fully accommodated beyond their expectations in Cabo San Lucas with its numerous restaurants, bars, and discos.

Sport Facilities

The picturesque beach in front of the resort extends for miles in both directions, but is generally too rough for swimming. Guests who wish to swim in the sea or partake in water sports are directed to Santa Maria Bay, and Lovers Beach, which offer the best snorkeling opportunities.

There are lounge chairs on the beach, as well as palapa-sheltered hammocks. The four infinity-edged swimming pools are located above the beach around the resort and include winding rivers, heated Jacuzzis, and a swim-up bar. Cold towels and frozen sorbet are provided to guests lounging around the pool areas. Guests wishing to take a nap by the pool can even arrange with a pool attendant for a wake-up call.

The spa-fitness facility is most impressive. The glassed-in fitness center offers numerous cardiovascular and exercise machines with personal TVs, as well as free weights. The his and hers spas have changing rooms, steam, sauna, Jacuzzis, and four treatment rooms, each with showers opening to solarium areas. Spa treatments available include a variety of massages, wraps, and facials.

An 18-hole Robert Trent Jones championship golf course at Cabo Real, a short walk from the resort, is utilized by Las Ventanas al Paraiso and several near-by hotels and boasts a picturesque 15th hole on the sea that abuts the resort.

In addition, there are two illuminated tennis courts and the concierge can arrange horseback riding, water sports, desert Jeep outings, off-road Hummer excursions and marine wild life expeditions.

Miscellaneous and Environs

There is a small boutique and jewelry store at the resort; however, shoppers can also explore the numerous handicraft, curio and jewelry shops, boutiques, and vendor stalls in Cabo San Lucas and at San Jose del Cabo.

A motor boat ride around El Arco, the dramatic rock outcropping at the tip of the cape, and the home of seals and pelicans, with an opportunity to swim and snorkel at a small sand beach is a must for all visitors at Los Cabos.

The resort offers a dramatic setting for weddings and special events.

It is possible to take taxis to the airport and to Cabo San Lucas, or the resort can arrange private transportation. If you plan to explore the area or take several trips to the towns, you may find it more convenient to rent a car when you arrive at the airport.

A private villa development owned by Las Ventanas al Paraiso surrounds the resort and is in a continuing development stage.

Although at times it is breezy, it seldom rains and Los Cabos boasts an average of 350 days of sunshine each year.

Affluent couples wishing to vacation in Mexico and who prefer an upscale, casually sophisticated property with extremely luxurious accommodations in a picturesque, quiet, refined setting will find Las Ventanas al Paraiso truly their windows to paradise.

Las Ventanas al Paraiso
Km 19.5 Carretera Transpeninsular CSL-SJC
23400San Jose Del Cabo, BCS Mexico
Tel. (52)624-114-2800
Fax (52)624-114-2801
In US-888-767-3966
Web: www.lasventanas.com

CANCUN

THE RITZ-CARLTON, CANCUN

Ritz-Carlton's first venture into Mexico commenced in April 1993 with the opening of the 365-room Ritz-Carlton, Cancun, abutting 1,200 feet of Caribbean beach in the midst of the recently developed Cancun hotel zone. The nine-story structure faces the sea with three wings stretching out into an "E"formation. Between the beach and hotel building are two free-form pools, a heated whirlpool, outdoor gardens, and a small restaurant and bar for lunch and snacks.

The interior of the hotel is very akin to the elegant decor found in the other Ritz-Carlton resorts plus wrought-iron railings, a five-story interior atrium soaring to a stained-glass dome, and local art thrown in to create a nuance of Mexican flair.

Although the physical hotel building is similar to Ritz-Carltons around the world, the staff is more than 95 percent Mexican. Service is a notch above most other Mexican hotels and resorts, and attitude is superior and exemplifies the Ritz-Carlton tradition.

Accommodations

Each of the 365 air-conditioned rooms and suites located in the three wings has a patio or balcony with ocean view, either a king- or two queen-size beds with hacienda-style headboards, Drexel furnishings, color televisions with international channels, radio-alarm clocks, in-room safes, travertine marble baths with twin sinks, separate shower stalls and tubs, private toilet compartments with telephones, makeup mirrors, portable hair dryers, and plush terry-cloth bathrobes.

The 50 executive and terrace suites offer more space, and the accommodations located on the second and third floors have larger balconies that include a lounge chair. The eighth and ninth floors are designated the "club rooms" and include the usual Ritz-Carlton club amenities (i.e., special concierge service and complimentary breakfast, snacks, hors d'oeuvres, and cocktails throughout the day and evening).

The resort can accommodate groups from 8 to 1,050 in its 27,000 square feet of meeting and function space, which includes a beautiful patio area that surrounds one of the outdoor swimming pools, a courtyard, 11,481 square feet of ballroom space, numerous conference rooms, and a boardroom.

Restaurants, Lounges, and Entertainment

The Restaurant Fantino is elegantly decorated in European grand hotel style and includes an intimate, private alcove that seats 14 guests. The cuisine is Mediterranean.

The Club Grill features fresh fish, seafood, and prime meats in richly appointed surroundings with music for after-dinner dancing. Three dishes I found exceptional were the pepper duck in a honey-tequila sauce, lobster lasagnettes, and diced Belgium Endive with smoked salmon and caviar in a light lime truffle-oil dressing. This is one of the finest restaurants in Mexico. Both of these restaurants received AAA Five Diamond awards in 2006.

The (indoor/outdoor) Café offers buffet and à la carte breakfasts, as well as lunch, dinner, and snacks, combining Mexican and all-American fa-

vorites. The Lobby Lounge is an ideal place to enjoy your margarita while watching the sunset, or your before- or after-dinner cocktail accompanied by piano music. The lounge offers 120 different varieties of tequila. Snacks, sandwiches, Mexican specialties, and exotic drinks are served on the patio between the pools and beach.

Sport Facilities

The 1,200-foot stretch of powder-fine white-sand beach lapped by aqua blue breaking waves is an ideal spot to lounge and sun. However, the waters are not always safe for swimming due to the strong undertow. Many guests opt to sun on one of the comfortable lounges spread around the two free-form swimming pools, the heated whirlpool, and the gardens.

The fitness center includes an aerobic room, a small gymnasium with free weights, exercise machines, three step machines, four treadmills and rowing machines, his and hers steam and saunas, and massage, manicures, hairstyles, and facials by appointment.

The three illuminated tennis courts are located above the garage, next to the pro shop. The resort can arrange tee times at a variety of nearby golf courses and can arrange a variety of aquatic sports at nearby facilities as well.

The Kayanta Spa (a Mayan phrase meaning "to be reborn") offers water rituals, massage therapies, body treatments and facials.

Miscellaneous and Environs

The resort is located in the heart of the newer Cancun hotels, 15 minutes northeast of the international airport, 5 to 10 minutes from many shopping centers and restaurants, and 20 minutes from downtown Cancun.

There is a boutique and newspaper-sundry shop on premises. Major shopping malls in the hotel zone include La Isla, Kukulkan, a 5-minute walk from the resort, and Plaza Caracol, a 10-minute bus or taxi ride.

The concierge can arrange day excursions to the Mayan archaeological ruins at Chichen Itza or Tulum, a half-day horseback riding excursion on jungle and beach trails at Rancho Bonita, jet skis, blade runners, and deep-sea fishing at Aqua World Marina, a day trip to Isla Mujeres or Cozumel, and a 40-minute drive to the not-to-be-missed Xcaret – a picturesque archaeological park that includes a not-too-difficult 30-minute swim down an underground river through prehistoric grottos and caverns, lounging and swimming in mild warm waters and natural pools, trained dolphins, horseback riding, botanical gardens, snack restaurants, and an archaeological museum.

The Ritz-Carlton, Cancun is unequivocally different from the hundreds of other hotels and resorts that line the beaches of Cancun. Accommodations are more spacious, the decor is more elaborate, the atmosphere (though casual) is far more sophisticated, dining is more upscale, and service is more concerned. The overall experience could be described as being at a typical Ritz-Carlton that happens to be located in Cancun and staffed with locals, rather than being at a Mexican-style resort. For vacationers wishing to explore Mexico and enjoy the ideal climate and beautiful beaches but requiring luxury, comfort, and insulation from some of the more typical tourist complaints, The Ritz-Carlton, Cancun offers the best of all worlds.

The Ritz-Carlton
Retorno del Rey #36
Zona Hotelera
Cancun, Quintana Roo 77500 Mexico
Tel. +52 998-881-0808
Fax +52 998-881-0815

FOUR SEASONS RESORT PUNTA MITA

Located on the Bay of Banderas, just north of Puerto Vallarta, on 45 acres of Pacific ocean-front amidst a 1,500-acre, private coastal development of hotels, resorts, private homes, golf courses and beaches, the sprawling Four Seasons Resort Punta Mita opened its doors in 1999. The main hotel structure, the 13 low- rise casita buildings, the restaurants, pool and spa blend with the environment and meander down a gentle slope surrounded by lush vegetation, all offering ocean views. The property is owned by Strategic Hotel Capital Corp, a U.S. real estate development firm, but is under the experienced and expert management of Four Seasons Hotels and Resorts.

85% of the clientele are from North America and 70% are leisure travelers. The resort is a 45-minute drive from Puerto Vallarta International Airport and an hour's drive from town.

The reception area is located in the main building along with the concierge desk, the gift shop, the main dining room, and the cultural center which houses the library, videos, and internet facilities, and is the site for various lectures and enrichment programs. The low-rise buildings housing the casitas and suites are spread along tropical slopes and ravines. The free-form pool, three-meal-a-day restaurant and adjoining sea-food/beverage bar sit just below the main lobby, only steps away from the ocean. The spa/fitness center, children's play room and family game room are also centrally located nearby. Transportation is provided on a regular basis to the Golf Club House for golfers, and those wishing to use the four tennis courts or dine at Tale of the Whale Restaurant.

Service is spectacular with over 550 employees looking after 140 guest rooms.

Accommodations

The 140 guest rooms which include 26 expansive suites are spread among 13 hacienda-style, low-rise buildings, most with views to the ocean. All accommodations are air conditioned and furnished in the manner of a luxurious Mexican home filled with modern conveniences. Every unit sports a large, private terrace or balcony and includes a king or two queen beds, a walk-in closet, a private safe, coffee maker, TV and DVD, ceiling fans, two-line hands-free telephones, a clock radio, a choice of down or non-allergic pillows, an iron and ironing board, an umbrella, and an oversized marble bathroom with a deep soaking tub, separate glass-enclosed shower, enclosed toilet compartment with an extension phone, an illuminated makeup/shaving mirror, a double vanity with twin basins, a hairdryer, bathrobes, slippers and Four Seasons' signature toiletries. Standard casita rooms measure 650 square feet with the balcony and the 26 luxury suites range in size from 1500 to 2,800 square feet, all with private plunge pools. High season rates start at $445 and increase to $4,635 for the three-bedroom Presidential suite. Tariffs reduce somewhat off season and golf, spa, honeymoon and other packages are offered at additional savings.

Washers and dryers are located in most buildings and available for guest use. The 2,600-square-foot ballroom can accommodate 225 persons for receptions and 175 for banquets. There are three addi-

tional meeting rooms for smaller events, and several outdoor reception areas.

Dining and Enterteinment

Ketsi is the casual indoor/outdoor restaurant near the swimming pool overlooking the beach that serves all three meals, emphasizing Mexican specialties and fresh seafood. Only a few steps away is the unique Nuna Bar where guests can enjoy imaginative cocktails and oysters on the half shell, stone crab claws, ceviche, shrimp and scallops.

Breakfast, lunch and snacks are available at the golf club restaurant, Tale of the Whale. In addition there is around the clock room service, as well as food and beverage service brought right to your lounge chair both at the pool and on the beach.

For dinner, Aramara is the fine dining venue featuring Chino/ Latino cuisine and fresh seafood either in the main restaurant, on an outside terrace or in a special private dining room that can accommodate up to 14 persons. There is musical entertainment at all restaurants in the evening and special theme dinners are featured throughout the week.

For $500 per couple, guests can opt for the "Romantic Dinner" served under the stars either on the beach or on "The Rock", a grassy knoll outcropping with spectacular views extending between the resort's two beaches. The menu is arranged in advance with the chef and includes all beverages and an after-dinner campfire. Management suggests this is the perfect opportunity to propose or celebrate an anniversary.

Sport Facilities

All 18 holes on the private, Jack-Nicklaus-designed golf course have ocean views. Eight front the ocean, and an optional 19th hole features a 199-yard, "over-the-ocean" drive to a green set on a rock outcropping on a natural island.

At the clubhouse there are lockers, a pro shop, a driving range, a pitch and putt facility, the Tale of the Whale Restaurant and four tennis courts (two hard tru and two artificial grass) which are illuminated for night play. Transportation through the Punta Mita property to the golf course from the main lobby is provided on a regular basis. A second 18-hole course is scheduled to be built in the future as additional resorts and homes are completed in the development. There are golf and tennis pros and a complementary golf clinic is held once each week.

The large, free-form infinity swimming pool surrounded by comfortable lounges adjacent to a hot tub and the Nuna Bar overlooks the resorts two tan-sand beaches. At the beaches are numerous additional lounges and protective palapas umbrellas to shade the sun. Attendants circulate around the beach and pool throughout the day to serve snacks, meals, drinks and complementary cold towels, evian spritz, bottled water and popsicles.

Water sports that can be arranged include coral reef snorkeling, scuba diving, sailing, deep-sea fishing and non-motorized water vehicles. The resort can also make arrangements for horseback riding, ATV tours and dune buggies.

The spa/fitness center encompasses an exercise room with a full range of cardio-vascular and weight training equipment many with personal TVs, men and women's changing rooms with steam and showers, a beauty salon, nine treatment rooms surrounding an outdoor courtyard and two "couples treatment suites", each with its own steam, sauna, shower, Jacuzzi tub and out-door terrace. In addition to the cost of the treatment, these suites exact an additional $100 per hour charge. Yoga and aqua aerobic classes are offered, as well as nature hikes.

Miscellaneous and Environs

The resort will provide transportation from the Puerto Vallarta International Airport at a cost of $175 round trip per vehicle. It is also possible to rent a car at the airport and the drive takes about 45 to 60 minutes depending upon traffic.

On premises are gift shops and a golf and tennis boutique with Four Seasons' signature items. The daily shuttle service into the town of Puerto Vallarta costs $30 per person. Considering the charges to and from the airport and town, it may be more economical and convenient to rent a car.

As at other Four Seasons'-managed resorts, the supervised "Kids For All Seasons" program is offered year around for children 5-12 years of age. The center features arts and crafts, TVS, VCRs, DVDs, a snack and beverage pantry, an outdoor playground and children's swimming pool, movies and video games. All restaurants offer children's menus and babysitting services are available at hourly charges.

Vacationers seeking a luxurious, full-facility Mexican resort with expansive, comfortable accommodations, exceptional dining and service, away from the hustle and bustle of the city will be delighted with Four Seasons Punta Mita.

Four Seasons Resort Punta Mita
Punta Mita, Bahia de Banderes
Nayarit, 63734, Mexico
Tel. 52 329 291 6000
Fax. 52 329 291 6060
www.fourseasons.com/puntamita

CHAPTER SEVEN

HAWAII

HAWAII (BIG ISLAND)
Four Seasons Resort, Hualalai
Hilton Waikoloa Village
Mauna Kea Resort
Mauna Lani Bay Hotel

KAUAI
Hyatt Regency Kauai Resort & Spa

LANAI
Four Seasons Resorts Lanai

MAUI
Four Seasons Resort Maui at Wailea

OAHU
JW Marriott Ihilani Resort and Spa
Kahala Mandarin Oriental

Four Seasons Resort Lana'i at Manele Bay

cre for acre, there are more lavish resorts in Hawaii than anyplace else in the world. It was difficult excluding a number of hotels that probably would have qualified by default had they been located in other countries. In any event, I have attempted to select the most lavish, unusual, and picturesque properties for your consideration.

The flavor of the experience varies somewhat from island to island. Oahu (Waikiki) is a teeming, bustling, cosmopolitan area overrun with tourists, containing several excellent hotels and restaurants. The Kahala Mandarin Oriental and JW Marriott Ihilani Resort and Spa offer an opportunity to visit Oahu and avoid the maddening crowds. Maui has defined resort areas that are more posh, elegant, and spread out than those on Oahu. In addition, there are many scenic side trips to enjoy. However, Maui is no longer quiet and pristine; hotels, condominiums, and commercialism now inundate the island. Kauai is the charmer, having the best beaches and the most picturesque places to visit, as well as being the least populated. The Big Island of Hawaii covers a vast territory, with interesting volcanoes, waterfalls, and lush valleys. The hotels have been built up around the towns of Hilo and Kona. The five resorts reviewed are set off by themselves along the Kohala Coast on the Kona side of the island. Lanai boasts two of the most highly acclaimed sister resorts in the world.

FOUR SEASONS RESORT HUALALAI

In September of 1996, the Four Seasons Resorts' management team opened its second luxury Hawaiian property on the Kohala coast of the Big Island only 10 minutes north of the Kona International Airport. Two hundred forty-three ultra-deluxe guest accommodations located in 36 low-rise bungalows, a residential community, a championship Jack Nicklaus-designed, 18-hole golf course, one of the world's most fully equipped health club-spa complexes, five unique swimming pools, various restaurants and public facilities sprawl over 625 choice acres formed from a 19th century eruption of the Hualalai volcano. Abundant remnants of ancient lava flows intermingled with lush, tropical foliage and an impressive collection of Hawaiian art and artifacts combine to create one of the most beautiful, lavish, Hawaiian-theme, full-facility resorts in the Islands.

On arrival, guests are greeted with cold oshibori towels, fresh orchid leis, and tropical juices, and then escorted to their bungalows by friendly, knowledgeable bellmen who conduct a golf-cart tour of the property prior to settling you in your accommodations. This extremely attentive, customer-friendly service permeates every facet of the resort from the waiters, waitresses, and maids to the attendants at the pools and sport facilities.

The resort is owned by a joint venture headed up by Kajima Kona Company, a large construction firm, which is currently developing a very expensive residential villa and home-site community overlooking the golf course and ocean.

Accommodations

The 243 rooms and suites located in the 36 two-story structures are spread along the ocean in five distinct crescent communities (four of which sporting its own pool and cabana area), resulting in the resort appearing less crowded and more intimate.

The 600-square foot standard rooms are located either ground level or on the second floor of eight-unit bungalows. Although the room rates range from $625 to $925 European plan, there is no charge for one child under 18 sharing the room; and, various golf, spa, and meal packages are also available.

Every guest accommodation is air-conditioned with a large outdoor lanai furnished with table and lounge chairs, and features a walk-in closet, a king or two double beds with down comforters encased in duvets, 42" plasma televisions with cable and CNN, a clock radio, DVD player, a refrigerated private bar, a sitting area, a private safe, several telephones with voice mail, and giant bathrooms with double vanities, magnifying mirrors, hair dryers, private toilet compartments, separate shower stalls and tubs, fluffy white towels, terry robes, cotton yukata robes, and slippers. Other amenities include expensive soaps, shampoos and lotions, coffee makers with packages of Kona coffee, irons and ironing boards, and umbrellas. Fax machines are available on request. Many of the first floor rooms have outdoor garden showers secluded by surrounding lava rock walls.

The 24 Four Seasons Executive Suites and four Deluxe suites are larger and even more luxurious and include elegantly furnished living rooms. These

accommodations range in price from $1,050 to $8,350 for the magnificent, one-of-a-kind, three-bedroom Presidential Villa located in a private bungalow overlooking the ocean.

Complimentary laundry machines for the convenience of the guests are located in small buildings spread throughout the bungalows.

In the Four Seasons tradition, group-meeting-convention facilities have not been neglected. Twenty-seven thousand square feet of flexible conference space features 15,500 square-feet of outdoor function areas, including a lava-rock amphitheater that can accommodate 380 persons for a reception or 300 for dinner.

Restaurants, Lounges, and Entertainment

In addition to 24-hour room service for those who prefer to dine on their lanai, there are also three, resort-attire, panoramic restaurants. Pahui'a ("aquarium" in Hawaiian) is the resort's signature dining facility, where 184 guests can dine by candlelight indoors or on a patio right on the ocean in a romantic Hawaiian setting surrounded by lush, tropical foliage accessible by a bridge spanning a natural alkaline pond. The dinner menu features local, Asian, and western cuisine with emphasis on fresh Hawaiian fish and seafood. Breakfast is also served here à la carte or buffet-style. The Danish, croissants, muffins, and banana bread are "to die for", and also available are a wide choice of breakfast specialties.

Beach Tree Bar and Grill, located between the ocean and pool, offers lunch and dinner in a casual setting featuring salads, sandwiches, grilled specialties, and Hawaiian entertainment with cocktails at sunset. At the 134-seat Hualalai Grille by Alan Wong, above the golf club house and open from 11:00 a.m. to 9:00 p.m., golfers and resort guests can look out at the golf course and enjoy the latest creations in Hawaiian regional cuisine.

Right before sunset, torches are lit throughout the resort creating a foreground for the blue sea and skies as they become slowly illuminated by the colorful Hawaiian sunset. Sipping a beverage on your

lanai at this time of the evening while witnessing this spectacle is a highly recommended pre-dinner pastime.

Sport Facilities

The center of activity is the Hualalai Sport Club & Spa, where guests can enjoy an outdoor lap pool, a fully equipped exercise facility with cardio-vascular machines located both indoors and on a porch, free weights, and an impressive range of exercise equipment, fitness classes, yoga, Tai-Chi, sand volleyball, basketball, a climbing wall, and eight Rebound Ace Surface tennis courts (four lighted for evening play), together with such court-side amenities as pitchers of ice water, sport drinks, and fresh towels with teaching pros, clinics, and tournaments. Spa facilities include massage therapy, body treatments and wraps, facials, a beauty salon, a sport shop, and men and women's relaxation areas that offer sauna, steam, indoor and outdoor showers, outdoor whirlpools, lockers, and changing rooms with all amenities.

In addition to the lap pool at the Sports Club, there are four additional uniquely-styled pools, one for each crescent of bungalows. The most unique is a lava rock pool filled with brackish water and tropical fish for snorkeling. The two largest pools are the free-form Sea Shell Pool, with a small adjoining children's pool, and the rectangular Beach Tree Pool, which is surrounded by a teak deck. Each pool complex includes a separate heated whirlpool. All pool areas feature comfortable lounges, large canvas umbrellas, and cabanas spread around the pool and adjoining lawns. Attendants set you up at the location of your choice with beach towels, ice water, cold face cloths, and Evian spritzes.

The resort is built around the 18-hole championship Jack Nicklaus Signature golf course which includes numerous holes overlooking the sea and is home to the PGA Tour MasterCard Championship at Hualalai. The first hole plays directly at the Hualalai volcano and borders a jet black lava flow. Other holes thread through deep bunkers and sand traps, weave around lava formations, and play over ancient fish ponds while skirting the shoreline. The golf facilities also include a 320-yard driving range and practice area, locker rooms, a pro shop, and bag storage area.

The one-mile paved path that extends along the ocean past the golf course is ideal for joggers and those wishing to enjoy a scenic walk.

Unfortunately, the government environmental regulations have prevented the resort from constructing an appealing beach-swimming area. Although there is a small section that is semi-protected from the waves and undertow, it is quite shallow and inundated with pebbles and rocks. Guests may prefer one of the four ocean front pools, adjacent to four of the (five) crescent communities.

Miscellaneous and Environs

Within the resort there is the Hualalai Trading Company, a shop offering gifts, sundries, bottled beverages, and gas for your car. Sport wear is sold at the Sports Club and golf pro shop. The numerous shopping opportunities in Kona are only a 25-minute drive from the resort.

Four Seasons Resort Hualalai has had the advantage of watching the development of luxury resorts built over the past several decades. Cleverly, it has assimilated the best features of each of its predecessors and emerged with a picture-perfect property offering the most comfortable accommodations, the very finest service, a complete range of sport facilities, and fine dining in a charming, idyllic, tropical Hawaiian environment.

Four Seasons Resort Hualalai
P.O. Box 1269
Kailua-Kona, Hawaii 96745
Tel. (808) 325-8000
Fax (808) 325-8100
Web: www.fourseasons.com/hualalai

HAWAII (BIG ISLAND)

HILTON WAIKOLOA VILLAGE

In the fall of 1988, this resort, formerly the Hyatt Regency Waikoloa, opened for business, acknowledged to be the most ambitious and most expensive resort ever built. Developed by the Hemmeter Corporation of Honolulu, other investors, and the Pritzkers (owners of Hyatt Corporation) at a price tag of $360 million, this fantasy property was carved out of 62 acres of jagged lava and is located at Waialua Bay along the Kohala Coast, 19 miles from the Kona International Airport, near the town of Kona on the Big Island of Hawaii.

The massive resort complex includes a spectacular main lobby with an impressive flagstone stairway leading down to the lagoons, a giant convention center, three separate low-rise hotel buildings, numerous free-standing restaurants, and swimming pools. The surrounding lagoons are stocked with tropical fish, birds, dolphins, swans, cranes, flamingos, Chinese pheasants, lush gardens, tropical trees, and foliage, all connected by a series of waterways.

Transportation around the resort (which adds an extra dimension to the experience of staying here) includes a one-mile-long museum walkway that takes you past $7 million dollars worth of Oriental and Pacific art pieces, mahogany canal boats (which seat 24 each) that traverse the lagoon waterways, and two air-conditioned, Swiss-made tubular trams.

Sound like Disney World? Well, it is and it isn't! There is no question that the resort was not intended to be a quiet, pristine hideaway, and that everything is done to excess. However, this is an ingeniously well-thought-out project where pool areas are never crowded, there are no long lines to get into restaurants, every room has a romantic balcony view, and guests are not stumbling all over one another.

In the early 1990s, the resort encountered financial difficulties and in 1993, it was sold to a partnership that included Hilton Hotels, at a fraction of its original cost.

Accommodations

Of the 1,240 guest accommodations spread over the three low-rise towers, the majority have views of the ocean and the remainder look out toward extinct volcanoes. Each 530-square-foot standard room is decorated with light woods and soft pastels. Every room has either a king-size or two double beds, color cable televisions, clock radios, service bars, walk-in closets, small safes, irons, ironing boards, coffee makers, hair dryers, and a bathroom/dressing area stocked with numerous upscale amenities for use during your visit.

Proceeding to your right as you leave the main lobby, passing by the convention center and Imari restaurant, you first reach the ornate Palace Tower. The 358 guest accommodations located here include 24 suites, plus two special Presidential suites. All Presidential suites at Hilton Waikoloa Village are lavishly furnished with expensive period pieces and antiques and have giant, formal living rooms and dining rooms, service kitchens, and two bedrooms--each with marble baths that contain Jacuzzi/bath and saunas, a powder room, and a large patio area.

As you proceed on past Donatoni's Restaurant, you come to the Ocean Tower, which is composed of three circular Polynesian-style connected tiers

that border the ocean and golf course and encircle gardens and lagoons dotted with exotic birds and statues. There are 565 guest rooms at the Ocean Tower, which include 22 suites, one Presidential suite, and 130 Executive Floor rooms. As at other Hiltons, for a modest supplement, Executive Floor guests receive special concierge services, a complimentary breakfast, beverage service, early evening hors d'oeuvres and cocktails, and extra room amenities. The Palm Terrace Restaurant and Boat Landing Pavilion and Food Court Bar are also located here.

The third hotel building, known as the Lagoon Tower, is to your left as you leave the main lobby and is proximate to the Dolphin Lagoon, Kona pool and water slide, the tennis gardens, Orchid Café, Kamuela Provision Company, Kohala Spa, and the shopping area. Located at this tower are 227 additional rooms, including seven suites and three Presidential suites. The convention facility is composed of 21 meeting rooms, a 24,760-foot grand ballroom, and two auxiliary ballrooms, as well as 45,000 square feet of indoor and 100,000 square feet of outdoor pre-function space.

Restaurants, Lounges, and Entertainment

Because there are so many restaurants to choose from, it may take you several days to cover them all. Breakfast is served at The Palm Terrace, Boat Landing Food Court, Malolo Lounge, and Orchid Café; lunch at Orchid Café, Kamuela Provision Company, Lagoon Grill, Boat Landing, Malolo Lounge and Kirin; and dinner at The Palm Terrace, Kamuela Provision Company, Imari, Kirin, Malolo Lounge and Donatoni's.

The Orchid Café, below the Lagoon Tower fronting the large Kona Pool, is a casual open-air restaurant serving meals with a California-style menu and an adjoining soda shop for ice-cream specialties.

The Palm Terrace, located at the Ocean Tower and accommodating 272 people, looks out at cascading waterfalls and a tropical pool. Meals include Polynesian and American dishes served both a la carte and buffet-style. The Palm Terrace, the Orchid Café, and the Lagoon Grill offer special children's menus that are very reasonably priced. Donatoni's, considered one of the best Italian restaurants in the Islands, features a delicious variety of northern Italian offerings in elegant European-style dining rooms and outdoors on a lanai overlooking the waterways. The fare includes numerous imaginative pastas that can also be ordered as appetizers, traditional Italian entrées, and a nice selection of wines (including some exceptional Italians).

Imari is an authentic Japanese restaurant offering three types of Japanese dining – teppanyaki, shabu shabu, and sushi bar. On Friday evenings guests can enjoy "Legends of Pacific" a dinner show/luau with dancing under the stars at Kamehameha Court.

Kirin Chinese Restaurant is located on top of Donatoni's. Kamuela Provision Company offers Pacific Fusion cuisine along with a wine bar featuring 40 different wines by the glass. Malolo Lounge located next to the Main Lobby is the perfect gathering place for all three meals, as well as, cocktails. Jazz entertainment is featured nightly from 9:00pm to 1:00am. Numerous casual bars and lounges are located around the property and at the pools.

Sport Facilities

The tennis facility includes eight courts in a garden setting, a pro shop, and a 432-seat exhibition stadium. Teaching pros are available for lessons and to conduct clinics, and they will arrange tournaments for groups and conventions.

Championship golf is offered at the adjacent 18-hole Waikoloa Beach Golf Course, designed by Robert Trent Jones, Jr., and at the King's Course. A $16-million, 18-hole course, designed by Tom Weiskopf and Jay Moorish, opened in late 1989 with its own clubhouse and pro shop. An on-site 18-hole seaside putting course offers family fun and excellent warm-up for serious golfers.

Unfortunately, there is no long stretch of white-sand beach at the Hilton Waikoloa Village. However, there is a small beach that runs along the lagoon where you can swim or rent small kayaks, paddleboats, and snorkeling equipment. The resort will shuttle you to nearby Anaeho'omalu Beach. This is a "so-so" public beach that services the hotels and the condos in the Waikoloa area. A better choice is Hapuna Beach, six miles away, which is considered by many to be one of the top beaches in the world.

Most guests prefer the awesome complex of swimming pools. The pool architects borrowed designs from Hyatt's watering holes at Cerromar, Grand Cypress, and Maui to come up with an endless variety of aquatic possibilities. The largest pool area, the Kona Pool, located along the Lagoon Tower, has thundering waterfalls, an exciting 175-foot water slide that winds down a cliff, Jacuzzis, a rope bridge, a water volleyball area, and a sandy-bottomed children's pool, and is surrounded by bars, snack shops, a sand volleyball court, restaurants, and lounge chairs.

Adjoining this is the Dolphin Lagoon, where an organization called Dolphin Quest provides trained experts who operate a supervised program for guests who wish to experience tame, trained dolphins. This is a very popular activity at the resort and children and teens need to make reservations, while adults are accommodated through a lottery if space is available.

Next comes the protected swimming lagoon and sandy beach. From here, you can cross a bridge leading to a second pool complex called the Kohala River Pool, set between the Ocean Tower and Palace Tower, consisting of a number of small pools with currents, a Jacuzzi, several small water slides, a number of separate lounge areas, a bar, and a snack shop/hot dog stand.

The resort has a day camp for its guests between ages 5 and 12, Camp Menehune. For a fee, the youngsters get lunch and a T-shirt, and enjoy supervised activities such as wildlife tours, lei making, hula lessons, snorkeling in the lagoon, a visit to the dolphins, swimming, boating, and similar activities.

Joggers can take a three-mile paved circular route within the Waikoloa Resort development or start at the paved path behind the Ocean Tower, which extends to the walk in front of the resort. You can continue along the walk either to the left in the direction of the King's golf course, or to the right in the direction of the Beach Course. Here you can head down to the nature path, which ends at Anaeho–omalu Beach. Now you have the option to double back or return by an extremely rocky path along the sea.

Bicycle rentals, scuba diving, and snorkel sails can be arranged through the Red Sail Sports Activity desk next to the Lagoon Grill.

Miscellaneous and Environs

Within the Lagoon Tower, a short walk from the main lobby, is a shopping arcade that includes men's and women's boutiques, sportswear shops, a sundry shop with logo items, jewelry stores, art galleries, and the Kohala Sports Club & Spa. The 25,000-square-foot spa is elegantly furnished with exercise and aerobic rooms, a racquetball/squash court, exercise machines, men's and women's saunas, steam, and dressing-room facilities. It offers facials, herbal wraps, loofah treatments, a variety of massages, and a hairdressing salon. There is also a quaint Hawaiian-style wedding pavilion fronting Waialua Bay, where guests can tie the knot. The resort also has the Waikoloa Wedding Planner Atelier where you can plan your wedding with the assistance of the Director of Romance.

Whether or not a mega-resort such as this is your cup of tea, you will be impressed and overwhelmed with the planning, engineering, and total "awesomeness" of this one-of-a-kind property. The Hawaiian Islands offer an endless choice of hotels and resorts to suit every taste; however, for couples, families, and business groups seeking an endless variety of good restaurants, a large selection of activities and facilities, an elaborate, exotic man-made environment, along with friendly, efficient service and comfortable accommodations, the Hilton Waikoloa Village has no equal.

Hilton Waikoloa Village
425 Waikoloa Beach Drive
Waikoloa, Big Island, Hawaii 96738
Tel. (808) 886-1234
Fax (808) 886-2900
www.HiltonWaikoloaVillage.com

MAUNA KEA RESORT
MAUNA KEA BEACH HOTEL,
HAPUNA BEACH PRINCE HOTEL

Considered by travel magazines and most experienced travelers to be one of the finest resorts in the world, Mauna Kea Beach Hotel has represented a standard of excellence since it opened in 1965. Spread out over 1,800 hillside acres on the Kohala Coast of the Big Island of Hawaii, overlooking a large crescent-shaped, white-sand beach, the property was originally developed by conservationist Laurance S. Rockefeller, whose goal was to create the most luxurious resort in Hawaii. In 1978, Mauna Kea Resort was purchased by UAL, Inc., at which time Westin Hotels and Resorts assumed the management. In 1988 the resort was sold to Seibu Railway of Japan, and now is managed by Prince Resorts Hawaii.

The grounds represent an ambitious landscaping project. During construction, more than one-half million plants of almost 200 varieties were imported to enhance the natural beauty of the setting. The hotel itself possesses a museum-quality collection of 1,600 Asian and Pacific art and artifacts displayed in the buildings, gardens, and grounds. Among the works are a seventh-century Indian Buddha, primitive wood carvings from New Guinea, Ceylonese batiks, Fijian tapas, and a famous collection of hand-stitched Hawaiian quilts.

The view of the beach and floral paths from the terrace and restaurants is absolutely beautiful, a perfect area for photographing the sunset.

The hotel closed down in 1994 to permit a total renovation of guest rooms and common areas and reopened in January 1996. At a cost of over $30 million, new plumbing, electrical, and air-conditioning systems were installed, guest rooms refurbished, bathrooms updated, sprinkler systems installed, and handicapped facilities added. However, much of the flooring, wood furniture, door locks, and bathroom fixtures were not replaced and still have the look of the 1960s. Parts of the common areas and guest facilities also were not modernized during the restoration.

In August 1994 a 350-room sister property, Hapuna Beach Prince Hotel, opened on 32 oceanfront acres directly south of Mauna Kea Beach Hotel fronting Hapuna Beach, considered the Big Island's most desirable strand of beach. Although the layout is somewhat similar to Mauna Kea Beach Hotel, having been built three decades later, it is considerably more modern with more desirable guest accommodations and state-of-the-art facilities which include an 18-hole Arnold Palmer/Ed Seay-designed golf course and club house, a large free-form pool, an impressive fitness center with spa facilities, and very attractive indoor and outdoor meeting facilities.

The two properties offer a diverse range of attractive sport opportunities and dining options, and guests at both hotels enjoy reciprocal signing privileges.

Accommodations

Mauna Kea Beach Hotel's 300 guest rooms and 10 suites are similar except for location. They are spacious and furnished with willow and teak furniture, ceramic tile floors, floral cotton bedspreads, and original paintings created for each room. Each has its own large private lanai, refrigerator, safe, bathroom (most with double vanities), closets, cotton bathrobes, slippers, and hair dryers. Coffee makers,

mini-bars, irons, and ironing boards are available on request.

The 350 spacious guest rooms, which include 36 luxury suites, at Hapuna Beach Prince Hotel all boast ocean views from private lanais. The standard guest rooms contain the same features and amenities as those at its sister hotel except the design, furnishings, and fixtures are newer and more modern, as are the bathrooms. The 36 suites are 1,200 square feet with a separate parlor. The incomparable 8,000-square-foot, free-standing Hapuna Suite has its own private driveway and porte cochere, four bedrooms each with private bath and lanai, a full-service kitchen, an elegantly furnished living room, dining room and den, a private swimming pool, plus 24-hour suite attendants. This one-of-a-kind accommodation will set you back $5,500 to $7,000 per night (depending on how many people you care to share it with).

The convention/meeting facilities for the two hotels include The Hapuna Ballroom, which can accommodate 900 people in a theater or reception set-up, as well as numerous outdoor gardens and areas for receptions, theme parties, and dining events.

Restaurants, Lounges, and Entertainment

Although MAP is optional, guests generally do not stray far from the premises; however, there are restaurants in nearby communities for those seeking a change of pace. A breakfast of local fruits, delicious fresh-baked rolls, muffins, and pastries, and rich Kona coffee can be enjoyed on your lanai after it is delivered by the courteous service staff. You can even have your own toaster. Breakfast is also served indoors and outdoors both à la carte and buffet-style at The Pavilion at Manta Ray Point at Mauna Kea Beach Hotel and at Ocean Terrace at Hapuna Beach Prince Hotel.

The lavish Sunday brunch served alfresco on The Terrace at Mauna Kea Beach Hotel is world famous. More modest luncheon fare is available at the Hau Tree near the beach, at the 19th-hole Clubhouse Restaurant adjoining the golf course, as well as Arnie's at the Hapuna Golf Clubhouse.

At dinnertime at Mauna Kea Beach Hotel, guests can select from The Pavilion at Manta Ray Point, featuring indoor and outdoor dining with music, and entertainment, or the lovely Ceylonese-inspired restaurant, The Batik, with a separate kitchen serving food à la carte. (MAP guests are given an allowance toward these meals.) The latter offers island specialties, fish and seafood, grilled meats, and classic Continental cuisine, and has music for dancing, in season. I believe you will find The Batik a rewarding dining experience.

In the evening at Hapuna Beach Prince Hotel, The Coast Grille & Oyster Bar features a vast selection of fresh fish and seafood plus an oyster bar; Hakone Steak House and Sushi Bar offers authentic Japanese cuisine alongside meaty steaks, chops and western fare in a tranquil setting à la carte and buffet style, as well as a 12-seat sushi bar.

Every evening, there is Hawaiian music and hula dancing at the Copper Bar at Mauna Kea and the Reef Lounge at Hapuna. On Tuesdays, the resort features an authentic Hawaiian luau under the stars ocean side, with native dancers and performers, and on Saturdays there is an "all you can eat" clambake Oceanside, with lobster, crab claws, prime rib and other fare.

Sport Facilities

Few resorts offer more in the way of sport facilities and activities than Mauna Kea Beach Hotel and Hapuna Beach Prince Hotel. At both, impressive stretches of light-tan-sand beach abut crystal-clear waters. Guests enjoy a wide range of water sports, which include snorkeling, scuba diving, boogie boarding, and windsurfing. The freshwater pools at both hotels are the site of snorkeling classes, scuba instruction, and swimming lessons. There also are sand volleyball courts.

Mauna Kea Beach Hotel's 18-hole Robert Trent Jones, Sr., golf course is highly rated by golf enthusiasts around the world. It covers 230 acres and has a water hole traversing the Pacific surf. Excellent instructors are available for private lessons and group clinics are conducted throughout the week at the driving range. There is a fully stocked pro shop and an informal restaurant for snacks right next to the course. This is one of the most scenic golf courses in the world, more mature than the others in the area.

The Arnold Palmer/Ed Seay-designed 18-hole championship links-style course at Hapuna Beach Prince Hotel is nestled into dramatic natural contours of the land from the shoreline to 700 feet above sea level, offering spectacular views of the Kohala coast and majestic Mauna Kea and Mauna Loa. Located at the clubhouse is Arnie's, an excellent restaurant for lunch and snacks. Unlimited golf packages are available throughout the year.

The tennis program is also tops. The Seaside Tennis Club at Mauna Kea Beach Hotel is built on descending levels of a gentle hillside and includes 13 plexipave all-weather courts. There is a pro shop, a tennis clinic, ball machines, teaching pros, and regularly organized tournaments for guests. There is a charge for court time unless you take one of the tennis packages.

Those wishing to keep fit and trim will appreciate the state-of-the-art fitness center and spa at Hapuna Beach Prince Hotel, which includes various exercise and cardiovascular equipment, aerobic classes, steam, sauna, massage, locker rooms, and spa facilities. At Mauna Kea Beach Hotel, there are also two separate, adjacent rooms divided into cardio/free weight equipment and a new Life Fitness 10-station circuit.

If this is not enough, the hotels will also arrange deep sea sport fishing, whale watching in the winter, horseback riding, and helicopter flight-seeing rides over waterfalls, volcanoes, and surrounding scenic points of interest.

Miscellaneous and Environs

There are seven shops at the two hotels, offering a wide selection ranging from fine jewelry and art to resort wear, souvenirs, and sundries.

Mauna Kea Resort is a 30-minute drive from Kona International Airport. Aloha and Hawaiian Airlines run daily flights from all of the islands, and United has two nonstop flights daily from California to Kona. Japan Airlines also offers daily flights.

By and large, Mauna Kea Resort is secluded and not accessible to any nearby towns. Everything needed for a great vacation is located on the premises. Many guests bring their children so they can enjoy an exquisite family vacation. Special family promotional rates are available during the summer months, with half-priced children's programs from May to September.

This may be one of the most complete and casually elegant resort complexes in the world. Its well-heeled guests return year after year to enjoy this widely acclaimed property, its magnificent beaches, its excellent service, award-winning restaurants, championship sport facilities, comfortable guest rooms, and diverse range of activities for all members of the family.

Mauna Kea Beach Hotel
62-100 Mauna Beach Drive
Kohala Coast, Island of Hawaii 96743
Tel. (808) 882-7222, (800) 882-6060
Fax (808) 880-3112
Web: www.maunakeabeachhotel.com
www.PrinceResortsHawaii.com

Hapuna Beach Prince Hotel
62-100 Kauna'oa Drive
Kohala Coast, Island of Hawaii 96743
Tel. (808) 880-1111, (800) 882-6060
Fax (808) 880-3112
Web: www.hapunabeachprincehotel.com
www.PrinceResortsHawaii.com

MAUNA LANI BAY HOTEL & BUNGALOWS

After a 25-minute drive from the Kona Airport, your taxi weaves down the access road from the highway, past the lava deposits and golf courses, and up to the modern garden entrance of the 3,200-acre Mauna Lani Bay Hotel & Bungalows. A beautiful Hawaiian girl greets you with a kiss, places floral lei around your neck, and directs you through the magnificent atrium lobby, with its trees, flowers, waterfalls, ponds stocked with tropical fish, and bird-cage elevator. You sit down in front of a rosewood desk and are given a glass of fresh orange juice while registering.

The Mauna Lani Bay Hotel opened its doors in February 1983. With respect for the Hawaiian culture, it has preserved the picturesque ancient outdoor fishponds, as well as the historic fishing and dwelling caves located on the property. The open-air lobby area, shaped like an arrow leading from the front entrance to the beach, is an artistically beautiful creation blending the best of modern design and nature.

Accommodations

Over 90% of the resort's 324 guestrooms, 14 suites and five exclusive bungalows offer ocean views and all feature private lanais, a refrigerator, remote-control color television with in room movies, clock radio, ceiling fan, modern bathroom with his and hers sinks, and various amenities, including hair dryers, magnifying mirrors, scales, cotton robes and slippers, and a separate toilet compartment. The 14 suites have the same facilities plus a second sitting room with its own bathroom, a wet bar, and a separate tub and shower in the master bath.

Five ultra-deluxe 4,000 square-foot beachfront bungalows are located immediately to the right of the hotel building with their own separate entrance allowing the patrons who are dropping from $5,200 to $5,900 per night more privacy and exclusivity. Each has two bedrooms, elegantly furnished living rooms that include a Sony entertainment system with a 50" flat-panel television, CD, DVD and VCR player, a fax machine and fully stocked bar, dining rooms, guest powder rooms, and two identical, giant bathrooms, each of which includes separate vanities, hydrotherapy tubs, separate toilet closets with bidets, walk-in closets, skylights over separate shower stalls that also have steam, and special blend bathroom amenities, a private outdoor terrace with a pool, Jacuzzi, gas barbeque, lawn furniture, as well as a fully stocked butler's pantry with complimentary wines and liquors and 24-hour butler service.

The ballroom seats 400 banquet-style or can be sectioned off into several smaller rooms. There are four additional rooms with all the equipment necessary for conferences.

Restaurants, Lounges, and Entertainment

Breakfast is served at the indoor/outdoor Bay Terrace--the main dining room – or through room service. In the morning, guests look out over colorful, lush, flowering gardens, lagoons, and palms while they enjoy freshly squeezed juices, island fruits, mouth-watering pastries, a variety of breakfast items, and freshly brewed Kona coffee.

Sandwiches, salads, and drinks are served at lunch time at The Beach Club and lunch and dinner are offered at the recently renovated Ocean Grill and Bar, located midway between the hotel's beach and pool. A full complement of dishes is served at noon and in the evening at The Gallery, the casual clubhouse restaurant adjoining the pro shop on the golf course.

The Canoehouse Restaurant with an outdoor lanai on the beach surrounded by streams, lagoons, and gardens, features award-winning Pacific Rim cuisine, lighter dishes, seafood, and grilled meats with a local Polynesian flair in a casual atmosphere. This is one of the best restaurants in the Islands.

A Hawaiian trio entertains in the atrium lounge near the Bay Terrace each evening. The Honu Bar is a popular venue before and after dinner for cocktails, coffees, cigars, board games, music, and dancing.

Sport Facilitie

There is a fairly large free-form freshwater pool and two outdoor Jacuzzis – one for adults and one for children – located between the hotel and the three-mile stretch of white-sand beach, the waters of which are surrounded by a protective reef. At the beach, you can arrange for scuba diving, snorkeling, windsurfers, small sailboats, kayaks, glass-bottom boat rides, and deep-sea fishing. The Beach Club, about one-half mile from the hotel, accessible by shuttle or by paths along the ocean and fish ponds, offers soft white sand, a protected swimming area, and a small restaurant and bar. There are 10 excellent plexi-pave tennis courts at the Tennis Garden and six more at the Racquet Club, with a well-stocked tennis shop, teaching pros, and ball machines. There is a charge of $6 per person per hour to play.

Two 18-hole championship golf courses were built on a lava bed, and various lava deposits form natural hazards on these picturesque courses that overlook the sea. There is a golf shop with an adjoining restaurant, a driving range, and teaching pros. The courses are rated by numerous magazines as among the most scenic in the world.

In addition, there are bicycles for rent, a volleyball court on the beach, a sauna in the hotel, and an exercise parcours. Joggers will enjoy running along the shaded trails that meander through the ancient fish ponds. Those wishing to run for a longer distance can take the two-mile road out to the main highway or continue past the Beach Club and run along the paths that skirt the golf course and the Mauna Lani Point Condominiums.

At the Racquet Club, there is a health spa with steam rooms, exercise equipment, Lifecycles, treadmills, a lap pool, locker rooms, an aerobics room, an executive putting course, and a general store.

Miscellaneous and Environs

Mauna Lani Bay Hotel is a self-contained resort, fairly well secluded from any towns or other resorts. The 23-mile drive from the Kona Airport costs about $50 by taxi. Also, you can rent a car at the airport or hotel and use it for sightseeing on the island.

A special children's program, Camp Mauna Lani, is conducted year-round.

In addition to a men's and women's hairstylist, there is an Asian antique store, an art gallery, a sundry shop, a boutique, and a jewelry store.

Mauna Lani Bay Hotel is an elegant, modern, comfortable resort, ideal for families that can afford the tariffs, featuring fine cuisine, friendly service, and a wide range of facilities on the Big Island's developing Kohala Coast.

Mauna Lani Bay Hotel
68-1400 Mauna Lani Drive
Kohala Coast, Hawaii 96743
Tel. (808) 885-6622, (800) 367-2323
E-Mail: reservations@maunalani.com
Web: www.maunalani.com

GRAND HYATT KAUAI RESORT & SPA

This lovely $220-million, low-rise resort set on 50 oceanfront acres in the Poipu Beach District on the garden island of Kauai opened in late 1990.

The Grand Hyatt Kauai Resort & Spa departs somewhat from the design of the other Hyatts built in Hawaii and has more open areas, taking advantage of the scenic views. Frankly, it is less gimmicky than the Hyatts built in Maui and Oahu; it is less crowded and more in sync with the environment. The public areas are still quite elegant and tastefully done with beautiful, floral gardens, open-air courtyards, and Hawaiian artwork. Adjacent to the resort is the 210-acre, 18-hole, link-style championship Poipu Bay Golf Course and various residences.

Accommodations

Seventy percent of the 602 air-conditioned guest rooms afford ocean views, with the remainder looking out to gardens and the mountains. Regency Club rooms offer VIP service, which includes special concierge services, complimentary breakfast, beverages, late-afternoon hors d'oeuvres, and special guest room amenities. Thirty-seven of the accommodations are designated suites, including two magnificent Presidential suites.

Since the rooms and suites are spread among numerous wings, often a considerable distance from a particular facility, guests may prefer to choose a wing more accessible to a certain area of the hotel.

Every accommodation includes a small separate sitting area, remote-control color television with cable, private service bar, and an in-room safe. The decorations are more casual than some of the new Hawaiian resorts and include plantation-style furnishings, white ceiling fans, and pastel earth tones. The bathrooms are average in size with combination tubs and showers, double marble sinks, hair dryers, and robes. The bathrooms in the suites are larger and feature a small television, Jacuzzi tubs, and separate shower stalls.

Meeting and banquet facilities are extensive with 19 rooms, a 14,200-square-foot Grand Ballroom, and several outdoor theme party areas. There is also a business center near the lobby servicing guests' business requirements seven days each week.

Restaurants, Lounges, and Entertainment

The Ilima Terrace overlooks Keoneloa Bay and offers family dining in an open-air, protected area and on a terrace for all three meals. On Sundays, a lavish Sunday Champagne Brunch is featured. Dondero's offers regional Italian cuisine in an ornate, marble-floored dining room and on an adjoining terrace overlooking the pools and sea. A special private dining room here can accommodate parties of up to 14 people. Dondero's is considered one of the better Italian restaurants in Hawaii.

Those wishing a more tropical dining experience will enjoy Tidepools, a casual restaurant surrounded by a freshwater lagoon overlooking the bay. It features Pacific-Rim specialties, fresh fish, seafood, and steaks.

For lunch, guests not wishing to dine at Ilima Terrace can have salads, snacks, sandwiches, and grilled entrées at the Dock by the pool or Kupono

Café at ANARA Spa (which offers healthy entrees and a variety of fresh juices).

In the evening, guests enjoy having drinks at the various lounges and bars where they can watch torch lighting ceremonies and Hawaiian entertainment. Later in the evening, they can relax in Stevenson's Library with an after-dinner drink or cigar while listening to the soothing sounds of jazz or challenging their partner to a game of billiards or various table games.

Sport Facilities

Although the 500-yard white-sand surfing beach in front of the resort is often too rough for swimming, Hyatt Regency Kauai Resort & Spa, in the Hyatt resort tradition, boasts one of the most imaginative swimming complexes in existence. Near the top of the outdoor gardens are several picturesque pools with bridges and colorful flowers and plants in an area designated "adult swimming pools". From these pools, a unique river with a slight current meanders down a cliff through lava rocks, grottos, and pools all adorned with greenery, until you reach a twisting water slide that affords an exhilarating ride as it descends to the main pool below, which surrounds a heated Jacuzzi. Immediately across from this pool area is a protected saltwater lagoon surrounded by flowers, plants, and black lava rocks that fronts the beach. This is a delightful area to swim in warm, calm waters. Walkways up and down this complex surrounded by waterfalls and lovely landscaping permit guests the opportunity to enjoy and photograph this scenic area.

The Poipu Bay Resort 18-hole link-style golf course, designed by Robert Trent Jones, Jr., is adjacent to the property and runs along the ocean. The course, which hosts national tournaments, includes a clubhouse with a pro shop, locker rooms and a restaurant.

The resort also has four tennis courts with a pro shop and teaching professional. Arrangements can

be made by the resort's concierge for deep-sea fishing, snorkeling, board surfing, kayaking, hiking, mountain biking, horseback riding, sailing, scuba, wind and body surfing, and helicopter rides over the island.

One of the major facilities is the 25,000-square-foot ANARA Health and Fitness Spa, which has a weight room with Paramount machines and cardiovascular equipment, a 25-yard lap pool, and separate areas for men and women that include Turkish steam, Finnish sauna, Swiss showers, whirlpools, open-air lava rock shower gardens, and a variety of treatments such as Swedish massages, Shiatsu, Aromatherapy, Lomi Lomi Reflexology, botanical baths, herbal wraps, hydrating facials, seaweed and body masks, as well as a full-service beauty salon and spa café.

A Camp Hyatt program is available for youngsters ages 3 through 12 for $45 per day and offers a full-day of supervised activities, lunch, and a T-shirt.

Miscellaneous and Environs

The resort is a 20- to 30-minute ride from the airport, and visitors may prefer renting a car in order to have transportation to visit the multitude of fascinating tourist sites on Kauai. "Don't miss" excursions should include Waimea Canyon, Fern Grotto on the Waialua River, and Lumahai Beach near Hanalei Valley (where South Pacific was filmed). Numerous retail shops offering fine art, apparel, jewelry, gifts, and sundries are located at the resort. Other opportunities for shopping exist at various shopping centers around the island.

Kauai is possibly the most beautiful and lush of the Hawaiian Islands, offering the most diverse scenic explorations. Visitors wishing to luxuriate in a more typical Hawaiian setting with extraordinary sport facilities, comfortable accommodations, and fine food and service will want to make the Grand Hyatt Kauai Resort & Spa their headquarters.

Grand Hyatt Kauai Resort & Spa
1571 Poipu Road
Koloa, Kauai, Hawaii 96756
Tel. (808) 742-1234
Res. (800) 233-1234
Fax (808) 742-1557
Web: www.Kawai-hyatt.com

LANA'I

FOUR SEASONS RESORT LANA'I AT MANELE BAY AND THE LODGE AT KOELE

In 1922, the world's largest pineapple producer, Dole Food Co., bought the 141-square-mile island of Lanai for $1.1 million. Castle & Cooke, Inc., built, and owns, two of Hawaii's most luxurious and unique resorts. On April 1, 1990, The Lodge at Koele opened its doors, followed by Manele Bay Hotel in May of 1991. Originally managed by Rockresorts, and then by Castle & Cooke Resorts, LLC, presently Four Seasons Resorts has assumed management.

Ownership has described The Lodge at Koele as a country estate of a world traveler and Manele Bay as a gentlemen's beachside villa, creating two different island environments. The Lodge at Koele is located in the highlands of Lanai and could be considered a combination of an English manor house and rustic hunting lodge surrounded by gardens and forested hills. The setting is not typically Hawaiian and is reminiscent of the countryside in England or Scotland, with cooler, breezier weather than its sister resort on the ocean. Behind The Lodge at Koele is a beautiful landscape with gazebos, ponds, flowers, and lush theme gardens stocked with a variety of exotic plants, flowers, and bushes running up the hillsides. The focal point of the hotel is the Great Hall, with its 30-foot-high beamed ceiling, two stone fireplaces, and unique antiques, furnishings, paintings, sculptures, and artifacts from Asia and the Pacific. This is a warm room where guests lounge and enjoy cocktails and coffees before and after dinner.

By contrast, Manele Bay is an exquisite beach resort set on a cliff above the ocean, with Mediterranean and South Pacific overtones. The nine wings of this tropical paradise are connected by walkways that wind through lush floral gardens filled with a vast variety of lovely scented flowers, exotic plants, trees, and gazebos. Running through these gardens are lovely Koi-filled streams fed by numerous thundering waterfalls and traversed by small Japanese-style bridges. Although Manele Bay boasts all of the facilities and amenities of other Hawaiian resorts, the atmosphere is less congested and more private and refined.

Here again, the focal point of the hotel is a magnificent hall called the Kailani Terrace, which is decorated with even more exotic furnishings, art, and artifacts from around the world than its counterpart at The Lodge at Koele. It is surrounded by the two main restaurants and overlooks the swimming pool. The remainder of the resort rambles over vast acreage, all of which is built on the cliff and hills leading down to the ocean.

Some guests are charmed by the cooler, country atmosphere of The Lodge at Koele while others prefer the more typical beach-style resort at Manele Bay. Which ever your choice, all facilities at both resorts are available to all guests and you are encouraged to make use of the different sport and dining options on a daily basis. A shuttle bus transports guests on the 20-minute ride between the two resorts throughout the day and evening.

Accommodations

Manele Bay is composed of nine two-story wings housing 236 guest rooms and suites connected by walkways that wind through the tropical floral gardens described earlier. The Lodge at Koele has 102 rooms and suites located in a two-story manor

house with wings extending on either side, half of which look out at the pool, flowering gardens, and hilly, wooded highlands.

At Manele Bay, all rooms and suites are air-conditioned, decorated in a tropical theme in warm golden tones enhanced by rich cherry and rattan furnishings, contain a combination of European, Asian, and Pacific furnishings and art, and include a four-poster king-size bed, color, cable, remote-control television with DVD player, refrigerator, mini-bar, private wall safe, comfortable sitting area, and an oversized bathroom featuring double marble vanities, private toilet compartments, separate shower stalls and bathtubs, hair dryers, robes, slippers, makeup mirrors, and numerous personal amenities. The mini-suites and full suites are considerably larger and more expensive, and several in the main building include personal butler service.

The rooms and suites at The Lodge at Koele are "country" in decor with an abundance of wood. They contain many of the same features and amenities as those at Manele Bay. They are somewhat smaller, however, and the bathrooms have single vanities and combination tub-showers. The lanais are less private, have hardwood furniture, and lack the appeal for secluded lounging. There are ceiling fans but no air-conditioning; however, the weather is much cooler and breezier here than at Manele Bay and air-conditioning would be seldom needed. The suites are a great deal larger and include fireplaces.

Although most writers and periodicals have lauded The Lodge at Koele, in my opinion, the accommodations at Manele Bay Hotel are the best bet for creature comfort and luxuriating.

Over 51,000 square feet of indoor and outdoor conference space at Manele Bay that can accommodate groups up to 300 persons, sits on a hill next to the tennis center and looks out to the ocean.

Restaurants, Lounges, and Entertainment

Although some guests choose to enjoy meals on their private lanai, the resorts also offer a welcome variety of dining options.

At Manele Bay there are two restaurants. The main restaurant, Hulopo'e Court, offering breakfast, lunch and dinner, and the more formal Ihilani, serving dinner only. Both feature elegant indoor dining rooms and protected outdoor verandas that look down to the pool and ocean. In the evening, the illuminated pool framed with tall palms, glittering Hawaiian torches, and a star-studded sky offers a romantic backdrop for the superior repast, embellished by fine china, silver, and linens, which are featured at both restaurants.

At Ihilani resort wear is recommended for men and the spotlight is on contemporary Italian cuisine using the freshest seafood and island fruits and vegetables. Those guests wishing to dress casually will be well rewarded with a similar romantic atmosphere at Hulopo'e Court where the emphasis is on Hawaiian cuisine prepared with fresh island ingredients.

Coffee and tea are available throughout the wings of the hotel. Lunch, snacks, and exotic drinks are served at the Pool Grille and golf clubhouse.

The Terrace Restaurant, which sits between the Great Hall and colorful outside gardens at The Lodge at Koele, offers all three meals in a casual yet refined environment. Immediately adjoining the Terrace Restaurant is the octagonal Dining Room, the signature restaurant at the resort. The gourmet cuisine is hearty with numerous game and meat selections, as well as local seafood and delicious artistic dessert creations. Presentation of each dish proves to be imaginative, and quality and taste bear out the restaurant's highly acclaimed reputation. Jackets are required for men here at dinner. Lunch and dinner are also served at the Golf Club.

Since there are no other restaurants of note on the island (other than Henry Clay's Rotisserie at the Hotel Lanai), guests may prefer to opt for MAP at $100 per person per day or FAP for $125. Considering the relatively high prices for various offerings, this could result in a bit of a savings. Meal plans for children are $35 for MAP and $45 for FAP.

An English-style high tea is available in the Terrace Dining Room at The Lodge at Koele each afternoon, and musical entertainment is featured at both hotels during the evening. There is a movie theater in Lanai City.

Sport Facilities

Both properties boast outstanding, picturesque golf courses. The 18-hole championship course at The Lodge at Koele, known as "The Experience at Koele," designed by Greg Norman and Ted Robinson, is a dramatic mountain course set against a backdrop of forested green hills and steep valley gorges where golfers by-pass ponds adorned with tropical flowers and small waterfalls.

The 18-hole Jack Nicklaus-designed course at the Manele Bay Hotel, known as the "Challenge of Manele," was built on hillsides overlooking the ocean with several over-the-water holes. Both courses have fully stocked pro shops and teaching pros. Golfers will also appreciate the 18-hole executive putting course at The Lodge at Koele.

Manele Bay Hotel features a three-court tennis complex with a pro shop, tennis instructors, and tennis clinics, while The Lodge at Koele has three courts situated between the main building and the riding stables. Trail rides are offered (at an extra fee) each morning and afternoon.

The swimming pool at Manele Bay is most inviting, attractively illuminated at night and surrounded by comfortable lounges, two heated Jacuzzis, and the grill and bar. The Lodge at Koele has a smaller heated pool and a Jacuzzi that sit in the gardens behind the main building. The beach at Manele Bay enjoys a picturesque setting, and while it is often a bit rough for swimming, it offers good snorkeling possibilities.

Manele Bay Hotel offers a fitness center and movement studio with exercise equipment, cardiovascular machines, and a steam room, and a variety of massage and beauty care treatments including hairstyling, nail care, facials, and makeup applications. Snorkel, scuba, deep-sea fishing, hiking, and 4-wheel vehicle excursions can be arranged. There is also a small workout/exercise facility at The Lodge at Koele near the pool.

Joggers will enjoy running along the paths at both golf courses and The Lodge at Koele offers bicycles, croquet, and lawn bowling. Each day a printed sheet of daily activities is given to the

the "Kids For All Seasons" program and new Teen Center.

Although many guests come to relax and luxuriate, a full complement of facilities and activities is available and guests are encouraged to utilize both properties.

Miscellaneous and Environs

Visitors to Lanai have a choice of six daily commuter flights on Island Air. A shuttle bus from the resort meets guests at the airport and takes charge of your luggage and transport. The airport is a 10-minute ride from The Lodge at Koele and 30 minutes from Manele Bay. The resorts also furnish regular shuttle service between the two properties throughout the day and evening.

There is a logo and sundry shop at each hotel and regular shopping excursions are offered by ferry to Maui.

Although there are a few points of interest around the island, Lanai does not offer the plethora of scenic wonders found on the Big Island, Maui, and Kauai. The location of these two uniquely different sister resorts on a relatively small Hawaiian island where there is little else of interest creates the special, private-island feel that guests find so appealing and that entices them to take advantage of the diverse facilities and dining experiences offered at each property on a daily basis.

Visitors to the islands seeking a more intimate, refined, and upscale Hawaiian resort with the most comfortable accommodations and top dining will find The Lodge at Koele and the Manele Bay experience the ideal relaxing vacation.

guests. Activities range from golf and tennis clinics to horseback and hiking excursions and half-day and full-day organized activities for children under

The Lodge at Koele und Manele Bay Hotel
One Manele Bay Rd.
P.O. Box 630310
Lanai City, Hawaii 96763
Tel. (800) 321-4666, (808) 565-2000
Fax (808) 565-2483
Web: www.fourseasons.com/lanai

MAUI

FOUR SEASONS RESORT MAUI AT WAILEA

In March 1990, Four Seasons Resorts opened its first Hawaiian property in Wailea, on the southern coast of Maui, where the weather is the sunniest and the beaches among the best. Set on 15 oceanfront acres, surrounded by golf courses and mountains, the eight-story, U-shaped, light-sand-colored buildings and roofs frame magnificent, sculptured floral gardens filled with coconut palms, crimson bougainvillea, classic fountains, and sparkling pools with cascading waterfalls. Both the inside and outdoor public areas exude elegance, yet the environment is quiet, casual, and relaxing – unlike some of its more bustling neighbors.

The interiors of the buildings are open and airy, having been specially designed to capture the island's fragrant breezes and offer dramatic views of the ocean, neighboring islands and the West Maui mountains. Island influences are reflected in the interior design and embellished by the furniture, paintings, screens, sculptures, and handicrafts. Service is typical of the Four Seasons standard, providing a more upscale, attentive experience than most other Hawaiian resorts.

Accommodations

Eighty-five percent of the 380 air-conditioned guest rooms offer ocean views, with the others looking out to the golf course and mountains. Every accommodation includes at least one large lanai with comfortable lounge chairs and a dining table. Each is appointed with deeply cushioned rattan and wicker furnishings done in soft white and gentle sunset hues, and includes a ceiling fan, remote-control color television with VCR/DVD, a refrigerator and cus-

tomized private bar, a private electronic safe, a sitting area, a CD/clock-radio, and luxurious marble bathrooms with separate shower and soaking tubs, private toilet compartments, magnifying mirrors, hair dryers, soft terry-cloth robes, twin basins, and numerous personal care items.

The average room is 600 square feet. Those desiring more spacious accommodations can opt for one of the 36 executive suites, 21 one-bedroom suites, 16 two-bedroom suites, the Illima suite, or the 5,000-square-foot Maile suite.

For an additional fee, you can be located on the club floors and obtain access to a private lounge with complimentary breakfast, afternoon tea, sunset cocktails and hors d'oeuvres, after-dinner liqueurs and desserts, and special concierge services.

The 20,000 square feet of meeting and function space can accommodate 10 to 700 guests and includes a 6,930-square-foot ballroom. The oceanfront luau grounds can service 400 people for banquets and 500 for receptions.

Restaurants, Lounges, and Entertainment

The Pacific Grill, affording both sheltered indoor and open-air dining, looks out to the pool, gardens, and sea. Breakfast is offered both à la carte and buffet-style, and rotisserie, wok, and grill items from the Pacific Rim are featured at dinner. Lunch, snacks, and tropical libations are available by the pool. Ferraro's offers Italian cuisine by the sea for dinner.

The resort's former signature restaurant, Seasons, has been replaced with a branch of Wolfgang Puck's Spago.

There is a Lobby Lounge and a Game Room featuring big-screen television, board games, and a pool table.

For $750 per couple, the ultimate romantic dinner is available and encompasses dining on a private lawn overlooking the ocean on a table set with fine linens, crystal, and china. The exclusive menu is arranged in advance with the chef and is accompanied by fine champagne.

Sport Facilities

The focal point of the resort is the 40-by-80-foot formal pool framed around a bubbling central fountain, flanked at each end by a heated whirlpool and surrounded by comfortable lounges protected by Moorish-style, semi-sheltered cabanas. A grass lounging area connects the pool to the resort's sandy beach, which is ideally situated in an area permitting calmer waters than many of Maui's beaches. At both the pool and beach, Four Seasons Resort Maui at Wailea employees provide attentive service, plush terry-cloth towels, refreshing wet face towels and ice water, Evian water, and pineapple juice. Equipment for most water sports is available. A smaller free-form pool fed by a waterfall emanating from lava rocks sits in front of the restaurants and flows into a small children's pool with a small connecting water slide.

The resort shares its desirable beach with the adjacent Grand Wailea Resort, which was originally a Hyatt and includes an exotic water playground complex. Guests may enjoy meandering over to this neighboring property and sampling the exotic pools, streams, grottos, and waterfalls.

There are two tennis courts located off the sixth-floor level of the resort illuminated for night play, and guests have use of the 11-court Wailea Tennis Center on request. Also, arrangements can be made on five outstanding golf courses in the area, including the Wailea Golf Club across the street from the resort's entrance. Walkers and joggers will be intrigued by the two miles of paved path that runs along the ocean in front of the resorts, homes, and condos located in the Wailea area.

The new health and fitness spa, completed at the close of 2002, includes free weights, cardiovascular equipment, men's and women's locker rooms with steam and numerous massage services and body treatments, as well as classes in aerobics, yoga, pilates, aquacise, and power walking.

The Kids For All Seasons program provides complimentary year-round supervised activities for children 5 through 12. A separate teen program is also featured during peak seasons.

The concierge can arrange sport fishing, helicopter rides, and horseback and one-day tours of the other islands by boat or plane.

Miscellaneous and Environs

Visitors fly into the airport at Kahului to take the 30-minute ride to the resort. There are numerous shops at the resort offering men's and women's apparel, logo items, beachwear, jewelry, art, and sundries. Shopping centers are located in Wailea, Lahaina, and Kanapali.

On the island of Maui you may wish to visit the Haleakala Crater, the largest dormant volcanic crater in the world, tour the 2,000-foot Iao Needle, which rises from the beautiful Iao Valley, walk through the historic, charming whaling village of Lahaina, or take the scenic winding drive to Hana, stopping to visit the Waianapanapa Cave and black-sand beach and the Seven Sacred Pools.

Travelers to Hawaii wishing to enjoy the ultimate luxury property in a lovely Hawaiian setting with impeccable service, fine dining, lavish accommodations, a first-class spa, and good facilities will prefer Four Seasons Resort Maui at Wailea to the other possibilities.

Four Seasons Resort Maui at Wailea
3900 Wailea Alanui
Wailea, Maui, Hawaii 96753
Tel. (808) 874-8000, (800) 334-6284
Fax (808) 874-6449
Web: www.fourseasons.com/maui

OAHU

JW Marriott Ihilani Resort and Spa

The 640-acre Ko Olina Resort and Marina development is located on the sunny western shore of Oahu, a 25-minute drive from the Honolulu International Airport. The Ko Olina area was originally designed to encompass several resorts, luxury condominiums, residential estates, a yacht and sports club and a shopping center surrounded by protected sandy environs, a championship golf course, and mountain backdrops.

In December of 1993, JW Marriott Ihilani Resort and Spa opened its doors – the first luxury resort to be built on Oahu since the former Kahala Hilton – complete with ultra-posh, spacious accommodations, a championship golf course, a tennis club, a sophisticated spa, and top food and service. The resort was originally owned and operated by subsidiaries of Japan Airlines. Today it is owned by an insurance company and managed by JW Marriott. Set on a tranquil, crescent-shaped, tan-sand beach dotted with coconut palms, the JW Marriott Ihilani Resort and Spa offers a welcome option to the bustling hotels of Waikiki. Ihilani means "heavenly splendor" and Ko Olina translates to "fulfillment of joy." The 17-story glass-domed atrium dominates the 387-room, uniquely shaped hotel.

Service is attentive, accoutrements are state-of-the-art, the mood is relaxed and sophisticated, and the setting is one of the most idyllic on the island. Fifteen percent of the clientele are from Japan and the balance are from the United States.

Accommodations

The 17-story main building and adjoining four-story wing house 387 lavish rooms and suites. Every air-conditioned accommodation includes a large lanai with teak porch furniture, a ceiling fan, remote-control color television with cable and an in-house movie library, an electronic safe, a mini-bar, screened, louvered balcony doors, CD radios, a sitting area, a state-of-the-art telephone system that controls the alarm clock, lights, fan, and temperature of the room and translates into six languages, and deluxe marbled bathrooms that feature Yukata (bright Japanese-styled) robes, a hair dryer, a make-up mirror, double vanities, a separate toilet compartment, soaking tub, separate glass enclosed showers, and numerous exotic complimentary soaps, lotions, and amenities. Eighty-five percent of the rooms afford ocean and lagoon views. The smallest accommodation measures 640 square feet and the luxury suites measure from 1,069 up to the 4,000-square-foot Presidential suite located on the top floor. For $4,500 per night occupants of this suite enjoy a lanai that encircles the suite, a formal living room and dining room, a library, a kitchen, 24-hour butler service and round trip limousine transfer, and every other amenity one can imagine.

The 10 one-bedroom, 1,440-square-foot Ihilani suites, which go for $1,400 per night are also quite luxurious, with large whirlpool tubs, a foyer, guest powder room, large living room and Lanai, and spectacular ocean views. The meeting facilities include a 5,530-square-foot ballroom that can accommodate up to 400 guests, seven additional ocean-view meeting rooms, and an 897-square-foot executive boardroom. An 18,318-square-foot meeting pavilion offers additional meeting and banquet options.

Restaurants, Lounges, and Entertainment

Naupaku Terrace is a 140-seat restaurant offering breakfast, lunch, and dinner in a casual, protected open-air setting overlooking the pool and lagoon. The Poolside Grill and Hokulea Lounge on the other side of the pool is open for lunch, snacks, and exotic libations.

Roy's Ko Olina Restaurant located at the Golf Club open for lunch and dinner offers diners a stunning view of the lagoon, waterfalls and the 18th hole of the golf course. The restaurant is the 33rd in the chain of Roy's Restaurants featuring Hawaiian Fusion Cuisine. Traditional Japanese cuisine is featured at Ushio-Tei, a quiet oasis in an authentic setting adjoining a peaceful Japanese garden.

The signature restaurant of the hotel, Azul, consists of a more formal, elegantly decorated lounge area and dining room and specializes in creative Mediterranean dishes from the south of France, Spain, Greece, Italy, Morocco, and Lebanon. There is a good wine list and prices are very, very steep. Guests here may enjoy dinner in the main dining area, in a private dining room, or on the terrace for romantic al fresco dining at the water's edge. In the evening there is live entertainment in the Hokulea Lounge, a good spot to watch the sunset.

Sport Facilities

Separating the hotel and crescent-shaped, palm-lined protected beach cove is a pool area comprised of a small circular pool, comfortable lounge chairs, a small poolside bar and grill, and an attentive service staff. Three additional crescent-shaped beach lagoons lie to the left of the resort, and the path connecting these lagoons offers the best opportunity for picturesque strolls and jogging.

The 18-hole Ted Robinson-designed golf course, highly rated by Golf Digest, contains 16 different water features, an often photographed 12th hole that sits atop a rock garden with waterfalls and lovely landscaping, teaching pros, and a large clubhouse that includes a fully stocked pro shop and Roy's Ko Olina restaurant.

Perhaps the main facility at JW Marriott Ihilani Resort and Spa is the magnificent 35,000-square-foot, four-level health spa with six tennis courts (four illuminated for night play), an outdoor lap pool, a spa café, men's and women's locker-lounge areas, cardiovascular and exercise equipment, a fitness program that features yoga and Tai-Chi, spa treatments that range from Shiatsu and Lomi-Lomi massages to a 180-jet Thalasso tub, seaweed masks, herbal wraps, Vichy showers, grand jets, and needle showers. There is a charge for tennis classes and spa treatments; various spa packages are available.

Miscellaneous and Environs

The shopping arcade includes signature sportswear and logo items, jewelry, apparel, sundry, tennis pro and golf shops.

Visitors may wish to rent a car and explore the numerous points of interest on the island such as the monument at Pearl Harbor, the Polynesian Cultural Center, and the fine restaurants and numerous shops and hotels in the Waikiki area. The JW Marriott Ihilani Resort and Spa is presently one of the premier class resorts on Oahu, located in the more secluded, Ko Olina Resort & Marina area. Those seeking a relaxing sojourn or a few days' respite from itineraries to other Hawaiian islands, the South Pacific, or the Far East will appreciate luxuriating in this upscale property that features very comfortable, fully complemented accommodations, excellent service, great golf and spa facilities, and fine dining.

JW Marriott Ihilani Resort and Spa
92-1001 Olani Street
Kapolei, Hawaii 96707
Tel. (808) 679-0079
Fax (808) 679-0080
1-800-626-4446 (US and Canada)
e-mail: ihilani.reservaton@marriotthotels.com

OAHU

KAHALA MANDARIN ORIENTAL

This resort basks on a quiet beach between Diamond Head and Koko Head craters in the luxurious Kahala District, about 10 to 15 minutes from Waikiki. Emerald mountain peaks form the backdrop, an 800-foot golden-sand beach is in the foreground, and a tropical lagoon stocked with performing dolphins, tropical fish, and turtles is in the middle. Opened in 1964, this magnificent property has been the standard of excellence for resort hotels on Oahu ever since. Mandarin Oriental acquired a 40 percent interest in the property in 1995 and assumed management from Hilton. A $75-million renovation was commenced at that time and the hotel reopened in March 1996.

What makes this experience unique is the management's dedication to pleasing the guests and the extra touches that are included to ensure that this goal is achieved. This is apparent from the moment you arrive, when the doorman takes your bags, the desk clerk calls you by name, and the courteous bellman escorts you to your room, where a fully stocked mini-bar, toiletries, suntan lotion, slippers, and plush robes await you.

The Kahala Mandarin Oriental offers the best opportunity to vacation on the island of Oahu and visit the numerous points of interest without staying in the overcrowded Waikiki area.

Accommodations

The 364 renovated guest rooms, including 33 suites, are among the largest, most comfortable, and best equipped to be found anywhere in the world. All rooms are oversized (550-square feet), tastefully decorated with light natural colors, teak parquet floors with hand-loomed Tibetan area rugs, four-poster, canopied king beds or two double beds, private safes, and feature CD/alarm-clock radios, 27-inch color televisions with cable, in-house movies, refrigerators with personal bars, bathrooms with separate showers and bathtubs, his and hers sinks and vanities, double closets, bathrobes, slippers, umbrellas, and a number of expensive toiletries and extras. Two hundred eighty-eight rooms are in the high-rise main building, and the remainder stretch out at ground level, overlooking the lagoon, golf course, and beach. Fifty percent of the rooms have lanais.

Among the accommodations are 33 regular suites – which include large parlors, lanais, wet bars, and guest baths – four junior suites, and the one-bedroom Presidential and Governor suites with giant living rooms, dining rooms, kitchens, expensive furnishings, luxurious bathrooms, and all amenities.

Conference/meeting facilities include a boardroom, three small meeting rooms, a banquet or conference room seating up to 250, and a ballroom with pre-function areas accommodating up to 800 and overlooking a lava-rock waterfall and garden.

Restaurants, Lounges, and Entertainment

Breakfast is available in the rooms or on the lanais. All three meals, daily buffets and a special Sunday brunch are offered at Plumeria Beach House, a casual, open-air restaurant overlooking the beach and ocean. Native fruits, baked rolls and muffins, and freshly brewed Kona coffee highlight the breakfast repast. The luncheon and dinner buffets here,

which include many gourmet salads, sushi, shashimi, and Pacific Rim hot dishes, are most impressive. Salads, sandwiches, and snacks are also served at the snack bar by the pool. Hawaiian hula is performed nightly at sunset.

Hoku's is the signature, all-ocean-view restaurant open for lunch and dinner, which features an open kitchen, tandoori oven, Chinese woks, kiawe wood grill, and oyster and sushi bars. The executive chef and his staff have created, arguably, the best gourmet restaurant in the Islands. Here guests enjoy unique cuisines featuring a combination of European cooking techniques with Asian influences and fresh local ingredients from the Islands. You can opt for the five-course degustation menu that permits you to create your own tasting combination of dishes. Some outstanding choices may include: shrimp with a crispy sweet potato crust on a remoulade sauce; Tandoori-oven Nan bread topped with tomatoes, goat cheese, and basil or smoked salmon, pineapple, and horseradish sauce; grilled lobster in lemon butter on a bed of pesto risotto; herb crust-

ed Onaga in a cream spinach and red wine sauce; breast of crispy duck on red wine cabbage with mashed potatoes encrusted in fritters, and a tasting of desserts including chocolate mousse cake, crème brûlée, Tiramisu, apple tart, and Hawaiian ice creams and sorbets.

Cabanas Seaside Grill is a casual, classy café where your meal is enhanced by the sound of the surf and your view of the Hawaiian starlit sky.

The open-air Veranda is designed in the tradition of a classic plantation home and offers afternoon tea, a curry buffet, and nightly entertainment.

A stylish eatery, Tokyo-Tokyo offers private tatami rooms, "robata-style" dining (where meals are brought hot from the grill and serviced on a wooden paddle), as well as al fresco dining.

Sport Facilities

All sport facilities are not on the premises; however, the hotel has a lovely pool and an 800-foot golden-sand beach, picturesquely bordered by two tropical islets. There are pedal boats, kayaks, lounging rafts, snorkeling, and scuba lessons, as well as a children's program called Kahala Keiki Club, providing an educational and entertaining discovery of the Hawaiian culture.

Chi Fitness Center provides exercise equipment, separate men's and women's sauna, steam, and Jacuzzi, and massages available in treatment rooms, on the beach, or in the privacy of your room. Yoga and fitness classes are offered in an outdoor gazebo. Unfortunately, there are no tennis or golf facilities that belong to the resort. Tennis players can be accommodated at the Hawaii Tennis Academy, about a 10-minute drive from the hotel. Arrangements will be made for golfers to be transported to several of the numerous courses on the island, including Luana Hills Country Club. There are no reciprocal privileges with the adjoining Waialae Country Club, whose golf course surrounds the rear of the hotel, and you can use the facility only if you are sponsored by a member or book a lesson with one of their professional staff.

If you rent a car, you will be able to drive to surf and snorkeling beaches or to other spots for deepsea fishing, yachting, and horseback riding, none of which are available on the property.

Miscellaneous and Environs

Located on the premises are men's and women's boutiques, several jewelry and import shops, a souvenir and sundry store, and a beauty salon. You are less than a mile from the Kahala Mall, and the ho-

tel offers shuttle service to Waikiki, the Kahala Mall, and the Ala Moana Shopping Center numerous times daily.

Those who especially enjoy the dolphins and wish to be close to the pond and pool area can request a "Dolphin View" room with a lanai right on the dolphin pond. Guests 13 and older may enjoy an Adult Dolphin Quest Encounter, which is carefully supervised by expert animal behaviorists. The interactive experience includes shallow-water interaction and awesome underwater views of these special mammals. Younger children can enjoy the 30-minute Children's Dolphin Discovery, which is offered for small groups ages 5 to 12.

Because taxis are rather expensive, you may prefer to rent a car in order to explore the points of interest on the island. These include the Arizona Memorial at Pearl Harbor, the Polynesian Cultural Center, and the fine restaurants and numerous shops and hotels in the bustling Waikiki area. A National Rental Car desk is conveniently located in the main lobby.

For those about to tie the knot, the Kahala Mandarin Oriental has charming wedding facilities, including a wedding chapel gazebo on the beach and offers an attractively priced romance package. The resort is located approximately 20 minutes from the airport, and many travelers avail themselves of the Kahala Mandarin Oriental as a stopover en route to the Far East and the South Pacific. This is unquestionably one of the more beautiful and comfortable luxury resorts in Hawaii, offering the very finest in dining, service, and accommodations.

Kahala Mandarin Oriental
5000 Kahala Avenue
Honolulu, Hawaii 96816
Tel. (808) 739-8888
Fax (808) 739-8800

CHAPTER EIGHT
THE SOUTH SEAS, AUSTRALIA, AND THE FAR EAST

AUSTRALIA
Hayman Resort (Great Barrier Reef)

FIJI
Vatulele Island Resort
The Wakaya Club
Westin Denarau Island Resort & Spa

INDONESIA
Amanresorts, Bali, (Amandari, Amankila, Amanusa)
Four Seasons Resort at Jimbaran Bay, Bali
Four Seasons Resort at Sayan, Bali
The Ritz-Carlton, Bali Resort & Spa

MALAYSIA
Shangri-La's Tanjung Aru Resort

SINGAPORE
Shangri-La Hotel, Singapore

TAHITI (French Polynesia)
Bora Bora Lagoon Resort
Bora Bora Pearl Beach Resort
Hotel Bora Bora
Intercontinental Le Moana Resort Bora Bora
Intercontinental Resort & Spa Moorea
Le Meridien Bora Bora

THAILAND
Amanpuri (Phuket)
Banyan Tree (Phuket)
Mandarin Oriental Dhara Dhevi, Chiang Mai
The Oriental (Bangkok)
Shangri-La Hotel, Bangkok

Shangri-La's Tanjung Aru Resort

The Far East offers some of the most exotic and lavish resorts in the world. For those wishing to stay from a few days to a week, I have selected those properties that offer deluxe accommodations and numerous facilities. Each affords visitors an opportunity to enjoy resort life while absorbing the surrounding culture.

AUSTRALIA

HAYMAN

Situated on its own tropical island (one of the Whitsunday group) located off the northeastern Queensland Coast of Australia, a 60-minute boat ride from the Great Barrier Reef, Hayman is Australia's premier world-class resort. The property was built at a cost in excess of $350 million (Australian), $9 million of which was devoted to the purchase and planting of thousands of full-grown tropical plants and lush vegetation. The end result was the creation of a classical, elegant low-rise resort hotel set on a lovely private island, boasting an endless range of facilities and amenities, surrounded by tropical trees, verdant floral gardens, dynamic ponds and pools, and a magnificent azure sea.

The guest rooms and other buildings are connected by open-air, partially covered walkways that curve around a large water complex that includes three swimming pools. The public rooms and penthouse suites include numerous antiques and objets d'art along with the elegant traditional furnishings.

Accommodations

The 244 guest accommodations are spread among four wings with private balconies or patios affording views of the swimming pools, lagoons, tropical gardens, beach and sea. The pool wing has 86 rooms and 6 suites, while the lagoon wing has 70 rooms, 12 suites, and 11 luxury penthouses. In addition, there are 32 palm wing rooms and 10 beach front rooms, 16 retreat rooms and 1 beach villa.

All of the guest rooms have a residential feel brought about through furnishings with muted tones and simple lines augmented by the use of exclusive art, tropical plants, and subtle lighting.

There is quite a difference in the size of the various accommodations. The palm wing and beach front rooms are the smallest, with smaller bathrooms and shower stalls without tubs. The rooms in the pool wing are smaller than those in the lagoon wing and have shower-bathtub combinations rather than separate shower stalls. Although the pool wing accommodations overlook the larger swimming pool complex and are often the favorite of first-time visitors, the lagoon wing rooms are far more spacious, with lavish marble bathrooms and separate dressing room areas, and offer more seclusion.

Features include a king- or two queen-size beds, both air-conditioning and ceiling fans, refrigerators with fully stocked mini-bars, private room safes, color television with cable and movie-link attachments, radios, clocks that can convert world times, irons and ironing boards, and marble bathrooms with hair dryer, robes, slippers, magnifying mirrors, and personal toiletries. (As noted above, the bathrooms in the lagoon wing are especially desirable.)

The 11 luxury penthouse suites that sit atop the lagoon wing, ranging in price from approximately $2,800 per night for a one bedroom to $4,500 for a three bedroom, are among the most lavish accommodations to be found anywhere in the world. Each is done in a different theme (e.g., French, Italian, Japanese, etc.) and includes numerous antiques, elegant furnishings, fantasy bathrooms, and extensive patios.

The Beach Villa features a plunge infinity pool, an enclosed private courtyard, an outdoor shower and entertainment area with a day bed, a refreshment bar, a separate guest bathroom, a 42" plasma screen television and state of the art sound system and personalized concierge service.

Restaurants, Lounges, and Entertainment

In addition to around-the-clock room service, Hayman has four restaurants, as well as the more casual Lanai and poolside dining areas. Breakfast, which

is included in the room rate, is served buffet style in the indoor/outdoor Azure restaurant on the beach.

The signature restaurant, La Fontaine, is a formal salon with Louis XVI-style furnishings, Waterford crystal chandeliers, classic French cuisine, an extensive wine list, and piano music – a sharp contrast to the resort's tropical setting. A smaller, separate dining room for parties up to 16 is furnished with English Regency period furniture, an 18th-century fireplace, a 24-karat gold dome, and a 16th-century clock from France. The resort occasionally offers special events, as well as gourmet degustations in the kitchen, known as the "Chef's Table."

La Trattoria features fresh pasta and pizza in an authentic peasant-style Italian restaurant, with indoor and outdoor seating, checkered tablecloths, a rustic air, and a nightly band for listening and dancing.

Another restaurant, the Oriental, has a Japanese decor with Japanese gardens and a special Japanese dining pavilion and features Chinese, Malay and Thai cuisines.

For conversation and cocktails, a popular area is The Club Lounge, a dignified setting with Louis XV and Early American high-quality reproductions and nightly entertainment. The club-like environment extends to an adjacent library, card room, and billiard room, the latter furnished with antique tables.

In addition to dinner dances, barbecues and seafood buffets, guests can enjoy dance bands and professional entertainers.

Sport Facilities

The resort's proximity to the Great Barrier Reef, Whitsunday Passage, and the incomparable coastal seas and fringing reefs surrounding the island ensures excellent opportunities for scuba diving, snorkeling, game fishing, and most water sports.

Some of the finest diving and snorkeling on the Barrier Reef is at Bait Reef Marine Park with everything from spectacular wall dives and high-powered drift dives to exploring the calm shallow lagoons or numerous canyons and tunnels of the reef. Wherever you look, the reef explodes with an extraordinary variety of color, pattern, form, function and interaction. Diving is available to both the experienced and novice vacationer, but rules are strictly enforced. Passage to the reef is an extra-charge excursion utilizing one of Hayman's launches or Cruise Whitsundays Wave Piercer. The cruise to Whitehaven Beach on Tuesdays and Thursdays for a day of swimming and sunning on a beautiful, white-sand beach with a barbecue lunch is also popular, as are the evening sunset cruises.

Water sports include catamaran sailing, dinghies, sail boating, water-skiing, charter yachts, small boat rides and reef walking. Helicopter and seaplane flights over the reef can also be arranged. There is a significant charge for most of these exciting adventures.

In addition to a golf target range and 18-hole putting green, there are tennis courts illuminated for night play, squash courts, and a health facility that includes a full gym, aerobic classes, massage and sauna. The resort recommends several walking paths around the island that range from one-half to five miles. Joggers will prefer the path behind the resort that extends from the marina to the end of the beach and the road immediately above it.

Miscellaneous and Environs

Guests fly into Sydney, Melbourne, Cairns, Mackay or Proserpine, transfer to a flight bound for Hamilton Island, and then board any one of Hayman Resort's super luxury yachts – Sun Goddess, Sun Paradise, or Sun Eagle – that will be waiting at the pier adjacent to the airport. The resort's white-clad staff makes you at home, serves champagne, and clears up check-in activities during your 40-minute ride to Hayman Island. The clientele is a mix of domestic and international from all around the globe.

Located at the resort are high-fashion boutiques, stores specializing in signature items, men's and women's hairstylists, medical services and betting facilities for off-track racing.

Hayman Resort is Australia's premiere world-class, luxury resort featuring a variety of restaurants offering excellent food and service, elegant accommodations, and full sport facilities in idyllic surroundings, convenient to the Great Barrier Reef, one of the world's most exotic marine habitats.

Hayman
Great Barrier Reef, Australia
North Queensland, 4801
Australia
Tel. (61-7) 4940-1234
Fax (61-7) 4940-1567
www.hayman.com.au

FIJI

VATULELE ISLAND RESORT

Situated 30 miles off the south coast of Viti Levu (the principal island in the 300-island Fiji group), amidst 60 acres of coconut plantation, fronting a ¾ mile-long, white-sand beach and lagoon protected by an offshore reef, is the incomparable Vatulele Island Resort hideaway. This romantic retreat accommodates a maximum of 19 couples in spacious 2,000-square-foot villas stretching across its picture-postcard-perfect South Pacific beach, nestled amongst tropical foliage to provide maximum privacy for pampered guests.

Built by the Emmy-award-winning Australian television producer Henry Crawford for a 1990 grand opening, the resort provides a casual experience in extremely comfortable accommodations, serviced by 110 extremely warm and friendly Fijians who reside in one of the four native villages spread along the island. The staff personally attend to all their guests' needs, including settling them in their villas, arranging special excursions, and supervising all meals, cocktail hour, activities, arrivals and departures. Upon arrival, photos of each couple are taken and displayed with their first names so that the service staff will be able to address you personally. Jackets, ties and shoes are not required. This all combines to create a friendly homey atmosphere where you feel more like a private house guest at a party on someone's island hideaway rather than a hotel patron.

The resort does require a four-night minimum stay. Children under 12 are not permitted except on certain specially designated family weeks. The tariff for this hedonistic experience starts at $1,026 per couple per night in low season and $1,338 in high season, and includes taxes, all meals, alcoholic and nonalcoholic beverages, island excursions and all activities except scuba diving and massage.

Accommodations

The 17 uniquely designed, Fijian-style villas with thatched roofs, locally referred to as "bures", include a large bedroom with king-size bed, a makeup vanity, stocked wet bar, private wall safes, bathrobes, hair dryer, ample storage and closet space, a large sitting room, large sprawling bathrooms with both indoor and outdoor showers, a private tiled terrace with hammock facing the beach, a private walkway to the beach, and your own padded lounge chairs, ideal for witnessing the spectacular evening sunsets.

In keeping with the get-away-from-it-all environment, there are no telephones, newspapers, radios, or televisions.

The resort also offers two premium villas, Vale Viqi (the grand honeymoon bure) and a spectacular villa known as The Point. These residences enjoy the best view of the beach and are the only accommodations with air conditioning and freshwater plunge pools.

Restaurants, Lounges, and Entertainment

Meals are available in your villa or on the open-air terrace outside the large central pavilion overlooking the lagoon. In the evening, guests mingle for complimentary cocktails and hors d'oeuvres before joining each other at a long banquet-style table to enjoy dinner under the stars with added illumination by lanterns and candlelight. Although the num-

ber of selections is limited, the menu varies daily and the cuisine is an imaginative combination of Fijian, Western and Asian creations accompanied by white and red wines.

Those wishing more privacy or a special romantic experience can take a boat ride for a private picnic breakfast or lunch at lovely Long Beach; or for total seclusion, they can be alone on Nooki Nooki Island, a small islet with a white-sand beach surrounded by interesting rock formations. Private dinners are also served in a jungle cave or the resort's wine cellar.

Tipping is not expected or accepted; however, guests may make a contribution to the employee's annual bonus funds at the conclusion of their visit.

Sport Facilities

Vatulele Island Resort's protected lagoon is ideal for swimming, snorkeling, scuba, sailing and other water sports. Five-day scuba certification courses are available. Fiji is considered one of the world's top-four dive destinations, and scuba diving is one of the main draws to this resort. Vatulele is a PADI-certified, Gold-Palm, 5-star resort with two resident instructors. Tennis and volleyball are offered. All equipment is supplied. Hikes to natural caves, grottos and pristine beaches are a favorite pastime for guests. Hikers and joggers can follow the scenic, wooded path that leads from the resort to the villages. The red prawn walk past 3,000-year-old rock paintings and petroglyphics, through a jungle forest to a grotto filled with the fabled, sacred red prawns is a recommended excursion. The 30-minute kayak trip (or 5-minute motorboat ride) to explore and/or snorkel the colorful grottos and volcanic rock formations between the resort and Long Beach is also a must for those who appreciate aquatic beauty.

Miscellaneous and Environs

All guests can reach Vatulele Island Resort on a daily scheduled charter flight that leaves Nadi Domestic Airport at 11:30 a.m., arrives at Vatulele at noon, departs the island at 12:20 p.m., and returns to Nadi at 12:50 p.m. The cost is $450 (including tax) per person with a 33-pound baggage allowance. It is possible to arrange for a charter flight as well. Guests can leave their excess luggage at the resort's Nadi airport office.

Fijian wedding ceremonies, complete with a Fijian minister, choir and wedding feast, are popular here. Many couples choose Vatulele Island Resort for their honeymoon.

Vatulele Island Resort is more than a tropical island resort. The friendly staff, the special attention given to each guest's needs, and the conviviality that prevails among the 19 couples who occupy the comfortable, sprawling villas combine to create special warmth. When departing guests board the seaplane on the beach in front of the resort and the staff sings the Vatulele farewell song, there is scarcely a dry eye in the crowd. For lovers, honeymooners and those resort aficionados wishing a very special South Sea island experience, a sojourn at Vatulele Island Resort should prove very rewarding.

Vatulele Island Resort
Worldwide Reservation Office
Nadi Airport, Fiji
Tel. +679 6720300
e-mail: info@vatulele.com
www. Vatulele.com

FIJI

THE WAKAYA CLUB

Wakaya Island – encircled by a coral reef encompassing five square miles, and composed of lush emerald rain forests, soaring cliffs, and 32 sparkling white beaches – is one of the 300 tropical islands located in the South Pacific between Tahiti and Australia. In 1973 David Gilmour acquired the island and built a village for over 140 Fijians (the employees and their families), centered by a quaint, 19th-century-style church and schoolhouse. On the most desirable 200 acres at the northwest end of the island, he constructed the incomparable Wakaya Club as an extension of his own island home for a maximum of 18 guests to luxuriate in eight 1,600-square-foot, secluded bures (bungalows), as well as one 2,400-square-foot Governor'S Bure. Amiable Rob and Lynda Miller oversee the property.

The resort's bungalows, set in a former coconut plantation, stretch along a white sandy beach fronting a turquoise, coral-ridged sea, surrounded by forests filled with Banyan trees, rare tropical birds, deer, goats, horses and pigs. The service staff of friendly, dedicated Fijians lives in the nearby village and contributes to the charm of The Wakaya Club experience. There is a ratio of 12 service staff to each couple. In addition, there are European- and Asian-trained chefs overseeing the preparation of meals at the Palm Grove Dining Pavilion with its soaring 60-foot cathedral ceiling. The clientele is a mixture of Australians, North Americans, Europeans, and Asians.

$1,900 to $2,300 (plus tax) per couple, per night, covers accommodations, all meals, alcoholic and nonalcoholic beverages, laundry services and all sports – including golf, tennis, croquet, two one-tank dives per day, snorkeling, hand-line fishing, and the use of required equipment. (It does not include deep-sea fishing, spa treatments, massages, or air transfers.) The Governor's Bure goes for $2,800 per night and Vale O for $7,600. Children under 16 are only permitted when the resort is fully sold out or where one party leases all accommodations. A minimum five-night stay is required.

Accommodations

Each of the nine 1,600- to 2,400-square-foot hideaways on the lagoon consists of a rattan-furnished living room with a four-stool, fully stocked complimentary wet bar and CD player, a bedroom with a king-size four-poster bed, a sea-view deck, a private safe, and an immense bathroom area with a six-foot soaking tub, a private outdoor shower enclosed in a lava-rock wall, twin vanities, toilet and bidet, and such extra amenities as cotton bathrobes, hair dryers, toiletries, an iron and ironing board and straw hats for the sun.

Each bure displays warm opulence with woven bamboo matting on the walls, built-in cabinetry, desks and furnishings crafted from Fijian Yaka wood, ceiling fans, and hardwood floors with overlaid fiber rugs. All bures are air conditioned and are heavily landscaped for privacy. Laundry is retrieved daily and returned freshly pressed on a tray strewn with tropical flowers.

Another option is the 12,000 square-foot Vale O, which sits atop a hill and can accommodate from one to three couples for $7,600 per night. This accommodation comes with a chef, housekeeping staff, on-call driver, private swimming pool, Jacuzzi,

internet connection, its own telephone and fax numbers, and night-lit tennis court, as well as full use of the resort facilities and amenities.

Restaurants, Lounges, and Entertainment

Dining is available in your bure or at the open-air Palm Grove Dining Pavilion, which includes an open deck with dining gazebos. Breakfast and lunch are served on the deck overlooking the lagoon. Guests frequently opt for a picnic on a private white-sand beach, which can be easily arranged.

On request, a dinner menu will be made available at lunchtime as a suggestion for the evening fare. Guests can place special orders if they wish to deviate from the proposed menu. Special dietary requirements will also be accommodated.

About 7:00 p.m. most guests congregate for cocktails at the Pavilion, followed by a romantic candlelight dinner. The cuisine is described as a combination of Continental, Indian, Italian, Chinese, and Fijian, with emphasis on local game, fish, seafood, and produce. Wines are imported from Australia, California, and New Zealand. In addition, guests can opt to have dinner served in their bure or by candlelight on the beach.

Once each week, the villagers perform a meke ceremony consisting of traditional Fijian songs, dances and a typical "lovo" feast.

Sport Facilities

The main attraction, of course, is the endless opportunity for participating in a vast variety of water sports, including a leisurely swim in crystal-clear waters, some of the best scuba and snorkeling in the world, glass-bottom reef boat rides and sport and deep-sea fishing. This is an ideal location to learn how to scuba and to obtain your international four-day Padi-dive certification. There is also a small, freshwater, grotto-like pool for those who can tear themselves away from the beaches. The beach in front of the resort is quite small. A five-minute walk will bring you to lovely Homestead Beach. In addition, arrangements can be made to

be transported to Vunitavola or Tuburua beaches, both only a 10-minute drive away, where you can arrange a private picnic lunch.

The Wakaya Club boasts a nine-hole, pitch-and-putt golf course that is never crowded based on the limited number of guests. In addition, there is one Wimbledon-Tex tennis court that is illuminated for night play, a croquet lawn, boccie ball and billiards.

The resort provides golf clubs, tennis rackets, scuba and snorkel gear, and all other necessary equipment gratis. Thus, guests need not include these items in their luggage allotment. The only charge not included in your daily rate is for deep-sea fishing expeditions, massages and purchases from the boutique.

The island offers excellent opportunities to explore pristine beaches and archeological sites dating back to 700 b.c., as well as for nature hikes through tropical rain forests to view tropical vegetation, as well as wild horses, pigs, deer, and exotic birds that abound on the island.

Miscellaneous and Environs

United States guests generally fly from Los Angeles, where Air New Zealand, Quantas and Air Pacific offer wide-bodied jet air service to Nadi airport on Viti Levu, Fiji's principal island. Nonstop service is also offered from Australia and certain other cities in Southeast Asia and the South Pacific.

From Nadi airport, it is a 30-minute flight on a Cessna Grand Caravan aircraft at a charge of $960 round-trip per couple plus 10 percent VAT. From Suva airport, travel time is 12 minutes and the cost

is $480 round trip. The baggage allowance is 95 pounds.

Guests may enjoy visiting the nearby Fijian village, where the employees live with their families, and seeing David Gilmour's private collection of 19th-century Fijian engravings and paintings housed in the club's recreation building.

The Wakaya Club is unique among the tropical resorts in that it only accommodates 18 guests, who have access to areas of lush grounds and facilities that could service three or four times as many patrons. The friendly staff provides a certain Fijian charm, which creates the feeling that you are on your own private plantation.

Sophisticated, discerning vacationers wishing to luxuriate in sumptuous Fijian-style villas while enjoying friendly service, as well as a full complement of water sports and other facilities in a very casual, idyllic beach and island-woodland setting will surely find The Wakaya Club their little bit of paradise.

The Wakaya Club
Island Office
P.O. Box 15424
Suva, Fiji
Tel. 6793-448-128, Fax 6793-448-406
E-mail: info@Wakaya.com.fj
USA and Canada—tel.1-800 828-3454
Australia—tel.1-800-126-205
Great Britain—tel.0-800-968-986

WESTIN DENARAU ISLAND RESORT & SPA

Conveniently located 20 minutes from Nadi Airport, the Westin Denarau Island Resort & Spa (formerly the Sheraton Royal Denarau Resort and the Regent), which first opened in 1975, sits on a long strand of beach on the shore of Nadi Bay, adjacent to the resort's Golf and Racquet Club. The property is designed like a Fijian village and blends into the island atmosphere, with two-story guest units stretching out from the island-style open-air lobby and restaurants that are cooled by sea breezes and colorfully decorated in bright Fijian decor. The facility is managed by Starwood Hotels & Resorts Worldwide, Inc. The grounds of the resort are crisscrossed by covered walkways and studded with brilliantly colorful hibiscus, bougainvillea, and frangipani. In the evenings, torchlights illuminate the palms and sand along the beach, as well as the outdoor pool and gardens, creating a beautiful, romantic Melanesian setting. In 2005 a $22 million refurbishment program was launched by Starwood for this resort and its two adjoining properties, the Sheraton Fiji Resort and the Sheraton Denarau Villas.

Accommodations

Two hundred seventy-four air-conditioned, spacious, contemporary guest rooms, decorated in a Fijian décor including, bright native wall hangings, soft natural fabrics, colorful tiles and wicker, in two-story units, stretch out across the beach. Each has a balcony or verandah, a radio, a 32" LCD, flat-screen TV with international channels, high- speed internet connections, a Bose DVD player and sound system (upper-level rooms only),refrigerator/mini-bar, double sink, complimentary tea and coffee maker, toiletries, robes and slippers, and a modern tile bathroom with a double-headed shower. These rooms are clean and cool and do not suffer from the clammy mustiness so prevalent in the small tropical units in many of the other hotels. The management provides hair dryers; and converters for electrical appliances can be purchased in the sundry shop. There are six luxury suites with separate sitting rooms and three large facilities for meetings, banquets and conventions.

Restaurants, Lounges, and Entertainment

Breakfast, featuring Western dishes, is served in the rooms or at the semi-open-air Ocean Terrace; and lunch is available at The Steakhouse overlooking the beach. Both of these restaurants and the Hamacho Japanese restaurant offer dinner. On Saturday

evenings, there is a buffet-style native feast, with a "Meke" dance performance that is similar to a Hawaiian luau in the Verandah restaurant at the adjacent Sheraton Fiji Resort. On Friday nights a Seafood buffet is featured in the Verandah Restaurant. Prices for all foods and beverages are quite high, even at breakfast.

Every evening, there is a local band that plays romantic music for dancing in the Meke Lounge, overlooking the palm-lined pool and beach. Those not wishing to sit at a table can sprawl out in a deck chair by the pool and still hear the music. A fire-walking performance is presented on Wednesday evenings.

Sport Facilities

A lovely freshwater three-tier swimming pool is located by the beach, overlooking the ocean complete with numerous comfortable lounges, umbrellas, and a Jacuzzi. The beach has soft, gray sand and the water, though clear, is not blue. However, the warm waters are fine for swimming and water sports.

Hikers and joggers can enjoy several picturesque routes. If you go left along the beach past the Sheraton Fiji, you can proceed for approximately two miles to where the beach ends and then return. An alternative route would be to go for about a mile up the road leading out of the hotel to the front gate, past the marina, turn right, and continue for a mile on a road bordering the golf course, which ends at the beach, where you turn right and go for another mile along the sea before you return to the hotel.

The hotel provides complimentary windsurfing, Hobie cats, paddleboats, kayaks, and archery equipment; water-skiing is available for an additional charge. Snorkeling and deep-sea fishing can be arranged. There is a small uninhabited tropical island about one kilometer away from the beach accessible by a small motorized craft. There are only a few primitive facilities here, and there is not much to do except bring a picnic lunch packed by the resort or walk around the rim and look back at the resort. However, if you ever wanted to be by yourself on an uninhabited island – for whatever reason you can conjure up – this is your chance. Shuttle service is provided three times daily; if you wish to return at a different time, however, be sure you make definite arrangements to be picked up. There are many little islands far more beautiful to explore that offer good beaches and facilities. To visit these islands, you will have to make more elaborate arrangements and devote an entire day.

Adjacent to the hotel is the 18-hole championship Denarau Golf Course and the Denarau Golf and Racquet Club. Preferential green fees are offered to guests. An international-size lawn bowling green and children's playground are also available.

At the Racquet Club there are four illuminated all-weather courts and six grass courts, a resident tennis pro, a tennis shop, a snack shop, and ball machines.

The resort provides numerous adult and children's activities during the day. They range from volleyball games and other games to palm-tree climbing, fire walking and a torch-lighting ceremony.

In 2006, the Heavenly Spa was introduced, a sanctuary created for indulgence and rejuvenation of body, mind and spirit, beautifully designed and peacefully nestled amidst 1300 square meters of lush meditation gardens filed with flora and native birds. The Spa is composed of 12 therapy suites and rooms overlooking a lily lagoon which winds around the spa complex, as well as, changing rooms, sauna, steam, Vichy, Swiss- jet and outdoor showers, hydrotherapy tubs and geisha bath-pools. Adjacent to the spa is the Westin workout facility and a 25-meter horizon-style pool.

Miscellaneous and Environs

On the premises are a sundry shop, a unisex boutique featuring island garments, and a shop offering foreign imports.

The Westin Denarau Island Resort & Spa is only a 20-minute drive from Nadi Airport and a 5-minute drive from the town of Nadi, where there are numerous native shops. One mile east of the resort is a marina where guests can charter boats to the Mamanuca group of out-islands or for deep-sea fishing and scuba.

Adjacent to this resort are the Sheraton Fiji Resort and the Sheraton Denarau Villas. These properties are also operated by Starwood Hotels & Resorts Worldwide, Inc. and are part of the renovation program described above. Guests at all three properties have reciprocal use of the various facilities.

As mentioned earlier, there are many activities for children, as well as a playground, a shallow children's pool, and baby-sitting services for the day or evening. This is a charming, friendly property with many facilities, conveniently situated, taking full advantage of its natural tropical setting.

Westin Denarau Island Resort & Spa
P.O. Box 9081
Denarau Island, Fiji
Tel. 679-750000
Fax 679-750259
In U.S.—tel. 866-478-2777

INDONESIA

AMANRESORTS, BALI
(AMANDARI – AMANKILA – AMANUSA)

Singapore-based Amanresorts, the inspired creation of entrepreneur-visionary Adrian Zecha, has created a triumvirate of fantasy hideaways situated in three different areas on the lovely tropical island of Bali. Each perfectly romantic resort has its own distinct flavor, and visitors frequently divide up their vacation time between the properties, as well as at Amanjiwo, located with a natural amphitheater in the verdant countryside of central Java, and at Amanwana, a luxury tented resort on the nearby Indonesian island of Moyo. Irrespective of your choice, you will be greeted at Denpasar Airport and transported in an air-conditioned limousine by one of the amiable, concerned staff while enjoying a refrigerated towel and cold drink. Complimentary transfers are also provided between the three Bali properties.

Amandari ("peaceful spirits") is perhaps the most well known, having opened in 1989, and was designed in the style of a typical Balinese village. It is nestled above a 250-foot river gorge overlooking terraced rice paddies with pathways descending to the Ayung River and Valley. Located near the artist's colony of Ubud, a 45-minute drive from the airport, Amandari treats its patrons to the ultimate tranquil mountain experience in an idyllic Balinese setting amongst the serenity, culture, and arts for which Bali is best known. This is "numero uno" for many well-traveled exotic resort aficionados.

Amankila ("peaceful hill"), the most isolated of the three properties, is a two-hour drive from Denpasar. It opened in March 1992 and is located on a bluff overlooking a private beach on the eastern coast of Bali, near the villages of Manggis and Karangasem. Here, guests enjoy a secluded, romantic, elegant beach/sea-oriented hideaway in total privacy.

Amanusa ("peaceful isle"), perched on a grassy hillside overlooking the Indian Ocean, Bali Golf and Country Club and the Nusa Dua resort area, is only a 20-minute drive from the airport. Of the three Amanresorts, this offers the most sport options and is most proximate to the more popular hotels, restaurants, and beaches of Bali. The ultraluxurious villas, extraordinary common areas, imaginative design, and total panorama from every nook and corner make this the favorite retreat of many of its well-traveled clientele.

The Balinese designed entrance lobbies, reception areas, indoor/outdoor connecting stairways, and restaurants in all three properties are ingenious architectural masterpieces, creating an almost futuristic aura.

Because guests receive free transportation between all three resorts, you will want to select the setting that best reflects your idyllic vacation mood and then take advantage of day or overnight visits to the other properties.

Accommodations

At Amandari, there are 30 air-conditioned duplex and single-level terrace suites, each surrounded by a walled garden and connected by floral walkways (illuminated by lanterns in the evenings) to the other resort facilities. The 12 duplex suites each have a spacious sitting area opening to a private patio with a spiral staircase leading from the bathroom-wardrobe area to an intimate second-level bedroom with its own second toilet and sink compartment. The one-level suites have even larger sitting areas and feature sliding-glass window walls. Each of the eight most expensive accommodations boasts large, private swimming pools. The most expensive accommodations are the one-bedroom and two-bedroom Amandari Suites and the three-bedroom Amandari Villa.

Every suite has a bamboo palm thatched roof, marble floor, day beds, beamed ceilings, furnishings of sandalwood and rattan, an outdoor dining terrace, a canopied king-size bed, lavish wardrobe-bathrooms with separate toilet compartments and shower stalls, twin closets and vanities and a small outdoor marble tub enclosed by a Balinese-style wall. The suites at all three properties feature cotton robes, slippers, hair dryers, and numerous other amenities available for the guests' comfort and equipment, such as refrigerated mini-bars, private room safes and sophisticated music systems that accommodate cassettes and compact discs that can be borrowed from each resort's library. The top-of-the-line "Amandari Suite" boasts the largest pool and most desirable view, and is sold as a one-bedroom for $1,900 per night or as a two-bedroom for $2,600.

The 34 free-standing luxury suites at Amankila meander along a hillside and are elevated to take advantage of scenic views. Linked by walkways to the resort's restaurants, pool and beach, each unit combines the grace of traditional Balinese decor with the modern elegance of terrazzo, native timbers and mirrored glass. Like the other properties, every accommodation includes a spacious bedroom, king-size bed, sitting area, indoor and outdoor writing desks and divans, a large bathroom with twin vanities, closets, separate shower and toilet compartments, a large soaking tub looking out to a lily pond, a hair dryer, magnifying mirror, and numerous amenities, outdoor terraces with protected dining pavilions, and a spectacular view. The extra-spacious, two-bedroom Amankila Suite and nine additional units have large private pools. All units have a clean, modern feel and are extremely comfortable.

Amanusa's magnificent 35 air-conditioned villas are extremely spacious with outdoor living areas that reflect the ultimate in romantic splendor. Each is constructed with thatched alang-alang roofs, marble stone, marble floors with rich teak woods and rattans. The focal point of the sleeping rooms is a white canopied, four-poster, queen-size bed set opposite a sitting area with a day bed, small dining table, and armoire that houses the mini-bar, music system and satellite television.

The gigantic bathroom-dressing area is separated from the bedroom by a stone wall and has twin closets and vanities, a separate toilet compartment (with telephone) looking out to gardens, both an indoor and outdoor-garden shower, and a sunken bathtub that is situated to appear as though it floats on a lily pond.

The bedroom opens out into a small enclosed garden court that contains a dining table and chairs for outdoor dining. On the other side of the villa, an expansive patio has a double lounging bed covered by a canopy. Eight units include large swimming pools that are illuminated at night.

Restaurants, Lounges, and Entertainment

All three resorts have bars, lounges, and 24-hour room service. The romantic nature of the accommodations, garden dining tables and private patios often tempt guests to dine in the privacy and comfort of their villas.

The menus at all three resorts include a variety of Asian, Indonesian, and Western cuisine, which is among the best in Bali.

Amandari's singular restaurant has floor-to-ceiling windows surrounded by a lower-level, protected open-air patio set above the picturesque pool, looking out to the terraced rice paddies, tropical jungle and river gorge. In the evening, a traditional Indonesian band renders hypnotic "rindik" music from their perch set across the illuminated swimming pool. The diverse selection of Western and Indonesian cuisine here is as outstanding as the setting.

Amankila's lovely main dining room is semi-open-air, looks out at the sea and features Indonesian and Western selections creatively intermingled under the direction of a French chef. Lunch and snacks, which include an eclectic mix of salads,

sandwiches, and Asian favorites, are also served down at the beach near the unique mirror-like pool which is surrounded by flowers and giant palms, creating a pleasing environment in which to enjoy your meal. At Amanusa, guests have a choice between the panoramic terrace restaurant that looks out to the golf course and sea, featuring both Thai and Indonesian specialties or the elegant, modern glassed-in Italian restaurant that offers Italian favorites in the evening by the pool. The Thai and Indonesian cuisine is among the best I have ever experienced.

In each restaurant at all three resorts, presentation is imaginative, the cuisine is top-notch, service is attentive, and the views are spectacular.

Sport Facilities

At Amandari, on-property sport facilities are limited to one flood-lit tennis court, an attractive swimming pool that appears to spill over into the adjoining rice paddies, and a recently constructed health club where guests can book a variety of massages and beauty treatments and enjoy the sauna, steam, and limited exercise equipment. Amandari will arrange tee times at Bali Handara Kosaido Country Club set in an extinct volcano, located an hour-and-a-quarter from the resort. Early morning play is recommended so as to avoid frequent early afternoon showers. At Amankila, a three-tiered pool below the lobby appears to float above the sea, while a very long second pool is located within a spectac-

ular coconut grove at the beach club. The half-mile fine-sand beach, with warm waters for swimming, is an enjoyable locale to spend the day. Snorkeling and diving gear, windsurfers and Hobie Cats are available. Half-day cruises on an outrigger can be arranged to dive sites, as well as to neighboring beaches and islands. Two tennis courts will be added in the near future. In the meantime, tennis is arranged at a hard court five minutes away.

Sport facilities at Amanusa include two flood-lit tennis courts and mountain bikes, and the resort will arrange tee times for guests at the 18-hole Bali Golf and Country Club that surrounds the resort. In addition to a large attractive pool and outdoor swimming deck, guests can be transported to its beach area below. It is only a five-minute golf cart ride to the Beach Club, which has a small restaurant that provides light meals and refreshments with washrooms and showers nearby. Guests may relax in one of the nine grass-roofed huts scattered along the beach front, or choose from a number of sun beds. The beach is protected by a fringing coral reef and is considered one of Bali's finest. Those wishing to work out at a health club or use sauna or steam will be accommodated at the Bali Hilton, adjacent to Amanusa's Beach Club.

Of course, guests at any of the Aman properties are welcome to utilize the facilities at the other locations.

Massages can be arranged in your villa at all three resorts.

Miscellaneous and Environs

Each resort has a boutique and craft shop and a library stocked with books, newspapers, cassettes, and compact discs for use in the bungalows.

Major tourist attractions around the island include the famous Temple Besakih, which lies on the slopes of the holy mountain, Gunung Agung, 36 miles from Denpasar, as well as the various villages that specialize in Balinese crafts. At Mas, you can watch master wood-carvers making graceful Balinese statues; at Ubud, you can visit an artist colony; and at Celuk, the natives work with gold and silver. All of these villages are near Amandari.

Most visitors will want to witness the Balinese dance performances offered in various villages, the colorful "Barong" and the hypnotic "Kecak" being the most popular.

Each of the resorts will arrange personal guided excursions to various sites in Bali, accompanied by refreshments and a picnic lunch. Additional places you can arrange to explore include Goa Gajah, a Buddhist monastery and the oldest relic of Balinese art, the Holy Springs at Tirta Empal, the Petula bird sanctuary, the collection of paintings at Neka museum, the spectacular rice fields at Sebata or Sideman-Putung, the monkey forest at Kedaton, the temples at Pura Luhur and Tanah Lot, the botanical gardens of Lila Graha, and snorkeling at Lovina Beach or Bali Barat.

Amandari will organize one-to-two-hour guided treks along rice terraces, native villages and temples, as well as a two-and-a-half-hour climb up Mt. Gunung Batur and rafting along the Agung River, a unique and exhilarating way to experience Bali's wildlife, waterfalls, rapids, and rice fields.

For a few-night diversion, some Amanresort guests in Bali opt to visit Amanwana ("peaceful forest"), a 20-unit tented-camp-property abutting an excellent snorkeling (not swimming) beach surrounded by lush tropical forests on the island of Moyo, east of Bali. Guests may travel non-stop from Bali to Amanwana in an air-conditioned Cessna Caravan amphibian. This state-of-the-art floatplane, operated by Travira Air, lands in the bay directly in front of Amanwana. Flying time is 65 minutes. Alternatively, guests may charter the Cessna Caravan. Although the accommodations have many of the facilities and amenities similar to the other Aman properties, they are smaller, do not have private patios, and the resort itself is quite simple without the stunning design, architecture, imaginative pools, and gardens found at the three Bali charmers. Snorkeling and diving is the main attraction, in addition to the possibility of enjoying a very casual, tranquil few days in this jungle-beach setting.

Whichever Amanresort you choose as your tranquil hideaway while exploring Bali, you will be rewarded with luxurious, comfortable accommodations, excellent cuisine, attentive service, and the ultimate in a scenic, romantic environment.

Amanresrts, Bali
Amanresorts Corporate Office
1 Orchard Spring Lane
#05-01 Tourism Court
Singapore 247729

Amanresorts Corporate Office and
United States contact numbers:
Tel.(65)6883-2555
Fax(65)6883-0555

United States:
Toll Free Nationwide (800)477-9180
Web: www.amanresorts.com

INDONESIA

FOUR SEASONS RESORT AT JIMBARAN BAY, BALI

Descending down 35 acres of terraced hillside and tropical landscaped gardens to a wide expanse of sandy beach on the northeast slopes of the Bukit peninsula, overlooking Jimbaran Bay, is the uniquely beautiful Four Seasons Resort on the magical island of Bali. The 147 luxuriously appointed villas, each with its own private plunge pool and floral gardens, are built into the hillside to afford incomparable views and total privacy for their fortunate occupants. Originally built by the Regent Hotel chain and completed in 1993, it became a Four Seasons Resort when Four Seasons acquired Regent Hotels. The mix of clientele includes North Americans, Australians, Europeans and Asians, creating a very cosmopolitan environment.

On arrival, the sweet smell of frangipani wafting on the gentle breezes, a cool tropical drink and a refrigerated towel revive travelers as they are swiftly checked in and whisked to their romantic villas. Public facilities include exotic affinity-edged swimming pools, a tennis-health-spa club complex, four semi-open-air restaurants, a boutique, gallery, library and lounge, a private beach and a main lobby reception area.

Accommodations

The 139 deluxe 2,152-square-foot villas and even larger (6) two-bedroom and (2) royal villas are airy, sumptuous, spacious and fully air-conditioned with marble floors, vaulted ceilings with ceiling fans, outdoor gardens, private 26-square-meter plunge pools, separate, open-air, semi-protected living-dining areas with refrigerated mini-bars, a wardrobe-dressing area with private wall safes, romantic bedrooms with canopied king-size beds, writing desks, oversized color remote-control televisions, DVD/VCR players, clocks, cassette/compact disc music systems, and bathing pavilions complete with an oversized soaking bathtub, double vanity, both an indoor and an outdoor shower, a private toilet, makeup mirrors, hair dryers, a large umbrella, numerous amenities and robes and slippers for use during your visit. Pressing, cleaning and laundry are available daily at very reasonable prices.

Banquet facilities can accommodate up to 90 people, and the resort is ideal for small, high-level incentive and business groups.

Restaurants, Lounges, and Entertainment

Dining at your private villa is available around the clock. The lovely indoor/outdoor dining room, Taman Wantilan, with panoramic views of Jimbaran Bay, is open for breakfast and dinner, offering a choice of contemporary Western fare and Indonesian specialties. Typical Sumatran or Balinese rijsttafel dinners can be arranged in advance. Adjacent is a private dining pavilion that can accommodate parties of 12 or less. Warung Mie is a charming specialty restaurant, accessible by a foot path over lily ponds that features a variety of noodle creations from all over Asia.

The Pool Terrace Café is open from 11:00 a.m. until 6:30 p.m., and features local Indonesian favorites, salads, sandwiches and snacks.

P.J.'s on the beach offers alfresco seaside dining with an emphasis on fish and seafood prepared to

ing are available. Although the water is warm and inviting, many areas are frequently out-of-bounds for swimming due to the danger of black coral. In addition to your lovely, romantic, in-villa plunge pool, the resort offers a large 34-meter swimming pool that appears to spill over the terrace into a free-form, tropically gardened soaking pool below, adjacent to nearby hot and cold spa pools and the pool café, which serves lunch, snacks, and drinks.

Tennis enthusiasts will appreciate the two flood-lit tennis courts at the Spa and Tennis Club, which also offers a teaching pro, assorted exercise and cardiovascular equipment, aerobic classes, a plunge pool, a variety of massage and body treatments, beauty services and men's and women's dressing facilities with showers and saunas.

Bicycles are available, as well as a full children's program and prearranged tee times at nearby golf courses.

Miscellaneous and Environs

Although there is a nice selection of merchandise in the combination craft shop-boutique on premises, visitors will want to explore the hundreds of shops and stalls in the vicinities of Nusa Dua, Sanur and Kuta Beach, as well as the artist colonies at Ubud, Mas and Celek. The resort, while enjoying a secluded location on Jimbaran Bay, is only 15 minutes from Denpasar Airport and 20 minutes from the Nusa Dua resort area.

Experienced resort connoisseurs and loving couples requiring spacious, romantic accommodations, creature comforts, seclusion, fine food and superior, attentive service in a picturesque, romantic setting while visiting the tropical paradise of Bali will be delighted with the Four Seasons Resort at Jimbaran Bay, Bali.

your specifications, Western or Asian-style and pizza. The menu is eclectic and the beach setting is charming.

Indonesian rindik music is featured each evening, and traditional Balinese music and dance programs are performed twice weekly. Compact and DVDs for use in your bungalow are available in the library/lounge.

Sport Facilities

The sandy beach at the foot of the terraced hillside extends for three miles, affording an attractive expanse for long walks or invigorating jogs. Complimentary windsurfing, sailing, surfing and snorkel-

Four Seasons Resort at Jimbaran Bay
Jimbaran, Denpasar, 80361
Bali, Indonesia
Tel. 62-361-701010
Fax 62-361-701020
www.fourseasons.com/jimbaranbay

FOUR SEASONS RESORT AT SAYAN, BALI

In February 1998, Four Seasons Resorts opened their second property in Bali on 18 acres of verdant, rolling hillside nestled in the central highlands, overlooking dense palm forests and terraced rice fields rising from the rushing currents of the sacred Ayung River, near the popular artist community of Ubud. Guests enter this secluded, intimate hideaway across a teak-and-steel suspension bridge that spans the river gorge and opens onto an infinity-edged elliptical lotus pond that covers the roof of the main hotel building. Looking out over this pond has been described as akin to standing on a small lake, suspended in air, floating 250 feet above rivers, rice fields and jungle. Guests then descend down a staircase to the lobby of this three-level, futuristic enclave and are immediately treated to a 180-degree panoramic view of the dense tropical surroundings. One could describe the decor as Balinese-modern; however, with a little stretch of the imagination, you can envision a unique Indonesian fortress straight out of a James Bond movie. Paths meandering through the valley immediately beneath the main hotel bring guests to the 42 private, free-standing villas disbursed throughout the grounds, each with its own private plunge pool, outdoor shower and large sun-deck/dining/lounge area. The paths terminate at the Riverside Café and the main, kidney shaped pool which borders the river below. Clientele from all over the world come to enjoy this uniquely designed, enviously situated, especially romantic Balinese property.

Accommodations

In the main hotel building there are 5 one-bedroom Sayan suites and 13 terrace suites, each exquisitely accented with rich teak and Balinese natural stone with large balconies and comfortable lounge chairs looking out to the river and hillsides.

The beautifully-designed terrace suites contain an upper-level parlor with a dining, lounging and terrace area, as well as a guest bathroom, television, stereo, telephone and fully-stocked mini-bar. Accessible by a private staircase is the lower level that includes a bedroom with a king-size bed, another large sun deck with lounge chairs and protective umbrellas, and a sumptuous bathroom with double vanities, terrazzo floors and soaking tubs, separate glassed-in showers, toilet compartments, a hair dryer, magnifying mirrors, Balinese-style robes and slippers, and larger walk-in closets with generous storage and private safes.

The one-bedroom Sayan suites are a bit larger with the parlor and bedroom/bathroom areas on the same level, separated by an entry foyer.

For the ultimate Sayan experience, you can opt for one of the 37 one-bedroom or two two-bedroom villas or the one-of-a-kind, three-bedroom, "Royal Sayan" villa, all of which are spread throughout the densely vegetated valley. The one-bedroom villas are entered from a deck with an Alang-Alang roof surrounded by lily ponds. You descend a stone staircase to the entry way that opens up into a semi-open air, protected sitting area with a couch, chairs,

fully stocked mini-bar and dining table, which adjoins the large sun deck that has two additional lounge chairs and an umbrella to block out the sun. All of this surrounds two sides of a delicious, plunge pool that is otherwise bordered by tropical vegetation. Inside the villa is a large bedroom with television, CD player, and a writing desk adjoining the lavish bathroom/dressing room complex, which is similar to those in the main hotel except a bit larger with an outdoor shower.

The two-bedroom villas include an additional bedroom with twin beds, as well as its own private terraced deck and bathroom. The Royal Sayan Villa is positioned in the most desirable location with stunning views of the surrounding landscape and the river valley. Upstairs are two bedrooms and a lounge area and downstairs is the location of the master bedroom, elegant dining room and living room. The spectacular 470 square-foot plunge pool is surrounded by lush gardens. The decor includes a rare collection of treasured Indonesian artwork.

Meeting facilities include a conference room with a connecting patio that can accommodate 16 for a boardroom set up and 30 for banquet seating.

Restaurants, Lounges, and Entertainment

Although most luxury resorts offer 24-hour room service not frequently utilized at dinner time, Four Seasons Resort at Sayan, Bali is atypical in that many guests elect to avail themselves of this opportunity in order to enjoy the especially romantic environment and panoramic views from their accommodations, which include the sounds of birds and the rushing Ayung River.

The main, three-meal-a-day restaurant, Ayung Terrace, offers an imaginative conglomerate of pan-Asian and Indonesian specialties and delectable breads and dessert preparations, both in the dining room and on an adjoining terrace which enjoys 180-degree, breathtaking views of the valley and river gorge. We found the quality of the cuisine exceptional during our last visit. There is also a small interior dining room that seats eight people.

Above the Ayung Terrace, enjoying the same spectacular views, and adjacent to the lobby is the Jati Bar and Lounge featuring afternoon tea, and cocktails during the evening until midnight. A Rindik trio plays from 5:00 p.m. and 7:00 p.m.

Lunch, snacks and an early dinner are served at the Riverside Café, a casual, open-air restaurant shaded by an Alang-Alang thatched roof and umbrellas, situated immediately above the kidney-shaped pool and Ayung River. Salads, sandwiches, char-grilled meats and fish, as well as pizzas hot from the wood-burning oven are featured.

Alternative, heart-healthy-low fat cuisine is offered on all menus.

Sport Facilities

The very attractive health spa includes an exercise facility looking out over the valley stocked with free-weights, cardiovascular and exercise machines, CDs, three soaking-pools at various temperatures, four treatment rooms with their own sinks, cabinets and bathtubs (one with two beds for a double massage), a beauty treatment salon, and luxurious men's and women's locker rooms with saunas, steam and showers. One tennis court will be added in the future and hiking expeditions, river rafting, kayaking, nature walks, and cycling through the Ayung River valley can be arranged.

Ideally positioned beside the river is a large infinity-edge, kidney shaped swimming pool surrounded by lounge chairs and immediately below the Riverside Café. Those wishing to enjoy a beach environment can arrange to spend the day at Four Seasons' sister resort at Jimbaran Bay.

Miscellaneous and Environs

The property is located 22 miles north/northeast of the International Airport in Denpasar; however, allow yourself an hour of traveling time. Chauffeur service is available and cars can be rented with an international driver's license. The hour ride between Four Seasons Jimbaran Bay and Sayan is complimentary for guests transferring from one resort to the other. Most major airlines servicing Asia fly into Denpasar, as well as to Jakarta.

There is a small shop off the lobby and at the spa visitors will want to devote at least half-a-day ex-

ploring the quaint artist community at nearby Ubud, where they will find excellent art and craft galleries, as well as boutiques and antiques.

Many guests who visit Bali prefer to divide their visit between Sayan and the Four Seasons property at Jimbaran Bay, where they can enjoy a tropical beach-front environment with expanded facilities in equally luxurious accommodations.

The combination of modern, exquisitely comfortable facilities with a Balinese flavor, the overwhelmingly lush, verdant tropical jungle setting, together with Four Seasons commitment to fine dining and service cannot miss putting this resort on every knowledgeable travelers "top ten" list.

Four Seasons at Sayan
Sayan, Ubud,
Gianyar, Bali 80571, Indonesia
Tel. 62-361-977-577
Fax 62-361-977-588
www.fourseasons.com/sayan

THE RITZ-CARLTON, BALI RESORT AND SPA

The Ritz-Carlton management professionals opened their first Asian resort in late 1996 on 190 acres of richly vegetated bluff overlooking the Indian Ocean in Jimbaran, Bali, Indonesia. The 290-room, four-story, double-wing hotel building flanked by 48 thatched-roof private villas, enclosed with volcanic rock and limestone walls with private plunge pools is set in the midst of lavish gardens filled with palms, hibiscus, frangipani, lantana, crotons, plumeria, and monkey pod plants, as well a lily ponds stocked with Koi fish, Indonesian statuary and lush vegetation. Marble stairs and paths with spouting fountains and waterfalls cascade from the elegant open-air lobby down a cliff to the infinity-edge pool complex and ocean.

Breaking from its traditional furnishings and standard Ritz-Carlton logo carpeted hallways, The Ritz-Carlton, Bali Resort and Spa has gone Balinese with Indonesian inspired furnishings, artifacts, antiques, limestone carvings and marble flooring throughout the public areas and guest accommodations with most public areas opened and looking out to the panoramic landscape and breathtaking sunsets.

But, make no mistake, this is still 100 percent Ritz-Carlton, exuding casual elegance and boasting possibly the most friendly, gracious, and efficient service staff to be found in Indonesia. The international clientele is a mixture of Japanese, North American, European and Southeast Asian with an abundance of honeymooners taking advantage of this romantic property.

Accommodations

Two hundred ninety air-conditioned Balinese-design-influenced guest rooms and suites, each with a generous-sized balcony looking out to the ocean, are spread over two four-story wings connected by protected walkways. Forty-seven of these accommodations are on the Ritz-Carlton Club Floor where, for an additional $60 per night, guests enjoy club privileges, including five daily meal presentations, concierge services, a free Balinese massage, a round of golf on the 18-hole putting course and numerous other extras. In addition, the resort offers 84 one-bedroom (3,200 square foot), two-bedroom (4,300 square foot), and three-bedroom villas, all boasting three-sided panoramic windows to the sea. All villas feature oversized, private plunge pools. Each villa includes a courtyard, separate parlor with additional television and CD player, elegant Indonesian-style bedrooms with canopy-four-poster beds, vaulted ceilings with ceiling fans, panoramic outdoor gazebos for massage, dining or just watching sunsets, ultra-posh marble bathrooms with an outdoor garden shower, a lily pond and many other amenities.

All of the non-villa, non-suite, oversized accommodations are identical, except for views; and all feature marble floors, private safes, ceiling fans, remote-control cable televisions, stocked mini-bars, light-weight cotton robes, umbrellas and lovely marble bathrooms with separate glassed-in shower stalls, tubs, toilet compartments with extension phones, hair dryers, magnifying mirrors, and numerous up-scale amenities.

Although rack rates for other accommodations range in price from $275 to $2,400 per night, the resort offers numerous attractive packages throughout the year ranging from $165 to the $1,050 "Bali Blue Sky", and there is no charge for children 12 and under.

The 6,404-square-foot ballroom provides meeting and banquet space for groups up to 500 and can be divided into three breakout rooms with very attractive outdoor function space. Theme parties are offered frequently in the outdoor gardens.

Restaurants, Lounges, and Entertainment

In addition to around-the-clock room service in your guest room or on your balcony, the resort offers numerous other dining opportunities, including specially-orchestrated, romantic diners on the Balinese-designed wedding gazebo at the edge of a cliff or on your own private bungalow.

Padi, an open-air pavilion restaurant that appears to float in lily ponds, serves breakfast in the mornings and authentic Thai cuisine for dinner. Near the pool is Sami Sami, a casual cliff-side restaurant and bar with three separate dining pavilions open for lunch and dinner, featuring Italian cuisine.

For a different experience, the sand-floor Kisik Bar, half-way down to the beach, set on a cliff overlooking the ocean, offers beverages and freshly grilled seafood on banana leaves.

The spot for afternoon tea, before-dinner cocktails, and hors d'oeuvres while watching the sunset, as well as after-dinner libations is the open-air Damar Terrace, surrounded by ponds and romantically illuminated by candlelight.

Bands and singers perform nightly in the gardens near the restaurants.

The intimate Martini Club is located in the Cliff Villa Complex overlooking open terraces and the Indian Ocean. Featured here are 35 classic and contemporary Martini selections, ideal for pre- or after-dinner relaxation.

C-Bar, an outdoor lounge with music serves exotic drinks and Oriental inspired fare from lunch to sunset and beyond.

Dava, with a contemporary and sleek design resembling a Lotus flower, with white marble floors and a unique slate stone dragon-skin wall serves up modern European cuisine at dinner time.

Refreshing beverages and an all-day menu of snacks and café cuisine is available at H²O, a café on the Cliff Villa poolside deck.

Sport Facilities

In the center of this resort complex is an imaginative, two-level outdoor pool, adorned with limestone statuary, where the upper level with its infinity edge spills over to the lower level with a waterfall effect. Adjacent to the lower level is an aquarium filled with colorful tropical fish and several children's pools that feature a 30-meter water slide that twists around floral gardens. Comfortable lounges and umbrellas encircle both pools; and the super-attentive staff provides towels, cold cloths, drinks, and water-spritz to enhance guest comfort. Also adjoining the upper-level pool are whirlpools and semi-open-air massage areas.

On premises is an 18-hole putting golf course, three lighted tennis courts, bicycles, table tennis, and a newly expanded, highly regarded, air-conditioned spa facility that includes an aerobic room, cardiovascular machines, free weights, sauna, steam, a locker-shower area, and sumptuous indoor/outdoor massage and body treatment rooms, villas and suites.

A "Ritz-Kids" program is available for families traveling with children, as well as a fully stocked, supervised playroom.

The beach at the bottom of the steep hill beneath the resort is not recommended for swimming. The resort provides regular transportation to Kubu beach, a three-minute drive away. After descending 184 steep steps (I counted them) guest are treated to a rather pristine beach with warm waters and mild surf, as well as friendly beach attendants to provide towels and drinks and arrange transporta-

tion back to the hotel. Taking along a picnic lunch (provided by the resort) is recommended. This venture is definitely limited to those who are physically fit and do not suffer from acrophobia.

Serious golfers can be transported to the golf course in the Nusa Dua area.

Miscellaneous and Environs

Seven small shops at the property offer boutique-signature merchandise, Balinese art, jewelry and sundries.

Visitors flying into the International Airport at Denpasar, a 15-minute ride away, can arrange transportation with the resort or can take an inexpensive taxi ride.

Bali offers an abundance of cultural excursions to artist villages, cultural dance performances and local temples, which are described in other chapters.

In addition to its lavish floral gardens, unique Indonesian influenced designs, imaginative pool complex, excellent dining venues, comfortable accommodations (including especially romantic villas), the element that most sets this resort apart from the competition is its unparalleled level of friendly, efficient Ritz-Carlton-style service.

Travelers to the unique island paradise who seek the ultimate in comfort, beauty, and service will be highly rewarded at The Ritz-Carlton, Bali Resort and Spa.

The Ritz-Carlton, Bali Resort and Spa
Jalan Karang Mas Sejahtera
Jimbaran, Bali 80364, Indonesia
Tel. 62 (0)-361-702-222
Fax 62 (0)-361-702-455
www.Ritz-Carlton.com/resorts/bali

MALAYSIA

SHANGRI-LA'S TANJUNG ARU RESORT

This luxury resort spreads over 25 acres of choice coastal property in a bay off the South China Sea on the northern coast of Borneo. The southern portion of Borneo, Kalimantan, is Indonesian, whereas the northwestern section is divided up between the Malaysian states of Sabah and Sarawak and the independent sultanate of Brunei. Kota Kinabalu is the capital city of Sabah, and the resort is located within a few minutes of the Kota Kinabalu International Airport, and only 10 minutes from the center of the city.

Operated by Shangri-La Hotels and Resorts, the Tanjung Aru Resort represents one of the few luxury resorts to be found on Borneo. The semi-open-air lobby and the other public rooms are tastefully decorated creating an informal Malaysian atmosphere. The outside grounds are lush with plants and flowers, creating an ideal tropical setting. This is a most romantic location, ideal for those who appreciate enchanting sunsets and virgin beaches on small uninhabited islands with crystal-clear, warm water.

Accommodations

All of the 500 guest rooms and suites have balconies, most of which overlook the sea and the lovely islets that dot the bay, providing a unique pristine refuge for swimmers and snorkelers.

The Kinabalu Wing, which was completed in late 1993, contains 223 guest rooms and 19 suites. The rooms and suites on the sixth floor are designated Horizon floor rooms and receive special services and amenities for an extra cost. Each room has a built-in refrigerator stocked with soft drinks and

liquors, direct-dial telephones, writing desks, sitting areas, hair dryers, multi-channel piped-in music, and satellite television with a variety of in-house video movies. The deluxe suites are particularly desirable; offering spacious bedrooms with four-poster canopied king-size beds, a separate living room, dining room, marble bathroom/wardrobe with private toilet compartments and Jacuzzi bath, and a magnificent stretch of balcony especially designed for watching sunsets and star gazing. Children under 12 can stay in the room with their parents free of charge, and there are baby-sitting facilities and daily children's activities.

The four-storied Tanjung Wing, resembling a starfish, surrounds a lush tropical garden overlooking the beach and nearby islands. All of the rooms and suites are luxuriously decorated and include down-feathered duvets and pillows, hand-tufted rugs and carpets and feature high speed internet access and built-in data ports.

There are conference facilities for up to 900 guests in a grand ballroom and several smaller meeting rooms. Those celebrating an anniversary or honeymoon should opt for one of the deluxe suites.

Restaurants, Lounges, and Entertainment

Café TA TU located on the ground floor of the Main Lobby with floor to ceiling windows also has outdoor seating. The restaurant features a wide variety of live cooking stations, a luxurious buffet spread, efficient service and is open from 6:00 a.m. to 11:00 p.m.

The Shang Palace at the Kinabalu wing serves authentic Chinese dishes.

The elegant Peppino Restaurant, with its unique artwork, serves an impressive selection of authentic Italian fare for dinner throughout the week.

The singing groups that play at cocktail hour, in the various restaurants at dinner, and in the lounges in the evening are exceptional. The Borneo Lounge and Bar overlooking the landscaped gardens and South China Sea, is a delightful venue to relax and enjoy drinks and light snacks while listening to a live band. The Sunset Bar is an ideal spot to watch the sunset over the sea.

Blue Note features a live band for dancing, as well as a cozy lounge section.

Pulau Bayu, which sits on the edge of the beach surrounded by the sea, serves typical Malaysian fare from 6:00 p.m. until 10:00 p.m. daily. This is another great spot to watch the sun set and have cocktails. A cultural performance and Sabahan buffet are featured on Saturday evening.

Sport Facilities

The 150-meter beach in front of the resort is delightful for swimming, and there is a three-mile expanse of not-very-attractive beach to the left of the resort that is suitable for jogging. The resort offers sailing, windsurfing, boating, water-skiing, scuba diving and deep-sea fishing. The two large free-surface tension swimming pools, whirlpool, and children's pool complex are well suited for casual lounging and swimming. Drinks, snacks and ice cream can be ordered right at the pool.

In my opinion, an outstanding experience is a boat ride to one of the numerous uninhabited tropical islets that sit out in the bay and are available by shuttle service from the hotel. All the islets offer an opportunity to walk barefoot on pristine white sandy beaches and swim and snorkel in clear, warm waters with coral reefs and tropical fish. The closest is Mamutik, where there are picnic and changing facilities, a small beach and clear, deep waters. The smallest, Sulug, has shallow waters with a gradual drop off, and it is the most secluded. Gaya is the largest and the location of Police Bay. Manukan, though not as beautiful as the others, offers the best

snorkeling and was chosen by the government to be developed with full facilities, a restaurant, swimming pool, and tennis court. Probably the best all-around choice is Sapi, which has toilets, changing facilities, a lovely beach, and warm waters with a gradual drop-off. It is the site, along with Gaya and Mamutik, used by the resort for picnics and parties. My only comparable experience was exploring the Yasawa group of islands near Fiji.

There are four tennis courts and a fitness center offering exercise equipment, sauna, steam baths, Jacuzzis, and massage. Guests have access to a 9-hole golf course near the resort, as well as an 18-hole golf course six miles away. There is a 9-hole pitch-and-putt practice course in the gardens on the property.

Miscellaneous and Environs

The resort will help you arrange tours to Kinabalu National Park, where you will find Southeast Asia's highest peak, Mt. Kinabalu, towering 4,001 meters above the lush tropical jungles of North Borneo; to the sulphur baths at Poring Springs, an area complete with rain forests, waterfalls, and caves; to the orangutan sanctuary at Sepilok near Sandakan; and to the turtle sanctuary at Selingan.

In Kota Kinabalu, you can visit the gold-domed state mosque, an example of contemporary Islamic architecture, and drive out to Tuaran Village, where the locals live in houses on stilts suspended above the water.

Sabah can be reached by air and is a two-hour flight from Singapore and Kuala Lumpur, two and a half hours from Hong Kong, and five hours from Tokyo.

Shangri-La's Tanjung Aru Resort is a modern tropical resort in an area of the world seldom visited by Western tourists. Those wise enough to make the adventure will be rewarded with pristine white sand, clear water islets, comfortable accommodations, beautiful surroundings, good food, attentive service and an opportunity to explore Sabah and other parts of Borneo.

Shangri-La has also recently opened the Rasa Ria Resort, set on Pantai Dalit Beach and surrounded

by 400 acres of lush tropical vegetation and nature preserve, featuring a wide range of water sports, an 18-hole golf course, tennis, horseback riding, a fitness center and a Kid's Club. We have yet to review the resort, but look forward to doing so for our next edition.

Shangri-La's Tanjung Aru Resort
Locked Bag 174
88744 Kota Kinabalu, Sabah, Malaysia
Tel. (6088) 225800, (6088) 241800
Fax (6088) 217155
Web: www.shangri-la.com

SHANGRI-LA HOTEL, SINGAPORE

Since the Shangri-La Hotel, Singapore opened its doors in 1971, it has been on everyone's "top Hotels of the World" list, including businessmen, bankers, travel agents and tourists. Unlike the other luxury Singapore hotels, the Shangri-La Hotel, Singapore is located away from both the commercial section and bustling Orchard Road, on 15 acres of choice private real estate accented with tropical gardens, foliage, pools, streams, waterfalls, and the fragrance of gardenias and jasmine. Yet, with all of its seclusive splendor, guests are only a 10-minute walk from the center of Singapore, which is undoubtedly the cleanest, most modern and most beautiful city in Southeast Asia.

The city resort-hotel is owned by a publicly traded corporation, listed on the Hong Kong stock exchange, with Malaysian and Singapore businessmen as the major stockholders. The corporation also owns the Shangri-La Hotel, Bangkok, the Shangri-La Hotel, Kuala Lumpur in Malaysia, the Rasa Sayang and Golden Sands resorts in Penang, the Tanjung Aru in Borneo and the Fijian Resort, as well as other hotels in this part of the world.

Shangri-La Hotel, Singapore is composed of three wings connected by protected walkways that surround floral gardens, the pool area, putting greens, tropical waterfalls, and Koi fishponds. The main lobby is vast with elegant appointments, artwork, and a lobby lounge. Frequent renovations over the years have kept this hotel/resort complex a step above the competition. Just when you think the decor and amenities in the rooms and the service throughout cannot get any better, it does.

Accommodations

The original Tower Wing, built in 1971, is 24 stories high with 458 frequently refurbished rooms and suites. The 9-story Garden Wing, built in 1978 and elegantly refurbished in 2000, has 148 rooms and 13 suites, all with rounded balconies covered with bougainvillea. The rooms in both of these wings include refrigerators, mini-bars, coffee- and tea-making facilities, iron and ironing boards, four-channel radios, televisions with a high-speed Internet connection via a wireless keyboard and CNN news, private safes, scales, alarm clocks, hair dryers, telephones in the bathroom, terry-cloth robes and kimonos, a morning newspaper, fruit basket, slippers and umbrellas for use while at the hotel.

The exclusive 17-story Valley Wing with private entrance and driveway, completed in 1985 and extensively refurbished in 2003, offers the most spacious and elegant accommodations. The 105 rooms and 26 luxury suites have all amenities found in the other two wings, plus a blend of Asian/ European-style furnishings in pastel colors, giant marble bathrooms with double vanities and separate shower stalls and baths, fresh flowers, and a complimentary full breakfast, cocktails, snacks, Champagne, wines and other beverages throughout the day. Although the rooms in the Valley Wing cost about $140 more than those in the Tower and $75 more than those in the Garden Wing, they may be well worth the extra tariff. All in all, there are some 750 guest rooms and suites. The magnificent Shangri-La suite goes for $3,300 a night and includes three bedrooms, a living room, dining room, a private gym, parlor, numerous bathrooms, and exquisite furnishings and artwork.

The 17th through 23rd floors of the Tower Wing were converted to the exclusive Horizon Club with its special club lounge featuring drinks, snacks, concierge, meeting facilities and other amenities.

There are approximately 23 meeting rooms and 2 ballrooms that can accommodate from 10 to 1,500 people. Audiovisual equipment and six-channel simultaneous interpretation systems are available. The 16,000-square-foot grand ballroom seats 1,300 for banquets and 1,500 theater-style. These facilities, together with the fine service and numerous restaurants and bars, make this an excellent choice for a Southeast Asian convention or corporate meetings of various sizes.

Restaurants, Lounges, and Entertainment

The Shangri-La Hotel, Singapore features a diverse choice of restaurants of exceptional quality geared to satisfy all levels of epicurean taste. The Line boasts individual open-concept kitchens that treat diners to the theatrics of food preparation "a la minute." The diverse selection of cuisine is offered in 16 different culinary styles throughout the day and evening. It is possible to order from this restaurant while sitting by the pool or terrace.

There are three excellent specialty restaurants available for lunch and dinner. Shang Palace serves up numerous Cantonese dishes in an authentic Chinese setting. Nadaman Japanese Restaurant, considered one of the top Japanese establishments outside of Japan, offers tatami rooms, sushi and tempura bars, teppan yaki grills, and à la carte dining. Afternoon tea is served each afternoon at the Rose Veranda.

Located on the twenty-fourth floor, with panoramic views of Singapore, is Blu Bar and Restaurant, featuring outstanding, California-style cuisine, specialty wines by the glass or bottle and live jazz entertainment.

Sport Facilities

In the lush garden, which is surrounded by the three wings of the hotel, there is a large, free-form swimming pool, as well as a children's wading pool and heated Jacuzzi. Behind the pool is a three-hole pitch & putt course and four all-weather illuminated tennis courts.

At the refurbished Fitness Center located at the Tower Wing lower lobby, you will find a well-organized, expertly staffed spa offering a variety of massage treatments, state-of-the-art exercise and cardiovascular equipment with entertainment systems, sauna, steam, hydropool and a luxurious locker and lounge area.

Miscellaneous and Environs

The resort is only a few minutes away from the numerous shopping complexes, restaurants and hotels of Orchard Road. On the premises, guests will find women's and men's hairdressers, sundry shops and several stores.

The beautiful Singapore Airport is only 20 miles away. Adjacent to the hotel is the 127-unit Shangri-La Apartments and a 550-car parking lot.

The Island of Singapore is situated at the southern tip of the Malay Peninsula, only 85 miles north of the equator, so it has a warm, tropical climate that generally varies from the mid-80s during the day to the mid-70s at night. Having been a British Colony for 140 years, it gained its independence in 1959. Its population of three million is mostly Chinese with a mixture of Malay, Eurasian, English, Indian and Pakistani thrown in. Most citizens speak some English, and you will find this the cleanest, most modern country in Southeast Asia.

Sightseers may wish to take in the magnificent botanical gardens (a good choice for walking and jogging), the Zoological Gardens and Night Safari Park, the Singapore History Museum, the Asian Civilization Museum, the Golden Hindu Temple, The Haw Paw Villa, China Town, The House of Jade, the food stalls in the street markets, the numerous shopping centers, the Jurong Bird Park, the cable-car ride from Mt. Faber to Sentosa Island, and the harbor cruise from Clifford Pier.

Shangri-La's Rasa Sentosa Resort

In March of 1993, the Shangri-La Hotels and Resorts group opened its second Singapore property on lovely Siloso Beach at the western tip of tropical Sentosa Island, which lies across from Singapore's World Trade Center and can be reached by a five-minute bus or panoramic cable-car ride. The main hotel building rises 11 stories in a semi-circle above imaginative free-form swimming pools and lush gardens leading to a white-sand, palm-studded beach with a protective cove lapped by calm, warm sea.

This is an upscale, yet very casual beach resort ideal for couples and business groups. It is also good for families traveling with children through Asia who wish to spend a few days or a week in a resort with a tropical setting and a full complement of facilities, proximate to the numerous family attractions found on Sentosa Island. These attractions include, Underwater World, a wax museum, Volcanoland, a multi-sensory exhibition in an ancient Mayan setting highlighted by a volcanic eruption, Fountain Gardens, featuring local plants and flowers with integrated color, light and music performances, typical Asian food stalls, bicycle paths running through tropical forests and nature parks, two golf courses, and several miles of white-sand reclaimed beach.

Two-thirds of the 459 air-conditioned guest rooms at Shangri-La's Rasa Sentosa Resort face the South China Sea, while the remaining rooms overlook the lush hills of Fort Siloso, and all have balconies. All have many amenities, including refrigerators, mini-bars, electronic room safes, remote-controlled color televisions with in-room movies, international direct-dial telephones, hair dryers, coffee- and tea-making facilities and tasteful furnishings. However, the rooms are a bit smaller and less elaborate than those at the Shangri-La Hotel, Singapore There are fewer dining options and overall it is a more casual, first class rather than deluxe experience. Regular, free shuttle service is offered between the two Shangri-La properties. Those seeking out a clean, modern, tropical atmosphere during their exploration of the Far East will want to include Singapore in their itineraries. Visitors to Singapore seeking the very best in accommodations, food, service and quiet elegance will prefer the Shangri-La Hotel, Singapore, while those who prefer a relaxing resort getaway will enjoy Shangri-La's Rasa Sentosa Resort.

Shangri-La Hotel
22 Orange Grove Road, Singapore 258350
Tel. (65)6 737-3644, Fax (65)6 737-1029
In the United States: 212-382-3155
E-mail: sls@shangri-la.com
Web: www.shangri-la.com

Rasa Sentosa Resort
101 Siloso Road
Sentosa, Singapore 098970
Tel. (65)6 275-0100, Fax (65)6 275-0355

TAHITI
(FRENCH POLYNESIA)

BORA BORA
LAGOON RESORT

In 1993, a Japanese entrepreneur constructed this $50-million dream resort on 16 acres of lushly vegetated property, bordered by white-sand beaches, on the northeast tip of Motu Toopua, a small islet (Motu) within the Bora Bora Lagoon in French Polynesia. The 50 over-water and 27 beach and garden bungalows built in the midst of lovely tropical gardens and towering palms look out across the lagoon to the verdant peaks of Bora Bora.

The resort's private launch meets guests as they arrive at the Bora Bora airport, and whisks them to this idyllic haven cooled by tradewinds and boasting one of the world's most romantic settings for sunsets and star gazing.

The central building, which houses the lobby, main restaurant, lounges and shop, is decorated with dark wicker, pastels and local art, and emanates a fresh, clean modern feel, superior to other resorts in this part of the world.

All of this pristine beauty does not come cheap, and the blend of North American, South American, European and Asian clientele can look forward to paying from $475 to $900 per night per couple for lodging, beverages and meals.

In 1997, the world-renowned Orient-Express Hotels took over management and in 2001 it acquired ownership, followed by numerous renovations. Orient-Express Hotels also manages Hotel Cipriani in Venice, Splendido in Portofino, and La Samanna in St. Martin.

Accommodations

The 77 bungalows (50 over water and 27 garden and beach), which include two beach suites with private pools and three connecting family bungalows, are arranged into three villages. Each roomy accommodation is at least 450 square feet, built in Fara (Tahitian Villa) style with pandanus roof, bamboo walls, polished yucca wood floors and sliding glass doors that open to private terraces. Other features include king or twin beds, writing desks, baths with separate showers and toilet compartments, mini-bars, private safes, hair dryers, tea and coffee makers, DVD players and daily laundry service.

All bungalows are air conditioned and the floor-to-ceiling louvered doors and windows permit cross-ventilation from the refreshing tradewinds. Additional circulation by the ceiling fans help to keep the rooms comfortable.

The over-water bungalows include glass coffee tables placed directly over an opening to the sea below, so guests can view and feed the colorful tropical fish.

The sunset bungalows are especially desirable because they afford stunning views of the sunset over tiny Motu Topu to the west, one of the most photographed tropical islets in the South Pacific.

Restaurants, Lounges, and Entertainment

A breakfast buffet and dinner are served in the main Otemanu restaurant, which hovers over the lagoon in a terraced design with open-air and protected areas for dining. At dinner, French-trained chefs prepare a variety of international and local cuisines.

Special theme evenings and native feasts accompanied by local entertainment are featured each week.

Lunch and dinner (from April to October) are available at Café Fare by the pool. Breakfasts (which are included in the room rate) include freshly baked pastries and croissants, fresh fruits and juices and a variety of more hearty fare. For lunch guests can enjoy grilled and barbecued fish, fowl and meats, as well as sandwiches, pizza and salads.

A guitarist-singer performs between 6:00 p.m. and 10:00 p.m. at the main lounge. Tahitian dance groups appear frequently. Billiards, Ping-Pong and darts are available at the game bungalow.

Food and beverages are imported from around the world, and are therefore quite expensive. Guests have the option to select a MAP arrangement for $55 (per person per night) or FAP for $80. Seven percent local tax is added to rooms only.

Sport Facilities

The quarter-mile of white-sand beaches are inviting; however, the clear, warm waters of the lagoon are not very deep and are better for snorkeling than serious swimming.

The resort provides snorkel and scuba equipment, windsurfers, outrigger canoes and other non-motorized water sports free of charge. For varying tariffs, deep-sea fishing, jet skis, horse riding, car and bike rental, scuba diving, sailing, para-sailing, glass-bottom boat tours, shark feeding, and cocktail, half-day and dinner moonlight cruises are also available, as is a picnic on a private motu.

In the middle of the property is an attractive free-form pool and an outdoor Jacuzzi.

In the spring of 2004, the Maru Spa opened with six treatment rooms set either waterfront or 12 feet above ground in the branches of two 40-foot Caoutchouc trees, offering a variety of massages, aromatherapy, scrubs, and beauty treatments.

Two tennis courts and a small gym with, aerobic machines, Nautilus and free weights round off the sport facilities. Jogging, bicycle and hiking paths may be added in the future.

Miscellaneous and Environs

Visitors fly into Papeete, Tahiti, from cities around the world, transfer to an inter-island 45-minute flight to Bora Bora, and are then met at the airport by the resort's private craft and transported across the lagoon to the dock in front of the main building.

On premises are a gift-sundry shop and a local crafts display.

Bora Bora Lagoon Resort is one of those casual yet elegant, low-key, get-away-from-it-all escapes from civilization, ideal for well-heeled honeymooners and in-love couples who seek comfortable tranquility, exotic views and outstanding sunsets. This is one of the top romantic resort destinations in the South Pacific.

Bora Bora Lagoon Resort
Motu Toopua, B.P. 175 Vaitape
Bora Bora, French Polynesia
Tel. (689) 604000/ 800-830-2409, Fax (689) 604001
United States Orient-Express Hotels
Tel. (800) 237-1236
within New York (212) 838-3110
E-mail: bblr@mail.pf
California: 16130 Ventura Blvd. Ste. 230
Encino, CA 91436
Tel. 818-379-2255, Fax. 818379-2259
E-mail: Sales@bblr.net

TAHITI
(FRENCH POLYNESIA)

BORA BORA PEARL BEACH RESORT

Situated on Motu Tevairoa, a 10-minute boat ride from Bora Bora airport and a 15-minute boat ride from Vaitape (Bora Bora's main town), looking out at azure blue waters and the verdant mountain tops of Bora Bora is the lovely Bora Bora Pearl Beach Resort. Operated by South Pacific management, this $20-million property opened in 1998 offering spacious over-water bungalows, as well as beach and garden-pool suites. The grounds are covered with beautiful tropical flowers and plants, and the restaurant, bar and common areas all enjoy magnificent vistas. All of the accommodations and structures, though typical Polynesian designs, have a more modern, fresher feel than many of the resort's competitors. In addition, Motu Tevairoa offers walking trails and numerous options for snorkeling.

Accommodations

All the bungalows are air conditioned and feature mini-bars, tea and coffee making facilities, DVD and CD players, LCD TVs, direct dial telephones, iron and ironing boards, safe deposit boxes, slippers, robes, hair dryers and magnifying mirrors.

For $750 to $850 per night, a couple can enjoy one of the 658-square-foot, over-water bungalows, each of which includes a king-size bed, a couch that can accommodate a third guest, a direct-dial telephone, a private safe, an overhead fan, a glass coffee table that slides open to permit you to feed the fish, spacious bathrooms with soaking tubs, separate shower and toilet compartments, glass vanities that look down to the lagoons, hair dryers, and robes, coffee/tea makers, and outdoor lanais

with open and sheltered areas, showers and ladders leading down to the lagoon.

The 20 garden-pool suites (at $580 per night) are very secluded and private with small plunge pools, gardens and sundecks. The 10 beach suites (at $750 per night) include outdoor gardens with heated Jacuzzis and indoor/outdoor bathrooms. At 786 square feet, these are the largest and most comfortable of the three options. All of the suites can accommodate families.

Restaurants, Lounges, and Entertainment

The main Tevairoa Restaurant overlooks the lagoon and offers breakfast and dinner featuring excellent international cuisine and several theme nights with cultural shows. Lunch is served by the pool at Miki Miki and guests can enjoy magnificent sunsets at the Taurearea Bar. Modified American Plan runs $85 per person and Full American Plan, $115. Continental breakfasts will set you back $23 and a full American breakfast, $25.

Sport Facilities

The Bora Bora Pearl Beach Resort offers a large range of complimentary activities, including a 5,220-foot free-form swimming pool with a small waterfall and two outdoor Jacuzzis, a floodlit tennis court, billiards, table tennis, badminton, miniature golf, a bacci ball court, kayaks, canoes and windsurfs. The resort also offers a PADI and CMAS diving center, catamarans for romantic cruises and an educational coral garden tour. Other activities such as jet skis,

snorkeling, deep-sea fishing, shark and ray feeding, parasailing can be arranged by the hotel's activity desk. Those in over-water bungalows can climb down their ladders to the clear, blue lagoon and walk for quite a distance toward the main island of Bora Bora, meander around the other bungalows and bridges or walk up to the main beach. Most of the water is about waist high and the sandy bottom is virtually free of stones and rocks.

In the spring of 2006 the 600 square-meter Manea Spa opened offering a large range of traditional Tahitian massage and beauty treatments. One suite and two double massage rooms are designed to accommodate couples. Also located here are two steam rooms, two saunas, a zen fare, a relaxation pavilion and a fitness room.

Miscellaneous and Environs

There is a game room, one boutique offering handy crafts, beach wear and black pearls and a 25-seat movie theater. The resort provides transfers by private boat shuttle from the airport and back for $28 per person one way, as well as complimentary boat service to the main island of Bora Bora.

Bora Bora Pearl Resort is one of the newest and most modern resorts in the Bora Bora lagoon, with a variety of extremely comfortable accommodations, expanded facilities, excellent dining and picturesque views. Many find this one of the best choices in the Bora Bora lagoon.

Bora Bora Pearl Beach Resort
P.O. Box 169 98730 Vaitape
Bora Bora, French Polynesia
Tel. (689) 605-200 Fax (689) 605-222
www.pearlresorts.com
e-mail: relations.clients@BoraPearlBeach.PF

TAHITI
(FRENCH POLYNESIA)

HOTEL BORA BORA

The Hotel Bora Bora sits on a white-sand beach bordering the world's most beautiful, protected lagoon, with a backdrop of tropical flowers and green-clad mountains, 10 minutes from the small village of Vaitape. It is here, at this casually elegant South Seas resort, that you can witness the most breathtaking sights imaginable. Each evening, from the lanai of your private thatch-roofed bungalow, you can watch the sun as it slowly sinks behind small palm-laden islets into the blue lagoon, all the while illuminating the entire sky with streaks of bright orange, yellow, and purple.

Bora Bora is one of the small picturesque islands making up French Polynesia. The first white man to set foot on Bora Bora was Captain Cook in 1777. He was followed by English, Spanish, Dutch, and French explorers. Today, it is a French territory.

The hotel opened in 1961 with 18 thatched bungalows, a restaurant and a bar. Thirteen more bungalows were added in 1967, and the resort was enlarged again in 1972 and 1978. Ownership and management thereafter changed to Amanresorts, Ltd., which owns other prestigious properties throughout Southeast Asia, including Amanpuri and Amandari. Today, there are 54 luxurious garden, beach and over-water bungalows and suites, a central main building housing the restaurant, bar, boutique and offices, a sport complex and three lovely long white-sand beaches. The guest accommodations were all totally renovated, upgraded and enlarged in early 1994, and room capacity was reduced from 83 to 54. The atmosphere is casual and relaxed; coats and ties are never required. Most activities and sport facilities are complimentary; how-ever, the room tariffs and prices for food and beverages are very high. This is a casual, elegant resort for vacationers seeking sophisticated seclusion.

Accommodations

Each of the 54 air-conditioned, Polynesian-style individual bungalows and fares are nestled among tropical gardens, on the beach, or resting above the lagoon and include thatched pandanus roofs, overhead fans, four-poster, king-size beds with attractive mosquito netting in the villa-type bungalows and king-size beds in the other accommodations, wood plank floors, screened doors and windows permitting natural air ventilation without bugs, refrigerated mini-bars, private safes, coffee and tea makers, radio/CD players (bring you own CDs), large sitting areas, outdoor lounging porches, and bathroom-dressing rooms with free standing soaking tubs, shower stalls, toilet compartments, and hair dryers. There are no televisions. Times Fax (newsletters) are provided to guests daily.

Rates for bungalows start at $700 per night. Some are spread among tropical gardens, while others are located on the beachfront with patios facing the sea and nearby hammocks. Over-water bungalows go for $950 per night and sit over the shallow waters of the lagoon and have bi-level porches with showers and steps into the lagoon.

Fares (Tahitian Villas) at 1,200 square feet range in price from $850 to $950 per night and include both a full-size living room and smaller sitting room leading out to a large sundeck. The Fares in the gardens have pools, and/or Jacuzzi/pool combinations surrounded by rock garden walls for additional pri-

vacy. These are the most comfortable, luxurious accommodations.

There is quite a bit more wind on the left side of the property (as you face the beach) than on the right. Thus the bungalows on the windy side receive more ventilation; however, it also can be windy on the beaches and terraces. The beaches on the right side of the property receive far less wind and are more ideal for lounging.

The Raititi Lounge is the activities center for organizing and reserving excursions, as well as the library and the venue for tea time. There is no additional charge for children ages 2 through 11 years old who share a room with their parents.

Restaurants, Lounges, and Entertainment

All three meals are available through room service and are served in the Matira Terrace Restaurant. At lunch and dinner, sandwiches, salads and light fare are available at the beach bar. Once each week, there is a barbecue and native dance performance on the beach. Local musicians perform a few nights each week at the main bar. The restaurant-bar area, although frequently renovated, retains its original charming appearance.

Respectful, casual attire is acceptable at all times. The food is outstanding by South Sea standards and includes fresh bakery items and imaginative Continental, French, and Polynesian creations. Multi-course dinner menus offer a wide variety of mouth watering selections. MAP runs guests about $95 per day.

Sport Facilities

Guests can swim, sail, jet ski, snorkel and scuba in the waters surrounding the beach or take out their own outrigger canoe. In addition, the resort offers lei-making classes and snorkeling lessons, and will arrange para-sailing, water skiing, glass bottom boat trips, shark-feeding excursions, organized explorations of a barrier reef, horseback riding, helicopter excursions, deep-sea fishing, four wheel drive jeep safaris and private picnics on isolated island beaches. The sunset cocktail cruise on the resort's

50-foot Catamaran is a must for all guests and a photographer's dream.

There are two illuminated tennis courts at the sport complex, a volleyball court, and a half-basketball court. Joggers and bicyclists can follow the road for several miles into the town, Vaitape, or go for miles in the opposite direction, which is more picturesque, or they can take the 19-mile main road around the island. Motor scooters, Jeeps and standard cars can also be rented by those wishing to explore the island. Whatever your choice of transportation, a journey around the island will prove very rewarding.

Miscellaneous and Environs

Overseas flights land in Papeete, Tahiti, each day. After a 45-minute flight on a commuter airline to the airport at Bora Bora, the resort's private launch takes you across the lagoon to its property.

Bora Bora is one of the most beautiful tropical islands in the world. It boasts a mild climate – temperatures range from the mid-70s to the mid-80s – picturesque green-clad mountains, a blue lagoon dotted with tiny pristine islands, an unspoiled native environment and incredible sunsets. The wet season is from December to February and can extend into March, April and May, though it seldom rains all day.

The Hotel Bora Bora is situated perfectly on this lovely island, providing guests with very comfortable, luxurious accommodations, seclusion, fine dining and concerned service in a casual South Seas atmosphere.

Hotel Bora Bora
B.P. 1 Nunue 98730
Bora Bora, French Polynesia
Tel. (689) 60-44-60, Fax (689) 60-44-66
In the United States
Tel. (818) 587-9650, (800)477-9180
Fax (818) 710-0050

TAHITI (FRENCH POLYNESIA)

InterContinental Le Moana Resort Bora Bora

Set between two beautiful white-sand beaches at Point Matira on the main island of Bora Bora, a ten-minute drive from the small town of Vaitape, lies one of French Polynesia's most romantic, Tahitian-style resorts. Built in 1987 as the Moana Beach Park Royal, impressive renovations took place from 2000-2002 after the Intercontinental chain assumed management. Fifty spacious, junior-suite bungalows stretch out over the clear, aqua waters of the lagoon and 14 abut the white-sand beach. Two of the beach bungalows and two of the over-water bungalows linked by lounges are available as "full suites."

The central hotel complex is composed of a reception lobby, a rambling open air protected restaurant with an adjoining outside terrace, a bar and cocktail lounge, an activity/game room, a picturesque, two-tier swimming pool, a black pearl store and an all-purpose sundry shop and boutique, all of which are surrounded by tropical plants and floral gardens. Other than the beach, water sports, and excursions, the property offers no additional sport or recreational facilities.

Accommodations

The 50 junior-suites-size over-water bungalows are connected by bridges, and each has a bi-level terrace with a shower and ladder leading down into the clear turquoise waters of the lagoon, ideal for swimming and snorkeling. The 14 beach bungalows are located along the white sand beach, only a few steps from the water, and have the same features as the over-water units. All bungalows are air conditioned, have separate sitting rooms, bedrooms

and bathroom/dressing room areas with double vanities, tub/shower and toilet compartments, as well as private safes, refrigerated mini-bars, hair dryers, ceiling fans, coffee-tea makers, bathrobes, DVD players, CD players, direct dial phones with voice mail, iron and ironing boards and two televisions with CNN and movies in French and English. The coffee tables in the sitting areas of the over-water bungalows have removable glass tops permitting guests to feed the fish from inside the bungalow, creating their own private aquarium. As mentioned earlier, two of the over-water bungalows and two beach bungalows are connected by a lounge and can be offered as full suites.

Although rates vary from year to year, beach and over-water bungalows range in price between $500 and $880 per night. Food, beverages and activities are also quite expensive, as is the case all over French Polynesia.

Restaurants, Lounges, and Entertainment

All meals are served in the semi-open air Noa Noa Restaurant, or on the adjoining terrace. We found the dining experience in the evening quite excellent for Polynesia and this is certainly one of the best hotel restaurants in these islands. The gourmet cuisine included French and Continental fare with Polynesian accents. Several evenings each week the resort features either barbecue or seafood buffets with Tahitian entertainment.

In addition to the folkloric shows, there is music for listening nightly. Of course, there is room service and guests can elect to dine in their bungalows

around the clock. Snacks and drinks are also served on the beach. For $55 per person, romantics can have breakfast delivered to an over-water bungalow by outrigger canoe.

Sport Facilities

Water sports include jet skis, catamarans, outrigger canoes, Kayaks, snorkeling and water-skiing. Arrangements can be made for diving, sport, fly and deep-sea fishing, as well as sailboat excursions. The beach is ideal for swimming. Here the waters are clear, free of coral and rocks, yet filled with colorful tropical fish. The newly constructed two-tier swimming pool with a small waterfall overlooks the beach and the lower tier has a sandy bottom.

Bicycles and cars can be rented at the hotel.

Miscellaneous and Environs

There is a boutique-sundry shop located on premises. In Bora Bora, there is little shopping except for the occasional pareo, souvenir, black pearl or grocery stores that pop up along the main roads.

One of the best ways to explore Bora Bora is by bicycle along the scenic main roads that run around the perimeter of the island. On one side you have multi-hued lagoons, while on the other, colorful tropical plants, flowers and soaring verdant-green mountain peaks.

Air France, Air Tahiti Nui, Air New Zealand, and other international airlines fly into Papeete daily from diverse parts of the globe. From Papeete, Air Tahiti offers short propeller flights to the various islands. Arrival by air into Bora Bora is especially pleasant since the airport is located on a Motu and transportation to the resort is by motor launch across the lovely blue lagoon with the mountain peaks of Bora Bora in the distance.

A second Intercontinental Resort in Bora Bora is scheduled to open in 2006 with 80 overwater villas on a motu, to be named: InterContinental Resort & Thalasso Spa Bora Bora.

For many, the name Bora Bora conjures up dreams of a tropical paradise, with blue lagoons, white sand beaches, lush flora and lovely native girls dancing to the beat of drums. Although this may not be exactly what visitors find, Bora Bora is one of the most lush and beautiful islands in the world. Travelers to French Polynesia requiring comfortable and full-amenity accommodations, overwater bungalow options and idyllic settings will enjoy the Intercontinental Le Moana Resort Bora Bora which offers one of the best swimming beach and over-water bungalow complexes on the island, along with exceptional dining.

InterContinental Le Moana Resort Bora Bora
B.P. 156-98730 Bora Bora
French Polynesia
Tel. (689) 60-49-00
Fax (689) 60-49-99
borabora@interconti.com
www.borabora.interconti.com

TAHITI (FRENCH POLYNESIA)

INTERCONTINENTAL RESORT AND SPA MOOREA

InterContinental Resort and Spa Moorea (formerly Moorea Beachcomber Parkroyal), is advantageously situated on a mini-peninsula on the northwest tip of the island, where cool trade winds sweep through the bungalows that meander around turquoise lagoons, small sandy beaches, giant coconut palms, and tropical gardens with rising emerald green mountains as a backdrop. The semi-open-air Polynesian-style main building houses the reception area, tour desks, several shops, the resort's main bar and two restaurants which look out over a swimming pool to the lagoons. The overall setting is most impressive and picturesque.

Accommodations

Forty-eight air-conditioned, hotel-style rooms and one large suite are located in a two-story building adjacent to the main hotel, 44 beach and garden bungalows are scattered around the lagoons and floral gardens, and 50 over-water bungalows connected by bridges meander over the lagoon. All accommodations were recently renovated, upgraded, air conditioned and include a sitting area, remote control television with CNN, a refrigerated mini-bar, a private safe and bathrooms with double vanities, hair dryers, tubs, showers and separate toilet compartments. The hotel rooms and garden bungalows have twin beds convertible to queen-sized and all the over-water and beach bungalows have king sized beds.

Although rates vary from year to year, beach, garden and over-water bungalows range in price between $440 and $880 per night.

Restaurants, Lounges, and Entertainment

All three meals are served in the semi-open-air Fare Hana Restaurant overlooking the pool. Breakfast is also served buffet-style at the Fare Nui Restaurant, with scenic views over the lagoon and reef, and, over-water bungalow guests can arrange to have breakfast delivered by outrigger canoe. The theme of dinners at Fare Nui Restaurant vary throughout the week and are served buffet-style three times each week; and, several times each week, special Tahitian barbecue and fish feasts are featured here or on the beach along with local entertainment and dance groups.

Dining is quite expensive, as it is throughout French Polynesia. MAP and FAP are available, but do not result in any significant savings.

Sport Facilities

Water sports include jet skis, catamarans, outrigger canoes, Kayaks, wave runners, snorkeling and water-skiing. Arrangements can be made for diving, sport, fly and deep-sea fishing, para-sailing, as well as sailboat excursions and a sunset cruise. .

There is a heated swimming pool, a children's wading pool and a main beach at the resort, plus several additional small beaches on the lagoons. The aqua and turquoise waters are inviting but better for snorkeling than swimming, and it is best to wear snorkeling slippers because of the underwater coral and other sea life. The main aquatic attraction here is the exceptionally well supervised Dolphin Quest operation run by the same organization

as the original at Waikoloa Hilton on the big Island of Hawaii. Guests have the unique opportunity to pet, feed, and play with trained dolphins in the lagoons below the over-water bungalows.

The resort has recently started a sea turtle conservation program and has created a nursery and an outdoor care center specially adapted for sea turtles that is open to visitors.

There are two tennis courts and bicycles, motor scooters, standard cars and "Fun Cars" are available for rent.

The Helene Spa is quite unique, set in exotic gardens. Numerous massages and body treatments are available together with river showers, river baths, Jacuzzi and natural therapies based upon plants, flowers and fresh fruits. All of the treatments are also available for couples. Prices for one hour start at $250 per person.

Miscellaneous and Environs

There is an all purpose boutique/ sundry shop located at the resort, as well as a black pearl and jewelry store. On the remainder of the Island of Moorea there is little shopping except for the occasional pareo, souvenir, black pearl or grocery stores that pop up along the main roads.

One of the best ways to explore Moorea is by bicycle or Moped along the scenic main roads that run around the perimeter of the island. On one side you have multi-hued lagoons, while on the other, colorful tropical plants, flowers and soaring verdant-green mountain peaks.

Air France, Air Tahiti Nui, Air New Zealand, and other international airlines fly into Papeete daily from diverse parts of the globe. From Papeete, Air Tahiti and Air Moorea offer short propeller flights to the various islands. There is also a regular ferry service from Papeete. Inter-Continental Resort and Spa Moorea boasts the most expansive gardens, lagoons and tropical vegetation of any resort in all of Polynesia. Combined with its idyllic setting, comfortable accommodations, concerned service and numerous facilities, it offers the best resort experience in Moorea.

InterContinental Resort and Spa Moorea
P.O. Box 1019
Tiahura 98729, Moorea
French Polynesia
Tel. (689) 55-19-19
Fax (689) 55-19-55

TAHITI
(FRENCH POLYNESIA)

LE MERIDIEN
BORA BORA

In 1998, Le Meridien hotel chain opened one of Bora Bora's largest and most modern resorts on the southern tip of Piti Aau Motu, with 85 over-water bungalows connected to the motu by bridges and 15 beach bungalows looking out over a blue lagoon to the majestic peak of Mount Otemanu on the main island of Bora Bora. Accessible only by the resort's private launches, the resort boasts lovely white-sand beaches, protected lagoons for swimming and snorkeling, paths to explore, and expanded public areas. The clientele is a mixture of French, European, North American and Japanese. French reigns as the principal language; however, all of the staff speak English. A unique feature of the resort is the fact that it is a turtle sanctuary where turtles breed and swim free in the lagoon.

Accommodations

Each of the 82 air-condtioned over-water bungalows, furnished in hard woods with louvered doors and a thatched roof, includes a matrimonial bed that can convert to two singles, as well as a lounging couch that converts to a third bed when needed, an overhead fan, a glass floor looking down to the sea (covered at night to keep out the light) a makeup table, a walk-in closet with a dresser and private safe, a refrigerator/mini-bar, satellite television with BBC, HBO, and English and French movies, a coffee/tea maker, a direct-dial telephone, a spacious bathroom with double vanities, bathtub, shower stall, toilet compartment, hair dryer, bathrobes and slippers, and a patio with an outdoor shower and ladder that leads down to the lagoon.

The 15 air-conditioned beach bungalows are very similar except they do not have glass floors. In addition to the lounge chairs on the attached deck, there are two additional lounges right on the sandy beach.

Restaurants, Lounges, and Entertainment

Le Tipanie restaurant is opened for breakfast and dinner, overlooks the interior lagoon, and is well known for its French and local cuisine. One portion of the restaurant serves buffet style, while the other offers a gourmet a la carte menu. During the week, special buffets, barbecues and Polynesian shows are offered, as well as a special candlelight soiree. All three meals are served at Le Te Ava by the white-sand beach and swimming pool, and cocktails are offered at Le Miki Miki Bar, the place to watch the sunset over Mount Otemanu. Casual attire is acceptable at all restaurants. Modified American Plan is available for $78 per person and room service is offered around the clock.

Sport Facilities

The main attractions of the property are the lovely white-sand beaches and warm waters and protected lagoons for swimming and snorkeling. Guests in the beach bungalows can step right out on to the sandy beach and enjoy the clear, warm waters of a protected lagoon. Those in the over-water bungalows can descend ladders from their attached decks into the sea. The abundance of water sport possibilities both at the resort and arranged by the activ-

ities desk include snorkeling, windsurfing, kayaks, surf bikes, pedal boats, Hobie Cats, scuba diving, ray feeding, jet-skiing, deep-sea fishing, parasailing, water-skiing, and visits to a lagoonarium. Horseback riding, and helicopter rides can also be arranged. There is a wellness center offering various massage treatments. Unfortunately, there are no tennis courts or fitness center. nor spa facilities.

Miscellaneous and Environs

There is a sundry-souvenir shop and black pearl store at the resort. Launch service is provided to and from the airport (an approximately 20-minute ride). A five-minute shuttle takes guests to the hotel's pier on Bora Bora. From the pier it is an additional 20- to 30-minute taxi or bus ride to the main village of Vaitape. Most guests rent cars here. Internet connections are available near the activity desk and guests can send and retrieve e-mails for a small charge.

Le Meridien also opened a resort near Papeete, on the main island of Tahiti, composed of 158 lagoon-view guest rooms and suites spread over seven, four- to six-story connected buildings, plus 12 over-water bungalows. The property includes a large free-form traditional pool and a sandy-bottom

pool, two restaurants, a small beach, a tennis court, and two shops. Although the hotel is fresh and modern, with lovely floral outdoor grounds, enviable views to the lagoon, and first-class, full-amenity accommodations, it would best be described as a comfortable overnight retreat for guests planning on longer sojourns to Le Meriden Bora Bora.

Visitors to Bora Bora seeking the most modern and comfortable accommodations, sandy beaches, a superior lagoon for swimming and snorkeling and spacious grounds with a Gallic flavor will be pleased with Le Meridien Bora Bora.

Le Meridien Bora Bora
B.P. 190 Vaitape
Bora Bora, French Polynesia
Tel. (689) 60-5151
Fax (689) 60-5152
In United States
Tel. (310) 793-0025
Fax (310) 793-8825
E-mail: sales@lemeridien.tahiti.com

THAILAND

AMANPURI, PHUKET

Amanpuri, which means "place of peace," is situated on 77 tropical acres of a coconut plantation overlooking a palm-fringed, picturesque beach lapped by the calm, crystal-clear waters of the Andaman Sea on the Thai Island of Phuket. Forty Thai-style bungalows and 30 private villas perched on hills meander down to an attractive midnight-blue mirror-like pool surrounded by the open-air lobby, restaurant and lounge areas, which are reminiscent of a traditional Thai village. Owned and operated by Amanresorts, Ltd., this incredibly picturesque property opened in 1988 and rapidly became a coveted retreat for the rich, famous and loving couples willing to pay the freight for a few nights in paradise.

Guests are greeted by a local Thai hostess who conducts a quick tour of the grounds before settling guests into their bungalows, where they are officially "checked in."

Although this is a very exclusive and expensive property, the atmosphere is totally laid-back and casual. The fortunate patrons, a mix of Europeans, Asians and North Americans, all appear to be in love, not only with each other, but also with this idyllic, romantic hideaway.

Accommodations

Forty air-conditioned private bungalows set on stilts running up and down the hills and cliffs above the sea are connected by winding paths. Each features a large sundeck with outdoor dining terrace, king-size beds, separate bath, shower and toilet compartments, electronic safes, stocked refrigerators, hair dryers, compact disc stereo systems and daily supplies of fresh flowers, fruits and cookies. Thirty private villas that enjoy the most desired views of the sea (and evening sunsets) include two- to six-bedroom bungalows, provide additional space, larger terraces, giant his and hers bathrooms and wardrobes, as well as Thai-style dining rooms, living rooms, and very large, dazzlingly beautiful private pools. The entire villa can be leased as a unit. It is ideal for small conferences and meetings. The bungalows and villas are spacious and comfortable, reflecting a traditional Thai design.

Because most of the rooms are located on hills and are a good walk from the main lobby, restaurants, and beach, golf carts are available to transport guests on request.

Restaurants, Lounges, and Entertainment

Room service is available around the clock for those romantics who prefer to dine on their private dining terrace. The villa guests have cooks available who will personally prepare their meals.

Overlooking the pool are two Thai-designed open-air restaurants. The Thai restaurant serves all three meals, and the adjoining structure features an Italian menu in the evening, including wood-burning oven pizza. For variety, an outdoor barbecue is available several nights each week on the beach, weather permitting. For $500 per person (for two people) or $400 per person (for three people), guests can book the all-day lunch excursion on the Sea Lion, the resort's Chinese junk that cruises in Phang Nga Bay. The excursion commences with a

speed boat ride from the resort's nearby jetty, around the bay (described below), to the Sealion.

Snacks and beverages can be ordered on the beach or by the pool throughout the day.

The superb executive chef, Daniel Lentz commands a staff of locals who turn out a wide variety of Thai and other Southeast Asian cuisines. Those wishing to sample an assortment of Thai dishes may opt for a special tasting dinner, which will include traditional Thai soups, salads, curries, fish and desserts.

The wine list offers a nice selection of French and Italian wines at very steep tariffs. You may prefer to opt for the local Singha Beer, which is easier on the pocketbook and better designed to cool down the palate for those indulging in the spicy Thai delicacies.

Dress is always casual. Service is slow but friendly, and the overall dining experience could be described as relaxed. Do not come expecting European efficiency and be prepared to deal with a local service staff that has only a rudimentary exposure to English. Most guests come for R & R and are content with the leisurely paced meals and romantic setting.

To accompany your dinner, musicians play traditional Thai background music by the pool across from the restaurants. There is no other evening entertainment. Complimentary Thai pancakes, fruits and cakes are offered late each afternoon by the pool.

Sport Facilities

If you can drag yourself away from the perfectly dreamy beach with its backdrop of towering coconut palms, comfortable lounges and beach attendants providing cold refresher cloths, ice water, food and beverages, you may wish to swim a few laps in the attractive main pool that sits between the restaurants, lounges and main lobby.

Tennis is available on six floodlit courts that sit on a slope above the sea. Equipment, coaching, and playing partners are available. Water-skiing, speedboats, snorkeling, diving and elephant safari rides through the jungle can be arranged by the resort. Five excellent golf courses, including the Blue

Canyon championship course, are located on the island The resort will provide transportation, arrange tee times and provide complimentary golf clubs. There is an exercise room on the beach with an assortment of equipment; and a world-class spa sits atop a hill overlooking the sea. The spa offers numerous massage and therapy treatments and includes impressive sauna, steam and changing rooms.

An absolute must is a half- or full-day excursion on one of Amanpuri's selection of cruise vessels. These include a 60-foot, 20-passenger Bluewater 60-day cruiser, and other luxury and fast vessels are available for private two- to three-day charters.

At various extra charges, these vessels will transport guests to exceptional tropical beaches and small island paradises with coral gardens to snorkel and dive, or on sightseeing tours around the island and surrounding sea. A favorite tour is the Phang Nga Bay cruise, which passes through unique geographical phenomena comprised of a labyrinth of forested, limestone pillars that rise out of the Andaman Sea. Your cruise will pull into a bat cave, pass through picturesque caverns created by rock formations, skim along a mangrove-lined tropical river, and visit a Thai fishing village and Koh Peng Kan, the tiny island location of numerous scenes from the James Bond movie, "The Man with the Golden Gun."

Miscellaneous and Environs

There are direct flights in and out of Phuket from Bangkok, Kuala Lumpur, Singapore, Jakarta, Hong Kong and Tokyo. The resort provides complimentary transportation by private car to and from the airport.

The Gallery features Thai silks, leather goods, and decorative handicrafts and jewelry. The shops in Phuket Town and Patong are limited, and serious shoppers are best off saving their baht for shopping splurges in Bangkok. However, the little stalls across from Patong Beach offer an impressive array of "knock-off" designer purses, watches and similar items.

Places of interest on Phuket include: the Nam Tok Sai Waterfall in the Khao Phra Toew Park, a national forest and wildlife preserve, the Marine Station, with its display of more than 100 species of fish, the amusements and productions at Phuket Fantasea and the Thai cultural performances at the Thai Cultural Village.

Amanpuri is an exclusive, one-of-a-kind, romantic treasure with possibly the most uniquely beautiful setting in the world. The spectacular yet casual environment, comfortable exotic accommodations, and opportunity to explore unusual pristine islands, beaches, and dive sites in luxury vessels makes this resort the favorite retreat for well-heeled resort aficionados visiting Southern Asia.

Amanpuri
Pansea Beach
Phuket 83000, Thailand
Tel. (076) 324-333
Fax (076) 324-100
E-mail: amanpuri@amanresorts.com
Web: www.amanresorts.com

THAILAND

BANYAN TREE, PHUKET

This uniquely romantic and luxurious all-villa resort property located on Bang Tao Bay, in the exclusive Laguna Phuket integrated resort area opened in September 1994. The 149 spacious villas encircle a lagoon and each villa is surrounded by lush walled gardens to insure privacy. Laguna Phuket is owned by Laguna Resort and Hotels Public Company, Ltd., and includes Sheraton Grande Laguna Phuket, Dusit Laguna, Laguna Beach Club, Laguna Phuket and Allamanda, in addition to its premiere property, Banyan Tree Phuket.

The golf course and spa located at Banyan Tree Phuket are available to guests staying at all of the hotels in Laguna Phuket and are situated on the same long stretch of white-sand beach. Transportation between properties is available by shuttle buses or on boats that traverse the lagoon.

The clientele is a mix of European, Japanese and Southeast Asians with a sprinkling of North Americans and Australians. Approximately 10 to 20 percent come for business meetings and conferences while the balance are vacationing couples seeking a romantic, restful environment. The predominantly Thai staff has a smattering of various languages; however, English-speaking guests must make allowances. Temperatures range from 70 to 90 degrees Fahrenheit and the monsoon season is from September through October.

Accommodations

The exquisitely designed villas sprawl along the banks of the main lagoon that connects all of the resort properties in Laguna Phuket.

The 36 Deluxe Villas include open-air sunken bathtubs and landscaped, walled gardens with outdoor Jacuzzis. The 34 Pool Villas boast a 30-by10-foot private swimming pool and Thai-style sala (patio), each perfect for dining, star gazing and watching the sunset.

For the ultimate romantic/hedonistic experience, you can opt for one of the 13, 1,815-square-foot Spa Pool Villas. The spacious outdoor gardens surround a 33' x 13.2' heated lap pool adorned with plants and flowers which includes a therapeutic Jacuzzi and two thalassatherapy beds. Behind the pool is a semi-covered lounge and massage area, several of which overlook the lagoon, while others over-look your own private babbling waterfall.

All accommodations have exotic Thai-style king-size beds that look out to the pool and/or gardens, expensive Thai art and artifacts, large separate walk-in shower and toilet compartments, sumptuous outdoor sunken soaking tubs, dining areas, color televisions, hair dryers, separate his and hers double sinks and vanities, numerous closets, fully stocked mini-bars and in-room safes.

The Pool Villas and the Spa Pool Villas come with video machines and CD/DVD players, which also can be requested in the other villas. The Spa Pool Villas include many other facilities and amenities including a Thai-style bed room that appears to be floating amidst a lily pond, a steam-room shower, an outdoor shower, a separate parlor with a writing desk, an entertainment area, flat-screen TV, an espresso-cappuccino machine and every conceivable toiletry and special amenity. These accommodations were clearly designed for loving couples. Families or non-intimate friends would best opt for

one of the two-bedroom villas. 22 larger Water-Pool Villas will be completed by the close of 2006.

Many visitors have chosen Banyan Tree Phuket for business meetings and small conferences. The two meeting rooms can accommodate up to 100 people and group banquets can be readily arranged.

In my opinion, the Pool Villas and Spa Pool Villas are the most desirable, romantic, luxury accommodations to be found anywhere in the world.

Restaurants, Lounges, and Entertainment

Banyan Tree offers 24-hour private dining in your villa and the Banyon Café at the golf course is open from 7:00 a.m. to 6:30 p.m. offering salads, sandwiches, Thai and Asian dishes. Watercourt, adjoining the lobby and overlooking the lagoon, serves an international buffet breakfast and dinner with Mediterranean and international dishes, in a relaxed, outdoor atmosphere with panoramic views of the lagoon.

Tamarind restaurant located at the Banyon Tree Spa by the main pool specializes in healthy spa cuisine with an emphasis on seafood.

The resort's signature restaurant is the charming Saffron, serving authentic and creative Thai cuisine, with a nouvelle presentation. Lunch, snacks and drinks are also available at Sands on the beach.

Although there is no formal entertainment, musicians often perform in the lobby bar.

For a change of pace, guests can enjoy dinner on the Sanya Rak, a long-tail boat with a nightly dinner cruise featuring Western and Thai cuisine.

Sport Facilities

Across from the lobby entrance is the 18-hole Laguna Phuket Golf Club. The golfing opportunities include a teaching pro, driving range, putting green and chipping area.

Tennis buffs can enjoy the two illuminated tennis courts, (one hard court and one grass court). Games and equipment can be arranged. Also available are, volleyball, bike tours, a swimming pool and an imaginative outdoor freeform pool with water jets and bubble mats.

The Banyan Tree Hotels and Resorts organization is well known for its impressive spa facilities that have been opened throughout Southeast Asia. The award-winning Banyan Tree Spa Phuket is Asia's first and largest Oriental Garden Spa, which provides a wide range of massage, body, and beauty treatments. Facilities include sauna, steam and Jacuzzi. Spa treatments are available both in traditional treatment rooms and in private, semi-open-air spa pavilions, referred to as Thai Salas. Charges vary for the different spa treatments and combination packages are available. Also located next to the Banyan Tree Spa is a fitness center with free weights and cardiovascular machines.

Miscellaneous and Environs

The resort provides chauffeur service for the 30-minute drive to and from the airport for approximately $20 each way.

A beauty salon and souvenir, boutique, and sundry shop are located in the main building, a pro

shop is at the Laguna Puget Golf Club, and there is additional shopping at Canal Village located on the lagoon between the Sheraton and Dust Laguna. Tours to other islands can be easily arranged with Laguna Travel and Tours for sightseeing, snorkeling and scuba diving.

Other Banyan Tree resorts are located in Bantan, Indonesia, Mahe, Seychelles, Bangkok, Thailand and Maldives Vabbinfaru and Ringha, China.

Phuket is certainly one of the most idyllic and popular resort areas in this part of the world and the lovely Laguna Phuket resort complex is possibly the most beautiful and desirable section of Phuket, away from the masses of tourists. Banyan Tree Phuket is the premiere property in Laguna Phuket, offering its guests a complete selection of facilities, a luxury spa, the most lavish and comfortable accommodations, and has been the recipient of numerous awards. Travelers to Southeast Asian destinations will be well rewarded if they elect to detour to Banyan Tree Phuket for a few days or weeks of rest, relaxation, and romance in ultimate tropical splendor.

Banyan Tree
33 Moo 4, SriSoonthorn Road, Cherngtalay
Amphur Talang, Phuket, 83110, Thailand
Tel. (66-76) 324 374
Fax (66-76) 324 375
E-mail: Phuket@banyantree.com
Web: www. Banyantree.com

MANDARIN ORIENTAL DHARA DHEVI, CHIANG MAI

Situated among 60 acres of verdant, tranquil landscaped gardens with lotus ponds and rice terraces, emulating a royal city of the 13th century Lanna Kingdom, the Mandarin Oriental Dhara Dhevi ("Star Goddess") provides its guests a truly unique, cultural, yet hedonistic experience. Here, one can savor the highest level of luxury and service together with exquisite dining, shopping and spa facilities in a secluded resort environment within close proximity to historical and cultural sights.

The resort is located only six miles from Chiang Mai International Airport where there are direct flights to and from China, Singapore, Bangkok, Taiwan and Myanmar. From late October to the end of February, temperatures range from 53 F. in the evenings up to 82 F. during the day, whereas during the remainder of the year they range between 71F. and 95F.

Accomodations

144 Villas, Pavilions, Colonial Suites and Theme Suites with 20 different styles of accommodations ranging in size from approximately 666 square feet to 7,000 square feet spread throughout the property. All feature traditional Lanna architecture, extensive museum-quality artifacts and antiques, as well as, high-tech entertainment centers.

The pavilions are reconstructions of traditional Thai-style houses, whereas the villas are authentic Northern Thai rice houses made out of teak wood. The two-story villas include whirlpool tubs, separate shower stalls, an outdoor deck or terrace and a Thai Sala. Many have private pools.

The Colonial Suites are located in two-story buildings. The upper floor suites offer spacious balconies, while ground-level suites enjoy direct access to lush gardens. All suites have a separate adjoining living room and private verandah.

The 3,990 square-foot Penthouse Spa Suite inspired by a royal palace in Myanmar offers its own private spa where guests can enjoy spa services in the privacy of their palace, a king-size bedroom, living room, dining room and pantry. The 3,970 square-foot Dhara Devi Suite is a three-story apartment with a central Pagoda Tower and a private wine cellar and swimming pool; and the Chiang Mai Suite features a private 4,330 square foot swimming pool. The 6,890 square-foot Royal Villa is a six-bedroom self-contained private retreat with three private pools and three Jacuzzis going for $6,000 per night.

All accommodations include on-call butler service, 24-hour in-room dining, a work desk with internet access outlets, fax-machines on request, two IDD telephone lines with voice mail, remote control TV with DVD player and DVD library, Bose C/D player with a C/D library, a radio, twin or king beds, a fully stocked private bar, an in-room safe, a spacious bathroom with a whirlpool tub, a separate walk-in shower, a hair dryer, an illuminated vanity mirror and bathrobes, slippers and exclusive bathroom amenities, tea-and coffee making facilities, an iron and ironing board and daily fresh fruits and flowers.

The resort has numerous meeting and event facilities including a 5,591 square-foot Grand Ballroom that can accommodate 900 for a reception, 700 theater-style and 360 class-room style; and a re-

ception for up to 1,200 participants can be arranged on the Khong Khao lawn.

Restaurants, Lounges and Entertainment

The resort offers a plethora of dining options ranging from relaxed meals poolside and in-suite dining to fine Asian and European culinary experiences in architecturally unique buildings reflecting the opulence of the past 700 years of Lanna history.

Le Grand Lanna features northern and classic Thai cuisine for lunch and dinner both alfresco on the terrace cooled by mist-spraying fans and in enclosed air-conditioned salons. In the evenings there is live classical Thai entertainment.

Cantonese and contemporary Chinese cuisine (including dim sum at lunch time) is served at Fujian in a two-story mansion graced with priceless objets d'art. A degustation supper menu offers miniature portions of the chef's signature dishes.

For nouvelle and classic French cuisine, dinner at the dramatic Farang Ses Restaurant with accompanying piano music is a must. Sitting at one of the outdoor tables on the terrace while watching the sun set over rice paddies affords one of Thailand's most romantic dining experiences.

International favorites are offered throughout the day and evening at Akaligo in the hotel's main lobby and at Rice Terrace in the villa lobby area. Snacks and beverages are available at the lobby bar and the Loy Kham Pool Bar.

Guests can learn the art of preparing Thai cuisine each morning from Monday to Saturday at the Thai Culinary Academy with optional visits to the market place to purchase ingredients.

Sport Facilities

There are two swimming pools. Loy Kham near the fitness center is a free-form pool looking out to paddy fields with an adjoining bar and sun terrace offering snacks, drinks and a spa menu. A second large heated pool is set in the gardens next to the Colonial Suites.

The 32,800 square-foot, palace-like Holistic Center offers a wide range of therapeutic treatments and spa services in 25 treatment rooms and suites. These include a variety of massage therapies, scrubs, reflexology, Rhassoul with Thai herbal mud, Watsa, body polish, facials, Indian holistic and hand and foot treatments.

Also on the premises are a state-of-the-art fitness center, two air-conditioned squash courts and two outdoor tennis courts. Joggers and walkers can enjoy paths running around the property skirting paddy fields, private villas and gardens.

Miscellaneous and Environs

The resort is only a five-minute drive to the city center. Sankampaeng, not far from the property, is

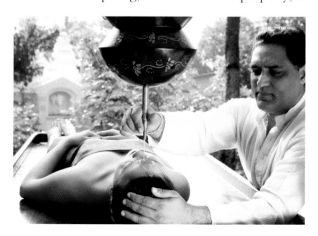

Chiang Mai's major shopping area for quality handicrafts, silk, cotton weaving, woodcarving, jewelry, silverware and lacquer. Other shopping meccas can be found at Baan Tawai (in the Hang Dong district) for wood carvings and basket weaving, at Baan Celadon to view a local pottery workshop, Bo Sang for waxed parasols and the Night Bazaar in the heart of the city is the destination for handmade products and souvenirs from the villages.

The most popular natural and cultural attractions include the National Park, orchid farms, waterfalls, natural caves and elephant camps, numerous Wats (temples) and the National Museum. Several tours and excursions have special appeal such as the bi-

cycle ride to a local village, temple and archeological site, as well as, the half-day, balloon flight complete with a Champagne breakfast, river raft trip and elephant ride.

The cultural center offers a regular schedule of programs, events, lectures and exhibits; and at the library guests will find a selection of books, DVDs and C/Ds.

At the Lanna Kid's Club a unique morning and afternoon program of activities, arts and crafts allow children the opportunity to experience Thai culture and traditions.

Mandarin Oriental Dhara Dhevi, Chiang Mai is an excellent retreat for travelers to Thailand wishing to experience the Thai culture and history while luxuriating in lavish accommodations surrounded by beautiful scenery, enjoying a variety of fine cuisine and being pampered by impeccable service.

Mandarin Oriental Dhara Dhevi
51/4 Chiang Mai
Sankampaeng Road
Moo I.T. Tasala A. Muang
Chiang Mai 50000, Thailand
Tel. +66(53) 888-888, Fax.+66(53) 888-999
www.mandarinoriental.com
e-mail: MOCNX.reservations@Mohg.com

THAILAND

THE ORIENTAL, BANGKOK

This venerable, world-famous hostelry was originally built in 1876 on the same panoramic site it occupies today along the banks of the colorful Chao Phraya River ("River of the Kings"). The Garden Wing was added in 1958 and the River Wing in 1976. Presently owned and operated by the Mandarin Oriental Hotel Chain, The Oriental in Bangkok has hosted royalty, statesmen, politicians, authors, and famous personalities over the years. Since 1981, it has consistently been rated one of the top 10 hotels in the world (and often "numero uno") by travel writers, travel magazines and business consultants. The Mandarin Oriental group also operates highly rated establishments in Hong Kong, Jakarta, Macau, Manila, Singapore, Kuala Lumpur, London, Honolulu, Miami, San Francisco and Surabaya.

What makes The Oriental so special is its sumptuous accommodations, superb cuisine, aristocratic charm, pampering service and enviable location, which permits a full river view from most guest rooms, restaurants and from the gardens and pool area. This is the hotel in Bangkok to "see and be seen," an oasis for expatriate Westerners, wealthy travelers, dignitaries and personalities. Management aspires to provide a top level of service, attending to guests' every need and whim, and accomplishes the task better than any other establishment in Bangkok.

Accommodations

The 359 guest rooms and 34 suites are spread among the three wings. Eighty-four of the accommodations have balconies looking out to the river. The most romantic rooms with the best river views are rooms ending in numbers 11 and 12 on each floor of the River Wing. For the ultimate in pampering, opt for a suite on the 16th floor. Butler service throughout the hotel includes unlocking your door, unpacking your suitcase, straightening your clothes and bringing you a cold drink, as well as attending to your every need.

The original Author's Wing, which includes the Joseph Conrad, Somerset Maugham, James Michener and Noel Coward suites, plus three superior rooms, is known throughout the world and frequently depicted in travel magazines. The decor of each suite is different, containing elegant original furnishings and antiques. Many of the rooms in the Garden Wing are split-level, and all have been recently refurbished. Equally lavish accommodations are the rooms and suites in the River Wing.

Each guest room and suite has twin beds (or a king-size), a Bose stereo system and C/D player, color television with in-house movies, stocked mini-bars, refrigerators, hair dryers, dressing tables, a writing desk, high-speed internet access, a complimentary morning newspaper, fresh fruits and flowers, robes and slippers for use during your visit and numerous amenities. All rooms and suites are lavishly decorated with beautiful woods, fabrics and furnishings.

The Royal Ballroom can accommodate 1,000 for a cocktail party and 350 for a banquet. The Ballroom can be subdivided into three separate facilities. There are also two additional conference rooms.

Restaurants, Lounges, and Entertainment

In addition to 24-hour room service, The Verandah indoor/outdoor coffee shop is open from 6:00 a.m. until midnight. The Verandah offers buffet and à la carte Continental and full-course breakfasts each morning (with delicious fresh bakery items), lunches, dinners and snacks – all overlooking the river.

Lord Jim's on the mezzanine floor above the lobby is a seafood specialty restaurant featuring a buffet lunch and à la carte dinners. Ciao, an outdoor Italian restaurant, is located on the marble terrace in front of the Author's Wing gardens, serving antipasto, pasta, pizzas, ice cream and coffee.

There is a nightly barbecue at the outdoor Riverside Terrace below The Verandah. For a change of pace, guests can take the five-minute hotel barge across the river to the Sala Rim Naam Thai Restaurant, which offers a buffet lunch of Thai specialties and a traditional Thai set dinner with classical Thai dancing. This is the best Thai restaurant in Bangkok.

Unquestionably, the grand culinary experience at The Oriental is the magnificent recently redecorated The Normandie, which is perhaps one of the best French restaurants in Asia. Here you can enjoy a romantic candlelight dinner accompanied by soft piano music while looking out the panoramic glass windows to the boats floating up and down the river. The offerings are imaginative, the wine list extensive, the service impeccable, and the prices steep. Those opting for the degustation menu will be richly rewarded.

The Bamboo Bar, more or less the "Harry's Bar" of Bangkok, is decorated in the Asian colonial fashion, featuring a jazz band with singer, pre-dinner cocktails and hors d'oeuvres, nightly entertainment, and local color. Teas, cakes and snacks are served in the Author's Lounge, and exotic drinks, sandwiches, imaginative salads and Asian cuisine are available during the afternoon by the pool.

The hotel also has a cooking school on Monday through Thursday tutoring guests in the art of preparation of Thai cuisine. On Friday and Saturday, guests can participate in a hands-on experience in a Thai kitchen.

Sport Facilities

Between the River Wing and the river are colorful gardens and two swimming pools. Immediately across the river (five minutes by hotel barge) is the Spa, Health, and Beauty Center, which was completed in 1993 at a cost of over $4.5 million and recently renovated during the summer of 2005. The facility includes a wide variety of spa programs, a special restaurant featuring gourmet spa cuisine, a full complement of treatments such as massage, aromatherapy, reflexology, seaweed, herbal wrap, collagen repair facials, bust firming, foot treatments and sauna, steam and whirlpools. The Oriental Spa is one of the most luxurious facilities of its kind in the world and has been voted as such by top publications. Guests obtain their treatments in one of the 10 elegant private rooms or 4 suites, each decorated in dark teaks with a massage area, private steam room, and shower. The three regular suites and spacious Oriental suite also include whirlpools and saunas and feature marble treatment tables.

The adjacent sport center features two illuminated tennis courts, two indoor squash courts, a changing room and sauna, state-of-the-art exercise and cardiovascular equipment, aerobic and yoga classes and a half-kilometer outdoor jogging track.

The hotel will arrange golf for its guests at many golf clubs located 45-60 miles from the property. Joggers will prefer running in Lumpini Park, about a mile from the hotel, where the pollution level is at the lowest in the city.

Miscellaneous and Environs

There are a number of shops, both at the hotel and immediately across the street, offering Thai silks, jewelry, watches, handicrafts, antiques and designer merchandise. Also at the hotel one can find a beauty and barber salon, medical center, business service center, a day care center for children 3-12, baby-sitting services, a flower shop, travel agency and full concierge service. The hotel's barge also transports guests to the River City Shopping Center- Ca five-minute ride.

Visitors to Bangkok will not want to miss visiting the exquisite Royal Palace and the adjacent Wat Phra Keo, home of the Emerald Buddha, the Wat Arun, Temple of the Dawn, Wat Traimitr, housing the Golden Buddha, Jim Thompson's House, the National Art Gallery, the National Museum and the morning markets along the Klongs. A barge ride down the Klongs to view the floating market and people living on the river is a must. The barge departs from right in front of the hotel.

Bangkok is a fascinating Asian destination with an abundance of daytime and evening activities. It is also a very hot, busy and polluted city. Exploring Bangkok will be best enjoyed if done in a leisurely fashion over a number of days. The Oriental offers visitors and tourists the ideal opportunity to luxuriate at one of the world's finest, most lauded resorts while enjoying possibly the best dining, service and accommodations in this part of the world.

The Oriental
48 Oriental Avenue
Bangkok, 10500, Thailand
Tel. +662-659-9000
Fax +662-659-0000
E-Mail: bscorbkk-reservations@mohg.com

THAILAND

SHANGRI-LA HOTEL, BANGKOK

Shangri-La Hotel, Bangkok, which opened its doors in 1986, is another gem of the Shangri-La Hotels and Resorts. Other Shangri-La resorts in this book include the Shangri-La Hotel, Singapore and the Tanjung Aru Resort in Malaysia.

Typical of this chain, the resort was constructed in the most ideal location in the city, on the banks of the Chao Phraya River ("River of Kings"), only 10 minutes from the main business section and shopping centers, yet set off in a quiet area. The hotel completed a $22 million renovation in early 2003. Most guest rooms, all public rooms and restaurants, the magnificent glass-enclosed lobby, the health club, the lush gardens and pool area all enjoy an uninterrupted panoramic view of the picturesque river.

The Shangri-La Hotel, Bangkok offers a deluxe experience, lavish accommodations and superior dining in an extremely elegant, modern environment that has a clean, fresh feel and never seems as crowded as other large hotels in Bangkok. The inside decor is lavish yet tasteful. The rooms are the last word in comfort and detail, from the exquisite furnishings right down to the wall safe, scales, hair dryers, robes and slippers. Relaxing in the gardens by the pool next to the river is a welcome change of pace in this crowded city. The restaurants offer a wide variety of satisfying dining experiences, while the hotel's surrounding streets are a shopper's paradise. Service is quite good by Bangkok standards, but not all of the staff speak English fluently.

Accommodations

All of the 799 rooms are beautifully decorated with a mixture of Western and Asian decor and include twin or king-size beds, color television with in-house movies and satellite television, direct-dial telephones with bathroom extensions, writing desks, makeup mirrors, large marble and mirrored bathrooms with scales, coffee and tea makers, hair dryers, robes and slippers, wall safes, refrigerators, well-stocked mini-bars, separate sitting areas and bedside remote controls for the lights, TV, radios and window curtains.

Seventy-three of the deluxe rooms and suites in the Shangri-La wing and all 129 rooms and suites in the Krungthep Wing have balconies. The 85 rooms on the Horizon Floor receive special amenities. Thirty-seven of the 41 suites designated as standard suites have connecting parlors, while the five special suites contain a living room, dining room, balcony, kitchen and two bedrooms. The Krungthep Wing has 16 suites, including the stunning Presidential suite.

The Grand Ballroom can accommodate up to 1,600 guests, and there are 27 additional meeting rooms. The business center offers secretarial, telecommunication and photocopy services.

Restaurants, Lounges, and Entertainment

Both room service and the Next 2 Café & Terrace are available 24 hours a day. The Next 2 Café & Terrace serves buffet breakfasts lunches and dinners,

with six different food stations offering Asian and international cuisine, as well as a la carte spa cuisine items. Next 2 Café also offers seating under the stars on the riverside terrace.

Gourmet Chinese dishes are featured for lunch and dinner at the Shang Palace, as well as dim sum at lunch time.

You will want to try Thai cuisine at Salathip, the lovely Thai restaurant that sits out on the banks of the river next to the pool. It is open for dinner only. Here you can sample an assortment of classic Thai

dishes and listen to Thai classical music and dance. The award-winning Angelini features Italian cuisine in a bi-level Venetian setting overlooking the pool and river, while Edogin, the Japanese Restaurant, serves sushi, teppan yaki and other Japanese delicacies.

Sport Facilities

Two large outdoor pools sit in lovely gardens by the river. Surrounding the pools are numerous lounge chairs and a pool bar for drinks. Most of the hotel's restaurants are only a few steps away.

Two tennis courts and two squash courts are located atop the 550-car parking lot. The courts are of good quality compared to most found in big cities in Asia.

At the health club, you can enjoy numerous exercise machines and bicycles, which are positioned to permit you to exercise while looking out over the river. There are modern sauna, steam, hydropool and massage facilities here, as well as a daily aerobic class.

CHI spa, the first of Shangri-La's new spa brand, opened in June 2004.

Inspired by the legend of "Shangri-La" this sanctuary of tranquility is one of the most luxurious private spa suites in Bangkok and is based upon the ancient healing traditions and philosophies of China and the Himalayas. The extensive menu offers over 35 specialized body, water, massage and facial therapies. Each spa experience takes place in one of nine private suites, with views of the Chao Praya River, complete with an infinity bath with color therapy, herbal steam and shower, relaxation lounge and changing, toilet and vanity areas.

Miscellaneous and Environs

An exclusive feature of the Shangri-La Hotel, Bangkok is its location next to Bangkok's sky train, which provides rapid travel to all parts of the city and a half-hour highway access to the airport. Limousine service is also provided to and from the airport for about $46. The hotel offers a complimentary shuttle boat to the River City Shopping Complex. In addition, day and evening dinner cruises can be

organized on the hotel's own Horizon Cruise II boat.

Connected between the two wings of the hotel is an upscale shopping center with numerous shops featuring Thai silks, jewelry, handicrafts, antiques, and made-to-order tailoring. In addition, there is a hairdresser, a sundry shop and a 24-hour medical clinic.

Great shopping bargains await the guests in the streets surrounding the hotel or at any of Bangkok's large shopping complexes. (See the entry on The Oriental for a description of sightseeing and places of interest in Bangkok.)

Discriminating travelers who especially enjoy spacious, immaculately clean and comfortable accommodations and lavish surroundings in a picturesque setting, as well as the finest in food and facilities, will consider the Shangri-La Hotel, Bangkok one of their more rewarding experiences in Asia.

Shangri-La Hotel
89 Soi Wat Suan Plu New Road
Bangrak, Bangkok 10500, Thailand
Tel. (662) 236-7777
Fax (662) 236-8579

CHAPTER NINE

AFRICA AND
THE INDIAN OCEAN

Prince Maurice, Mauritius

MALDIVES

FOUR SEASONS RESORT MALDIVES AT KUDA HURAA

The Maldives, referred to by Marco Polo as "the flower of the Indies", lying 450 miles southwest of Sri Lanka, consist of 1,190 tiny, palm-decked coral islands trailing down the Indian Ocean, divided into 26 atoll clusters, overlapping the equator.

Four Seasons Resort Maldives occupies its own private island paradise in the North-Male atoll, surrounded by a white-sand beach lapped by crystal-clear waters reflecting azure and turquoise hues. Palm and sea grape trees, tropical flowers, and plants line the beach and surround the hotel lobby, restaurants, pool, as well as the 96 beach-front and over-water guest bungalows.

The property was originally opened in 1996 as Kuda Huraa Reef Resort, appealing primarily to serious scuba divers who sought a pristine, luxury property in the Maldives. Four Seasons took over in 1998 and made numerous additions to the bungalows, adding private plunge pools, and outdoor showers and decorations, as well as upgrading the restaurants and dining and introducing the Four Seasons' standard of service. Additional renovations and rebuilding was undertaken following the Tsunami in 2004. The resort now not only features one of the best diving programs in the world, but offers an idyllic, deluxe, private-island experience for its international clientele, which originally was largely British, German, and Japanese, but is now attracting upscale resort afficionados from all corners of the globe. This is an extremely picturesque venue that lends itself to watching sunrises and sunsets, as well as leisurely daytime walks around the island that can be easily negotiated in 20 minutes.

Many guests just park themselves on a comfortable beach chair or relax on a rubber raft in the sea. Others participate in the variety of sailing, fishing, and diving excursions that operate daily.

Accommodations

There are 96 Maldive-inspired bungalows, all with teak-planked or terra-cotta tile floors and furnishings, including 58 beach bungalows and suites, with secluded plunge pools, each surrounded by lush vegetation, located only a few steps from the sea, as well as 38 deluxe over-water bungalows accessible by a wooden bridge. Half of the over-water bungalows are positioned to enjoy the sunrise and the other half the sunset. Fifty-seven of the 58 beach bungalows feature secluded private plunge pools and there is one two-bedroom Suite with its own beach area ideal for a traveling family.

All accommodations include a king or two twin beds, a private electronic safe, a refrigerator/mini-bar, a tea and coffee maker, a hair dryer, cotton robes, bathtubs and showers, DVD and C/D player, satellite television, and outdoor patios with lounge chairs and a clothes drying ramp.

The over-water villas are spacious and quite pleasant, with separate indoor lounge areas, writing desks, wardrobe areas, and sumptuous bathrooms. The outdoor porches feature lounges, dining table, showers, and steps leading down to the sea. Six of the over-water bungalows and one of the beach villas are designated as suites, thus affording additional space, comfort, and amenities.

Restaurants, Lounges, and Entertainment

Next to the pool is the semi-protected, three-meal-a-day, Café Huraa featuring Asian, Western, and Continental à la carte dining and themed evening buffets. Immediately adjacent is Baraabaru Specialty Restaurant, offering romantic, table-light dinners with innovative cuisine from Sri Lanka, India, and the Maldives.

The Reef Club, near the over-water bungalows, offers breakfast to guests residing in that area. Salads, sandwiches, grilled meats, fish, Italian and pizza from a wood-burning oven area available at dinner. At 6:30 each evening, this is the location to watch the fish feeding, followed by a spectacular sunset.

Cocktails and refreshments are served throughout the day and evening at the Nautilus Lounge, off the lobby. This is also the locale for nightly musical entertainment. A special romantic dinner can be arranged on a small promontory extending from the pool area looking out to the ocean. In-bungalow dining is available around the clock.

Sport Facilities

The affinity pool looks as though it is spilling over into the sea and has a swim-up bar, adjacent children's wading pool, and outdoor Jacuzzi. The beach is picture-card perfect. However, there is an abundance of coral and stones both on the beach and in the warm waters, making it advisable to wear protection on the feet (for those of us with "tender feet").

All forms of watersports are available including canoes, kayaks, water-skiing, catamarans, windsurfers, fishing boats, snorkeling equipment, and boogie boards.

The main highlight of the water-sport program is the diving availabilities. The resort has a Padi/IANTP-certified instruction center with Nitrox (enriched air) diving tanks. Instruction for beginning, intermediate, and advanced divers is offered, along with four daily boat dives. Attractive diving-resort packages are available.

Four Seasons has renovated the fitness-spa facilities, bringing them up to the standard of its other exotic resorts, with a full-range of exercise equipment, and a bevy of indoor and outdoor massage and beauty treatments. A new free-standing spa, situated on its own private island, was added in 2001, accessible only by boat. Five spacious, cream-colored spa pavilions are set on stilts over the water, each with an outdoor courtyard and massage beds positioned so that face cradles look out to the sea. The spa pavilions are designed for couples and feature outdoor garden showers, private soaking tubs, and indoor shower/steam rooms.

The resort owns a 39-meter, 11-stateroom catamaran that can be booked by guests for exploration of the lagoons, for dives in remote regions, for snorkel and swimming in turquoise waters teeming with neon-colored sea-life, as well as for picnics on private sandy beaches. Aboard the catamaran, passengers will find two sun decks with Jacuzzi, a restaurant with indoor and outdoor seating, a bar and a library and lounge.

Miscellaneous and Environs

There is one boutique-souvenir-sundry shop on premises and the resort offers several excursions to the capital island of Male each week; however, the Maldives are for romantics, nature lovers, and divers, not for serious shoppers. Excursions to neighboring islands, sunset sails, fishing trips, and other aquatic adventures are offered daily.

Daily flights come into the International Airport on Huhule Island from major hubs in Europe, Asia, and Africa. From the airport it is a 30-minute motor launch ride to the resort on one of its numerous speedboats ($120 for adults and $60 for children round trip).

During the second half of 2006, Four Seasons opened a second resort in the Maldives occupying the entire 18-acre island of Landaa Giraavaru in the Baa Atoll accessible by seaplane from Male International Airport. The resort is comprised of 102 thatched beach villas, water villas and suites. Facilities include four restaurants featuring Asian, Indian, and Arabic cuisine, as well as fresh fish and seafood items, a 10-pavillion spa sanctuary with garden and ocean settings, three swimming pools, a state-of-the-art gym, tennis courts, a PADI dive center, and facilities for children and young adults. We look forward to personally reviewing this new resort prior to our next edition.

The Maldives are a required visitation for any seasoned traveler who seeks out exotic and beautiful, pristine beaches and for watersport and dive enthusiasts. Those of you who appreciate the more upscale Four Seasons brand of comfort, attentiveness, and imagination will prefer to spend their visit to the Maldives at Four Seasons Resort Maldives at Kuda Huraa.

Four Seasons Resort Maldives
at Kuda Huraa Island
Maldives
Tel. (960) 444-888
Fax (960) 441-188

ISLAND HIDEAWAY AT DHONAKULHI

Set on its privately-owned, uninhabited virgin island of Dhonakulhi in the North Maldives, an archipelago of small coral islands located in the Indian Ocean 357 miles south of India, Island Hideaway at Dhonakulhi debuted during the summer of 2005. This crescent-shaped, densely vegetated island, surrounded by white-sand beaches touching crystal-clear turquoise waters of a shallow lagoon, remains 95% untouched. The remainder of the island, is occupied by the resort. Guest villas are tucked into lush greenery and scattered along the beach at least 100-feet apart, providing the ultimate in privacy and uninterrupted, panoramic lagoon vistas. This ultra-luxurious island retreat boasts some of the most spectacular and lavish accommodations to be found anywhere in the world.

Accommodations

43 villas are available in six different designs and styles. Every accommodation is air conditioned and includes large bedrooms with luxury mattresses and bed linens, walk-in closet areas, ceiling fans, satellite TV, DVD and C/D, coffee/cappuccino, espresso machines, generously stocked full-size bar/refrigerators, IDD telephones, personal safes, internet access, daily international newsletters, an outdoor terrace, and en-suite bathrooms with some form of indoor/outdoor bathing facilities, double vanities, hairdryers, mosquito repellants, bathrobes, slippers, complimentary toiletries and drinking water, umbrellas, torches, and dedicated guest-use bicycles.

Each of the two "Hideaway Palaces" sprawls over 1,420 square meters of land, located on a natural sand bank and is composed of exclusive villas surrounded by a number of infinity pools. Each has three bedrooms, an indoor dining pavilion with a roof terrace, a lounge and cinema pavilion with a DVD library, an open-air dining pavilion, a pantry pavilion for preparation of snacks and beverages by a private butler and a Maldivian Swing pavilion with a wide two-person swing for enjoying the daytime and evening scenery.

Each of the five "Jasmine Garden Villas" is set on 705 square meters of beach-front with its own private infinity swimming pool and garden area. The indoor-outdoor master bathrooms include two-person bathtubs. These luxurious villas also have an open-air, dining pavilion that sits atop the pool, a roof terrace, a guest toilet and shower, day beds and a Maldivian Swing pavilion.

The 20 "Dhonakulhi Residences" are scattered along the white-sand beach front, each sitting on 550 square meters of land with an open-air living area, an outdoor Jacuzzi splash pool, indoor/outdoor bathrooms with two-person bathtubs, an alfresco garden dining pavilion, a roof terrace and a Maldivian swing pavilion.

Two 236-square-meter "Spa Water Villas" are erected on stilts in the shallow turquoise-blue lagoon. Each has its own exclusive ocean-view treatment room (serviced by Mandara Spa therapists), sauna, steam room, outdoor bathtub and shower and sundeck with lagoon access. Seven "Raamba Retreat Villas" are dotted along the beach front each occupying 385 square meters, while the seven "Funa Pavilions", also located on the beach occupy

176 square meters. These contain all of the facilities and amenities described above, as well as two-person, hand-crafted Jacuzzi tubs, outdoor garden showers, and patios facing the beach with sun beds.

Restaurants, Lounges and Entertainment

The emphasis throughout the resort is on fresh fish and seafood, as well as a variety of international selections. Maldivian cuisine is featured at the Matheefaru Restaurant and authentic Asian cuisine and seafood specialties at Gaafusi. All restaurants are located near the beach affording panoramic views.

Alternately guests can dine in the privacy of their villas, directly on the beach or at a nearby sandbank indulging in a romantic, candle-lit Robinson Crusoe experience.

Meeru Bar on the beach with a deck extending over the water offers exotic drinks and snacks with live music and cultural shows on some evenings.

Sport Facilities

The infinity swimming pool which faces the ocean with attached Jacuzzi and children's pool is the center of daytime lounging. Just about every imaginable water sport is offered including water skiing, snorkeling, diving, windsurfing, canoeing, para-sailing, Hobicats, speedboat trips and game fishing. The Meridis Dive Center features Padi-certified scuba instructions for adults and children over ten years of age, and offers guided snorkeling and diving excursions.

Tennis, volleyball on the sand and bicycling are also available, as well as a fitness center and yoga pavilion.

Hideaway Spa by Mandara features a sun, sand and sea theme with internal waterways, waterfall walls, and open areas with sand floors. The two Lagoon Spa Villas offer private ocean views, double treatment rooms, private bathrooms with steam shower, outdoor dip pools, day beds, personal sound systems and lagoon access. The four spa Land Treatment Rooms are surrounded by waterways with open-to-air double treatment rooms, private bathrooms with steam shower, 2-person baths

and an outdoor relaxation area. The two Spa Water Villas (residences) are described under accommodations. A variety of Mandara treatments and therapies are available including massages, body packs, detox, facials manicures and pedicures.

Miscellaneous and Environs

Also at the resort is a library stocked with books, games, C/Ds, DVDs, along with a cyber café; the Hideaway Bazaar with arts, crafts, souvenirs, and essential travel accessories and toiletries; Sifani of London jewelry boutique and a Mandara Spa shop; and "Tender Hearts", Kids Club.

Day trips to uninhabited islands for swimming, and picnicking can be arranged, as well as, private charter photo flights.

Guests fly into the international airport at Male, the capital city. From here they take a 45-minute scenic flight to a domestic airport at Hanimaadhoo followed by a short speedboat ride to Dhonakulhi Island. Other options include a seaplane flight from Male or taking one's private yacht to the resort's fully equipped marina.

Island Hideaway at Dhonakulhi offers the dream vacation for well-healed travelers seeking a uniquely private island experience with ultra-luxurious, romantic accommodations, a plethora of water sports and fine dining and service.

Photographs: © Sakis Papadopoulos / Impressions

Island Hideaway at Dhonakulhi Maldives,
Spa Resort & Marina
Haa Alifu Atoll, North Maldives
Tel. +960-650-1515
Fax.+960-650-1616
e-mail: sales@island-hideaway.com
www.island-hideaway.com

MAURITIUS

ONE & ONLY
LE SAINT GÉRAN

Located on 60 acres of tropical gardens filled with swaying palms and colorful flowers on the golden peninsula of Belle Mare, set on the northeast coast of Mauritius, with the Indian Ocean on one side and a coral-sheltered lagoon on the other, fringed by nearly a mile-long white-sand beach, this recently renovated and remodeled, deluxe resort offers its discerning clientele the finest dining and the most facilities of any property on the island. The magnificence and striking beauty of One&Only Le Saint Géran, the flagship of the One&Only Resorts International chain, is immediately apparent from the moment you enter the impressive, Mediterranean-style, arched gateway and lobby, with its whitewashed walls, clinging flora, and tropical fishponds. Then step out to its imaginative, free-form swimming pool that winds around the indoor and outdoor dining terraces and bars, leading to the sparkling sand and clear, calm, aqua waters of the sea.

The accommodations are deluxe; dining and service are the best in Mauritius; facilities include a nine-hole golf course, Givenchy Health and Beauty Spa, every conceivable water and land sport; and evenings start with romantic gourmet dining, followed by dancing and entertainment. All of this luxury comes at a price, and in high season (January-April), a couple must part with $1,166 per night for a junior suite, $2,380 for an Ocean Suite, and $7,735 for the Grand Villa. (These rates include breakfast and dinner at the main restaurant, La Terrasse).

Accommodations

All of the 162, air-conditioned accommodations open onto sea or lagoon, with furnished terraces or balconies; ceiling fans; spacious dressing rooms; in-room, multimedia entertainment systems comprising stereo, satellite television, DVD/CD players, international direct-dial telephones with personalized voice mail, and e-mail access through the television system; electronic safes; mini-bars; large bathrooms with soaking tubs, walk-in showers, separate toilet compartments, hair dryers, and tasteful furnishings. In addition to 148 junior suites, there are 14 Ocean Suites with multiple patios, a sitting room, and a guest bath. For those wishing to deplete their children's college funds, the 622-square-meter Grand Villa with its private entrance, plunge pool, two guards and butler that can accommodate up to four adults and two children may be the choice. Thirty-seven butlers, as well as, room service are available at the disposal of guests around the clock.

Restaurants, Lounges, and Entertainment

The resort's grandest coup was its success in drafting Alain Ducasse (considered by many, the world's greatest chef and holder of three Michelin stars for restaurants in both Paris and Monte Carlo) to design and supervise Mauritius's premiere dining venue, Spoon de Iles, staffed with chefs personally trained by Ducasse. This fashionable and refined establishment, overlooking secluded tropical gardens and ponds, offers imaginative, international cuisine and a vast selection of vintage wines.

Set around the pool, overlooking the beach, is the resort's main, three-meal-a-day, indoor/outdoor, La Terrasse Restaurant. The offerings include Western, Asian, and Mauritian favorites, expertly prepared, and impeccably served, as well as theme

dinners with cabaret shows, buffets, and nightly entertainment. The tables set under umbrellas between the pool and beach are especially romantic and desirable.

Four bars are dispersed around the resort, one at the pool, one at the golf course, one at Paul and Virginie, and one at Spoon de Iles.

For a variation, guests can enjoy the delightful waterside restaurant and bar at Paul and Virginie, specializing in seafood preparations. The resort will also provide transportation to its sister hotel, One&Only Le Touessrok, where additional restaurants can be sampled along with that property's facilities.

In the evenings, One&Only Le Saint Géran features nightly dancing. The casino, open five nights a week, offers roulette, blackjack, and slot machines.

Sport Facilities

The picturesque, nine-hole (par 33) golf course, designed by Gary Player, abuts the premises with its adjoining pro shop and bar. Guests that prefer to play 18 holes can be accommodated at the 18-hole Bernhard Langer-designed course located at the sister-resort, One and Only Le Touessrok. The five, Peter Burwash-designed, floodlit, tennis courts and tennis club, together with the beach, pools, volleyball, bicycling, badminton, croquet, pony riding, table tennis, basketball and bocci ball facilities, and state-of-the-art fitness center, make this the best choice for sport-active vacationers. Watersports include Hobie Cats, catamarans, kayaks, laser sails, Pedalos, snorkeling, water-skiing, windsurfing, small-game fishing, aqua-gym sessions, and glass-bottom boat trips.

The 7,500-square-foot Givency Health and Beauty Spa beckons guests with a deep-blue lap pool, numerous relaxation and treatment rooms, body and facial massages, skin-peeling, hydro-jet treatments, Jacuzzi, sauna, steam, and herbal wraps.

The Kid's Only program accepts guests ages 4-11 for supervised activities, excursions, computer games, and evening meals. Younger children from two years old can also join in if accompanied by an adult or a baby sitter. A special meeting area and activities are also available for teenagers.

Miscellaneous and Environs

A full-service beauty salon is available at the Spa. Shops offering souvenirs, logo-branded items, beachwear, Givenchy products, Alain Ducasse products, sport accessories, and duty-free jewelry are also on the premises. Regular free shuttle service between Le Saint Géran and its sister hotel, Le Touessrok is provided and personal training and golf and tennis lessons are available. Le Touessrok underwent a 50 million dollar renovation in 2002 adding 98 new suites on adjoining Frangipani Island. We look forward to reviewing this property on our next trip.

Less than an hour's drive will take guests to the international airport as well as the principal town of Port Louis and the main tourist shopping area at Grand Baie.

Well-heeled travelers to Mauritius seeking an elegant, luxury resort that offers aesthetic beauty and a complete range of facilities and activities, as well as lavish accommodations, fine dining, and service, will certainly enjoy One&Only Le Saint Géran.

One & Only Le Saint Géran
Belle Mare, Mauritius
Tel. (230) 401-1688, Fax (230) 401-1668
e-mail: info@oneandonlylesaintgeran.mu

In United States: (954) 713-2500, (800) 223-6800
Web: www.oneandonlylesaintgeran.com

MAURITIUS

LE PRINCE MAURICE

The most charming and exotic property on Mauritius opened its doors in late 1998 on 60 acres of tropical gardens, with rare and lush vegetation on the northeast coast of the island, surrounded by secluded white-sand beaches and a calm, turquoise lagoon. The various bungalow-style accommodations and public areas overlook either the panoramic beach or a picturesque natural fish and mangrove reserve.

As you enter the semi-open-air reception area, you encounter a magnificent, infinity pool with a swim-up bar, surrounded by lily ponds that appear to drop off into the white-sand beach and bay. Uniquely, the decor of the accommodations, public buildings, and grounds compliment and meld into the scenic landscape, typifying the charm of the island, reminiscent of Amanresorts and Four Seasons properties in Southeast Asia.

Accommodations

Sixty-eight of the 76 junior suites are located in two-story buildings with thatched roofs, while eight are on stilts above the natural fish reserve. Each is air-conditioned with a patio or balcony and equipped with a hair dryer, mini-bar; television with internal DVD channels, Sky News, and DVD player, a stereo CD/cassette player, a radio, a telephone/answering/fax machine and an in-room safe. Those on the second level have A-frame roofs. The marble bath-

rooms are extravagant with double vanities, separate glass-in showers, toilet stalls, and bath- and dressing rooms.

The 12 senior suites are almost twice as large. Nine are located adjacent to the beach, with small private plunge pools, and three are on stilts over the natural fish reserve. In addition to the living room with a dining area, the bathrooms have separate his and hers vanity areas and outside gardens with soaking tubs. The singular Princely Suite is palatial with two swimming pools, kitchen facilities, two junior suites and one senior suite, and its own security guard.

All of this grandeur will set you back, in high season, $1,100 per night for a junior suite, $2,200 for a senior suite, and $7,034 for the Princely Suite. The prices are based upon double occupancy and include breakfast.

Restaurants, Lounges, and Entertainment

The main restaurant L'Archipel, attached to the main building, overlooks the pool and beach, with both protected and open-air sections. The menu offers a variety of international favorites. Located in a unique, natural environment, a bit of a walk from the main building, surrounded by mangroves, overlooking the natural fishpond is the unusual, floating, seafood/grill restaurant, Le Barachois, with five intimate connected decks, each set above the pond, open for dinner. Two lounges/bars emanate from the main building, offering libations and musical entertainment.

Sport Facilities

As mentioned above, the resort boasts a lovely infinity pool and one half-mile of white-sand beach lapped by calm turquoise water, ideal for sunning and swimming. In addition, guests can enjoy waterskiing, Pedalos, snorkeling trips, windsurf boards, kayaks, Hobby Cats, and glass-bottom boat rides free of charge; and fly-fishing, catamaran cruises and scuba diving can be arranged for a fee.

At the resort there are two floodlit tennis courts, bicycles, a practice putting green, and free green

fees are offered at Belle Mare Plage, on two 18-hole golf course, ten minutes away. Shuttle service is provided free of charge.

For children 4-10, there are game rooms, a private pool, a dining area, supervised activities, and babysitters.

The health spa and fitness center, situated in the lovely rear gardens, encompasses a small pool, a squash court, a fully equipped gym, Jacuzzi, sauna, steam, a hair dresser salon, and private rooms for massage and body treatments. Aerobic and yoga classes are offered. A Guerlain Institute offers scientifically researched beauty products.

Miscellaneous and Environs

The airport is a 50-minute drive from the resort, and the principal city of Port Louis is a similar distance. There are three shops on the property, including a logo shop, a jewelry store, and one that offers souvenirs and beach accessories. Many visitors prefer the shopping at Grand Baie where there are numerous shops and boutiques.

For travelers to Mauritius who seek intimate solitude and romantic, luxurious accommodations in a more exotic, panoramic setting with an abundance of upscale facilities, Le Prince Maurice will fill the bill.

Le Prince Maurice
Choisey Road, Poste de Flaque, Mauritius
Tel. (230) 413-9100
Fax (230) 413-9129

SEYCHELLES

RESORTS OF THE SEYCHELLE ISLANDS

Although this book is devoted to describing the world's most luxurious, self-contained properties, and many countries with great leisure destinations have been excluded because they do not boast resorts comparable to the others included herein, I must make an exception for the Seychelle Islands.

Friends often ask me which I consider to be the most beautiful and romantic resort areas in the world. Having spent a portion of my adult years searching the globe for the most idyllic locations offering a warm, mild climate, panoramic vistas, lovely beaches for long strolls and swimming, and an extremely romantic environment, I have settled on six areas: Bali in Indonesia, the Maldive Archipelago south of India, the out-islands of Fiji, the Amalfi Coast in southern Italy, numerous tropical islands off the shores of Malaysia and Thailand, along with my first choice – the incomparable Seychelles.

These very unique, dramatically beautiful tropical islands that encompass the 175-square-mile archipelago of the Seychelles are located in the Indian Ocean near the equator, 1,000 miles east of Kenya and at least 1,000 miles away from any other land mass. The islands were uninhabited until the mid-18th century, when France took possession. Over the years, the 115 islands (80 of which are still deserted) were settled by Europeans, Africans and Asians, and today the 70,000 inhabitants speak Creole, French and English and 90 percent live on Mahe, the largest island and the location of an international airport.

These islands are geographically unique in that most are of solid granite origin rather than volcanic rock, with dramatic cliffs that rise from the sea, carpeted with lush vegetation and interesting boulder formations, which were the debris of gigantic movements of the earth's crust thousands of years ago. The beaches in the Seychelles are the very best in the world, and the warm seas surrounding the islands offer countless opportunities for swimming, waters ports, snorkeling and diving. Several of the islands are home for rare species of seabirds and plant life found nowhere else in the world. The weather is hot and humid, with more wind and rain during the northwest monsoon season from November to April, with December and January being the worst months. From May through October the southwest trade winds bring drier and breezier conditions, with temperatures averaging in the low 80s.

Since this book is a guide to luxury resorts, I have described properties in the Seychelles on different islands that are considered the most upscale, offering the greatest amount of creature comforts together with envious locations. With two exceptions, most would not qualify as deluxe and none are bargains; however, each is the best to be found on their respective islands. They will not disappoint the experienced, understanding traveler who appreciates incredibly beautiful beaches and environs and who can make allowances for fewer facilities and amenities, apathetic service, and the absence of pampering.

The recent additions to the Seychelles resort scene – Lemuria, on the island of Praslin, and Banyan Tree, on the island of Mahe – would be considered ultra-deluxe properties and similar to the exotic resorts found in Bali and Thailand.

On the main island of Mahe, location of the capital city of Victoria, the most luxurious property is Banyan Tree. Set on lovely Intendance Bay, at the southwestern tip of the Island, on a most breathtaking white-sand beach, surrounded by palms, lush tropical forests and steep, protective mountain slopes, Banyan Tree is a serenely beautiful destination. Here guests can luxuriate in one of 47 stunning, plantation/colonial-style villas.

All of the air-conditioned villas have high sloping ceilings, airy verandahs, louvered doors, private pools, sun lounges, pavilions with living and dining areas, king size bedrooms, coffee and tea makers, TVs, private safes, IDD telephones and large bathrooms with tubs, showers, dual vanities, bathrobes and hair dryers. The villas range in size from 1,000 square feet up to 4,800 feet for the two-bedroom, Presidential Villa. In high season, prices range from $1,309 per night up to $4,172.

In addition to in-villa dining and picnics on the beach, there are three restaurants featuring Southeast Asian, International and local cuisine. The beach at Intendance is considered one of the top ten in the world. Also available are a variety of water sports, an attractive infinity pool, a gym and a world-class Banyan Tree Spa offering an assortment of Asian therapies and treatments.

One of the resorts on Mahe with the most facilities is the Plantation Club at Baie Lazare, also located near the southwestern tip of the Island. The property, situated on 180 acres of former coconut plantation, with lush grounds abounding with tropical flora, fronted by an impressive expanse of white-sand beach bordered by palms, granite formations and verdant forest is privately owned and operated.

Each of the 200 air-conditioned rooms and suites includes a split-level bedroom and sitting area, an outdoor balcony or patio with views out to the sea or the tropical lagoon, satellite television with a video channel, in-house radio music, a refrigerator, private safe, hair dryer and a wardrobe-dressing area. My first choice would be the refurbished, deluxe rooms which have large bathrooms with giant soaking tubs and separate glass showers, cathedral ceilings and teak furnishings. For families, the two-bedroom suites are very elegant and spacious, with separate living rooms and a second guest bathroom.

Sport facilities include two flood-lit tennis courts, a practice tennis court, volleyball, open-air badminton, a large free-form, fresh-water pool with an adjoining children's pool, a health center with sauna, Jacuzzi, massage and a very small exercise room, and water-front activities such as windsurfing, Pedaloes, canoes, Hobicats, snorkeling and a Padi-certified diving center with a full-range diving program for the beginner, as well as the advanced diver. The white-sand beach is panoramically beautiful with clear, warm waters. Unfortunately the ocean floor beneath the water has stones, coral and an occasional sea urchin.

The main dining room, Frangipani, opens up to gentle sea breezes for a buffet breakfast, as well as dinners with Creole and international cuisine and theme buffets. Lunch, snacks and beverages are served by the pool. Lazare's is an à la carte specialty-dinner restaurant featuring more upscale continental dining in an elegant romantic atmosphere with quiet musical entertainment. From 8:00 p.m. to 2:00 a.m. guests can try their luck at slot machines, roulette and blackjack in the hotel casino (the slots open at 2:00p.m.).

Both Banyan Tree and the Plantation Club are a 30- to 40-minute drive from the international airport, where car rentals and taxis are readily available. Helicopter service direct to Plantation Club's heliport is also possible.

Other hotels on Mahe include Meridian Barbaron Beach near Grand Anse, and Meridian Fisherman's Cove, Sunset Beach, Northolme, Berjaya Beau Vallon, and Coral Strand, all on Baie Beau Vallon. None of these establishments could be considered first-class. The best restaurants on Mahe, other than at Banyan Tree and The Plantation Club, include La Scala (Italian) and Le Corsair (French Creole) at Bel Ombre, Chez Plume (French Creole) at Anse Boileau, and La Perle Noire (French Creole) at Beau Vallon.

Of the numerous exquisite beaches that surround the perimeter of the island, Anse Intendance, the location of Banyan Tree Resort, is the most picturesque, with a half-mile of powdery sand and huge rolling waves framed by mountains, coconut palms, and takamaka trees. Beau Vallon at the northwest portion of the island is the busiest and most suited

for swimming and waters sports (but not the most beautiful), and Anse Royale on the southeast coast is also extremely picturesque and excellent for swimming and snorkeling.

Praslin, the second largest island, is accessible from Mahe by a 15-minute propeller flight, or a 2 ½-hour ferry-boat ride, and is most well known for its lovely 450-acre rainforest, the Valley-De-Mai, home of the botanical rarity, the Coco de Mer Palm, as well as such rare birds as the Black Parrot, Blue Pigeon, and Bulbul.

This seven-mile long island is surrounded by coral reef and boasts numerous silver-white-sand beaches. Cote d'Or and Anse Volbert make up a 2 1/2-mile stretch bordered by palm trees, several small hotels, and restaurants. Anse Lazio, sits at the

most northern tip of the island, accessible only by a rather primitive, bumpy road. This is a most picturesque, idyllic beach and the setting of palms, pines, seagrapes, granite rock formations and tropical flowers is absolutely, positively, breathtaking. The powder-white sand is firm and excellent for strolling and jogging, and the crystal-clear, warm waters are the very finest for swimming. Adjacent to this extraordinary beach is an excellent restaurant, Bon Bon Plume. Here, owner Richelieu Verlaque offers patrons exceptional fresh fish, seafood, Creole dishes and French wines in a casual, open-air restaurant overlooking the panorama of Anse Lazio.

For a big evening out, visitors head for the elegant casino on Cote d'Or, a beautiful, colonial-style building. Downstairs there is a separate room with dozens of slot machines and the main casino offering roulette, blackjack and poker. Upstairs is the location of a gourmet restaurant, Tante Mimi, one of the best continental restaurants on the island. There are several hotels of note on Praslin, including La Reserve, Lemuria, L'Archipel, Acajou, Coco-de-mer, and Chateau de Feuilles.

Possibly the most luxurious resort in the Seychelles, Lemuria opened in December 1999 on the northwest coast of Praslin, only a ten-minute drive from the airport. Surrounded by lush, rare vegetation and three white-sand beaches, washed by warm turquoise waters, the resort complex set on 250 acres includes a main reception building set on a hillside with 88 suites and nine villas located on the beach.

Each accommodation has a terrace or a balcony, a mini-bar, private safe, television, DVD/ stereo-cassette player, telephone with an answering machine and a bathroom with twin sinks, a deep soaking tub, a separate shower stall and cotton robes. The 80, 600-square-foot Junior Suites go for $870 per night in high season and the eight, 1,200-square-foot Senior Suites for $1,820. The eight, two-bedroom, 7,000-square-foot Pool Villas start at $3,220 and the 12,000 square-foot Presidential Villa with its own full-size swimming pool will set you back $9,320 per night.

A three-level pool cascades down to the sea. Sport facilities include an 18-hole golf course, two

floodlit tennis courts, a lounge, a meeting room, a children's club with babysitters, four bars, a spa-fitness center with state-of-the-art equipment, sauna, steam, Jacuzzis, massage and body treatment rooms, and a beauty salon. Numerous water sports are available, including Pedalos, snorkeling, sailing, catamarans, kayaks, and windsurfing. One of the three beaches surrounding the resort, Anse Georgette is considered to be among the most beautiful in the world.

There are three restaurants on premises: the Legend, offering international and local cuisine; the Sea Horse, featuring Mediterranean/Italian specialties; and a casual venue on the beach where guests can enjoy salads, grilled items, fresh fish and sea food. Rates include breakfast and meal plans are available.

Another upscale resort, La Reserve, is situated on a small bay between Anse Volbert and Anse Lazio, on the northwest side of the island. Thirty accommodations, consisting of 14 bungalows, 12 air-conditioned villas and four air-conditioned suites, are spread over tropical gardens on a small beach where picturesque rock formations are illuminated at night. Although the rooms and bungalows are tastefully furnished with long four-poster beds, verandas, refrigerator/mini-bars and bathrooms with shower stalls, hair dryers and magnifying mirrors, there are no televisions, radios, room safes or bathroom amenities. Facilities include one tennis court, a boutique, a colonial bar where afternoon tea is served, and a charming semi-open-air restaurant that jetties out over the water. Breakfast is served buffet style. Dinner varies from candle-lit dinner dances to Chinese and Creole buffets. Boat trips for

an out-island barbecue are also offered weekly. The dining experience at La Reserve is very satisfying.

In 1996, Acajou opened on the Cote d'Or, another absolutely perfect expanse of firm, powder-fine, white-sand beach with very calm, crystal-clear waters for swimming. All 28 of the air-conditioned guest rooms have wood-plank walls and ceilings, ceramic tile floors, tasteful furnishings, a small porch, cable television, a refrigerator, hair dryer, queen-sized bed, ample storage, a bathroom with a tub-shower combination, sink and toilet and a fresh, clean feel. Facilities include a small pool, an open-air restaurant and a bar.

A 30-minute boat ride from Praslin will transport you to La Digue, the most beautiful, pristine, and photographed of the developed Seychelle islands. The breathtakingly scenic Anse Source D'Argent is the most beautiful beach-setting in the world. Here, warm turquoise waters, with mild currents, lap silver-white-sand beaches inundated with tiny private coves interspersed with geometric gray boulder formations, palm trees, and other tropical flora, with verdant green hills in the background. This is the scenery that appears most often on postcard and brochures covering the Seychelles. Anse Source D'Argent is also the perfect choice for a romantic picnic. The more adventurous can ride bicycles or hire transport to Grande Anse and Petite Anse, two half-mile expanses of white-sand beach where the sea is beautiful, but with strong waves and currents. Visitors to these two beaches must be prepared to climb steep hills with precarious footing.

Unfortunately, there is only one hotel with any facilities on the island, La Digue Lodge. Situated on a peaceful stretch of while-sand beach with gardens filled with coconut palms, takamaka trees, and flowering plants, the 57 air-conditioned accommodations include refrigerated mini-bars, limited cable television, hair dryers, and ample bathroom and storage space.

The beach-front A-frames are the most desirable and feature two, small, upper-level loft areas for family members. Public facilities include the small open-air lobby, a small pool with lounges adjacent to the restaurant that serves lunch and snacks, boutiques, and the main, semi-open-air dining room that features buffet breakfasts and a fixed, table d'hôte dinner menu, both of which are included in the room rate.

Although I wanted to love this intimate, picturesque resort, which has great possibilities, our overall experience (several years ago) prevented leaving with a favorable opinion. Upon arrival we had bugs crawling around our refrigerator, closet, and bathroom. In the evening, there was no hot water in which to bathe or shave, and when we awoke in the morning we found our bathroom inundated with literally hundreds of bees that apparently crawled in through small openings in the walls and windows. When we complained to the general manager, he was extremely defensive and aggressively belligerent and made us feel we either had to endure, leave, or step outside and have a "shoot-out". Dining was mediocre at best and service tolerable, but far from gracious. Possibly, La Digue is best visited for a day by motor launch from Praslin until a suitable, tourist-friendly establishment is developed.

Although (other than Banyan Tree and Lemuria), few of the hotels and resorts afford the comfort, dining, and level of service of a luxury establishment, the Seychelle Islands are an absolute must for world-travelers who wish to experience the ultimate in panoramic scenery, idyllic beaches, and lush environs. I have no doubt that the Seychelles are destined to be discovered and acknowledged by travel periodicals and developed by major hotel chains. Why not beat the crowds and experience these unique, one-of-a-kind gems before the onslaught.

Banyan Tree, Anse Intendance
Mahe, Seychelles
Tel. 1-888-437-8456 (US)
+352-401-5678 (Seychelles)
www.BanyanTree.Mahe, Seychelles

The Plantation Club Resort and Casino
Baie Lazare, P.O. Box 437
Victoria, Mahe, Seychelles
Tel. 248-361-361, Fax 248-361-333

La Reserve
Anse Petit Cour, Praslin, Seychelles
Tel. 248-232-211, Fax 248-232-166

Lemuria Resort of Praslin
Anse Kerlan, Praslin, Seychelles
Tel. 248-281-281, Fax 248-281-000

Hotel Acajou
Cote d'Or, Praslin, Seychelles
Tel. 248-232-400, Fax 248-232-401

CHAPTER TEN

EUROPE

AUSTRIA
Hotel Schloss Fuschl

FRANCE
Auberge des Templiers (Les Bezards)
Chateau d'Artigny (Tours/Montbazon)
Chateau d'Esclimont (St. Symphorien-Le-Chateaux)
Chateau du Domaine St. Martin (Vence)
Chateau Les Crayeres (Reims)
Domaine des Hauts de Loire (Onzain)
Georges Blanc (Vonnas)
Hotel du Cap-Eden Roc (Cap d'Antibes)
La Cote Saint Jacques (Joigny)

GERMANY
Brenner's Park-Hotel and Spa (Baden-Baden)

GREAT BRITAIN
Chewton Glenn (New Milton)

GREECE
Astir Palace (Vouliagmeni near Athens)

ITALY
Grand Hotel Quisisana (Capri)
Hotel Cala di Volpe (Sardinia)
Hotel Cipriani (Venice)
Hotel Splendido & Splendido Mare (Portofino)
Il San Pietro (Positano)
Santa Caterina (Almalfi)
Villa d'Este (Cernobbio, Lake Como)

SCOTLAND
The Westin Turnberry Resort (Ayrshire)

SPAIN
Barcelo La Bobadilla
Byblos Andaluz (Mijas-Golf)
Castillo Hotel Son Vida (Mallorca)
Hotel Arts (Barcelona)
Hotel Formentor (Mallorca)
Marbella Club (Marbella)
Puente Romano (Marbella)

SWITZERLAND
Badrutt's Palace (St. Moritz)
Beau Rivage Palace (Lausanne)
Le Mirador Kempinski (Vevey)
Palace Hotel (Gstaad)
Suvretta House (St. Moritz)
Victoria Jungfrau Grand Hotel and Spa (Interlaken)

Chateau d'Esclimont, St. Symphorien-Le-Chateaux

Collectively, the resorts in Europe offer the best food, service, and traditional elegance in the world. However, few have the acreage, sport facilities, and variety of restaurants and entertainment that are found in the resorts of the continental United States, the Caribbean, Mexico, Southeast Asia, and Hawaii.

In spite of these shortcomings, a stay at a European resort can be an unforgettable experience. Only here will responsive, willing maids and room service come at the push of a buzzer; only here will a knowledgeable concierge make all your arrangements and solve all your problems; only here will three or four waiters scurry around your table at dinner to ensure the best service; and only here will you be treated with efficiency and respect by everyone at the hotel.

Having to dress for dinner and other formalities may not be compatible with many people's idea of a relaxing vacation. Others will find a sense of being ensconced in elegance and tradition a change of pace and enjoyable. Because the European establishments differ from country to country, the specific comments and qualifications prefacing each country may prove helpful.

FRANCE

Although there are not many properties that would qualify as great resorts under the definition set forth earlier, there are numerous charming, small châteaus and inns that offer exceptional cuisine and accommodations in picturesque surroundings that should appeal to resort afficionados. Therefore, I have included 10 of these properties that are spread throughout the provinces and can be visited during a one-week drive through France.

The itinerary I suggest will have special appeal to wine lovers and gourmets, as it passes through the major wine regions and goes past many of the highly acclaimed restaurants in provincial France. In my opinion, the dining experience in the restaurants of these resorts is more satisfying than in comparable restaurants in Paris and generally will cost half the price.

If you start in Paris, you can take the short drive to the Palace of Versailles, enjoy lunch nearby at Trois Marches (Michelin, 1 stars) and arrive a half-hour later at Château d'Esclimont, a 16th-century castle converted to a very special deluxe hotel.

If you drive south to Orléans and continue west to Onzain in the Loire Valley, you can spend the next day at the charming Domaine des Hauts de Loire. (Michelin, 2 stars)

The next day, take the short drive to Tours, explore the castles and vineyards of the Loire Valley, lunch in Tours at Charles Barrier (Michelin, 1 stars) or Jean Bardet (Michelin, 2 stars), and continue on 10 miles to Montbazon, where you can spend the night at Château d'Artigny.

Continuing south for 180 miles will bring you to the great wine region of Bordeaux. Wine enthusiasts may wish to remain an extra day in Bordeaux to have more time to explore the great châteaus of Medoc, Graves, St. Emilion, Pommeral, and Sauterne.

From Bordeaux, you can continue by plane, train, or car to the Côte d'Azur, where there is an abundance of highly rated restaurants, including Moulin de Mougins (Vergé-Michelin, 1 star) at Mougins, Louis XIV at Hotel de Paris in Monte Carlo (Ducasse-Michelin 3 star), and Le Chanteclaire at the Negresco in Nice (Michelin, 1 star). For the night, you can stay at Le Mas d'Artigny in St. Paul de Vence or at Château du Domaine St. Martin above Vence, (Michelin, 1 star) which are two small, charming, relaxed resorts with excellent restaurants in a picturesque area a few miles north of Cannes and Nice. Those who prefer more pomp and formality may prefer Hôtel du Cap at Cap d'Antibes, one of the most exclusive resorts in the world with exceptional dining and gardens.

If you are driving from the Bordeaux area to the Côte d'Azur and wish to take two days, I suggest an overnight stay at L'Ousteau Beaumanière in Les Baux-de-Provence, where there is an excellent restaurant (Michelin, 2 stars).

From the Côte d'Azur, you will head north to Paris, passing through the Rhône Valley and Burgundy. You may wish to stop for lunch in Valence at Pic (Michelin, 2 stars) on your way to Lyon. Lyon is a good home base for those wishing to explore the region. Before you reach Lyon, you can detour to Lake Annecy to spend a day at L'Eridan, renowned Chef Marc Veyrat's elegantly rustic Auberge overlooking the lake, where you can enjoy Veyrat's somewhat unique style of gastronomy (Michelin, 3 stars). At least one evening should be spent in Vonnas at the incredibly charming inn of cuisiner Georges Blanc. Here you will enjoy one of the best meals in France (Michelin, 3 stars), as well as one of the most beautiful properties. There are a number of other highly acclaimed restaurants in the Rhône Valley and Burgundy area, including Les Pyramides in Vienne (Michelin, 2 stars), Paul Bocuse in Collonges-au-Mont d'Or (Michelin 3 stars), Alain Chappel in Mionnay (Michelin, 2 stars), Auberge du Cep in Fleurie (Michelin, 1 stars), L'Esperance in Vezeley (Michelin, 3 stars), Troisgros in Roanne (Michelin, 3 stars).

From Burgundy, it is a short drive or train ride to Paris or Geneva, Switzerland. On the way back towards Paris, your final evening could be spent at Auberge des Templiers, an inn near the Loire Valley with cottages set in lovely gardens and superior service and dining (Michelin, 1 stars). This is certainly one of the most charming, heavenly places in Europe.

Heading north, you will enjoy an evening and fantastic dinner at Michel Lorain's hotel on the Yonne River, La Cote Saint Jacques (Michelin 3 star).

If you have one more day, a trip to Les Crayères in Reims is a rewarding detour. Situated in an elegant château in the heart of the Champagne region, Chef Didier Elena plies his culinary skills, creating a top dining experience (Michelin, 2 stars).

The 10 hostelries reviewed are not resorts in the same sense as the other establishments described in this book; therefore, you will not find the same variety of restaurants, sport facilities, shops, and activities. However, each offers superior accommodations, cuisine, service, and surroundings. For travelers to Paris with only a weekend or a few days to spend in the country, I would recommend the relatively short excursions to Château d'Esclimont, Auberge des Templiers, or Les Crayères.

For those seeking large grand hotels in resort areas, I can recommend the following: Cannes – Majestic and Carlton; Nice – Negresco; La Baule – Hermitage; Deauville – Normandy, Hotel de Paris – Monte Carlo; and the Palace at Biarritz.

GREECE

This country has more picturesque islands and charming towns than any other in Europe. Unfortunately, few of the hotels are of the caliber or offer the facilities and amenities required to be included in this book as great resorts. An exception, the Astir Palace complex at Vouliagmeni Beach near Athens, is a truly worthwhile experience, and I recommend it highly to my readers who tour the Greek Islands. This resort is a deluxe property by Greek standards, but may only be considered a first-class hostelry in other West European countries. This observation is not intended to detract from the desirability of the resort; however, visitors should not come expecting to experience accommodations, food, and service comparable to deluxe resorts in Switzerland, France, Italy, or Spain.

Other Greek Islands with beaches and numerous hotels include Corfu, Mykonos, Rhodes, Skiathos, Santotini, and Crete.

Villa d'Este, Cernobbio

ITALY

Although Italy is saturated with grand hotels, few other than those described herein qualify as great resorts.

For those who wish to stay at a resort in Italy for an extended period, I can recommend the Villa d'Este, in the breathtaking Lake Como area (one of the most complete resorts in Europe), the Grand Hotel Quisisana, on the floral island of Capri, the romantic, intimate San Pietro, near Positano, Santa Caterina in Amalfi, the elegant Hotel Splendido set on a hill overlooking Portofino, Hotel Cala di Volpe on Sardinia, and the charming Hotel Cipriani on Giudecca Island, a four-minute boat ride across the canal from San Marco Square in Venice.

SPAIN

The two main resort areas in Spain are the Costa del Sol and the island of Mallorca. Most of the hotels in these areas attract budget travelers from Northern Europe and Spain, and the beach towns are touristy and crowded. However, Spain boasts many notable resorts, six of which are described in this chapter.

Overall, the settings are romantic, the service is competent, the food is Continental, and the rooms are large. However, air-conditioning is always questionable and entertainment is limited. Fellow guests are most often Europeans. Although the weather is more reliable here than in France, Switzerland or Northern Europe, it would be wise to confine your visits to the late spring, the summer and early fall.

SWITZERLAND

The cities and villages of Switzerland contain many of the world's greatest hotels, with comfortable accommodations, excellent cuisine, friendly and efficient service and hospitality and a picturesque setting. There are numerous towns, such as St. Moritz, Gstaad, Interlaken, Montreux, Davos and Zermatt that are winter ski areas similar to those found in Colorado.

The establishments covered here are impeccable hostelries with a great deal of charm. During the winter ski season, they are usually filled to capacity with wealthy clientele from all over the world who seek a chic winter resort. However, those seeking fun in the sun during the summer months should know that the sport facilities found at most of the resorts do not compare with those in other areas of the world. They are often not complete, inconveniently located or just not "up to snuff." In addition, the weather rarely gets as warm as it does in southern Italy, Spain and Greece. In any event, weary travelers visiting Europe will enjoy and appreciate a sojourn to the properties listed. It will afford them a chance to rest and unwind in superior, friendly, comfortable, elegant picturesque surroundings.

Of the areas covered, Gstaad is a small charming typical Swiss resort village, St. Moritz is a cosmopolitan resort town with scenic beauty, Interlaken is a medium-size town set between numerous resort areas, and Lausanne is a resort area in the lake region reminiscent of the French and Italian Rivieras.

Those wishing to spend several weeks in Switzerland and to sample the diverse resorts included in this chapter can rent a car and drive through the country in a relaxed fashion. If you fly into Geneva and rent a car at the airport, you can drive to the Beau Rivage Palace in Lausanne or Le Mirador above Vevay in three-quarters of an hour. From Lausanne, it is less than an hour-and-a-half's drive through picturesque mountains and valleys to the Palace Hotel in Gstaad. Another hour-and-a-half drive through mountains will take you to the Victoria Jungfrau Grand Hotel and Spa in Interlaken.

Zurich is another hour or two away. From Zurich, you commence your journey down the eastern portion of Switzerland. The drive to St. Moritz could take from three to four hours. After visiting Badrutt's Palace and Suvretta House in St. Moritz, you can take a train or drive back to Zurich or Milan to fly home.

AUSTRIA

HOTEL SCHLOSS FUSCHL

Majestically set on a peninsula in lovely Lake Fuschl, surrounded by rolling hills and green forests, Hotel Schloss Fuschl is the premier full-facility, upscale retreat in Austria. The Castle of Fuschl was constructed in 1450 as a hunting lodge for the archbishops of Salzburg. In 1958, Carl Adolf Vogel purchased the Castle and converted it into a resort. The Max Grundig group (with hotels in Germany and Monte Carlo) acquired the property in 1977 and proceeded to make numerous improvements and renovations. Since 2001, the property has been part of the ArabellaSheraton group. The grounds consist of the main hotel, six lake-side cottages, a nine-hole golf course, a new spa complex, a fishery and a boat and sun deck area on the lake, all connected by lovely floral gardens, green fields, and wooded trails.

The property received an extensive renovation in 2005/2006 which encompassed a new annex housing a large spa, indoor pool, an elegant ballroom, and a gourmet restaurant; as well as renovations and redecorations to its wine cellar, tower suites, and the adjacent Jaegerhaus Hunting Lodge. A very impressive collection of old master paintings and objets d'art was also added. A second phase of renovations will include the Waldhouse

The lobby, lounge, and interior areas are rustic in decor, very typical of a hunting lodge. The restaurants (Castle Restaurant and "Imperial" gourmet restaurant), however, are elegant and take full advantage of the splendid views of the lake and surrounding hills and forests. All indoor areas are adorned with old masters from the "Schloss Fuschl Collection." The service is continental, yet friendly, and the general mood of the resort is perhaps a bit more relaxed than most European establishments.

Accommodations

Of the 110 guest rooms and suites, 65 are designated deluxe and grand deluxe rooms, 32 are designated suites, seven Tower Suites, and six Lake-Side Cottages. Six additional rooms and suites are located in the Jaegerhaus Hunting Lodge directly opposite the Castle Tower.

The rooms are all quite different in size, location, and decor. All rooms have air conditioning. Many have balconies and genuine antique furnishings, mini-bars, direct-dial telephones, remote-control color televisions, private wall safes, dressing tables and bathrooms with hair dryers and terry-cloth robes. The most desirable accommodations are the seven Tower Suites, which include expensive paintings, an abundance of valuable antiques, elaborate chandeliers and large, modern bathrooms.

Modern conference facilities with audiovisual equipment are available at the ArabellaSheraton Hotel Jagdhof, just 600 meters away. The 143 rooms of the Jagdhof, under the same management, offer a somewhat more casual atmosphere.

Restaurants, Lounges, and Entertainment

A buffet breakfast along with lunch and dinner are served daily in the Castle Restaurant, a bright, airy dining room with most tables enjoying panoramic views of Lake Fuschl through large picture windows. When weather permits, all meals are offered

on the adjoining outdoor terrace, which offers an even more dynamic setting. The lunch and dinner normally served in one of the elegant second-floor dining rooms are special treats because Hotel Schloss Fuschl has been voted one of the best hotel restaurants in Austria. The à la carte menu changes each season, and there are imaginative special appetizers, entrées, and desserts featured daily. Jackets and ties are required for men at dinner.

The superb cuisine, although Austrian in description, has Gallic overtones with an emphasis on fresh ingredients, miniature vegetables, extremely light sauces, and exotic presentations.

Although there is an assortment of European wines, Austrian vintages and French Bordeaux predominate. The Vinothek, a wine bar located in a historic vaulted cellar dating back to the 16th century, is the place to sample a large selection of rare wines. Wine tasting events are often held at sunset on the adjacent Diana Terrace.

The newly opened gourmet restaurant, "Imperial," offers innovative Eurasian fare under the supervision of Gault-Millau-honored chef Thomas M.

Walkensteiner. A special sampling menu is available as well as à la carte items.

Afternoon tea and pastries are served in the Yellow Salon and in the legendary Castle Bar. A cigar lounge with comfortable leather chairs and an open fireplace invites guests to enjoy an impressive selection of cigars and brandies.

For a change of scenery, guests can take the short walk up the hill to the ArabellaSheraton Hotel Jagdhof for typical Austrian cuisine and a less formal repast. We found dinner at the Jagdhof a charming experience.

Sport Facilities

The newly constructed Castle Spa features state-of-the-art facilities, a swimming pool, steam bath, sauna, whirlpool, and workout area.

A nine-hole golf course is located on Hotel Schloss Fuschl's property and offers rolling green hills and a picturesque view of the lake. Tee times can be arranged through the hotel. Only ten minutes from the resort, golfers can play 18 holes at the Eugendorf Golf Club.

Beneath the main hotel building on Lake Fuschl, guests can relax and sun on a private bathing pier, as well as swim, windsurf, fish, or take a ride in a rowboat or paddleboat on the lake. Mountain bicycles can be rented for those wishing to explore the surroundings. At the Castle Fishery arrangements can be made for a guided boat tour of the surrounding fishing waters which includes a rustic fisherman's snack.

The region surrounding Lake Fuschl offers miles of Nordic walking, jogging, and hiking trails. The eight-mile route leading around the lake begins at the Castle Fishery, where there is a sign with orientation tips.

The Castle Shed is home to a vintage Rolls Royce and antique carriage collection and can accommodate large gatherings.

Miscellaneous and Environs

Visitors to the castle may prefer to fly into Munich or Salzburg (the closest airports) or travel by train from Zurich, Frankfurt, or Vienna.

In addition to exploring the colorful small villages along Lake Fuschl and the surrounding suburbs, most guests will wish to spend some time in Salzburg, which is only a 15-minute drive from the resort. The Altstadt (old town) lies on the left bank of the city with the Mozartplatz in the center. Here you can have coffee, pastries, or a beer in numerous atmospheric cafés, such as Café Tomaselli, explore the numerous shops and boutiques, visit Salzburg Cathedral, a splendid Renaissance building with two symmetrical towers that is famous for its 10,000-pipe organ, or explore Residenz Place, which dates back to the 12th century, location of the impressive Baroque 17th-century Residenz Fountain and the 35-bell Glockenspiel. For a panoramic view of the city, take the express elevator from Gstättengasse 13 to Mönchsberg Terrace.

Hotel Schloss Fuschl offers its guests a rustic Austrian retreat in a picturesque setting with comfortable accommodations, attentive service, and exceptional cuisine.

Hotel Schloss Fuschl
A-5322 Hof Bei Salzburg, Austria
Tel. 43-6229-2253-0
Fax 43-6229-2253-1531
E-mail: schloss.fuschl@arabellasheraton.com
www.schlossfuschl.at
Web: www.arabellasheraton.com

FRANCE

AUBERGE DES TEMPLIERS

In 1939, the Dépée family purchased the historic site of this charming French inn. In the Middle Ages, a Commanderie of the Knights of the Temple stood here, and in the 17th century the main Manor House was built as a post-horse stage point, where guests stayed overnight. By 1946, the Dépées had converted the Manor House into a charming inn, preserving the original structure. Through the years, they added two dining rooms, numerous cottages, and a pool and tennis courts in the lovely gardens behind the manor.

The Manor House consists of a reception area, a lounge with bar and fireplace, a breakfast room, a patio, two dining rooms and seven guest rooms. The rooms have wood-beam ceilings, giant rustic chandeliers and expensive period furnishings. All the design and decorations are elegant and tasteful. Today the Auberge is owned and operated by Philippe Dépée . Although there have been numerous chefs over the years, the recipes and supervision of the kitchen and dining room are personally directed by the Dépées with total dedication.

The gardens and park behind the manor form a beautiful painting. The well-manicured lawns are dotted with trees and accentuated by colorful flower beds. Ivy and flowers adorn the walls of the manor and crawl up the several cottages that are tucked behind the trees and hedges. The veranda outside the dining room is surrounded by beds of roses and is a most charming place to enjoy breakfast or a candlelight dinner.

Accommodations

In the original Manor House and the newer cottages, there are a total of 22 air-conditioned guest rooms and eight suites that contain separate parlors. All accommodations are rustic yet elegant in design and furnishings and though different, all include air conditioning, a television with CNN cable, a large closet and wardrobe area, expensive period furniture and fabrics and a telephone. The modern bathrooms have colorful tiles, tubs with European shower attachments, double sinks, separate toilet compartments and terry-cloth robes and some have magnifying mirrors and hair dryers.

For the ultimate comfort, a couple can luxuriate in the grand apartment in the cottage to the right of the Manor House, which consists of a lovely bedroom with soft floral prints, a king-size bed and exquisite furnishings, a lavish bathroom with Jacuzzi tub, separate double shower, sauna, toilet-bidet compartment, double vanities and many mirrors, a vestibule with giant walk-in closets and a warmly furnished den with a fireplace. A weekend in these sumptuous, romantic accommodations will add a spark to any relationship.

Restaurants, Lounges, and Entertainmen

The two adjoining dining rooms are done in an elegant rustic country French decor and face out into the park. There are wood-beam ceilings, tapestries, large light fixtures, expensive fabrics and area rugs, and each table has flowers and a candelabrum. In the summer, dinner is also served outdoors on the terrace. When weather permits, salads and light offerings are served by the pool.

Amiable Maîtres d'Gilbert Chevalier and Guy Pelletier, who have been with the hotel for decades, will personally assist you with your food

and wine selections while you are enjoying cocktails and complimentary hors d'oeuvres in the bar or on the terrace. There is an extensive wine list with a marvelous selection of Burgundies, Bordeaux, and Rhônes from the Auberge's wine cellar. Gilbert, who speaks perfect English, personally oversees the service and presentation of food at every table in the dining room.

The cuisine is superb and the variety of game dishes, foie gras and souffles were the very best I have experienced. There is an à la carte menu, plus two fixed-price degustation menus. At lunchtime, guests can order the entire menu or opt for some of the imaginative lighter starters such as a delightful salad composed of a whole roasted lobster in a chalotte-flavored butter with Arugula, a delicate, flaky torte stuffed with slices of ripe red tomato, mozzarella and sautéed red snapper covered with a roux of mashed, ripe black olives, balsamic vinegar, oil and spices, or a sampling of duck foie gras with salad greens and an eggplant melange. In my opinion, Auberge des Templiers offers one of the better all-around dining experiences in the world.

Sport Facilities

In the middle of the gardens is a large swimming pool with lounges. Near the pool are two composition tennis courts, and there is a golf course in Sully-sur-Loire, a 15-minute drive from the resort. Guests can walk, jog or bicycle a few miles to a lovely stretch of woods and a small lake.

Miscellaneous and Environs

Les Bezards is only 98 miles from Paris at the beginning of the Loire Region. You can take Autoroute A-6 to Montargis and then turn on to Highway N-7, which runs right past the entrance to the resort. Highway A-77 also leads into Boismorand from the Dordives.

Auberge des Templiers is a marvelous choice for an overnight stay while driving through France; or,

if you are staying a few days, you can explore the nearby castles of the Loire Valley. Within 10 miles is the hunting museum and castle in Gien, and the castle at La Bussière. Gien is also the home of the world famous Faiencerie factory which can be visited by appointment. Within 10 to 50 miles, you will find such famous castles as Boucard, Blancafort, La Verrerie, Maupas, Méneton-Salon, Bourges,and Le Paiais Jacques-Coeur. In July and August, there is a historical drama from the days of the knights performed at St. Fargeau.

Auberge des Templiers is that special place, an idyllic private sanctuary where everything comes together harmoniously. The senses are treated to the fragrance of roses, the beauty of perfectly manicured lawns and flower beds, the sounds of chirping birds, and the taste of fine French cuisine. This resort is a most charming place to pass a few days in quiet, beautiful, floral surroundings while enjoying the most comfortable accommodations, as well as the very finest food and service. This is a total winner in every category and one of my personal favorite retreats.

Auberge des Templiers
45290 Les Bezards
Boismorand, France
Tel. 011-33-2-38-31-80-01
Fax 011-33-2-38-31-84-51
e-mail: auberge.templiers@wanadoo.fr
www.lestempliers.com

FRANCE

CHÂTEAU D'ARTIGNY

This magnificent château, surrounded by 50 acres of woods, sits on a hill overlooking the Indre Valley and the town of Montbazon. Montbazon is 140 miles from Paris and six miles from Tours in the heart of the Loire/Château country.

Different castles and fortresses have stood on this site since the eleventh century. Charmed by the beauty of the setting, the famous French perfumer François Coty bought the estate in 1912 and spent 20 years erecting the present château. In 1961, Château d'Artigny was purchased by René Traversac, a French real-estate entrepreneur, and converted to a castle hotel. It was the forerunner of his hotel chain – "LesGrandes Etapes Françaises", which includes Château d'Esclimont among others.

The palatial public areas are among the most elegant to be found in France, and the floral gardens provide a magical facade to this magnificent structure.

Accommodations

There are 32 guest rooms in the main chateau and nine more guest rooms and four suites in the Pavillon d'Ariane, situated a half-block from the château, and 10 deluxe rooms and two suites in Cite des Parfumes a building added in 2001. At the bottom of the hill, near the entrance to the property, are two other hotel buildings, Pavillon de Chasse, with three rooms, and Port-Moulin, with seven. The rooms in the main chateau, Cite des Parfumes and Pavillon d'Ariane are quite large, with high ceilings, elegant period furnishings, good closet space and modern bathrooms. The suites in the Pavillon d'Ariane are

the most impressive. The public rooms in the main chateau are very elegant, with expensive tapestries and objets d'art. There are also three conference rooms here that can accommodate up to 80 people; and four modern conference facilities on the first floor of Cite des Parfumes, the largest of which can accommodate 120 theater-style.

Restaurants, Lounges, and Entertainment

The main restaurant consists of two magnificently appointed rooms that look out over the valley. The food, service and atmosphere have been notable over the years. Breakfast is served à la carte, buffet-style or in your room. Cooking classes are offered once each month.

The wine list consists of an impressive collection of expensive, fine French wines. In addition, the salon bar offers an extensive variety of old ports, whiskeys and cognacs.

There is no music or entertainment on a regular basis. However, a number of musical concerts take place at the château during the fall and winter seasons.

Sport Facilities

On the property, there is a small freshwater swimming pool with lounges and a pool bar. Next to the pool, there are two tennis courts, a ping-pong table, and a small pitch-and-putt golf facility. A fitness/spa area was added in 2002 in the tunnel connecting the Pavillon d'Ariane with the main chateau. Located here are a steam room, sauna, Jacuzzi, massage

and changing rooms, a relaxation area and a gym with limited equipment. There are walking and jogging paths in the surrounding forests, and horseback riding is available four miles away. The nearest 18-hole golf course is eight miles from Montbazon.

Miscellaneous and Environs

There are no shops at the hotel, and the closest big city is Tours, seven miles away. A cigar lounge with a French pool table was recently added beneath the Pavillon Ariane. You may want to visit some of the famous châteaus in the nearby area: Chenonceaux (21 miles), where there is a sound and light presentation; Chateau de Blois (40 miles) Chambord (38 miles), which is surrounded by one of the largest parks in France; Chinon (26 miles); Amboise (23 miles); Loches (21 miles); Villandry (13 miles); and Azay-le-Rideau (12 miles). A nice day trip would include visiting the castles at Chenonceaux and Amboise, followed by lunch at Le Choiseul, a lovely (one-star Michelin) hotel restaurant which sits immediately east of the castle and is owned by Les Grandes Etapes Francaises.

Those interested in the wines of the Loire can visit the vineyards producing Muscadet, Anjou, Sancerre and Vouvray. (The last is the closest to Montbazon.)

When driving from Paris, take the Autoroute A-10 past Orléans to Tours, then follow N-10 for six miles to Montbazon. Château d'Artigny is a grand property that features excellent cuisine, fine service and elegant accommodations, and it is an ideal home base for exploration of the châteaux and vineyards in the area of the Loire.

Château d'Artigny
92 Rue de Monts,
37250 Montbazon, France
Tel. 02-47-34-30-30
Fax 02-47-34-30-39
E-mail: reception.artigny@grandestapes.fr

FRANCE

CHÂTEAU D'ESCLIMONT

This sixteenth-century castle is only a one-and-one-half-hour drive from the airports of Paris, providing a leisurely and unforgettable trip for travelers flying into or out of France. The resort sits in 150 acres of parks and forests surrounded by ancient stone walls. The lake around the main castle building – stocked with swans – and the Renaissance-style towers, façades, alcoves, open balconies, and sculptures add to the charm of this historical structure, built in 1543 by Etienne di Poncher. The castle was purchased by Les Grandes Etapes Françaises chain and converted into a hotel in 1981. The chain also owns Château d'Artigny and Le Mas d'Artigny, and all of the hotels are members of Small Luxury Hotels of the World.

Accommodations

The 53 rooms and four apartments are each unique and are located in the Castle, the Guards' Tower, the Hunting Lodge, and the Pavillon des Trophées. All of the rooms are large and comfortable, with high ceilings, picturesque views, mini-bars, refrigerators, television, makeup mirrors, country French furnishings, and modern bathrooms with hair dryers, magnifying mirrors, and terry-cloth robes. Rates are quite reasonable, ranging from 140 euros per night, for the least expensive, up to 890 euros for the luxury apartments.

There are seven meeting rooms, one of which can accommodate up to 250 persons for parties and affairs. The elegant and lavish apartments are especially comfortable and well worth the extra tariff.

Restaurants, Lounges, and Entertainment

The dining experience is one of the major attractions that entices affluent Parisians and world travelers to Château d'Esclimont. Lunch and dinner are offered in two elegant dining rooms overlooking the lake and gardens. The à la carte menu features an imaginative selection of fish, fowl, and meats. Special selections are featured daily, and there is a six-course degustation menu. A separate dessert menu offers an assortment of delicious pastries, soufflés, and sorbets. With your coffee there are complimentary fresh miniature tarts.

Breakfast is served Continental-style in the breakfast room, or buffet-style in one of the lounges, or in your guest room. The freshly baked croissants and rolls and freshly squeezed juices are exceptional.

There is a cocktail lounge for before- and after-dinner drinks. However, there is no music or entertainment. Once each month, from November through March, there are musical evenings with cocktails and a classical music concert followed by dinner.

Sport Facilities

A small, heated, outdoor swimming pool with lounge chairs is located near the Hunting Lodge, and there are two tennis courts in the park and row-boats to go up and down the river that runs by the château. The hotel also provides bicycles, and bicyclists and joggers will enjoy riding or romping around the park and forest trails. Ballooning over

the countryside and horseback riding can be arranged. Archery and skeet shooting are also available, as well as a small three-hole pitch-and-putt golf course.

Miscellaneous and Environs

The Cathedral of Chartres and the Castles of Maintenon and Rambouillet are located within 20 minutes of the hotel.

There are no shops at the hotel or nearby. Visitors are better off saving their francs for Paris. To reach the castle, take Autoroute A-10 from Paris to A-11 and exit at Ablis. From Ablis, take the road in the direction of Chartres. Go four miles to Exit D-18 toward St. Symphorien. You can arrange to pass through Versailles, and you may wish to stop there to visit the famous palace. Guests can also take a helicopter ride from either airport near Paris and be dropped off right in front of the château.

Château d'Esclimont is a charming homage to the Renaissance style, offering comfortable accommodations in a lovely setting with fine cuisine and service, and an opportunity for a few days of tranquil enjoyment.

Château d'Esclimont
28700 Saint Symphorien-le-Château
Tel. 011-33-2-37-31-15-15
Fax 011-33-2-37-31-57-91
E-mail: esclimont@grandesetapes.fr
Web: www.grandes-etapes-francaises.fr/chateau_esclimont

FRANCE

CHÂTEAU DU DOMAINE ST. MARTIN

High in the hills, a few miles above the medieval town of Vence, overlooking the Côte d'Azur, sits the very lovely 32-wooded acres of Château du Domaine St. Martin. Nestled among levels of trees, flowers, manicured lawns, and bushes are the impressive main hotel, six bastides, the remains of an ancient wall and drawbridge, two clay tennis courts, an underground car park and a charming pool area adjacent to the outdoor restaurant.

The property was originally the site of a fortified stronghold in the days of the Romans. Later, in 350 A.D., it was the residence of St. Martin, the evangelist bishop of Tours, from whom the property received its name. Then, in 1150 A.D., the estate was turned over to the crusaders returning from Jerusalem, and subsequently became a commanderie of the Knights of the Temple.

A family bought the estate in 1936 and converted it to a hotel in 1958. Five bastides were added in 1967, and a major renovation and room addition took place in the mid-1990s, bringing every accommodation to an ultra-deluxe level. Today, the resort is owned by the Oetker family, who also own Hôtel du Cap-Eden Roc in Antibes, Hotel Bristol in Paris, Brenner's Park-Hotel and Spa in Baden-Baden and Park Hotel in Vitznau.

The reception area, hallways and salons are all magnificently furnished with Persian and Flemish carpets, Aubusson tapestries, expensive objets d'art and antique furnishings from the period of Louis XV. The addition of lovely floral gardens in front of the entrance to the hotel has enhanced the overall magnificence of the property. The resort exudes history, elegance and style, while at the same time providing the highest degree of comfort.

Accommodations

In the main manor house are 32 deluxe accommodations, 31 designated as junior suites. All accommodations are air-conditioned, with exquisite antique and period furnishings, sitting areas, color televisions, and modern marble bathrooms complete with separate toilet and shower compartments, soaking tubs, double vanities, magnifying mirrors, hair dryers, terry robes and numerous amenities. All rooms are extremely spacious, and most have balconies or terraces looking out over the hills of Cap d'Antibes. Some of the junior suites can be transformed into a large apartment for families and friends traveling together, or for those requiring additional comfort. These are some of the most elegantly furnished rooms of any hotel in Europe.

The six additional apartments that sit above the resort on a private road also look down to the sea and are the shape of a traditional French bastide, so they are referred to as the "bastides." All of these apartments are magnificent, with very large bathrooms, closets and terraces, a private sitting room, and an impressive array of exquisite antique furnishings. The bastides afford guests total privacy.

Restaurants, Lounges, and Entertainment

Breakfast is available through room service or in the breakfast room. You may especially enjoy munching on fresh croissants and drinking your morning coffee or tea on the balcony of your accommodations while watching the sun rise over the French countryside.

Lunch is available in the dining room or informally at small linen-clad tables protected by umbrellas near the pool. Lighter salads, cold meats, cheeses and fruits, as well as heavier traditional fare, are available.

For dinner, gentlemen must wear jackets and ties. The amiable maître d' will take your order while you sip an aperitif on the terrace. In addition to a diverse selection of à la carte offerings, there are also two reasonable fixed menus, permitting guests to sample a number of preparations, cheeses and pastries.

All restaurant facilities that were recently redecorated offer magnificent views of the Côte d'Azur. On our most recent visit, we found the preparations to be exceptional, rivaling the finest restaurants in France. The ambiance of the dining room, the impeccable service, imaginative food presentation and superior cuisine combine to afford guests a most memorable culinary experience.

Sport Facilities

In addition to a very attractive infinity swimming pool and lounge deck area built in 1994, there are two respectable clay tennis courts. Joggers and hikers will enjoy the three-mile path (six miles round trip) that commences at the bottom of the road that leads up the hill to the resort. This romp will take you past large estates and wooded forests while looking out over the nearby villages and countryside. The resort will be adding spa facilities in the near future.

You are only a 40-minute drive from the golf course in Mougins or the beaches of the Côte d'Azur.

Miscellaneous and Environs

The resort is open from mid-February to mid-October and is located 20 minutes from the airport near Nice. If you are driving, you exit Autoroute A-8 at Cagnes-sur-Mer and head in the direction of Vence. You pass through Vence and at "T" Junction follow the signs marked "Route de Coursegoules." After about five minutes, you reach the road sign directing you to St. Martin.

Visitors will want to explore the charming towns of Vence and St. Paul de Vence, retreats for artists over the centuries and interesting places to explore art galleries, small bistros, or just walk around the souvenir shops and look out over the ancient walls at the countryside. No visit would be complete without driving down to the resort towns of Nice, Antibes and Cannes and spending a day browsing through the chic shops and colorful beaches.

Château du Domaine St. Martin offers travelers to the French Riviera scenic surroundings, exclusive privacy, ultra-luxurious accommodations, exceptional dining, impeccable service and a special ambiance not available at many other establishments. This is possibly the most elegant resort in Europe.

Château du Domaine St. Martin
Avenue des Templiers B.P. 102
06142 Vence Cedex
France
Tel. 33(0)4 93-58-02-02
Fax 33(0)4 93-24-08-91
E-mail: reservations@chateau-st-martin.com
Web: www.chateau-st-martin.com

FRANCE

Château Les Crayères

The Pommery Champagne family created the lovely, 17-acre park and terrace of this property in 1885 across the road from their cellars. In 1902 they built the magnificent chateau. The Gardinier family purchased the chateau and grounds in 1979, renovated the chateau and opened for business in 1983 after retaining renowned cuisinier Gerard Boyer to open his three-star Michelin restaurant on the premises. For 20 years, Boyer and his wife, Elayne, operated one of France's most exquisite properties and finest dining establishments.

The Boyers retired in 2002 and Boyer's sous chef, Thierry Voisin managed the kitchen until the arrival of Didier Elena in February of 2005. Elena had been working with Alain Ducasse for over 15 years. He now brings his talents and unique cuisine to Les Crayers.

The Gardinier family operates Les Crayeres, as well as their winery in Bordeaux, Phelan Segur.

The impressive château is furnished in an elegant, traditional decor and features a lovely outdoor patio surrounded by floral gardens overlooking a rambling park. Here guests can enjoy alfresco meals when weather permits.

Accommodations

In the main château there are 17 spacious rooms plus one apartment. In addition, two duplex apartments and another guest room are located in a nearby cottage. Every room has unusually high ceilings with French windows that look out to the park and surrounding gardens, giving the feel of Old World luxury not found in many similar properties that were built during this century. Each room is impeccably furnished, air-conditioned and heated, and includes a large sitting area, a writing desk, telephone, color television, refrigerator, mini-bar, giant wardrobe closets, fresh flowers, other amenities, and bathrooms with separate toilet compartments, bathtubs, showers, magnifying mirrors and terry-cloth robes.

Restaurants, Lounges, and Entertainment

Although the guest accommodations are among the more luxurious in France, most visitors are enticed to Les Crayères to experience the world-famous cuisine. The solicitous service staff will personally assist guests in ordering their meal while they enjoy complimentary local champagnes and hors d'oeuvres in the lounge.

During the spring and summer, you will appreciate dining on the outdoor patio or semi-covered veranda that separates the patio from the restaurant. In the evening, you can watch the sun set over the park from your dinner table.

On my most recent visit, I especially enjoyed the eggplant fritter in a tomato-chive sauce, a delicious small salad composed of tiny French string beans, foie gras, diced artichoke hearts, truffles, mushrooms and lobster, the smoky-flavored whole salmon swimming in a crème de caviar and arugula, a whole truffle en croute with sauce périgneux, a crusty fillet of beef in a bone marrow wine sauce, and the assortment of fresh cheeses and imaginative desserts, including an assortment of rich chocolate tasters that would launch a chocoholic into in-

stant ecstasy. The 60,000-bottle wine cellar is one of the most extensive in France and the attentive sommelier will assist you with your selection.

Adjoining the restaurant is an English-style bar and glassed-in patio, where cocktails and coffee are served. There is no music or entertainment at the resort.

Sport Facilities

Unfortunately, other than a tennis court set in the rear of the park, there are no other sport facilities on the property. A swimming pool and gymnasium are under consideration. Presently, the main event is luxuriating in sumptuous accommodations and around-the-clock dining.

Miscellaneous and Environs

While visiting Reims, you may wish to visit the famous cathedral, as well as one of the major cham-

pagne estates, which are nearby. Meandering along the pedestrian-only streets in the center of town with their numerous boutiques, brasseries and restaurants is also a good choice.

If you are driving from Paris, exit the Périphérique near Point Bercy and take Autoroute 4 to Reims, exiting at Reims-Rémi. Proceed left on Avenue Champagne until you reach the roundabout. Turn onto Avenue Gal Giraud, turn left on Avenue H. Vasnier, and you will be at the main gate to the château.

Visitors to France who are looking for the best accommodations, impeccable service, and one of the most perfectly magnificent French restaurants in France, set in a charming, tranquil locale will want to take the two-hour excursion to Château Les Crayeres.

Chateau Les Crayères
64, bd. H. Vasnier
51100 Reims (Marne)
France
Tel. 3-26-82-80-80
Fax 3-26-82-65-52
E-mail: crayeres@relaischateaux.fr
Web: www.LesCrayeres.com

DOMAINE DES HAUTS DE LOIRE

The Bonnigal family purchased this lovely wooded park in 1975, formerly the site of a feudal castle and Count Rostaing's hunting lodge. Located near Onzain, only minutes from the Loire River, this charming 19th-century French Auberge is an excellent place to relax and enjoy yourself while visiting the castles and vineyards along the Loire.

Le Manoir, the main building, originally constructed in 1860, has an impressive façade adorned with ivy, flowers and white shutters. The entry hall, lounge, and dining rooms are among the most attractive of any hostelry in France. Beamed ceilings, wood plank floors partially covered with magnificent Oriental carpets, period furnishings upholstered in soft pastels and floral prints, and antique brass pots brimming with colorful seasonal flowers tastefully blend to give this resplendent property a warm, homey atmosphere.

In 1980, La Residence and Le Pavillon, two additional buildings, were added by the Bonnigals, increasing the available accommodations from 15 to 32. Guests approach the property through an impressive wooded forest. Across from the manor house is a pond with swans, and behind the pond are the swimming pool, changing cabana and tennis court.

Accommodations

In Le Manoir, a spiral staircase leads up to 10 rooms and four apartments. Twelve rooms and six apartments are located in La Residence. Many of the country French-style guest rooms and suites are air-conditioned, and every accommodation has a mini-bar, private electronic safe, bathrooms with hair dryer, magnifying mirror and terry-cloth robe, and a color television that can receive CNN. Room and apartment rates range from approximately 130 to 430 euros per night. Each room is unique in size and decor, and there is a considerable difference between the less expensive and more expensive accommodations. The deluxe guest rooms and apartments are quite luxurious.

A conference facility can accommodate 60 people for a meeting, and one of the dining rooms can be reserved for private parties.

Restaurants, Lounges, and Entertainment

As described earlier, the three dining rooms are impeccably furnished, and tables are arranged with fine linen, Limoges china, delicate crystal, candles and fresh flowers – all of which orchestrate the perfect mood for Chef Remy Giraud's imaginative cuisine, which is presented with refinement under the direction of the most amiable maître d' Bernard La Croix. The chef, who boasts two stars from Michelin, is noted for his imaginative fish and seafood preparations and Boeuf Poche au Montlouis, his signature dish.

The "amuse bouche", (complimentary starters you receive gratis before the items you order) are amazing. On our most recent visit we were treated to a combination of escargot in a small, flaky pastry shell, tiny melon balls with finely grated ham in a liqueur sauce, a tapenade with chevre in another pastry shell and white amperages in a light cream truffle sauce. Appetizers of note included a slice of

delicate foie gras adorned with a celerie salad with cashews and fava beans in a creme fresh sauce with smoked duck crisps, as well as the tiny potatoes stuffed with caviar, walnut cream and leak sauce topped with shredded, deep-fried leek. Be certain to save room for the equally imaginative main course and desserts, as well as the devastatingly wicked cheese cart and tiny pastries. In addition to the à la carte items, several fixed-price multi-course menus, which run from 75, 95 and 155 euros, are featured daily.

Sport Facilities

The swimming pool is a bit more attractive than those found at most French resorts and is adjacent to a changing facility and bathrooms, as well as a single tennis court. Bicycles are available, there are several walking paths through the forest, and hunting, fishing and horseback riding can be arranged in the vicinity.

Miscellaneous and Environs

From Paris, take Autoroute A-6 to A-10 and continue on A-10 past Orléans to Blois. From Blois, take road N-152 for about 10 miles to Onzain. From Onzain, continue on D-1. The resort is located just after the boundaries of Onzain.

Situated in the middle of the Loire Valley, guests can conveniently visit the castles along the river, such as Amboise, Chenonceau, Chaumont, Cheverny and Chambord, as well as the vineyards that produce the wines of the Loire, which are featured at the resort.

Pierre-Alain Bonnigal and his well-trained staff are available to assure guests a most delightful sojourn. Domaine des Hauts de Loire offers a warm, comfortable, refined environment for travelers who appreciate superb cuisine and friendly, efficient service in surroundings most pleasing to the senses.

Domaine des Hauts de Loire
Route de Herbault
41150 Onzain, France
Tel. 02-54-20-72-57
Fax 02-54-20-77-32
E-mail: hauts.de.loire@wanadoo.fr
Web: www.domainehautsloire.com

FRANCE

GEORGES BLANC

This charming inn set in the beautiful floral village of Vonnas, in the heart of Burgundy, is surrounded by a lovely river filled with water lilies and swans, gentle bubbling waterfalls, thick green forests and colorful flowers. The warm homey interior is a combination of rustic country French decor, elegant antiques, Flemish tapestries, Bressan furnishings, fireplaces and sheer charm. During the past decades, the Blancs added an 11-room annex known as La Cour Aux Fleurs that is connected to the inn by a small bridge, and they converted a nearby building into a 10-room residence offering more modest, less expensive accommodations especially for families.

The standard of culinary excellence dates back three generations to when Jean-Louis Blanc opened the first restaurant in 1872. Since 1968, Georges Blanc and his wife, Jacqueline, have managed the establishment. They have modernized many of the facilities, enabling the restaurant and inn to receive the most prestigious ratings available, including three stars from Michelin, four toques from Gault et Millau, membership in Traditions et Qualité, and the top rating from Relais et Châteaux and Relais Gourmand. In my personal opinion, it is one of the very best dining experiences in the world. George's and Jacqueline's children are involved with the hotel and restaurant operation, awaiting their turn to carry on the family tradition.

Accommodations

The 27 rooms, suites, and apartments located in the inn, as well as the 10 rooms and 1 apartment in La Cour Aux Fleurs Annex, are all air-conditioned, tastefully furnished, and have refrigerator/mini-bars, private safes, color televisions with CNN, and marble bathrooms with hair dryers, magnifying mirrors and fluffy terry-cloth robes. Each accommodation has a different configuration and furnishings. Thirteen of the rooms in the inn and all rooms in the annex have king-size beds. The standard and deluxe rooms are very reasonably priced. You can upgrade to one of the two rustic-style bi-level rooms with a balcony on the river; one of the three junior suites; the full suite with a balcony on the river, two bathrooms with a walk-in closet, and a sitting room; or one of the 2 two-bedroom apartments for additional tariffs. The marble bathrooms in the deluxe rooms and suites are quite large, and have double vanities, separate showers, and tub and toilet compartments; eight have Jacuzzi tubs.

Guests and families wishing to experience the culinary excellence of Georges Blanc inexpensively can opt for one of the recently renovated 10 accommodations in the La Residence Des Saules, a building located about 150 meters from the inn. These accommodations are air-conditioned, comfortable and modern and each has a color television, a mini-bar and a separate sitting room with convertible sofa for children. Prices average around $150 to $175 per night. Thus, it is possible for a couple to spend the night and dine at L'Ancienne Auberge for as little as $220.

Restaurants, Lounges, and Entertainment

Breakfast is served in the guest accommodations or in the new, casual breakfast room, where you can enjoy freshly squeezed orange juice, melt-in-your-mouth croissants and brioches, and other tempting

pastries, cheeses, and sausage with good French coffee. The table is elegantly adorned with fresh flowers, and the view is of the charming surroundings and river.

Lunch and dinner are served in the formal main dining rooms. Guests are encouraged to walk through the immaculate kitchen and watch the greatest chefs in France meticulously prepare the very best of haute cuisine. Guests are also welcome in the impressive (130,000-bottle) wine cellar, which is stocked with a vast selection of recent and rare vintage Burgundies and Bordeaux and from other countries worldwide. Before dinner, most guests have an aperitif in the lounge or outdoor terrace, at which time they can study the menu and make food and wine selections.

Although you are free to order à la carte, Georges Blanc offers degustation dinners – four courses for 98 euros, six courses for 150 euros, seven course for 190 euros and twelve courses for 220 euros – that allow guests to sample numerous imaginative dishes at each sitting. Actually, two more courses are really included because all guests receive hors d'oeuvres (amuse bouche) before the meal and a mélange of miniature pastries after the meal without charge. Don't miss tasting the crêpe

parmentière au saumon et au caviar, a light potato pancake stuffed with slices of fresh salmon and caviar in a lemon zest beurre blanc sauce, the lobster mousse served in a spectacular green herb sauce, the Bresse chicken prepared in a sauce of cream and foie gras and freshly cooked garlic, the fabulous assortment of cheeses and pastries, and the special meringue filled with red currant sorbet decorated with raspberries floating in a fruit sauce accompanied by a thin apple tart.

The service is impeccable, the china, crystal and silver are the finest, and the ingredients are the freshest and the best available. Each offering is imaginatively displayed on the plate, accompanied by appropriate garnishes, creating a blend of compatible colors and shapes. The contrasting flavors of the food will overwhelm your senses. Whether you are a true or an amateur gourmet, this is the overall experience that other restaurants seek to fulfill but never quite accomplish.

The Blancs visit each table to make certain all is well with the food and service. Georges will be happy to provide an autographed menu or wine list. A recipe book, in French or English, can be purchased so you can attempt to duplicate some of your favorite dishes when you return home.

Recently, the Blancs added a quaint bistro with a charming outdoor terrace called L'Ancienne Auberge, designed to emulate the restaurant of Georges's ancestors in the early 1900s. Guests can enjoy typical Bressan-style cuisine (at its very best), as well as modestly priced wines for a fraction of the cost of the main restaurant. A complete four-course dinner costs 40 euros. This is a wise choice for lunch for those who plan to gorge themselves in the main dining room for dinner. We found our lunch here, the best French Bistro experience we had during our visits to France.

Sport Facilities

On the premises is an outdoor heated swimming pool with lounge chairs and bar service and a tennis court. A heliport is located just behind the pool. It is used by European businessmen who fly guests in to sample this extraordinary restaurant and inn.

Joggers will enjoy running through the charming village and along the winding rivers and country paths. There is a golf course five miles away, pitch-and-putt golf in the park adjacent to the inn, and horseback riding three miles away.

Les Serres du Soleil Spa opened during spring 2006 with a fitness room, relaxing room, hamam, indoor pool with Jacuzzi, and wellness, treatment and massage facilities.

Miscellaneous and Environs

Located on the main floor of the La Residence Des Saules are the Georges Blanc boutique and wine store. Here you can purchase gourmet foods including meats, pâtes, cheeses, breads, and pastries prepared in Georges's kitchen, wines from his vineyard, and kitchen accessories, fine crystal, china and signature items.

Vonnas is located about 11 miles from Macon, 215 miles from Paris and 30 miles from Lyon. Less than an hour from the vineyards of the Côtes de Nuit and Côtes de Beaune, and less than 30 minutes from the Beaujolais region, Vonnas is an excellent home base for exploring the vineyards of Burgundy. When driving to Vonnas, exit from Autoroute A-6 to A-40 at Mâcon and thereafter exit to N-79 in the direction of Bourg for about 7 miles until you reach D-80, which leads you right into town. The resort is about half way from Paris to the Cote d'azur and one hour from Geneva.

A visit to the domaine of Georges Blanc offers a chance to experience the very best of French cuisine and Continental service and charm, and possibly the world's finest restaurant. It is one of those once-in-a-lifetime opportunities that should not be missed, and any visit to the provinces of France is not complete without it.

Georges Blanc
01540 Vonnas, France
Tel. 04-74-50-90-90
Fax 04-74-50-08-80
E-mail: blanc@relaischateaux.fr
Web: www.georgesblanc.com

FRANCE

HÔTEL DU CAP-EDEN ROC

Located in the hills of the fashionable resort area of Cap d'Antibes, just east of Juan-les-Pins, in the center of the French Riviera, is that famous "dig" of the rich and famous, Hôtel du Cap-Eden Roc. The main hotel building, originally constructed in 1870 and called "Villa Soleil," sits in the middle of a lovely park with botanical gardens. About one block away, on the edge of a small cliff that leads to the sea, is Pavillion Eden Roc, the beach club/restaurant annex built in 1914. Both buildings have been continuously renovated throughout the years, and their use of white marble gives them a bright, airy feel that conceals their true age.

When passing through the main gate and driving up the road leading to the hotel, you get the sensation of entering a grand, private estate. The lobby is done with marble columns, a special staircase, and expensive antiques. Here, those who can afford the very high tariffs come "to see and be seen." The concierge shouts out "bonjour, monsieur" as you walk past his desk. The resort has hosted heads of state, royalty, and movie stars throughout the years. The atmosphere is elegant, sophisticated, and posh.

Hotel du Cap-Eden Roc is owned by the same group that owns Brenner's Park-Hotel and Spa in Baden-Baden, the Bristol in Paris, Château du Domaine St. Martin in Vence, and Park Hotel Vitznau in Switzerland.

Accommodations

The main building contains 90 guest rooms of varying sizes and decors, as well as four large suites. In addition, there are 32, very modern, large rooms at Pavillion Eden Roc, one large villa, and 32 cabanas near the sea. For $3,000 per night, you can luxuriate in Suite 644, the most desirable accommodation at the Pavillion, which includes a large patio with its own fountain and enviable view of the sea and coastline. Many movie stars and dignitaries have spent the night here. All guest rooms are spacious with a bright, fresh appearance, antique and traditional furniture, tasteful decorations, large wardrobes, a writing desk, and modern marble bathrooms that include double sinks, showers and bath, some with sunken tubs. There are no radios, televisions, refrigerators or mini-bars. The 32 bright and airy accommodations at Eden Roc are especially comfortable and enjoy a convenient location next to the pool and restaurant.

The banquet room seats 200, but the hotel accepts conferences and conventions during the months of April and October only. The 32 seaside cabanas with private patios can be rented by the day and are furnished with table and easy chairs, sun beds, mats and parasols. Toilets and showers are available within the cabana area, as well as, a small snack shop and service bar where you can telephone for drinks and also get towels.

Restaurants, Lounges, and Entertainment

The only restaurant is located in the Pavillion Eden Roc and includes a formal glassed-in dining room and an outdoor terrace, both overlooking the sea. Below the restaurant is the outside bar, which adjoins the changing rooms, pool and lounging area,

and a snack restaurant that is open in July and August. Having an elegant lunch alfresco, perched on a rock above the Mediterranean, affords a memorable experience. Breakfast on the patio of the main hotel building overlooking the park, gardens and sea is also very special. The croissants and baguettes are to die for.

The cuisine is best described as traditional French with Continental specialties, including offerings more familiar to American tastes than will be found in many other comparable restaurants in France. I found the repast exceptional. The cuisine was superbly prepared, imaginatively presented and impeccably served in a very picturesque setting. The restaurant seems to merit higher ratings than it has received from most other guides. Prices are very high, but the outstanding quality justifies the expense.

A piano player or small orchestra plays for your listening pleasure at dinner; however, there is no entertainment or dancing. Those wishing after-dinner excitement must seek out the discos and casinos in the surrounding villages of the French Riviera.

Sport Facilities

The heated saltwater pool at Pavilion Eden Roc Beach Club is built into the rocks on a cliff that drops into the Mediterranean. There are ladders and diving boards for those wishing to swim in the sea, as well as rafts a short distance away; however, there is no sandy beach. Yacht rides, water-skiing, fishing and windsurfing can be arranged. A pier accommodating yachts and small craft sits below the pool area.

There is a tennis complex consisting of five clay tennis courts in the park that extends from the main hotel building down to the sea, and tennis is very popular with the guests. The fitness center includes men's and women's private saunas, a steam room, massage facilities and a recently expanded exercise room with state-of-the-art cardiovascular equipment and free weights.

Miscellaneous and Environs

There is a hairdresser and boutique on the premises, and numerous fine boutiques, restaurants and shops can be explored in all the adjoining seaside villages that comprise the Côte d'Azur.

Management contends that the absence of radios, televisions, refrigerators, entertainment and a year-round snack restaurant is in keeping with the preferences of their long list of repeat clientele. Although I sorely miss such amenities, I can't argue with success.

Hôtel du Cap-Eden Roc is open from late April until the end of October. Bring along lots of travelers checks, because personal checks are not accepted without a letter of guarantee from your bank. In addition, credit cards are not accepted.

This resort is often patronized by wealthy European and American tourists, dignitaries and movie personalities who come to be pampered. It has been justifiably acclaimed to be the best in the world by many critics and knowledgeable travelers. Service is absolutely incredible. Those resort aficionados who enjoy an expensive, sophisticated, glamorous environment with posh accommodations, excellent food and impeccable service in a chic Côte d'Azur setting will call Hôtel du Cap-Eden Roc their home away from home.

Hôtel du Cap-Eden Roc
B.P. 29 Blvd. Kennedy
Cap d'Antibes 06601 Antibes, France
Tel. 493-61-39-01
Fax 493-67-76-04
Web: www.edenroc.hotel.fr
e-mail: reservation@HDCER.com

FRANCE

LA CÔTE SAINT JAQUES

Enjoying a prime location in the small village of Joigny on the banks of the River Yonne, La Cote Saint-Jacques attracts serious gourmet's from all corners of the world. It was here in 1945 that Marie Lorain opened a small bed and breakfast in the family residence. Commencing in 1958, Michel Lorain and his wife Jacqueline assumed the helm and inaugurated continuous expansions and improvements to the original manor house. Cuisinier Michel received his first star from Guide Michelin in 1971, his second in 1976 and together with his son, Jean-Michel, the coveted third star in 1986. The restaurant also boasts four toques from the Gault-Millau Guide.

Prior to joining his father, Jean-Michel trained at such renowned establishments as Troisgros in Roanne, Taillevent in Paris and Freddy Giardet in Crissier, Switzerland. Today, Jean- Michel and his lovely wife, Brigette, oversee the restaurant and hotel operations. The complex encompasses 10 rooms in the original building and 22 rooms in the new residence which is also the location of the reception, dining rooms, bar/lounge, signature boutique, indoor swimming pool, sauna and outdoor terrace. An underground tunnel running under the road connects the two buildings. The Lorain holdings also include a 20-acre winery, a 12-passenger river boat (at the disposal of hotel guests) and a contemporary-style, 50-room hotel built in 1993 on the opposite side of the river, appropriately named "La Rive Gauche".

Accommodations

The original hotel building housing 10 rooms sits across the road from the 22-room new residence connected by an underground cavernous-like tunnel. A majority of the rooms in the new residence offer balconies looking out to the river and each has air conditioning. Every accommodation at La Cote Saint Jacques includes a television, a refrigerator stocked with gratis water and soft drinks, a private safe, a hair dryer, and terry robes and slippers. Although the rooms and suites are quite comfortable, none could be described as lavish nor as well appointed as many of the other French properties described in this book.

The 42 rooms and eight mini-suites at La Rive Gauche are very simple; however a significant bargain at 60 to 105 euros per night. Also located here are two seminar/function rooms, a tennis court and a pleasant restaurant.

Dining, Restaurants and Entertainment

Certainly the "raison d'etre" for visiting La Cote Saint Jacques is to sample the outstanding gastronometry of Jean-Michel Lorain, one of the world's most creative and acclaimed chefs. The menu is extensive, as is the impressive wine list which includes dozens of premier and grand crus from the nearby village of Chablis.

The innovative starters may include a duck foie gras surrounded by a melange of spiced minced beet puree with green herbs and mixed garden greens, a warm lobster salad with tiny potatoes, herbed lettuce and sauce gribiche, or cream of frogs' legs, duck liver and fresh morels. Fish and seafood dishes feature sauteed tiny snails, celery and topenade stuffed in a crispy pastry shell with poached garlic froth, as well as breaded turbot filet

garnished in morels, whipped chestnut puree and a tart grape sauce. The chef's specialties include Bresse Chicken steamed in Champagne, and milk-fed veal chops accompanied by a puree of peas and bacon with truffled Jerusalem artichokes in a coffee flavored veal au jus.

You will not want to miss the degustation of fresh cheeses from the cart followed by one of the numerous dessert selections, several of which feature fruit and sorbet themes presented in pastry shells while others tempt with a variety of chocolate creations.

Breakfast is offered indoors and outdoors (weather permitting) in a small room and terrace overlooking the river. Lunch and dinner are served in two elegant main dining rooms which are separated by a small private room with a view to the kitchen that can accommodate special parties up to eight persons.

Sport Facilities

There is an indoor pool looking out to a terrace in the new residence and a sauna. A tennis court sits in the gardens at La Rive Gauche across the river and horseback riding, golf and fishing can be arranged. Since the majority of guests stay only for a night or two, sport facilities have not been a serious consideration. There is no charge for children under 12 years of age, babysitting is available, and children can enjoy a special game room, as well as the swimming pool.

Miscellaneous and Environs

Other than the signature boutique at the new residence, there are few shopping opportunities in Joigny. Guests can opt to take a short scenic cruise on the hotel's private river boat while sipping coffee or Champagne. Interesting half-day trips include the nearby wineries at Chablis, the art museums at Sens, the chateaux of Tanlay, Ancy de Franc and St.

Fargeau, the Pontigny Abbey and the Basilica in Vezelay.

You can reach Joigny in one-and-a-half to two-hours driving on autoroute A-6 from Paris or in a half hour driving north on N6 from Auxerre. In the alternative it is possible to travel by train from Paris through Auxerre.

La Cote Saint Jacque and the cuisine of Jean-Michel Lorain present serious gourmets with a most rewarding experience only a short drive from Paris.

La Cote Saint-Jacques
14 Faubourg de Paris
89300 Joigny
Tel. +33(0)3 86 62 09 70
Fax. +33 (0)3 86 91 49 70
Lorain@relaischateaux.com

GERMANY

Brenner's Park-Hotel & Spa, Baden-Baden

The world-renowned Brenner's Park-Hotel and Spa, with its Brenner's Spa and new Medical Spa is located in a rambling 87-acre private park and shaded by ancient trees on the banks of the murmuring River Oos along the Lichtentaler Allee in the resort town of Baden-Baden. The grounds of the resort are surrounded by miles of lush green parks with majestic trees, shrubs and colorful flowers connected by continuous paths along the river.

In 1872, Anton Brenner, a tailor for the Royal Court, acquired the property, which was subsequently expanded and redesigned by his son, Camille, and grandson, Kurt. From its inception, the property attracted illustrious dignitaries, statesmen and royalty, creating a glamorous aura that continues today. The Villa Stephanie, built in 1912, now houses the private clinic, Stephanie les Bains Clinic. Occupied by the French army after World War II, the hotel was refurbished in the early 1950s and sold to the Oetker family in 1969. They presently own and operate the property under the excellent direction of Frank Marrenbach. Other hotel/ resorts acquired by the Oetkers include Hôtel du Cap-Eden Roc and Château du Domaine St. Martin in the south of France, Le Bristol in Paris and Park-Hotel Vitznau in Switzerland.

In 1991, a more informal restaurant, several shops, and a 240-car garage (across from the main entrance to the hotel) were added; in 1999, a 4,300-square-foot addition was completed, expanding the resort's spa facilities.

Few hotels in the world offer the impeccable, concerned service found at Brenner's Park. From the moment your car pulls into the driveway and you are assisted with your luggage and settled into your posh accommodations, until the day of your departure, the pleasant, exceptionally trained staff seem dedicated to making your visit a memorable experience.

Accommodations

There are 100 spacious, high-ceilinged accommodations, which include 17 junior suites, 12 one-bedroom, and 3 two-bedroom suites, all elegantly furnished with very expensive, tasteful fabrics, period pieces, antiques and works of art. Fresh flowers, chocolates, wines and other amenities are in place upon your arrival. Every room and suite includes large closets, cable television, mini-bars and refrig-

erators, electronically operated window shades, sitting areas, writing desks, private safes and marble or tile bathrooms with tub, shower, double sink, hair dryer, magnifying mirror, telephone, and heat-

ed towel bars. These are possibly the most lavish accommodations in Europe.

The banquet, party and conference facilities can accommodate from 10 to 250. The royal suite has its own private staircase, a dining room and kitchenette equipped with a personal butler.

Restaurants, Lounges, and Entertainment

The elegant, yet intimate, Park Restaurant which looks out to the park accommodates up to 45 guests in the evenings featuring outstanding cuisine and service. Over the years, we have especially enjoyed the magnificent game, fish and seafood offerings with their imaginative presentation enhanced with colorful side-dishes and sauces. The wine list is extensive with vintages from around the world. The adjoining Wintergarten Restaurant, with tables both in the conservatory-like indoor area and outside in the gardens is open from noon until midnight offering a diverse selection of lighter fare, along with classical cuisine with a Mediterranean touch. Vegetarian and low-calorie cuisine is also available. The Park Restaurant at Brenner's Park has won numerous awards around the world. In the

morning, guests can enjoy an elaborate breakfast buffet in a non-smoking or smoking-permitted grand dining room. This is possibly the best spread of its kind we have ever experienced including a variety of delectable French and German cheeses, herrings, gravlox, cold meats, freshly squeezed juices and fruits, an assortment of cereals, freshly baked breads, rolls and pastries and champagne, as well as, omelettes, eggs and pancakes cooked to order.

Before and after dinner, guests may wish to relax in the Oleander Bar and Lounge and partake in alcoholic or non-alcoholic beverages, coffees, teas, espresso or cappuccino. Frequently, a piano player entertains with background music.

Sport Facilities

The hotel has a large, private, indoor swimming pool, looking out to forested paths and the river. The fitness center includes a room looking out to the gardens with cardio-vascular equipment, free-weights and exercise machines. In this area is a state-of-the-art relaxation facility with sauna, steam, bio-sauna, whirlpools, a fridgidarium, a relaxarium, and vitalizing showers.

The hotel will arrange tennis at the nearby Rot-Weiss Tennis Club, as well as, golf, horseback riding over scenic bridle paths, bicycling, fishing, balloon and glider rides.

The beauty Spa offers a variety of skin treatments, facials, massages, manicures, pedicures, makeup advice, and hair and beauty treatments. In addition, the "Kanebo Harmonizing & Care Beauty Spa" was opened in late 2003. This facility consists of four beauty suites set up along Asiatic lines which provide harmonizing and care applications developed with elements of traditional Asiatic medicine and Kanebo's holistic philosophy designed to appeal to the senses, as well as, caring for the skin. Featured is the "Seiketsu" which is a bathing ritual in two multi-jet tubs with whole body peeling as well as soft washes and stimulating scalp treatments accompanied by hot tea, peppermint compresses and refreshing whole body gel masks.

Brenner's Medical Spa includes a staff of physicians, dentists, and therapists who provide medical and dental care, nutrition counseling, medical preventative exams and a variety of physiotherapy training and procedures.

Miscellaneous and Environs

The charming resort town of Baden-Baden affords visitors picturesque hiking trails, art exhibitions, smart boutiques, a European-style gambling casino, and an 18-hole golf course and numerous fine restaurants and cafes. The lovely Lichtentaler Allee runs directly in back of the hotel paralleling the River Oos. Guests enjoy strolling along this forested and floral promenade.

For variety, guests will enjoy a visit to Strasbourg, on the Franco-German border, about 20 miles inside France, where they can visit the famous cathedral, browse through the fashionable shops, and dine at two of France's most renowned restaurants, Au Crocodile and Beuerheisel in the Park at Orangerie. At Au Crocodile, (Michelin, 2 stars), amiable Monique and Emile Jung will escort you through a degustation of Alsatian specialties and fine wines. Awarded the Grand Award by the Wine Spectator each year since 1993 for having one of the finest wine collections in the world, the restaurant offers one of the best all-around dining experiences in France. Emile, Monique, and their dedicated staff are gracious, humble hosts who make their guests feel welcome and special. This is a must for every aficionado of fine dining.

Baden-Baden is a 50-minute drive from Strasbourg, a 90-minute drive from Basel or Frankfurt, and 60 minutes from Stuttgart.

Brenner's Park-Hotel and Spa is a compulsory stop for experienced travelers who wish to experience this hotel's sophisticated environment, luxurious accommodations, fine cuisine and wines, impeccable service and Old World charm.

Brenner's Park-Hotel & Spa
An der Lichtentaler Allee
Schillerstrasse 4-6
D-76530 Baden-Baden, W. Germany
Tel. (07221) 9000, Fax (07221) 38772
E-mail:reservations@brenners.com
Web: www.brenners.com

CHEWTON GLEN (HOTEL, SPA & COUNTRY CLUB)

Ninety miles south of London, between Southampton and Bournemouth, and situated between the New Forest and the sea, is the location of Chewton Glenn, one of the most excellent resorts and spas in Europe, recipient of numerous international awards. Surrounded by 130 acres of glorious parks and woodlands, this converted English country estate offers travelers the ultimate charming, relaxed sojourn. Here you will find a combination of modern luxury, timeless charm and superb comfort.

The main building is an English manor house built in three wings covered with ivy and set in the midst of beautiful manicured lawns, shrubbery and colorful flowers. The warm and inviting public rooms offer a perfect coziness, affording a bright, airy atmosphere where, from every vantage, guests can look out at the surrounding landscape.

Although Chewton Glenn's origins date back to the days of the Normans, the present manor was first built in the eighteenth century. During the 1840s, the famous novelist Capt. Frederick Marryat visited here and wrote many of his novels, the most well known being The Children of the New Forest. Each guest accommodation is named after either a title character or ship from one of his books.

Col. Edward Tinker purchased the property in the early 1900s and remodeled it. After being converted to a hotel in 1962, Chewton Glenn was sold to its present owner, Martin Skan, in 1966. Over the years, the building has been extensively renovated and restored. Mr. and Mrs. Skan have devoted their energies to every possible detail with the aim of creating the perfect resort. Their efforts have certainly paid off, and critics, as well as guests, are quick to agree that Chewton Glenn uniquely accomplishes the total experience that has eluded its competitors.

Accommodations

The resort has 58 spacious guest rooms and suites, all uniquely designed and lavishly furnished with elegant country-English and antique pieces, and decorated in warm pastel tones with floral drapes and walls lined with mirrors, paintings and fine prints. Twelve rooms were added in 1990 in a connecting hotel wing, and six rooms and two suites were added in 2000. In 1998, the ten coach houses were renovated and air-conditioned. Six of these have lovely outdoor garden terraces.

Many of the accommodations have a private garden or balcony, and all include sitting areas, vanities, remote-control, color, satellite television, C/D and DVD players, personal safes, a trouser press, ice, mineral water, sherry, fresh fruit, homemade biscuits, and modern bathrooms complete with bathtubs, shower stalls, double sinks, magnifying mirrors, fluffy robes and slippers, and expensive complimentary toiletries from Moulton Brown.

The resort welcomes high-level business meetings and corporate retreats. The Lake Suite (conference room) can accommodate up to 100 theater style and 60 classroom style in comfortable leather chairs, and the private dining room can seat up to 24 for smaller dinner events.

Restaurants, Lounges, and Entertainment

The exquisitely decorated dining rooms are the perfect setting for one of the most rewarding dining

experiences to be found in all of England. Adjacent to the more formal indoor rooms is the bright, airy, glass-enclosed conservatory dining room, which is embellished with colorful flowers and plants and overlooks the pool and gardens. Every table is adorned with linens, Villeroy & Boch (basket pattern) china, Sheffield cutlery, fine crystal, and fresh flowers. On warm days, meals are also served on the terrace.

The superb cuisine is brilliantly presented, utilizing local products including fresh fish, game from the nearby New Forest and beef from Scotland. The resort has held one Michelin star continuously since 1984. The extensive wine list includes great vintages, as well as a wide array of more recent offerings from France and an extensive assortment of others from Italy, Germany and California – over 500 bins in all.

The service staff – from the maître d' and waiters to the sommelier and bar stewards – are professional, friendly, and efficient, affording truly impeccable service. Lunch and dinner are available on a fixed-price multicourse, gourmet menu, with numerous appetizing selections. Prices vary from $36 for a three-course lunch to $124 for a 5-course chef-selection gourmet dinner.

On our most recent visit, we started with medallions of lobster and scallops surrounded by a ginger cream sauce and fresh foie gras with a sherry vinaigrette. For entrées, we had fresh-grilled Dover Sole meuniere and roast saddle of English Lamb seasoned with thyme. This was followed by a selection of English and French farmhouse cheeses and an almond and prune tartlet served in an Armagnac sabayon sauce, accompanied by apricot sorbet in a pastry crust. An extensive vegetarian menu is also available.

Guests select their various courses and wine while enjoying a cocktail and canapés in one of the comfortable lounges, which are also the sites for after-dinner coffees and cordials. A piano player offers appropriate musical accompaniment in the main lounge on weekends. Healthy fare is served at the pool bar and lounge during the daytime.

Sport Facilities

On the estate are croquet and putting lawns, a small heated outdoor swimming pool bordered by colorful flowers, a 9-hole par-3 golf course (most holes average about 100 yards) and billiards.

In 1990, the resort added a health club that includes a Romanesque indoor pool, indoor and outdoor whirlpools, sauna, steam, massage, facial and body treatments, and a gymnasium with exercycles, treadmills and various other equipment. In 2001, additional treatment rooms and a relaxation suite were opened; and since that time facilities continued to be developed and expanded. Beauty treatments, manicures and pedicures are available at the Spa Grooming Lounge. The Chewton Glen Spa has received many accolades and is considered by many to be one of the U.K's best hotel spas. A tennis center with two all-weather outdoor courts, two indoor courts, and a full-time tennis pro is located a short walk from the main building.

In the vicinity are several 18-hole golf courses and riding stables. The hotel can arrange clay pigeon and game shooting, and fly-fishing on nearby rivers. Walkers and joggers will enjoy the adjoining forest paths and the picturesque seaside cliffs, a ten-minute walk from the hotel.

Miscellaneous and Environs

Visitors flying into Heathrow or Gatwick Airports can rent a car or make arrangements for the resort's limousine to meet them right at the airport. Although the limousine ride costs over $275 one way, the chauffeur can be a wealth of information and,

if time permits, he can be encouraged to take a side road that will take you within a stone's throw of Windsor Castle, Eton College and Ascot racecourse. The drive from London or the airports can be a bit confusing and can take from one- and- a- half to two- and- a- half hours depending upon traffic and how well you follow the signs. From London, it is possible throughout the day to take one of the trains from Waterloo station to New Milton, which is only a few minutes' taxi ride from the resort. Helicopters will be accommodated on the property's lawn.

There is a small gift shop next to the reception area. Unfortunately, the surrounding towns offer few shopping possibilities other than antique shops, jewelers and traditional English tea houses. About a mile away are Highcliffe and Barton-on-Sea, residential areas adjacent to cliffs overlooking the sea and English Channel. Five miles away is Lymington, linked by ferry to the Isle of Wight.

Visitors to Great Britain wishing the ultimate charming English experience will be well rewarded at Chewton Glenn, where they will be treated to some of the most luxurious, comfortable accommodations, beautiful surroundings, gourmet cuisine and impeccable, friendly service to be found anywhere in the world.

Chewton Glen
New Milton, Hampshire, England BH25 6QS
In U.S., toll-free
Tel. (800) 344-5087, Fax (800) 398-4534

In England
Tel. (01425)275341, Fax (01425) 272310
E-mail: Reservations@Chewtonglen.com
Web: www.ChewtonGlen.com

GREECE

ASTIR PALACE

The Astir Palace at Vouliagmeni, one of Greece's foremost resorts, is conveniently located only 20 miles from the center of Athens and 19 miles from the Athens Airport. Spread over 75 acres of pine-clad promontory, commanding magnificent views of the blue Aegean Sea, the Astir Palace offers an attractive alternative for travelers seeking a full-facility beach resort but not having the time or desire to fly or cruise to the myriad of Greek Islands.

Founded in 1951, the resort is owned by the National Bank of Greece. The resort complex, with a total of 549 rooms, is composed of 70 bungalows and three separate hotels, each of which stands on a cliff descending to the sea and has its own restaurants, pool, beach, and shops. Guests can avail themselves of the facilities at all the properties, as well as the tennis courts located between the hotels.

As you enter the front gate above the marina, you first come to the Arion, which opened in 1967 and since that time has been totally renovated. The adjoining Nafsika was opened in 1972, and in 1984 the more modern Aphrodite was added to the complex. The Aphrodite has the best pool and beach area, and is located several blocks from the other hotels. The 73 bungalows date back to 1960.

The three hotel buildings and bungalows were totally renovated and refurbished during 2003 and 2004 in preparation for the 2004 Olympics.

The grounds are extensive, adorned with manicured lawns, bushes and flowers. All accommodations and public areas enjoy spectacular, panoramic views of the impressive scenery and aqua-blue Aegean Sea.

Accommodations

The 525 guest accommodations are spread among the three hotel buildings, and the 73 bungalows extend along the cliff to the right of the Arion, each overlooking the beach and sea below. The bungalows, though secluded, are comfortable, with many of the same facilities as the rooms, but not as luxurious.

The 123 rooms and suites at the Arion are ample and recently furnished with tasteful, traditional decors, and each has a balcony or patio looking out to the sea or gardens. The penthouse rooms on the fourth floor are particularly inviting. There are radios, satellite televisions, direct-dial telephones with voice mail, private safes, refrigerators and mini-bars in all of the accommodations at all three hotels.

The 162 guest rooms and suites at the Nafsika are the largest of the three, with all units having generous balconies or patios overlooking the sea.

The Aphrodite is the newest and most modern. The rooms and bathrooms are not quite as large as the Nafsika, but they are airy and modern. Of the 165 guest rooms, 145 have balconies with sea views, whereas the other 20 have outdoor patios facing the opposite direction.

As described above, all of the accommodations at the resort were significantly renovated during 2003 and 2004.

A buffet-style breakfast is included in the room rates. All three properties have their own meeting rooms and banquet facilities. This is possibly the leading convention and meeting facility in the Athens area, and during the colder months, one of the three hotels remains open to accommodate this

market (as well as overnight romantics). Hi-tech conference facilities are located at each hotel. The conference center at the Nafsika can accommodate up to 550 persons theater-style.

Restaurants, Lounges, and Entertainment

Breakfast – consisting of fresh juice, fruits, rolls, cake, cold meats, cheeses, cereals, eggs and beverages – is served buffet-style at each hotel, or can be ordered through room service. Lunch is also served at each establishment, as well as at the snack bars and the picturesque Club House. On Sundays there is a Greek lunch buffet at the Kymata Restaurant, near the pool at the Nafsika.

For dinner, guests can choose among the charming Pergola outdoor garden restaurant at the Nafsika (which moves indoors to the elegant Jason dining room during the colder months), the outdoor balcony at the Club House seafood restaurant in the midst of the bungalows overlooking the sea, the more formal Grill Room at the Arion, or the indoor/outdoor Spila Restaurant at the Aphrodite.

Menus feature a combination of Greek and Continental offerings, as well as fresh seafood, and there is an upscale wine list. However, prices are quite high, especially for beverages.

Numerous lounges and bars are located throughout the complex, offering evening entertainment that varies from piano music to singers and small dance bands. Throughout the week, special theme dinners are featured, including barbecues, fish and sea food nights and Greek buffets.

For romantics, one of Greece's most charming, panoramic restaurants, Ithaki, specializing in fresh fish, epicurean fare, impeccable service, soft piano music and "to-die-for" atmosphere is located about a half-mile in front of the resort. When visiting Athens proper, you may enjoy the restaurant atop Mount Likovitis "Orizontes" which serves continental cuisine with incomparable panoramic views of the Acropolis and all of Athens.

Sport Facilities

The Astir Palace is a European beach resort, and among the main appeals to guests are the beach

and pool facilities, which include lounges, snack bars, water-skiing, sailboats and other water sports. Each hotel has its own private beach where the sea water is protected by natural rock formations. The beach area near the Aphrodite is the most secluded and picturesque. There are attractive, large pools at both the Aphrodite and Nafsika and a small outdoor and small indoor pool at the Arion.

Also at the Arion are a leased gymnasium, sauna and massage facility charging outrageous prices. Located between the Aphrodite and the other hotels are four illuminated tennis courts that are available for a $12 per hour charge. Six miles away is the 18-hole Glyfada golf course. Immediately below the complex is a marina with mooring for your yacht (if you insist upon bringing it along).

Miscellaneous and Environs

Numerous designer boutiques, jewelry and sundry stores, hairdressers and other shops are spread among the hotels. The shops, restaurants and historical sights of Athens are less than a 30- to 40-minute drive away.

The resort provides transportation to Athens twice each day, as well as between the three ho-

tels. As an alternative, guests may wish to rent a car to get around. Taxis are not terribly expensive; however, it is important to have some idea of the correct fare before embarking because the drivers frequently will tell you the meter isn't working, or will tamper with the meter during the trip.

The Astir Palace is a Greek-style resort located in a very picturesque area, offering a convenient, enjoyable alternative to the Greek Islands for travelers who wish to relax, sun and luxuriate away from the pollution, hustle and bustle of Athens.

Astir Palace
Apollonos 40
16671 Vouliagmeni/Athens
Greece
Tel. 30-2108902000, Fax 30-2108962582
www.astir-palace.com
e-mail: sales @astir.gr reservations@astir.gr

ITALY

GRAND HOTEL QUISISANA

Centrally located on the charming, cosmopolitan island of Capri, which lies off the coast of Sorrento, the Grand Hotel Quisisana is one of the most elegant and excellent hostelries in Italy. Travelers to Italy have not fully experienced this beautiful country if they neglected the area south of Naples – extending from Sorrento to Positano and Amalfi – or missed the hydrofoil ride to Capri. The Greek Islands may be charming, the French Riviera is chic, and Venice may be for lovers, but Capri has it all – charm, beauty, romance – and the Grand Hotel Quisisana offers an opportunity to enjoy this exquisite island in luxurious surroundings and spacious accommodations, with concerned service and fine Italian cuisine.

There are several possibilities for traveling to Capri, such as the hydrofoil ride direct from Naples, Amalfi, Positano or Sorrento, or a breathtaking excursion along the Amalfi Drive followed by a boat ride to Capri. Hotel porters will meet you at the dock and take your bags while you take the funicular railway or a taxi to the hotel. There is a charge of approximately 10 euro per bag for this service.

Accommodations

There are 148 lavishly decorated guest accommodations, which include 32 junior suites, six duplex suites and nine special sea-view suites, all decorated with marble, antique furnishings and Old World elegance. Most of these guest accommodations have balconies, and all are air-conditioned and include modern bathrooms, ceramic tile floors, private room safes, two-line direct-dial telephones, refrigerators, mini-bars, remote-control televisions with satellite channels and pay television, terry-cloth robes and slippers, hair dryers and other amenities. There are eight public rooms for meetings and banquets, one of which can accommodate 500 people.

Restaurants, Lounges, and Entertainment

For those who do not choose to take breakfast on their patios or balconies overlooking the sea, a buffet breakfast of fresh orange juice, crisp Italian rolls, croissants, rich coffee, and fresh fruits, cheeses, and meats is spread out on the terrace of the main dining room.

Lunch is served at La Colombaia, the charming outdoor restaurant adjoining the pool. Fresh fish and seafood, a variety of pastas and pizzas, mouth-watering veal and chicken creations, an assortment of fresh fruits, cheeses and pastries, and an exten-

sive Italian wine list are offered at this gourmet meal.

Dinner indoors or on the patio at the charming Restaurant Quisi is a romantic and most gratifying culinary experience. The resort's excellent chefs offer an imaginative menu featuring Italian cuisine accompanied by romantic music and expert service. This is one of the finest hotel restaurants in Italy. During the summer, dinner is also offered at Colombaia accompanied by sax music. Here an extensive menu including an array of salads and cold dishes is featured, along with wines available by the glass from the Intermezzo wine bar.

During high season you may dine at the Quisi Bar. Rendez-Vous serves continental cuisine and Quisi & Sushi offers Japanese fare.

In the evenings, the intimate Quisi bar features a piano player or a small combo for listening and romantic dancing. Inside the Quisi Bar is the Krug Room where guests can taste prestigious champagnes along with special canapés and other dishes. Your room rate includes breakfast. However, the prices for food and beverages can be quite high (depending upon the current exchange rate between the euro and your currency), so insist on checking prices before ordering so as to avoid any misunderstandings.

Sport Facilities

The center of activity during the afternoon is the lovely freshwater pool, where gracious European service people attend to your needs with lounges, towels and cocktails. The Spa at the hotel, Quisi Beauty, includes a Romanesque indoor glass-enclosed swimming pool and whirlpool, exercise equipment, sauna and steam (for a 20/30 euro supplement), massage and related facilities. The hotel has two tennis courts in its adjoining gardens, as well as a teaching pro.

Those who prefer a dip in the Mediterranean can be accommodated at Marina Piccola, accessible by a short bus ride or an exciting walk down the side of a steep hill that overlooks the picturesque Faraglioni Rocks.

Miscellaneous and Environs

The owners of the resort, the Morgano family, also own three additional properties, Scalinatella, Casa Morgano and Hotel Flora, all only a five-minute-walk away. Scalinatella and Casa Morgano are de luxe, boutique hotels; whereas, Hotel Flora is less luxurious and less expensive. These three hotels, although smaller, enjoy breathtaking vistas, and offer a bit more intimacy.

There are several chic European boutiques to the right of the entrance of the hotel, plus numerous other quality shops within a half-mile radius offering Italian linens, silks, high fashions, crystal and souvenirs.

No visit to Capri would be complete without a stroll through the colorful streets and passageways, a ride up the funicular railway, a relaxing aperitif in the main square, a cruise around the island or through the Blue Grotto, an excursion to the top of Anacapri, and a romantic dinner in an open-air garden restaurant with strolling guitarists playing your favorite Italian ballads.

Although inundated with summer tourists, my favorite time to visit Capri is during the months of June, July, August and September, when the weather is the mildest. The resort is open from mid-March to the beginning of November.

The Grand Hotel Quisisana offers its guests a comfortable pool and garden area, impeccable service, superb dining, sumptuous accommodations and Italian charm. You will love Capri and the Grand Hotel Quisisana – trust me!

Grand Hotel Quisisana
Via Camerelle 2
80037 Capri, Italy
Tel. (39) 0818370788
Fax (39) 0818376080
E-mail: info@quisi.com
Web: www.quisi.com

ITALY

HOTEL CALA DI VOLPE

Amidst rugged terrain, abutting emerald seas with a backdrop of mountain vistas, lies this uniquely-styled, luxury resort frequented by dignitaries, personalities, yachtsmen and upscale travelers from around the world. Originally developed in 1963 by the Aga Khan under the direction of French architect Jacques Couelle, who designed the property to blend discretely into the Sardinian landscape, Hotel Cala di Volpe was expanded in 1971 and acquired by ITT Sheraton through its Ciga subsidiary in 1994.

Actually, the Costa Smeralda, which covers 33 miles of the northwest coastline of Sardinia, is a pre-planned resort and residential area developed to blend into the environment. Hotel Cala di Volpe is one of three luxury resort hotels now owned by Colony Capital and managed by Starwood Hotels and Resorts (which acquired ITT Sheraton) together with an 18-hole golf course, a conference center, yacht moorings and various other properties. The guests emanate from around the globe; however, 75 percent or so are European and about 10 percent are from the United States.

To this observer, the style and feel of the property is best described as Mediterranean with a rustic, United States's southwestern--stucco and red-tile roof--decor and a fisherman/yachtsman motif. Considering the upscale clientele, high prices, and excellent cuisine, yet simplicity of design and absence of pretension, one could say that an initial physical inspection of the property does not unveil its true, understated elegance.

During the heart of the summer high season, rates run close to $2,500 per day for two with all meals included and an additional $1,400 for an ad-joining parlor. However, in the spring and fall, these rates reduce by over 50 percent.

Directly in front of the main hotel building is the slip for yachts, the pool and the poolside restaurant. The fine-sand beach with an attendant and umbrellas is about two-thirds of a mile walk away over a sand and dirt path or accessible by motor boat that departs from the yacht moorings in front of the hotel.

The resort is open from mid-April through mid-October. Meridiana Airlines offers flights from most major Italian cities and numerous European capitals to the airport in Olbia, which is 30 minutes from the hotel. The resort will arrange ground transportation upon request. Ferry service is also available from the Italian mainland, southern France and nearby Mediterranean islands.

Accommodations

Ninety percent of the 123 air-conditioned guest rooms and suites have balconies and all have Stucco walls and ceramic-tile floors, and include Sardinian-style, rustic furnishings, a double bed or two twin beds, a private safe, refrigerator, mini-bar, hair-dryer, direct dial telephone, remote-control LCD televisions with cable and DVD player, high-speed internet access (at a charge),separate showers and bathtubs, numerous amenities such as terry robes and slippers, fresh fruit, flowers and a bottle of local wine. The 15 junior suites also provide CD and video machines and extra amenities; and the grand Presidential suite boasts three double rooms, two living rooms, three bathrooms, a kitchen, a solarium and a private roof-top swimming pool.

Meeting and function facilities with one room that can accommodate 500 for a banquet, 600 for a cocktail party and 540 classroom style are located at the hotel and conference center at Porto Cervo Village, 10 minutes away.

Restaurants, Lounges, and Entertainment

The main dining room, adjacent to the hotel lobby, overlooks the bay and is open only for dinner featuring Italian, Continental and Sardinian fare. Breakfast and a buffet style lunch are served at the restaurant by the pool (only a few steps from the hotel). The barbecue, buffet-style luncheon is magnificent, with extensive gourmet offerings ranging from every variety of fresh salad and antipasto imaginable and fine imported cheeses to Sardinian-style pastas and entrees, barbecued meats, fowl and fresh fish. Since this extraordinary repast is included for guests on full-board, it should not be missed. Those visiting the resort must pay 120 to 160 Euro for the privilege of partaking.

Of course, room service is available for all meals, beverages and snacks; and picnic lunches can be arranged for boat and driving excursions.

To provide more variety for guests on full pension, the resort offers a dine-around program that includes meals at Hotels Pitrizza and Romazzino, Cervo Grill (grilled and flambe specialties by candlelight), Pescatore (seafood on a terrace overlooking the sea), and La Safina (located at the Pevero Golf Club).

Guests enjoy cocktails at the pool bar and on the terrace of the main lobby. Bar Pontile is the location for piano music and dancing with after-dinner cocktails and beverages. Night clubs in the area include Sopravento, Sottovento, Pepero, Smaila's Cabaret and Billionaire.

Sport Facilities

Located on property are three synthetic-grass tennis courts, a 9-hole putting green, an Olympic-size salt-water pool and a new fitness center equipped with state-of-the-art cardio-vascular machines, exercise machines and free weights. There are changing rooms with showers and a sauna at the fitness center.

The nearby 18-hole, Robert Trent Jones-designed Pevero Golf Club services all of the resorts in the area and is available by hotel shuttle.

Water skis and boat rentals can be arranged and there is motor-boat shuttle service to the resort's

beach, two-thirds-of-a-mile down the coast. The sand is soft, fine, and well maintained; the shimmering waters of the Costa Smeralda throw off varying shades of aqua, emerald and deep blue, and swimming and sunning is among the best found in this part of the Mediterranean. There are numerous excellent beaches along the Costa Smeralda, the most highly touted being the pink-sand beach at Budelli.

Miscellaneous and Environs

Several designer boutiques featuring men's, women's and children's clothing, jewelry and souvenir items are located at the hotel, as well as a hairdresser, and numerous additional shops can be found at the other Starwood Hotels and Resorts properties and in the town of Porto Cervo. Also in Porto Cervo are moorings for 650 yachts, making it possibly the best-equipped (and the most popular) marina in the Mediterranean.

Visitors to Hotel Cala di Volpe will want to explore the other Starwood Hotels and Resorts properties on the Costa Smeralda. Hotel Pitrizza features 51 rooms and suites overlooking the sea with its own private beach and pool set in the rocks, with moorings for small yachts and private boats. Romazzino ("Rosemary"), designed by architect Michael Busiri Vici, with 90 rooms and suites, all with private terraces, also provides a private beach and adjacent pool. These two deluxe properties are a bit smaller and more intimate then Hotel Cala di Volpe and guests at all three resorts enjoy visiting the others and partaking in the dine-around reciprocal program. Starwood Hotels and Resorts also owns the 106-guest room Cervo Hotel, Costa Smeralda Resort and the conference center near the port, which is open 12 months each year.

Well-heeled vacationers and yachtsmen seeking a sophisticated, yet casual environment in one of the Mediterranean's prettiest locales with excellent dining, fine service and sandy beaches will find Hotel Cala di Volpe piu simpatico.

Hotel Cala di Volpe
07020 Porto Cervo
Costa Smeralda
Sardegna, Italia
Tel. (39) (7890) 976111
Fax (39) (7890) 976617

ITALY

HOTEL CIPRIANI

The elegant Hotel Cipriani occupies three unique acres on the island called Giudecca, a stone's throw across the canal from San Marco Square. Guests can be transported around the clock to San Marco Square by the hotel's private launch. This is the ideal way to enjoy Venice, ensconced in comfort and luxury, in the midst of charm and tranquility, yet only moments away from all the action.

Since 1958, this deluxe resort has pampered its guests with the loveliest pool and terraces, the best food and service, and the most comfortable accommodations to be found in Venice.

The hotel was originally built in 1956 by Giuseppe Cipriani, owner of the famous Harry's Bar, located near San Marco Square in Venice. His desire to create a private retreat within easy reach of the square led him to acquire the original

acreage on Giudecca Island, four minutes away from the square by boat. In 1976, Orient-Express Hotels purchased the property and now operates it

through their experienced, amiable director, Dr. Natale Rusconi. Orient-Express Hotels also owns and operates the Hotel Splendido in Portofino, La Samanna in St. Martin; Bora Bora Lagoons in French Polynesia; and other resorts around the world, as well as the revamped collection of Orient Express trains.

In 1991, the Palazzo Vendramin del Cipriani, a fifteenth-century palace, was annexed to the property, creating 10 new luxury accommodations in an elegant, private environment.

The feel of the resort is that of a rambling country estate. Although it is open from the beginning of April through the end of October, the property is the most charming while the weather is mild. When weather permits, guests can enjoy sitting in the floral Casanova gardens, at the outdoor terrace restaurants, and around the large pool while looking out at the canals, lagoons and city of Venice. Over the years, Hotel Cipriani has hosted numerous dignitaries and heads of state, including Nancy and Ronald Reagan during the 1987 Summit meeting held in Venice.

Accommodations

All of the rooms differ in size. The hotel describes its accommodations as consisting of two single rooms, 41 standard and deluxe double guest rooms, 27 junior suites and 18 large suites, for a total of 88. In addition, there are two junior suites, six regular suites and three double rooms in the newly restored and renovated deluxe Palazzo Vendramin, the epitome of Venetian style. Some have private terraces or gardens, others enjoy magnificent vistas of San

Marco, and all feature a kitchen, bar, bathroom with whirlpool and television. Adjacent to the Palazzo Vendramin, Palazzetto Nani Barbaro offers an additional four junior suites and one mansard-type junior suite with breathtaking views of Saint Mark's basin.

Included in every air-conditioned room is a radio, color television with CNN, mini-bar, refrigerator, writing desk, vanity mirror, and bathrooms with hair dryers, tub, shower, expensive amenities and terry-cloth robes and slippers for use during your stay. Many of the superior rooms and suites have balconies, Murano crystal chandeliers, elaborate furnishings, and marble bathrooms with double vanities, private toilet compartments, bathtub Jacuzzis and televisions.

Special butler service is available in the Palazzo Vendramin and Palazzetto Nani Barbaro, where each suite has a full-facility kitchen. These are among the most elaborate accommodations in Italy--with prices to match.

All of the accommodations are tastefully furnished; however, the superior rooms and suites and those in the Palazzo Vendramin have far more expensive furnishings that include some antiques. There is a large conference room and a banquet room available for meetings and special occasions.

The recently acquired Granaries of the Republic, an impressive antique building next to the Palazzetto Nani Barbaro, offers banquet and meeting space.

Restaurants, Lounges, and Entertainment

Breakfast, which is included in the rate, is served either in your room, on your patio or in the main dining room, which includes a beautiful outdoor floral terrace on the lagoon for alfresco dining during the summer. Here you can enjoy fresh orange juice, Champagne, fresh berries and other fruits, cheeses, prosciutto, salami, eggs, rolls and various coffees while watching the boats pass by.

Before lunch, you may enjoy trying a Bellini, the special house drink, which consists of blended peach juice and Champagne.

Lunch is served informally at the indoor/outdoor restaurant by the pool, where you can order light salads, fabulous pasta or complete dinners. There is a special antipasto buffet offered. Sandwiches, salads and drinks are also available at a small snack bar by the pool.

Dinner is offered in the sophisticated main dining room, the Fortuny Terrace Restaurant , or on warm evenings a candlelight dinner is served outdoors overlooking the lagoon with the lights of Venice in the distance. A new wooden terrace built on the water, Cip's, is located on the ground floor of Palazzetto and offers simple, fresh Italian specialties including pizzas.

A piano player entertains for listening and dancing until 1:00 a.m. at the Seagull Bar, where guests

can enjoy after-dinner beverages, including rare liqueurs and cigars. There is also piano music at the small bar adjoining the Cipriani dining room earlier in the evening.

Sport Facilities

The Hotel Cipriani boasts a gigantic, heated, salt-water pool with an elaborate lounge/restaurant area overlooking the lagoon. The atmosphere is tranquil and scenic. Attentive employees will bring you towels and drinks while you sunbathe. There is one tennis court located in a beautiful garden setting, as well as a small, indoor fitness room with a treadmill, Exercycle and several other pieces of equipment. The health club offers sauna, steam, massage and a solarium.

Miscellaneous and Environs

There is one small boutique on the premises, as well as a ladies' hairdresser. Within four minutes, the private launch will transport you to the heart of the Venice shopping district. Guests can store cars during their stay at a garage facility in Venice. Those arriving by plane or train can take a water taxi that will drop them off right at the entrance to the resort. On request, a representative from the hotel will be at the dock by the airport to assist you. Prices for accommodations, dining and extras are quite steep. This brand of superior quality does not come cheap. Double rooms, including breakfast, range in price (in Euros) off-season from 625 to 815 euros and in-season from 815 to 1,330 euros. Suites go from 1,100 to 5,800 euros off-season and from 1,730 to 8,330 euros in-season. Various all-inclusive packages are available.

Venice is one of the most charismatic and unique cities in Europe with its winding streets and canals, famous San Marco Square, excellent shops, charming restaurants and tavernas and romantic gondola rides. For Cipriani guests dining out in Venice, an outstanding choice would be the outdoor terrace of Do Leone at the Londra Palace Hotel, only a few steps from San Marco.

The Hotel Cipriani affords visitors to Venice a truly superior experience, close to the heart of the city, yet on a private, tranquil island. Here you can luxuriate in elegant gardens and surroundings and extremely comfortable accommodations, while enjoying some of the best food and service in Italy.

Hotel Cipriani
Giudecca 10, 30133 Venice, Italy
Tel. 011-39-41-52-07-744
Fax 011-39-41-52-03-930
E-mail: info@hotelcipriani.it
Web: www.hotelcipriani.it

ITALY

HOTEL SPLENDIDO & SPLENDIDO MARE, PORTOFINO

This magnificent villa, which dates back to 1450, is set on a sloping hillside, with four acres of tropical trees and gardens overlooking the spectacular bay and small harbor of charming Portofino on the Italian Riviera, 23 miles south of the Genoa airport.

The property was the summer residence of the Baratta family from the 19th century until it was purchased by the Valentinis in 1901 and converted to a hotel. Sea Container Corporation, which owns the Orient Express, the Hotel Cipriani in Venice, Villa San Michele in Florence, and several other deluxe properties, bought the Hotel Splendido in 1986 and commenced renovations to the rooms and public areas. Furnishings are in the traditional Italian style, the corridors have decorative black-and-white marble floors, and the feel is typical Old World elegance.

The most unique feature of the resort, which has attracted politicians, dignitaries and entertainment personalities over the years, is the commanding view of picturesque Portofino that one can enjoy from most guest rooms, the outdoor restaurant, and the pool. However, the privilege of luxuriating in a deluxe hotel while gazing down at chic Portofino harbor does not come cheap, and minimum room rates, food and beverages run higher than at many other European grand properties.

In 1998, Splendido Mare opened its doors in a most convenient and desirable location on Portofino's famous Piazzetta, a picturesque, semicircular waterfront area where the various yachts dock. This added 16 additional, more modern accommodations, as well as an indoor/outdoor terrace restaurant to the Splendido properties.

Accommodations

The 65 guest accommodations consist of four single rooms, 27 doubles, 27 junior suites, and seven full suites. Fifty of these have balconies or terraces, and 10 have a view of the harbor from windows. Each room and suite is air-conditioned and has a color television with VCR attachment, a mini-bar/refrigerator combination, direct-dial telephones, a radio with cassette feature, a hair dryer, a scale, robes and toiletries. The newly renovated quarters have wall safes, scales, heated towel bars, and magnifying mirrors have been added to the bathrooms. Some of the standard rooms and closet areas are not very large when compared to the other European properties in this book; however, they are very tastefully decorated. The junior suites are larger, having added small sitting areas, and the recently renovated full suites are quite luxurious.

At Splendido Mare there are seven doubles, seven junior suites, and two full suites, all of which are air-conditioned, elegantly decorated and furnished, with direct-dial telephones, mini-bars, satellite television, hair dryers, scales, and most have balconies and private safes.

There are two meeting rooms, one of which can seat up to 80 theater-style.

Restaurants, Lounges, and Entertainment

In addition to 24-hour room service, meals can be enjoyed in the main dining room, which moves outside (when weather permits) to a protected patio that affords a panoramic view of the harbor and

surrounding areas. A buffet lunch is offered at a fixed price at the pool and features fish, seafood and meats, as well as salads, pastas, pizza from the oven and desserts.

The à la carte dinner menu offers numerous imaginatively prepared pastas and a variety of entrées. Service in the dining room is traditional Italian style, with the waiters taking great care in arranging the food presentation on each plate and making certain the appropriate silverware is utilized at each course. Dinner for two with a mid-priced Italian wine, after taxes, will easily set you back $225.

A piano player/singer performs throughout the evening in the lounge adjacent to the dining areas. There is no other entertainment.

Immediately below the Hotel Splendido, in the small harbor town of Portofino (a 10-minute climb down the hillside), are numerous restaurants, bars and cafés where you can sit outside and watch the yachts and the passing tourists. The indoor/outdoor Chuflay Bar Restaurant at Splendido Mare is an excellent spot to see and be seen while enjoying "Splendido-quality" cuisine and service.

Sport Facilities

A heated, saltwater pool sits on the hill surrounded by lounge chairs and umbrellas. There is a sundeck area above the pool and a small restaurant and bar adjacent to it. Below the pool deck is the beauty parlor, which is also the location of the gymnasium, saunas, and masseuse. The hotel has one tennis court with synthetic grass. Eighteen holes of golf and horseback riding are available five miles away in Rapallo. The hotel can arrange excursions to neighboring towns, as well as water-skiing from its motor launch.

Miscellaneous and Environs

There is a small, upscale boutique at the hotel, and in the towns of Portofino and nearby Santa Margherita you can browse through dozens of boutiques, souvenir shops, and leather, jewelry, and art stores.

To reach the resort, you can fly into Genoa and either rent a car or take a taxi for the 23-mile ride, or take a train to nearby Santa Margherita and obtain a taxi at the train station. If you drive from Nice to Portofino, it will take approximately two-and-a-half hours. When driving, you exit the autoroute after Genoa at Rapallo, and follow the signs that take you along the coast through Santa Margherita to Portofino. There is ample parking at the resort.

Portofino is undoubtedly the most picturesque and desirable location along the Italian Riviera, and the Hotel Splendido is the most elegant and sophisticated hotel in this area, offering its very affluent clientele fine service, dining and luxury in a breathtaking setting.

Hotel Splendido & Splendido Mare
16 Viale Baratta
Portofino 16034, Italy
Tel. 39 0185 267801
Fax 0185 267806
E-Mail: reservations@splendido.net
www.hotelsplendido.com

ITALY

IL SAN PIETRO

Tucked away in a cliff that descends to the sea, partially hidden by colorful flowers and lush green vines, lies the romantic, unique architectural wonder, the San Pietro. Access to the resort is off the breathtaking Amalfi Drive, one-and-a-half kilometers south of the charming seaside resort town of Positano.

San Pietro is the vision and accomplishment of Carlino Cinque, who conceived, constructed, owned and operated the resort until his death. It is now owned and operated by his niece, Virginia Cinque, and his grandnephews, Vito and Carlo Cinque. Since 1934, Uncle Carlino had owned and operated the smaller hotel Miramare in Positano. Starting in 1958, he hired contractors and laborers to blast away rocks and create his dream child, which opened its doors with 33 rooms in 1970. Today, the structure has been expanded to 62 rooms and larger public areas.

This is a special refuge conceived as a romantic hideaway designed for honeymooners, lovers and couples celebrating anniversaries and other occasions who seek tranquility, elegance, comfort and a spectacularly picturesque setting. Every private accommodation, as well as the public rooms and restaurants, overlook the sea and scenic, neighboring villages, with flowers lining every path and adorning every room. Floors are of decorative ceramic tile; and floor-to-ceiling picture windows enhance the enchanting view of the water and Amalfi coastline. This intimate gem captures the charm and quiet beauty so many lesser resorts have strived for. You can casually socialize with fellow guests who travel here from Europe, the United States and around the world, or you can enjoy total privacy throughout the resort.

Accommodations

Each of the 62 rooms and suites is uniquely different in shape, size and decor. Although they were built in the 1970s and 1980s, they have been renovated annually and are quite modern, with ceramic tile floors, elegant bathroom fixtures, and traditional Italian furnishings and wardrobes; and each has either an open or enclosed terrace overlooking the sea. Several new accommodations were competed in 1999 and sit atop the property with spectacular terraces and panoramic vistas. Included in each accommodation are an air-conditioner, refrigerator/mini-bar, double bed, telephone, television with a CNN channel, internet access for notebooks, a hair dryer, terry robes and slippers and a private room safe.

Twenty-two of the rooms are sold as special rooms. They are larger and generally have giant terraces, picture windows in the bathrooms, Jacuzzi soaking tubs and varying special features. One of the suites contains a large sunken tub with a stream of water flowing from the phallus of a Pompeii statue.

The standard rooms are generally smaller than the more expensive deluxe guest rooms and generally lack some of the special features. Repeating guests will wish to try different rooms on each visit, in order to appreciate the unique beauty of the hotel.

Restaurants, Lounges, and Entertainment

There is only one dining room, which includes two lovely outside terraces set on the cliff overlooking the sea. Dining by candlelight on these terraces, looking out at the moon and twinkling lights of Positano in the distance, is one of the most heavenly, romantic dining experiences you will encounter in your life. The restaurant recently received its first Michelin star. All three meals are served in the dining room. A Continental breakfast can be ordered and brought to the terrace of your room, and sandwiches, salads, and fruits are available at the bar by the beach.

The menu, which does not change from lunch to dinner, is quite extensive, offering almost every variety of pasta, veal and chicken dish, as well as fish, seafood, omelets and salads. A complimentary slice of mouth-watering pizza hot from the oven precedes every dinner. Jackets are recommended but not required for gentlemen; on warm nights, however, most guests dress casually but elegantly. Service is extremely friendly, and the experienced maître d' seems to be almost everywhere in his effort to please.

The large outdoor floral terrace that extends from the lobby is a perfect place for watching the sunset with a before-dinner cocktail or gazing out at the stars and scenic evening panorama with a cappuccino or after-dinner drink.

There is little entertainment other than a marvelous piano player and saxophonist who play background music during dinner and create an intimate setting for dancing afterwards.

Sport Facilities

An elevator from the lobby descends to the beach via a passage cut through the rocks. The beach is small, with black sand and pebbles, and is not a terribly comfortable place to repose. Above the beach is a large carved rock area with comfortable lounges, steps to the water, and a small bar serving drinks and snacks.

Near the elevator at the beach is one asphalt tennis court tucked into the cliff only a few feet from

the sea with a scenic backdrop of cliffs and greenery.

There is also a small swimming pool two floors above the lobby with an adjacent lounging area that looks out to the sea. This is more of a dipping pool than a swimming pool. A relatively small fitness center/spa was recently added with state-of-the-art equipment, a variety of massage and beauty treatments and a Turkish bath.

Miscellaneous and Environs

To get to the San Pietro, visitors can fly into Rome and either rent a car or take a two-hour train ride to Naples. From Naples, there are numerous options. The easiest choice would be to rent a car or take a taxi from the Naples train station. A taxi can cost anywhere from 100 euros on up. It is also possible during the summer months to take the Aliscafi (hydrofoil boat) from the harbor directly to Positano and then be transported by a small motor launch to the resort. The least expensive alternative is to take a local train to Sorrento, Meta, or Salerno, then a taxi to the resort. Trains do not go through Positano.

You do not want to miss traversing the famous Amalfi Drive, the highway that twists and turns up and down cliffs overlooking the sea between Salerno and Sorrento, dipping into numerous charming seaside resort towns, including Amalfi, Praiano, and Positano. The coastline road is somewhat dangerous for the novice, and I would recommend leaving the driving to a local and just sitting back and enjoying the scenery. If you take a taxi from Naples,

you can either get to the resort via Sorrento or you can take an alternative route through Salerno and Amalfi, which takes an additional 45 minutes.

Positano, which is a short ride or a long walk from the San Pietro, is a small seaside resort town of narrow streets lined with shops and restaurants winding down the cliff to the harbor and public beach. The hotel will transport you to the town in its private vehicles. Amalfi is also only a few miles away and is a charming spot, somewhat larger and easier to explore.

The San Pietro is a special seaside resort capturing the charm and scenic beauty portrayed by the media as indigenous to this part of Italy. Although it lacks some of the facilities and the variety of possibilities found at larger resorts, it is just perfect for world travelers seeking a sophisticated yet intimate, romantic, scenic retreat with fine dining, impeccable service and Italian charm.

Il San Pietro
Via Laurito 2
84017 Positano, Italy
Tel. (089) 87-54-55
Fax (089) 81-14-49
E-mail: info@ilsanpietro.it
www.ilsanpietro.it

ITALY

SANTA CATERINA

Located on the famous Amalfi Drive, only minutes from the town of Amalfi, the Santa Caterina sits on the top of a cliff enjoying a commanding view of this typical seaside Italian village. Two elevators extend down the hillside, transporting guests past terraced floral gardens and citrus groves to the blue Mediterranean. Located at sea level is the gym and the attractive beach club, which includes a swimming pool, sun-bathing area, bar, and charming outdoor garden restaurant, as well as easy access to the sea. A spa was added in 2004.

The history of this very special resort is as impressive as its scenic surroundings. In 1880, Giuseppe Gambardella built the original structure, which was destroyed Christmas Eve 1892 during a landslide of rocks from the adjoining mountains. Giuseppe's son, Crescenzo Gambardella, personally rebuilt the property in a safer location in 1904, constructing the original six guest rooms with the assistance of one laborer. Over the 20th century, the Gambardella family made numerous renovations and additions, bringing the resort to its present 62 guest accommodations.

During the Second World War, the property was occupied first by the Germans and subsequently by the British and Americans. Such notable entertainers as Glenn Miller and Artie Shaw entertained the American troops on the hotel's picturesque terraces.

Today the Santa Caterina is owned and managed by the most gracious and hospitable Giusi and Ninni Gambardella, the granddaughters of Giuseppe and daughters of Crescenzo. Most of their own children, Crescenso, Alessandro and Beatrice already work at the resort in various capacities and look forward to continuing the family tradition in future years. Dedicated Armando di Palma and a talented staff oversee the day-to-day operations.

During the past few years, the owners have spent millions constructing more elegant suites, renovating guest rooms, and expanding the park and gardens. As a result, this is one of the most charming and romantic properties in southern Europe.

Accommodations

Thirty-five guest rooms and 15 junior and full suites are located in the main building, with nine additional accommodations, between the junior suite and deluxe categories, in the Villa Santa Caterina, located in the center of orange and lemon groves. All accommodations are air conditioned and include original antique furnishings, hand-painted ceramic tile floors, remote-control televisions with satellite channels, refrigerators, mini-bars, private safes, private terraces, double beds, and modern bathrooms with Jaccuzi tubs, showers, hair dryers, heated towel bars and numerous amenities.

Two suites in the garden, known as LaFollia Amalfitana and La Casa Dell Arancio, are especially desirable, as well as several others in the gardens below the main building.

In 2005, another building was acquired and is the site of six additional modern rooms and suites.

Down the lemon grove path from the beach club restaurant sits the Juliet and Romeo honeymoon cottage where romantics can enjoy total privacy amidst the scenic splendor of the Amalfi coastline.

One of the salons can accommodate up to 80 people for meetings and conventions. Room rates

include a buffet breakfast. MAP and FAP are also available.

Restaurants, Lounges, and Entertainment

All three meals can be enjoyed in the casually elegant, scenic main dining room with its floor-to-ceiling glass windows overlooking the sea and town of Amalfi, spectacular marble and lapis floors, unique light fixtures, and lovely greenery. Service keeps in with Italian tradition, supervised by Giuseppi, the helpful, friendly maître d'.

Guests can choose from the vast selection of à la carte items, which includes dozens of antipasti, pastas, salads, omelet's, meats, fishes, cheeses, and desserts. The ingredients for all dishes are fresh, and each offering is prepared to order.

I especially enjoyed the Sauté di Frutti di Mare (mixed seafood sautéed in oil, garlic, and parsley), folloviello (a thin crêpe filled with mixed seafood, quickly browned with a rich lobster sauce), Crêpe Santa Caterina (a delicious cheese mixture in a crêpe with a light tomato sauce), the Sciatielli dello

Chef (a potato noodle in an eggplant tomato cheese sauce), as well as the exquisite dessert soufflés. The wine list is extensive, with numerous selections from the Campania area seldom exported to other parts of the world.

Meals are also available through room service on your terrace. The romantic outdoor garden restaurant overlooking the pool offers a panoramic view, and is surrounded by lush vegetation, flowers and lemon trees. Lunch, which is served here, ranges from oven-baked pizzas and imaginative pastas to grilled fish and meats.

Cocktails before dinner and coffee or liqueur afterwards are most enjoyable on the outdoor terrace adjoining the main dining room with its spectacular view looking down to the town of Amalfi. There is a piano player or small combo every evening.

Sport Facilities

Located at the attractive beach club, a few feet above the sea are a small pool bar, an area set up for sunbathing, and a bar serving various beverages and fruits. For the more hearty, swimming in the Mediterranean off the sun deck is possible.

Joggers and walkers can head toward Amalfi on the road outside the hotel; however, cars winding around the narrow road make this a bit hazardous. Fishing and boating excursions can be arranged in town. A small gym near the pool has several cardiovascular and exercise machines and free weights, and boasts panoramic views out to the sea and the town of Amalfi. The spa that was added in 2004, offers sauna, steam and a variety of massage, cosmetic, facial and hydrotherapy treatments, all at varying prices.

Miscellaneous and Environs

There are numerous shops in Amalfi. Shopping is somewhat better in Positano and Capri, both of which can be reached by a scenic hydrofoil or boat ride.

Visitors frequently take the 10-minute side trip to the grotto Esmeralda, where they can experience a short rowboat ride through a small cave with iridescent waters and stalagmite and stalactite formations.

Although there are numerous restaurants in Amalfi, those wishing to dine outside the hotel will be well rewarded if they take the short excursion to Ravello for lunch or dinner at Hotel Palumbo, where you will be treated to fine cuisine and a breathtaking panorama.

The resort is open all year round. Temperatures in the winter dip to the 50s and climb back to the 80s and 90s by mid-summer. Guests often rent a car and drive from Rome. It is possible to take a train from Rome to Naples and transfer to a train to Salerno or Sorrento and then hire a taxi to Amalfi. It is also possible to take a taxi from Naples. The resort can arrange a private car from Rome, Naples, Sorrento or Salerno.

As mentioned in other chapters, this is a part of Italy visitors should not miss. The warmth and dedication to making guests comfortable demonstrated by the family owners and staff make this a very special experience. Discerning travelers seeking an elegant, yet informal quiet retreat, a mild climate, an incredibly scenic setting, suburb service, and outstanding Italian cuisine will adore the Santa Caterina.

Santa Caterina
84011 Amalfi, Italy
Tel. 39 (089) 87-101-2
Fax 39 (089) 87 1351
E-mail: info@hotelsantacaterina.it
Web: www.hotelsantacaterina.it

ITALY

VILLA D'ESTE

The Grand Hotel Villa d'Este sits on the west shore of Lago di Como, a few miles north of the town of Como, 30 miles north of Milan. From your room each morning, you can look across the lake and watch the spectacular sunrise over picturesque lush mountain slopes that stretch down to the waters and are dotted with houses and villas. On warm evenings, you can dance under the stars on the patio in front of the hotel to a romantic Italian orchestra, while looking out at the same breathtaking panorama. Now, however, the sunlit villas have been replaced by thousands of twinkling lights.

Built by Cardinal Gallio in 1568, this princely estate was combined with an adjoining property and made into a hotel in 1873. Earlier in the 19th century, Caroline of Brunswick, wife of King George IV of England, had purchased the original residence and added the luxurious touches that make the hotel unique. Although the two main villas have been completely refurbished since World War II, the marble, the Romanesque Italian gardens, the period furniture, and the Old World elegance and charm remain intact.

Accommodations

The 154 air-conditioned guest rooms are furnished with tasteful Italian provincial antique and period pieces and are lavishly decorated. One hundred twenty-five rooms are located in the main building and 29 are located in the adjoining Queen's Pavilion. Some of the standard rooms are smaller than others. There are 54 junior suites and 9 one- or two-bedroom suites. The junior suites are similar to the double rooms, except they have sitting areas and more desirable views. All guest accommodations include mini-bars, private electronic safes, cable television, direct-dial telephones, high-speed internet connections and large marble bathrooms, many with Jacuzzi tubs. Commencing in the late 1990s, many of the rooms and bathrooms were renovated and nine new accommodations were added, all with walk-in closets and ultra-luxurious bathrooms.

The room rates, which include a full breakfast, can run quite high, depending upon the relative exchange rate between the euro and the dollar. From time to time, Villa d'Este also accommodates international conventions in its nine meeting rooms and four banquet rooms, with seating capacities ranging from 10 to 250, all with modern conference equipment.

Restaurants, Lounges, and Entertainment

Breakfast is available in the rooms (continental), or buffet-style at the Veranda restaurant, which has electrically controlled glass windows that overlook Lake Como. The complimentary breakfast buffet, which is most impressive, includes fresh fruits, juices, champagne, cereals, rolls, cheeses, meats, eggs, waffles and omelets of your choice.

Lunch and dinner are served in the Veranda, and dinner is also available at the more informal Grill. The Veranda menu has Continental and haute Italian cuisine while the Grill features meats, seafood and regional specialties. On warm evenings, the Grill serves meals alfresco on its patio overlooking the lake. Both restaurants have extensive wine lists

featuring a magnificent selection of Italian wines from the various regions of Italy. In the warmer summer months, a light lunch and drinks are served in the open terrace area near the pool.

On the elegant patio that extends from the front entrance of the main hotel to the lake, piano entertainment accompanies your pre-dinner cocktail and after-dinner coffees and liqueurs. On warm summer evenings a romantic Italian orchestra plays dance music. Watching the sun set or gazing out at the stars over Lake Como from this spot while the music plays is an incredibly romantic experience. In addition, there is a piano bar and a nightclub featuring dancing. Several times each summer, the resort features festive outdoor specialty events with cocktails, a set gourmet menu and entertainment. Food and beverages are very expensive.

Sport Facilities

Although most European resorts tend to fall short in this category, the Villa d'Este is an exception. In addition to an indoor freshwater pool and a children's pool, the large outdoor pool and heated Jacuzzi float on pontoons right on the lake. Arrangements can be made at the pool for waterskiing, sailing, fishing, windsurfing and canoeing.

This is one of the best tennis facilities in Europe, with eight beautifully maintained tennis courts on the hill overlooking the hotel.

Originally, the resort had its own private golf course, seven miles away. Today, it is no longer a private course. However, this course and several other regulation courses are within a 30-minute drive. There is a putting green on the premises.

A health club, gym, squash court, golf simulator, sauna, steam, whirlpool and massage room are next

to the indoor pool with underground access from the main hotel building. The Beauty Center offers a selection of massage, hydrotherapy and beauty treatments for the face and body.

Miscellaneous and Environs

In the hotel, there is a hairdresser salon, several elegant boutiques and a jewelry store.

Visitors may want to take the boat ride up Lake Como that stops off at historic and picturesque little towns and villages. The town of Como is a charming Italian resort village with numerous hotels, stores and pizzerias. There is a gambling casino on Lake Lugano, one half-hour away.

Most visitors fly into Milan, and then take the 45-minute drive north. However, trains will bring you right into the town of Como where you can catch a taxi to the hotel. On request, the hotel will arrange limousine service to and from the airport.

The Villa d'Este boasts an efficient, friendly service staff, features haute Italian cuisine in a superior atmosphere, offers a variety of sport facilities and entertainment, and puts it together in one of the more picturesque, charming, romantic settings in the world. Though "troppo, troppo caro", with many extra charges, this is among the best, most complete and chic resorts Europe has to offer.

Villa d'Este
Via Regina 40
22012 Cernobbio, Lago di Como, Italy
Tel. (011 39) 031 348890
Fax (011 39) 031 348873
E-mail: info@villadeste.it
Web: www.villadeste.it

SCOTLAND

THE WESTIN TURNBERRY RESORT

Set on a hill overlooking its own golf course and the sea, built in the style of an Edwardian country house, is the venerable Westin Turnberry Resort, Scotland.

The hotel was built at the turn of the century by a private railway company on land owned by the Marquess of Ailsa. It encompassed an 18-hole golf course. During both World Wars the hotel was requisitioned for use as a military hospital and golf course for an air base. Thereafter it was totally resurrected and renovated.

The hotel reopened in 1950 and a new Ailsa course was created by Mckenzie Ross. By 1954, still under the ownership of the railways, the Arran course was built. In 1983, the railway company sold the property to Sea Containers, who, in 1987, passed it on to a private Japanese family company. Subsequently, major renovations took place between 1989 and 1993, with an investment of over $33 million. Today, the resort is managed by Starwood Hotels and Resorts as part of the Westin hotel chain.

The three-story main hotel building, with two wings in a U-shaped configuration, descends down a hill to the golf course and sea with most public areas enjoying commanding panoramic views. The elegantly furnished reception area, lounges, drawing rooms, bar and restaurants that compose the ground level set the tone for this very traditional Scottish property oozing with Old World style and charm.

Forty-five percent of the clientele comes from the United Kingdom, 35 percent from North America, and 20 percent from other countries. Historically, better than 80 percent came to play golf; however,

the addition of an impressive spa facility and outdoor activity center has attracted more vacationing couples whose main interests are not necessarily golf oriented.

Accommodations

One hundred and thirty-two traditionally styled guest rooms and suites, each with different design and decor, are spread around the three floors and wings of the main hotel and the new free-standing spa wing. Forty percent have sea views. Every accommodation has traditional furnishings, a writing desk, lounging chairs, remote-control television, and bathrooms with tub, shower, heated towel bars, hair dryers, terry-cloth robes, magnifying mirrors and toiletries. There is no air conditioning (which would seldom be needed due to the climate and

winds off the coast), and no stocked mini-bars (but there is 24-hour room service and refrigerators in the spa rooms and suites).

The rooms and suites vary considerably in size and comfort levels. The three largest suites come with either one or two adjoining bedrooms and are enormous in size. The newer, smaller suites with

separate sitting rooms are cozier and more than ample for any couple requiring extra space. Seventeen newer guest rooms built in 1991 are located in the spa wing; eight have double beds. Fourteen other rooms in the hotel have double beds (three of which are of the elaborate four-poster variety); however, management anticipates adding additional queen- and king-size beds to accommodate its ever increasing population of vacationing couples. The more expensive accommodations have Jacuzzi bathtubs, three have balconies, and the large suites have fireplaces. A modernization program continues and guest room amenities could change in the future. Because of the differences from room to room, it may be prudent to obtain a description of the room in advance.

A few minutes' walk from the main hotel complex are 9 two-bedroom cottages and 12 six- to eight-bedroom lodges that can be booked for family gatherings, golf outings, or corporate entertaining.

There are several facilities that can accommodate conferences, meetings, and banquets. These are all elegantly decorated and not of the usual business conference variety. One room can accommodate up to 280 theater style and another, at the golf clubhouse, up to 80. More groups frequent the resort during winter months and most are golf oriented.

Restaurants, Lounges, and Entertainment

The Turnberry Restaurant, located in the main hotel building, is a large, formal, elegantly furnished dining room with large picture windows that look out to the golf course and sea. Breakfast is served here, as well as dinner, which is accompanied by soft piano music. Meals are served European-style by friendly young servers, many of whom have trained in France. The cuisine of Chef Ralph Porciani is described as classical French and Scottish. Dining selections are impressive and guests can choose from a multi-course fixed-priced menu or from numerous à la carte selections. Local fish, seafood and lamb are always featured. Many dishes are international in flavor and the extensive list of fine wines includes choices from around the world.

Lunch and dinner are available at the Terrace, located atop the spa building. This is also an elegantly decorated room, a bit less formal, with picture windows that look out over a railing to the sea, positioned in such a manner as to afford you the feel of dining on a cruise ship. The menu is described as "a modern twist on traditional dishes." I found the selections equally as interesting as those in the dining room, and the room a more intimate experience.

The casual, golf clubhouse dining room, known as the Tappie Toorie Restaurant offers all-day dining until 7:00p.m. Although ideal for golfers and those wishing a quicker meal, the food and service do not compare with the other dining rooms.

The small atmospheric cocktail lounge in the main hotel features a large selection of Scotch malt whiskies. The larger lounge, The Ailsa Bar, offers piano music during the evenings from 7:00 p.m. to 9:30 p.m., and a bagpiper plays traditional Scottish tunes outside the main building from 6:30 p.m. to 7:00 p.m. There are numerous other parlors and lounges where guests can enjoy coffee, tea, soft drinks and alcoholic beverages. Complimentary hors d'oeuvres are offered before dinner in the bars. Twenty-four-hour room service is also available.

Sport Facilities

The prime attraction of The Westin Turnberry Resort, Scotland is its world-renowned golf facilities, which include the 18-hole Ailsa course, home of numerous "Open Championship" tournaments; the new, highly acclaimed 18-hole Kintyre course; the 9-hole Arran Academy course; a 12-hole pitch-and-putt course; several practice putting greens; and a clubhouse with a fully stocked pro shop, a restaurant open for breakfast and lunch, and a meeting hall with an enclosed conservatory that can accommodate up to 120 persons. Although the fame associated with the Ailsa course – affording it high ratings among professionals in golf periodicals – is due to its challenging play, and although it enjoys numerous holes with engaging vistas of the sea, it is a "links course" and may appear a bit barren to those golfers accustomed to verdant-green, wooded golf courses.

Individuals and groups alike can experience the very latest teaching and practice facilities at the Colin Montgomerie Links Golf Academy, which features group golf clinics, personalized programs, individually tailored training, indoor teaching areas, 16 covered bays, and a state-of-the-art audiovisual theater with swing-analysis technology.

Another major facility at The Westin Turnberry Resort, Scotland is the elegant health spa, built in the early 1990s, that houses an inviting 20-meter, glass-enclosed, indoor swimming pool with an underwater lighting and music system, adjacent Jacuzzi, a well-equipped exercise room, men's and women's changing and relaxing facilities that include sauna, steam and Swiss shower, sun booths, as well as daily exercise classes, cholesterol tests,

hairdressers and other general beauty treatments, and a variety of massage and body treatments such as aromatherapy, hydrotherapy, deep cleansing, body polish, and algae and mud masks. There is a significant charge for all special spa and beauty treatments. As described earlier, also located at the spa wing are 17 guest rooms and the Terrace.

In addition, the resort offers two all-weather tennis courts, a jogging trail along the sea coast and golf course, two squash courts, and a billiard room.

The Outdoor Activity Center will assist in organizing off-road driving, salmon and trout fishing, archery, shooting, quad biking, falconry, mountain biking and horse riding.

Miscellaneous and Environs

Most visitors fly into Glasgow, Prestwick, or London Heathrow airports. The resort is a one-hour drive from Glasgow, 30 minutes from Prestwick, and an hour by plane from London. You can take a train to the town of Ayr, 17 miles north of the resort, where you can catch a taxi. The Westin Turnberry Resort does provide chauffeur service from Glasgow airport for roughly $150 each way.

On premises are a boutique, a knickknack shop, and a fully stocked golf/pro shop.

Sightseeing could include Culzean Castle, four miles to the north, Robert Burns's home near Ayr, 17 miles north, Glasgow, 53 miles north, and Edinburgh, 92 miles northeast.

The Westin Turnberry Resort is a golfer's paradise, offering comfortable accommodations, fine dining, sophisticated European-style service, and one of Europe's finest spa facilities, all in a panoramic, Scottish, coastal setting.

The Westin Turnberry Resort
Ayrshire, Scotland KA269LT
Tel. 011-44-(0) 1655-331000
Fax 011-(44)-1655-331706
E-mail: turnberry@westin.com
Web: www.westin.com/turnberry

SPAIN

BARCELÓ LA BOBADILLA

arcelo La Bobadilla is a very unique resort sanctuary located in the wooded foothills of Andalusia, 36 miles north of Malaga, and 42 miles west of Granada. Perched on a hillside in the style of a tiny Moorish village, the whitewashed buildings with red-tiled roofs, wrought-iron gates and balconies, and wooden-shuttered windows overlook shady patios, sparkling fountains, and orange and lemon trees. Scarlet, red and yellow bougainvillea climb the white walls, and pink and red geraniums cascade from the iron grills. The interior is distinctive, combining Andalusian style with contemporary elegance. Graceful Moorish arches, carved-wood ceilings, tiled floors and marble fountains adorn the lobby.

The resort was built in 1985 by Rudolf Staab, a German entrepreneur, whose dream was to create the ultimate understated, authentic, yet elegant Spanish resort get-away close to nature for travelers who desired luxury without pretense. Today the resort is owned by Barcelo Hotels.

The estate extends over 1,000 acres of scenic countryside with rivers, valleys, hiking paths and olive groves. Vegetables, fruits, and flowers for the hotel are grown on its farmland, and cattle, sheep and pigs are bred on its ranch.

Accommodations

Presently, there are 62 elegant bedrooms and suites, built in the "cortijo style," each uniquely different in architecture, design and furnishings. All of the spacious rooms and suites have either a balcony, terrace or garden. The giant bathrooms are especially luxurious and include marble shower stalls, handmade tiles, bathtubs, terry-cloth robes, hair dryers, magnifying mirrors and the finest amenities. Each room has a mini-bar/refrigerator, remote-control television with cable and CNN, private vault, spacious storage, a writing desk and direct-dial telephones.

The convention hall is located in a former Mediterranean-style church and can accommodate 120 theater-style or 20 in a smaller conference room. Various meeting and conference equipment is available.

Restaurants, Lounges, and Entertainment

There are two restaurants on the premises: El Cortijo, next to the main lobby and village square, serving regional cuisine; and the internationally acclaimed La Finca, offering gourmet "haute cuisine." Breakfast is available in your room or buffet-style at the breakfast lounge. Delectable fresh juices, breads, rolls, croissants and pastries are featured. Grilled and barbecued preparations are offered during the summer by the pool. There is a bar and outdoor grill restaurant at the swimming pool and a bar-lounge off the lobby of the main building. Room service is available around the clock. La Finca is a special experience, featuring an impressive selection of Spanish and international wines and the opportunity to sample the specialties of Chef Lutz Bosins.

Sport Facilities

Facilities include a lovely outdoor 1,500-square-meter swimming pool set in gardens surrounded by palm trees and comfortable lounges and umbrellas, an indoor heated pool and Jacuzzi, a fitness center with exercise equipment, Turkish baths and Finnish saunas, two tennis courts, table tennis, horseback riding with excellent horses and scenic trails, rabbit hunting (during season), pentanque, archery, clay pigeon shooting and bicycles. For hunting and shooting, guests must have a gun license.

Miscellaneous and Environs

From the airport in Malaga, visitors should take main road E 902/N 331 direction Antequera-Granada. At kilometer 35/40 from Malaga crossroads direction "Granada" (right-hand) and "Antequera/Sevilla" (on the left), take direction Granada, and turn off on the exit SALIDA (Salinas). At a distance of five kilometers direction Iznajar/VVA. de Tapia (C334) you will find on your right hand side the main entrance to La Bobadilla complex. To visit Granada, you would go back to A-92 and follow it for 40 miles to Granada, where you will want to explore the Alhambra district. Also located at the resort are a beauty parlor, a masseur and a boutique.

Visitors to Spain seeking ultra-luxurious accommodations, exceptional dining and a wide range of sport facilities in a picturesque, tranquil, typically Spanish country environment away from the crowds will adore this unique gem.

Barceló la Bobadilla
Finca La Bobadilla, Apdo. 144
18300 Loja (Granada) Spain
Tel. 34-958-321861
Fax 34-958-321810
E-mail: labobadilla.info@barcelo.com
Web: www.la-bobadilla.com

SPAIN

BYBLOS ANDALUZ

This luxurious, Spanish-style resort and spa, which opened in 1986, is located only a few minutes' drive from the town of Fuengirola, in the heart of Spain's Costa del Sol, about 20 miles from the Malaga airport.

Picturesquely set between two Robert Trent Jones golf courses, with the Sierra Blanca foothills for a backdrop, the resort offers its wealthy clientele a quiet retreat in contrast to the hustle and bustle of most of the hotels located along the Costa del Sol. The public areas are immaculately clean and tastefully designed in an Andalusian motif, with marble floors, white stucco walls, numerous courtyards, and fountains adorned with colorful ceramic tiles, plants, and Spanish objets d'art.

In addition to the sumptuous accommodations and comfortable lounge areas both inside and in the gardens, the Byblos Andaluz offers some of the most extensive sport and spa facilities found in Europe. The summer weather is warm and pleasant.

Accommodations

Of the 144 guest accommodations, 108 are mini-suites and 36 are considered full suites. However, even the least expensive room in the hotel is spacious and elegantly furbished and includes a large, private balcony, a separate sitting area, a dressing table, two twin beds or a queen-size, closets with wooden hangers, a refrigerator/mini-bar, a private safe, a separate toilet compartment, and a lavish bathroom with double sinks, separate tub and shower, a hair dryer, and terry-cloth robes. Although the full suites are larger and generally have

the better views, the accommodations designated as mini-suites are extremely comfortable.

The resort accepts business meetings and small conventions with facilities that include six separate salons, one of which is able to seat 150 theater-style, and another that can accommodate 400 for a cocktail party.

Restaurants, Lounges, and Entertainment

Le Naihac is touted as the premiere gourmet restaurant at the hotel, offering à la carte dining. The wine list consists mostly of Spanish offerings, with a few French selections thrown in at astronomical prices.

Byblos Andaluz is the less formal restaurant that is open for dinner. Breakfast and lunch are served buffet-style, and dinner offers regional specialties and several meats, fishes and pastas, as well as special diet items for guests who come to lose weight and for participants in the spa program.

In the winter, breakfast is served indoors at La Fuente Restaurant.

There is a small bar by the pool, and the St. Tropez Bar and Lounge next to the restaurants offers before-dinner cocktails, after-dinner cordials and features music nightly.

Sport Facilities

The extensive sport facilities include two 18-hole golf courses, a driving range, five tennis courts, two outdoor and three indoor pools, and a health spa known as the Thalassotherapy Center, which is im-

mediately adjacent to the main hotel. There is also horseback riding nearby.

The lovely outdoor pool and garden area is an extremely pleasant place to spend your day. Comfortable lounge chairs are spread throughout the landscaped gardens and look out at the golf course and foothills in the distance.

Two of the tennis courts are hard surface, and two are clay. Two are illuminated for night play, and tennis lessons can be arranged.

At the Thalassotherapy Center by La Prairie, there are three pools, one for rehabilitation treatment, one with therapeutic jet sprays, and a third for swimming. The gym has a few pieces of exercise equipment, but no state-of-the-art machines or organized exercise classes. After a compulsory medical exam, guests can enjoy a variety of spa treatments, including bubbling seawater baths, massage, jet showers, marine ultrasonic underwater treatments, pressotherapy to drain the lymph nodes, and algotherapy (in which seaweed and infrared rays are applied). A hairdresser is also located at this complex.

Miscellaneous and Environs

There is a small shopping arcade that includes high-priced men's and women's boutiques and a linen shop.

Excursions can be arranged to the towns of Granada, Sevilla, Ronda, Marbella, and Gibraltar.

Visitors generally fly into the international Malaga airport, rent a car, and follow the main road in the direction of Cadiz. After reaching the town of Fuengirola, you exit at the Byblos Andaluz sign and continue in a westerly direction for a few miles in the direction of Coin until you reach the entrance to the hotel and golf courses.

Most of the guests are European, with about 10 percent from the United States and other parts of the world.

The Byblos Andaluz is a unique, picturesque, peaceful retreat in the heart of Spain's Costa del Sol, offering its refined clientele very spacious and comfortable accommodations, a large selection of sport and spa facilities, fine dining, elegance, sophistication and a relaxed experience.

Byblos Andaluz
Urb Mijas Golf s/n
29650 Mijas Costa-Malaga
Spain
Tel. 34-952-47-3050
Fax 34-952-47-6783
E-mail: Comercial@byblos-andaluz.com
Web: www.byblos-andaluz.com

CASTILLO HOTEL SON VIDA

Perched on top of a hill on the original site of a thirteenth-century castle, surrounded by 500 acres of subtropical park and a golf course, affording magnificent views of lush surroundings and the town and bay of Palma, is this classic European resort. The main building is an ancient Spanish castle converted to a deluxe hotel.

In 1961, a Spanish company converted Son Vida into a hotel and added modern guest rooms in order to attract personalities from all over the world. In the 1970s, a luxurious new wing was constructed. From 1983 to 1991, Sheraton managed the hotel and many of the public areas, guest rooms, and bathrooms were refurbished, giving the resort the American-style comfort lacking in most Spanish hotels. However, the lobby, halls, public rooms, lounges and sitting rooms, with their marble floors, Oriental area rugs, antique furnishings and priceless art, have been left intact. They retain a feeling of Old World elegance. The Husa hotel chain took over in 1991. Although Husa still manages Son Vida, it is owned by a German investment group that also owns and operates Arabella Golf & Spa Resort, an impressive resort located about a half-mile away that shares the same golf course. Son Vida is open all year. During 2005 and part of 2006, the hotel underwent expansive renovations to all guest accommodations and public areas. Temperatures in February go down to the low 50s, and in the summer they reach the high 80s.

Accommodations

Most of the164 accommodations which include 12 suites have balconies that afford magnificent views.

The guest rooms have air-conditioning and heating, direct dial telephones, internet connectivity, oversized, flat-screen TV with satellite and movie channels, mini-bars, wall safes and a writing desk. Bathrooms include a steam shower and a choice of bathrobes and amenities from Hermes and Bulgari. Guests in the suites enjoy 24-hour butler service.

The conference facilities, with eight meeting rooms that can accommodate up to 400 people offer simultaneous translations, projectors, screens, hostesses and secretarial services.

Restaurants, Lounges, and Entertainment

Breakfast is available on the balconies from room service, or buffet-style in the Es Castell restaurant. Offering panoramic views over the Bay of Palma, Es Castell features Mediterranean cuisine for both lunch and dinner. During the warmer months, lunch is served on the adjoining open-air patio overlooking the swimming pool.

Es Vi, the charming bodega, features a choice of 800 wines.

In the evenings, the elegant bar, Armas offers piano music. It has an adjoining outdoor terrace with swings looking out at Palma Bay that is a delightful spot for before-dinner cocktails. Evening entertainment includes classical concerts, dance bands and folklore presentations. Guests can also relax in the George Sand cigar lounge; and during the winter months, afternoon tea is served at the Salon Real.

Sport Facilities

In addition to three freshwater pools, there is an indoor pool, sauna, steam room and gymnasium. A masseuse is available. The outdoor pool area is stocked with comfortable lounges, is adjacent to the bar and restaurant, and offers fantastic views for guests basking in the warm Mallorcan sun.

Below the pools are four tennis courts. Two 18-hole golf courses are available to guests with guaranteed starting times and reduced green fees. Both are near the hotel; and a riding stable is 15 minutes from the hotel.

A beauty farm offers facials, acupuncture, massage therapy and rejuvenating treatments. For the youngsters there is a playground and children's pool.

Miscellaneous and Environs

There is a jewelry and fashion shop at the resort, as well as, a men's and women's hairdresser. Several times each day, the courtesy bus transports guests into Palma and leaves them at Jaime III Street, the main shopping area.

Although some guests prefer to rent cars, the 5- to 10-minute taxi ride into Palma costs only 10 euros, and the 9-mile ride to the airport costs only a few euros more. The resort will arrange airport transfers and limousine service on request.

Son Vida offers its international clientele Old World elegance with up-to-date modern comforts, spacious accommodations and Continental food and service in subdued picturesque surroundings close to the Spanish resort town of Palma.

Castillo Hotel Son Vida
07013 Palma de Mallorca
Islas Baleares, Spain
Tel. +34.971-493-493
Fax +34.971-493-494
E-mail: info@hotelsonvida.com
Web: www.hotelsonvida.com

SPAIN

HOTEL ARTS BARCELONA

Rising 44 stories above the newly developed Olympia Marina Village, overlooking the sparkling waters of the Mediterranean is the magnificent Hotel Arts, a showpiece for contemporary Catalan and Spanish artists. Over 1000 innovative paintings, murals, sculptures and other objects d'art grace the public areas, as well as every guest accommodation. Set in front of the hotel, like a ship's maiden-head, is the famous sculpture of a fish by Frank Gehry that has become a modern-day landmark for Barcelona.

The hotel is owned by HOVISA, a subsidiary of Deutschebank, but managed by the Ritz-Carlton chain. The name "Ritz-Carlton" was not used so as not to confuse the property with another hotel in Barcelona named "The Ritz". After a pre-opening of a portion of the hotel in 1992 in time for the Olympics, the property officially commenced operations in 1994, and received major renovations and refurbishments in 2003-2004.

Although technically not a resort (as I define "resort" in this book) but a high-rise with an exposed glass and steel exterior, the property has extensive garden terraces enhanced with Mediterranean plants, olive and fruit trees, and is located adjacent to a vast expanse of beach and the Olympic Marina. Within short walking distance are dozens of small restaurants, and, from the hotel entrance, guests have direct access to the Casino of Barcelona.

The airport is a 20-minute drive from the hotel; and, a 15-20-minute walk will take you to the city center.

Accommodations

The 482 spacious, beautifully appointed accommodations are composed of 397 485-square-foot deluxe rooms, 56 645-foot executive suites, and 27 one-two-and three-bedroom, duplex apartments and two presidential suites ranging in size from 1,610 to 4,815 feet. 75 of the rooms and suites connect and four are designed for the physically handicapped.

The rooms and suites on floors 30-33 enjoy access to "The Club", a venue where for an additional $150 per night, guests enjoy five separate complimentary food presentations, soft drinks, and wines, newspapers, expedited check-in and check-out and special concierge service.

Every accommodation includes a vestibule, a state-of-the-art remote control cable television with C/D, DVD and stereo system, a private safe, a refrigerator/mini bar, P.C. and fax connections, two phones with voice mail, bed-side controls for all lights and window shades, enormous closet, dresser and storage space and a lounging area. Guests will be delighted with the large marble bathrooms that boast double vanities, a bathtub, a separate shower stall and toilet/bidet compartment, terry robes and slippers and an impressive assortment of toiletries and other bathroom amenities.

Located on the top ten floors with sweeping vistas of the city and sea, the giant duplex apartments, impeccably furnished and adorned with impressive art collections and flowers, can accommodate large families, several couples, as well as dignitaries traveling with an entourage. Each has a spacious living

room, a full-size dining room, an entry way with a guest bath and a fully equipped kitchen on the first floor with bedroom/bathroom suites on the upper level. Butler service and access to The Club lounge is also included.

The 14,000 square-foot ballroom with 4,600 feet of pre-function area can accommodate 1,350 persons "theater-style", 750 in a classroom arrangement and 1,000 for a banquet. This room can be subdivided; and, a 3,450- square-foot junior ballroom with 1,700 feet of pre-function space is also available.

Dining, Entertainment and Lounges

In 2004, the hotel recreated its dining options. The indoor/outdoor Café Veranda continues to serve extensive buffet breakfasts daily with a special brunch on Sundays. The semi-open air Marina Restaurant, pool-side, will offer seafood specialties, Tapas, salads, sandwiches and pizzas during the warmer months.

Enoteca, a fine-dining lunch and dinner restaurant (opened Monday-Friday) features Mediterranean cuisine, as well as, a wine list with over 350 great wines, an oenophile's haven.

The most "happening" venue in Barcelona for both lunch and dinner (Wednesday-Sunday) – the place to see and be seen – is Arola's, a casual, relaxed restaurant and bar featuring an extensive wine list and traditional Catalan cuisine designed by Madrid's two-star Michelin chef, Sergi Arola.

Bites offers tapas, sandwiches and salads throughout the day and a continental breakfast each morning. The locale for liquors, malt whiskeys and fine cigars accompanied by musical entertainment is The Bar, and for traditional "high tea" in the late afternoon, head for The Salon.

For variety, Barcelona offers a plethora of international restaurants throughout the city with dozens of small bistros within walking distance.

Sport Facilities

During the warmer months, the nice-sized swimming pool/lounge area overlooking the beach and marina is a delightful place to relax and soak up a

few rays while attendants provide chilled towels, bottled water and apples. Nearby is a hot plunge pool. Those who prefer a colorful beach and the sea are only a few steps away from the best public beach area in Barcelona.

Tennis, golf, bicycling, sailing and windsurfing can be readily arranged by the concierges. Presently there is a fitness center with cardio and exercise machines, large men and women's changing room/lounge relaxation areas with steam, sauna, and a solarium, and a hair salon. Located on the 42nd and 43rd floors is The Spa by Six Senses Spa at Hotel Arts offering body and facial treatments in eight treatment rooms along with wet areas which include sauna, steam, a vitality pool and ice fountain.

Miscellaneous and Environs

Hotel Arts is located in the center of Marina Village which was constructed for the 1992 Olympics. This is the most modern area of the city with excellent restaurants specializing in seafood and regional dishes, a small-craft marina, shops and a long strand of beach.

On the hotel premises are shops featuring jewelry, boutique merchandise, Hediar gastronomic products and gifts, sundries and logo items. There is a modern shopping center only minutes from the

hotel, and visitors to Barcelona will enjoy walking down the colorful Ramblas Promenade with its souvenir shops, boutiques, flower stalls, small restaurants and art displays.

Places of interest include the Picasso Museum, Gaudi's Sagrada Familia Church, The Gothic Quarter, and a panoramic ride on the aerial cable car.

Temperatures range from the 70s and low 80s in the summer down to the 40s and 50s in the winter.

Hotel Arts is one of the most exquisite hotel structures in the world offering its guests impeccable service and incredibly comfortable accommodations in Barcelona's most modern, upscale locale.

Hotel Arts Barcelona
Carrer de la Marina 19-21
08005 Barcelona, Spain
Tel. 34 93 221 1000
Fax. 34 93 221 1070

SPAIN

HOTEL FORMENTOR

From the moment you reach the top of the mountain and look out at the lovely peninsula of Formentor, where pine-studded hills reach down to crystal-clear waters, you realize you are observing one of the most scenic spots in the world. Hotel Formentor, with an enviable position near the beach and a mountain backdrop, marvelous gardens, and areas of dense forests, represents an ingenious blend of man-made elegance and unspoiled natural beauty. Whether you are sunning at the pool, dining at the outdoor balcony restaurant, or sipping a drink at the patio bar, you will be treated to a breathtaking panorama of tropical flowers, tall pines blue waters, and green-clad mountains.

Formentor is a peninsula located at the northeast portion of Mallorca, about 40 miles from the main city of Palma. For centuries, the area was owned by the Costa family, wealthy Spanish land barons. In 1929, Argentinean Adan Diehl purchased the land and built the original hotel, and since the day it opened it has been frequented by dignitaries from all over the globe. Winston Churchill, a frequent guest had a suite bearing his name. After experiencing numerous financial difficulties, the resort was purchased by the Buades family in 1954. They expanded some of the facilities, and the family continues to own and operate Hotel Formentor today. Over the years, various refurbishing and renovations have taken place.

Accommodations

There are 117 guest rooms, seven of which are designated superior. In addition, there are three, two-bed room and 15, one-bed room suites and one grand apartment. 15 of the rooms and suites have balconies or terraces that afford magnificent views of the gardens, mountains and sea. Each guest ac-

commodation includes twin beds convertible to a queen, ample storage, a writing desk, satellite television with CNN, a refrigerator/mini-bar, a private safe, a hair dryer and terry bathrobes and slippers.

Although the lobby, public rooms, and gardens are decorated with expensive marbles, antique pieces, and area rugs, the rooms are sparsely appointed and would not be considered luxurious. Because the prices here are not expensive by world standards, I would recommend a suite. Those traveling with children will find the suites especially preferable. The large marble-floored meeting area can accommodate up to 500 people, and the in-house movie theater seats 127.

Restaurants, Lounges, and Entertainment

Breakfast is served in the rooms or buffet-style at the main dining room, a semi-open-air balcony that looks out over the pool, forests, and beach.

Lunch is available in the dining room à la carte or at the beach restaurant, which features a large buffet.

Dinner is served in the main dining room, and jackets and ties are required here, as well as at the indoor/outdoor Grill Room by the pool. Food and service at the Grill Room are superior and more international. MAP is available at a reasonable separate charge. However, this does not apply to the Grill Room.

Tea, coffees, wines and other beverages are served in the terrace gardens throughout the day and evening. Also, in the evening there is piano music in the dining room and at the salon.

Sport Facilities

The pool area is picturesque, surrounded by flowers and trees. There are two freshwater pools (one with a shallow wading area), comfortable lounges, a bar, and a children's playground.

The beach, a few steps away, is one of the best in Spain. Lounges, umbrellas and cabanas can be rented. A small shop and the resort's beach-side restaurant are also located here. Water-skiing, sailing, and windsurfing are available.

Hotel Formentor has five tennis courts (two of which are illuminated for night play), a tennis pro and clubhouse, and a rather sparse miniature golf course. However, an 18-hole regulation golf course is located 10 miles away. Recently sauna, steam, massage, a hairdresser and a small exercise facility were added.

Miscellaneous and Environs

The drive from the airport near Palma takes about 60-70 minutes. Because there is little need for a car at the resort, you may prefer taking a taxi, which currently costs about $95. Those who wish to explore the numerous shops, restaurants, and large hotels in Palma can stay overnight in Palma, as commuting from Formentor is time consuming and expensive. On the premises are a designer boutique and a sundry-logo shop.

Don't miss taking a side trip to Drach Caves. They are among the most excavated and interesting caverns in the world, featuring fascinating arrays of stalactite and stalagmite formations, underground lakes, and an underground concert followed by a boat ride.

Hotel Formentor is open from spring through the fall. There is a high concentration of guests from Germany, England, and Spain. On my last visit, there were many children enjoying themselves with their parents.

The owners of Hotel Formentor have dedicated themselves through the years to preventing commercialism in the area and preserving this wonder of nature. They have resisted more profitable uses of the land. Those who seek a dignified Spanish resort in one of the world's most picturesque settings will enjoy the quiet elegance of Hotel Formentor.

Hotel Formentor
Playa de Formentor
07470 Puerto de Pollenca
Mallorca, Spain
Tel. 34 971-899-100
Fax 34-971-865-155

SPAIN

MARBELLA CLUB HOTEL GOLF RESORT & SPA

Continental, cosmopolitan, and sophisticated are all apt terms to describe this famous resort, known throughout the world for its international clientele, spacious and luxurious accommodations, beautiful grounds, and fine service. Located on the Costa del Sol on the Golden Mile between Puerto Banus and Marbella, this property boasts 300 days of sun per year, with temperatures ranging from the mid-50s in winter to the mid-80s in summer.

Built in 1954 by Prince Alfonso Hohenlohe as a haven for his personal friends, the Marbella Club Hotel, Golf Resort and Spa soon became popular with experienced travelers from France, Britain, Germany, Italy, and Spain, as well as the United States. The Marbella Club consists of numerous whitewashed Andalusian-style buildings, bungalows, and suites tucked away in the midst of subtropical gardens, a beach club, and a lovely outdoor patio restaurant. It is under the same ownership as Puente Romano, which was built in 1978, a half-mile away.

Accommodations

At a cost of millions of dollars, all existing accommodations were renovated and many new guest rooms were added in the mid-1980s, 1990s and early 2000. Presently, there are 84 deluxe rooms, which are extremely spacious with twin or double beds, sitting areas, balconies or terraces, closets, & mini-bars, radios, color satellite televisions, individual wall safes, tropical-style furnishings, and marble bathrooms. The 37 suites are similar, except they have separate sitting rooms. The 16 villas contain from two to five bedrooms with twin beds and separate parlors. All have private gardens, and some have private heated swimming pools. Villas most recently added are ultra-deluxe, decorated in shades of cream and light blue with fine fabrics and each includes a private garden and heated pool.

There is a convention facility designed to accommodate up to 120 people, and additional, larger facilities at Puente Romano.

Restaurants, Lounges, and Entertainment

The Marbella Club has three eating venues. Near the entrance to the property and the main lobby is the Winter Garden/Grill, with a summer outdoor garden patio. The outdoor terrace restaurant, with its pink tablecloths, cane chairs, Spanish tile, olive trees, palms, flowers, and chirping birds, offers the most beautiful, charming, romantic atmosphere imaginable. Here you can enjoy a buffet breakfast with fruits, juices, freshly baked croissants, breads, cheeses, Champagne and coffee, as well as a romantic candlelight gourmet dinner served Mediterranean-style with piano, guitar, or harp music in the background. Chef Juan Galvez boasts one Michelin star. The adjoining cocktail lounge is a favorite gathering place for before-dinner drinks.

At lunchtime, the beach club offers a sumptuous buffet featuring gazpacho, paella, grilled meats, fowl and fish, giant prawns and lobster tails, seafood, salads, cheese, and tempting desserts. There is also a snack bar at the upper garden pool.

In keeping with the Spanish tradition, lunch is served from 1:30 p.m. to 3:30 p.m., and most guests enjoy dinner between 9:00 p.m. and 11:00 p.m.

In 2003, the chic, casual MC Café was added featuring contemporary Euro-Asian-fusion cuisine between 10:00 a.m. and midnight. Guests can opt for modified American Plan for 85 euros or Full American Plan for 145 euros.

Sport Facilities

The resort has a fresh water pool in the gardens near its main restaurant (which is heated in winter) and another heated, fresh-water pool down at the beach club, where guests can enjoy drinks, snacks, or a buffet lunch. Unfortunately, the beach, like those all over the Costa del Sol, is not terrific; the water is a bit cool and the sand is not very inviting. However, the resort does bring in white sand for their area of the beach; and water sport enthusiasts can make arrangements for water-skiing, windsurfing, paddleboats, and catamarans. The club has its own pier, permitting small craft to dock.

There are nine golf courses in the vicinity of Marbella. The resort completed its own 18-hole, David Thomas-designed golf course in 1999, with reduced green fees for guests. There is a riding stable located here, exclusively for hotel guests. A spa facility was recently added at the beach club and offers a Thalasso-therapy indoor therapeutic pool, sauna, steam and various health and beauty treatments. An excellent tennis facility with an exercise room is available at the nearby Puente Romano Tennis Center, which belongs to the same company.

Miscellaneous and Environs

The resort is 37 miles from the Malaga airport and planes fly in regularly from Madrid and other European capitals.

There are numerous shops and an art gallery at the resort and additional shops at Puente Romano next door, as well as a very attractive shopping area at Puerto Banus, a marina village five miles south of Marbella, where visitors can stroll along a harbor filled with elegant yachts and surrounded by lovely architectural developments, charming restaurants, and shops.

Villa Tiberio, an exceptional, romantic Italian restaurant with outdoor gardens, is only a short walk from the hotel.

The Marbella Club is one of the most luxurious, picturesque, Continental-style resorts in Europe. Well-heeled guests from all over the globe make reservations at this special property months in advance in order to partake of the exceptional accommodations, fine dining and exceptional service.

Marbella Club Hotel – Golf Resort & Spa
Boulevard Prince Alfonso von Hohenlohe
Carratera de Cadiz 177
29600 Marbella, Malaga, Spain
Tel. (34) (95) 282-2211
Fax (34) (95) 282-9884
E-mail: hotel@marbellaclub.com
Web: www.marbellaclub.com

SPAIN

HOTEL PUENTE ROMANO

Several miles to the west of the resort town of Marbella, lying between the towering Sierra Blanca Mountains and the blue Mediterranean Sea, is the lush, elegant Puente Romano resort. Built in 1978 by the owners of the nearby Marbella Club, Puente Romano's low-rise, white-washed, Andalusian-style guest accommodations adorned with flowers are set amidst acres of trees, shrubs, waterfalls, pools, streams, and luxuriant gardens.

In addition to the shops, restaurants, and bars that surround the Plaza Romana near the lobby, there are three distinct pool areas, a large beach club with a restaurant and water sports, and a tennis-health club complex.

Accommodations

The resort is composed of 193 large demi-suite deluxe rooms and 81 suites spread throughout 19 acres of subtropical gardens. The furnishings are done in a tasteful Mediterranean Spanish style. Each guest room includes a large porch, several closets, beamed ceilings, an electronic wall safe, color satellite television, a separate sitting area, a pantry with refrigerator/mini-bar, and marble bathrooms with separate toilet compartments, double sinks, tub/shower combinations, and numerous complimentary amenities.

There are 12 meeting rooms, which can each accommodate up to 600 people.

Restaurants, Lounges, and Entertainment

At El Puente, next to the Plaza Romana below the lobby, guests can partake of a buffet breakfast, which includes fresh fruits, juices, rolls, meats, cheeses, and other breakfast fare and breakfasts can be enjoyed through room service on your patio.

Lunch is one of the highlights of the day. The buffet lunch at the beach club includes gazpacho, numerous salads, seafood, cheeses, paella, grilled meats, fish, Spanish delicacies, and an assortment of tempting desserts. Families with children may opt for the hamburgers, hot dogs, salads, and snacks served by the main pool and at the tennis club.

At dinnertime, El Puente offers an international à la carte menu and Roberto Ristaurante features haute-Italian cuisine. Nightly during the summer months, a variety of folklore shows accompany dinner at La Plaza Restaurant. At the Cascada Bar next to El Puente, there is a singer and piano player in the evenings.

Sport Facilities

There are three attractive swimming pools set in the gardens and a children's wading pool, each surrounded by comfortable lounges. The main pool, which is heated during the winter, has a drink and snack bar. There are also numerous lounges and an array of water sports offered at the beach club, including water-skiing, windsurfing, and catamarans in the summer.

The large tennis and fitness complex includes 10-tennis and 4-paddle courts, an exhibition court, and a pro shop. There is a sauna, Turkish bath, and masseuse here, as well as a gymnasium and Pilates studio.

As mentioned in the section on the Marbella Club, horseback riding is available two and a half

miles away, and the resort has special golf arrangements with several golf courses in the area.

Miscellaneous and Environs

The Malaga airport is 25 miles away. If you do not elect to rent a car, a taxi ride costs about $70.

There are numerous shops at the resort, including men's and women's boutiques, hairdressers, a florist, a drugstore, leather shops, realtors, and banks. Visitors will enjoy exploring the charming harbor town of Puerto Banus, five miles away, as well as the atmospheric cities of Seville, Granada, Cordoba, and Madrid.

Puente Romano is one of the most complete, lush, full-facility resorts in Europe. Couples and families will enjoy the lovely grounds, comfortable and spacious accommodations, and fine food and service.

Hotel Puente Romano
Carretera de Cadiz Km177
29602 Marbella, Spain
Tel. (34) 952-820-900
Fax (34) 952-775-766
E-mail: hotel@puenteromano.com
Web: www.puenteromano.com

BADRUTT'S PALACE

Ideally situated on a hill overlooking St. Moritz, surrounded by tall pines and the giant Rosatch Mountain Range, and across the street from shops and bistros, Badrutt's Palace is both a winter and summer resort.

Owned and operated by the Badrutt family since it opened in 1896, the original hotel has had numerous additions through the years. Although the main structure is quite old, the public rooms are lavishly furnished with antiques, and all the guest rooms have a fresh, modern feel. There are marvelous views of the lake and mountains from the porches of some guest rooms, from the restaurants, and from the lounging area around the pool. The resort is open from mid-December until the beginning of April, taking advantage of the winter ski season. It is also open during the warmest part of the summer, from the end of June until the end of September. In 1999, Rosewood Hotels assumed management.

Accommodations

There are 165 guest rooms, which include 30 full and junior suites. Each accommodation is a little different. The 20 rooms in the late 1980s' addition are more modern, whereas those in the original hotel building are more traditional. However, all are large and tastefully and originally furnished. They have antiques and modern pieces, comfortable beds with down pillows and quilts, radios, plasma televisions, complimentary mini-bars, direct-dial telephones with voice mail, large closets, modern bathrooms, makeup areas, seating areas, and welcome gifts of flowers, fruit cake, and mineral water. The full

suites, which are large apartments with separate bedrooms, living rooms, wardrobes, and porches, are furnished with expensive antiques and artwork. Most of the guest rooms facing the lake, and many facing the city, have a private balcony or terrace. Be certain to ask for a room facing the lake.

There are eight meeting rooms, the largest of which can seat 320 people.

Restaurants, Lounges, and Entertainment

For breakfast, you have your choice of room service, or you can dine in the restaurant looking out at the lake and mountains. Lunch is served in the elegantly beautiful main dining room and the grill room (in winter). These adjoin each other and look out at the lake. In the summer, lunch is also served on the outdoor porch of Chesa Veglia, a converted farmhouse that dates back to 1658, and on the outdoor porch by the pool, where you can order salads and barbecued meats. Drinks and snacks are available all day at the Acapulco Snack Bar, which overlooks the indoor pool. A lighter lunch is also served inside at the Acapulco Snack Bar, when it is not being served at the Acapulco Terrace, next to the outdoor pool.

Dinner is available year-round in the main dining room, Le Restaurant, and the informal Patrizier-stuben at Chesa Veglia. The Patrizierstuben offers excellent Swiss specialties and international food and wines in a casual atmosphere. In the winter, the formal grillroom and informal pizzeria at Chesa Veglia are also open, as is the rustic K-Bar and the Italian Trattoria in the main hotel. Wherever you

dine at Badrutt's Palace, the food is top-notch gourmet, the service is good, and the wine list will knock your socks off. When I last reviewed the resort, they were still featuring a nice selection of classified Bordeaux from the 1970s and 1980s, Burgundies from the 1970s and 1980s, and numerous other and more rare vintages. These bottles weren't available for any price at the specific châteaus when I was in France. During the winter, guests can enjoy the famous new-style cuisine at Nobu at Badrutt's Palace.

In the evenings, the Kings Club Disco opens at 10:30 p.m., the hot spot for nightlife in St. Moritz.

Sport Facilities

During the summer, you can enjoy three outdoor tennis courts, a small outdoor pool, a unique giant indoor pool with an adjoining cave-like kiddie pool, windsurfing, sailing, and fishing on the lake (a half-block down the hill), horseback riding and pony rides five minutes away, an indoor squash court, sauna, masseuse, a small gym, an indoor golf driving and putting facility, horse-drawn carriage rides, and two 18-hole golf course that are a 10-minute drive from the hotel. Joggers will be delighted with the 2½-mile run around Lake St. Moritz. There is an additional charge for most activities.

During the winter, the hotel has its own ice-skating rink and will shuttle you to 40 miles of ski runs, two bobsledding runs, and two sleigh rides only minutes away. There is a private ski school and ski rental on the premises.

This is a good resort for children. In addition to all of the other facilities described above, there is a playground, a children's counselor, video games, Ping-Pong, pony rides, the lake, and surrounding parks.

Miscellaneous and Environs

Badrutt's Palace owns numerous designer boutiques located in front of the hotel and across the street. Many other boutiques, watch and jewelry shops, and chocolate stores are in the area. A hairdresser and beauty salon are on the premises.

To reach St. Moritz, you can fly into Zurich or Milan and then take a three- or four-hour ride by car or train. Also, a private airport is located just 10 minutes from the hotel. There is also a scenic bus ride available from Menaggio or Lugano.

Badrutt's Palace is one of the more elegant traditional resorts in the world. It is an expensive but fashionable place "to see and be seen," popular with European aristocracy. It has fresh, comfortable guest rooms, good service, gourmet cuisine and wines, an unusually large variety of facilities for a European hotel, and a breathtakingly beautiful setting.

Badrutt's Palace
Via Serlas 27
CH-7500 St. Moritz, Switzerland
Tel. 41-81-837-1000, (800) 223-6800
Fax 41-81-837-2999
E-mail: reservations@badruttspalace.com
Web: www.badruttspalace.com

SWITZERLAND

BEAU-RIVAGE PALACE

This elegant, traditional European grand hotel, which originally opened its doors in 1861, is set in its own beautiful 10-acre park overlooking Lake Geneva in the heart of the Swiss resort area of Lausanne, Switzerland. But for the towering mountains across the lake, the abundance of green parks filled with beautiful flowers, and the moderation of tourists, this deluxe lakeside resort is reminiscent of the French seaside resorts at La Boule, Deauville, Cannes, Beaulieu, and Nice.

The reception area has ornate marble columns, and all the lounges and salons are expensively furnished with traditional pieces incredibly well maintained. Over the course of the last eight years, the hotel has undergone a comprehensive restoration program, which has instilled a renewed vibrancy. The program includes the addition of a 125-car underground parking lot. The $65-million renovation and updating of the rooms and public areas gave the entire hotel a fresh look, though it retains a traditional décor, and this is the factor that sets the Beau-Rivage Palace above many other European grand dames.

Accommodations

The hotel has 169 guest rooms that vary in size and décor, including 29 suites. Most distinctive are the seven lavish top floor suites, each created to be different and unique in style. Nearly all the rooms, bathrooms and suites were totally renovated, air conditioned, redecorated and modernized in the 1990s and are among the most comfortable quarters to be found in Europe.

Each guest room is air conditioned and spacious, with generous wardrobe space, tasteful French period furnishings, a mini-bar, cable television, private safe and modern bathroom with bathrobes and complimentary toiletries. Most accommodations have balconies and Jacuzzi tubs. The junior suites are extravagant, with exquisite furnishings, original antiques, crystal chandeliers, and stereos. The executive suites have everything previously described plus an enormous separate living room, guest bath, and hall space that must be seen to be believed. The Presidential Suite, Somerset Maugham, (re-

opened in 1998), is decorated in the Napoleon III style with a modern staircase to a private rooftop terrace.

There are 11 conference facilities that accommodate from 8 to 600 guests. The Grand Salon, with its stained-glass cupola, is one of the more impressive ballrooms in Europe. All of the conference and meetings rooms were elegantly refurbished and air-

conditioned between 1997 and 1998, and a new high-tech conference center was opened.

Restaurants, Lounges, and Entertainment

Both lunch and dinner are offered at La Rotonde, the gourmet restaurant overlooking the park with a breathtaking view of Lake Geneva and the French Alps, or informally at the Café Beau Rivage, a Parisian-style brasserie, and the "in place" of Lausanne for tasting French and Swiss regional cuisine. An additional restaurant exclusively for hotel and spa guests opened in 2006.

To meet with friends at cocktail time, guests can choose between the Bar Anglais, with its typically British décor, located on a patio overlooking the gardens, or the simply named Le Bar. Both provide musical entertainment with a piano player. In addition, there is a wine bar where an extensive choice of Swiss and French wines are served by the glass together with snacks.

The resort can arrange an exclusive dinner party aboard Le Montreux steamboat while cruising Lake Geneva.

Sport Facilities

In December 2005, the Beau-Rivage Palace opened its Cinq Mondes Spa. The 15,000 sq. ft. full-service destination spa has nine treatment rooms, including a private spa suite reserved for couples. The Cinq Mondes Spa combines traditional well-being and beauty rituals drawn from Japanese, Ayurvedic, North African, Taoist and Balinese techniques. The founder of Paris-based Cinq Mondes, Jean-Louis Poiroux, traveled the world for ten years to create

signature treatments from great traditions, including a Taoist Face Care-Massage and Bain Japonais d'Arômes et de Fleurs® (Total relaxation at the hammam, in a bath of colored light combining the benefits of chromotherapy and personalized essential oils). Cinq Mondes also offers beauty salon services.

The new spa space includes two swimming pools in the gardens, one indoor and one outdoor.

The Beau-Rivage also has a children's playground and two tennis courts. Joggers will appreciate the long path that winds around Lake Geneva immediately in front of the hotel. The concierge can arrange boat rides on the lake, water-skiing, horseback riding and golf on nearby courses.

Miscellaneous and Environs

On the premises is a jewelry store. The unique Olympic Museum is only a five-minute walk from the hotel. Lausanne is 36 miles from the airport in Geneva and an easy ride on the autoroute. The Beau-Rivage Palace is located right on the lake in the resort area of Ouchy. The immediate area consists of large public parks and gardens, numerous hotels, shops and indoor/outdoor cafés.

The proprietors of the Beau-Rivage Palace also own another lake-side hotel, La Residence, next door. This elegant, yet intimate, gem, surrounded by private gardens with its own outdoor pool and restaurants, offers 75 rooms and junior suites at tariffs considerably lower than its big sister. Guests at both establishments enjoy reciprocal privileges.

Couples and families traveling through Switzerland who are looking for an elegant, traditional, resort hotel with ultra-luxurious accommodations, excellent food, service and facilities in a pleasant typical European resort area will be pleased with the Beau Rivage Palace.

Beau-Rivage Palace
Place du Port 17-19
1006 Lausanne-Ouchy
Switzerland
Tel. (41) 21 613-33-33, Fax (41) 21 613-33-34
E-mail: reservation@brp.ch
Web: www.brp.ch

LE MIRADOR KEMPINSKI

This lovely country manor, set on a hillside 1,200 feet above Vevey on Lake Geneva (Lac Leman), between Lausanne and Montreux was built in 1904 and for decades was known as Hotel Mon Repos. In 1970, an American entrepreneur, Joseph Segel, acquired the manor house, changed the name, and spent the next 20 years developing and converting the facility into a world-class resort.

In 1990 the property was sold to Mariya Co. of Japan; however, Segel reacquired the resort three years later and embarked upon a $25-million renovation, which preceded the 1994 reopening of Le Mirador as one of Europe's most luxurious spa destinations. In 1998, the resort was acquired by LHS, a German corporation with headquarters in Atlanta, Georgia. In 2003, Le Mirador joined Kempinski Hotels & Resorts.

Although the property itself is only 12 acres, it is surrounded by vast expanses of pastures, vineyards, and wooded paths. To the left of the manor house is an annex built in the 1970s, the location of numerous guest rooms and a large garage, with an underground connection to the rest of the hotel. To the right are the indoor/outdoor pool, the casual Le Patio restaurant, the fine dining restaurant Le Trianon, the health club and the Givenchy Spa, all of which are also connected to the other buildings.

Public areas are richly appointed with elegant furnishings, period pieces, paintings, and other works of art. Almost every area, including the restaurants, lounges, pool, conference room, terraces, and guest rooms, enjoys panoramic views of the lake, villages, and surrounding snow-capped Alps.

The entire staff is extremely hospitable and helpful, and you will not experience any of the formality and stuffiness that exists in many comparable Swiss resorts.

The atmosphere is casual even though you are surrounded by elegance and every conceivable amenity.

Although this is an idyllic haunt for couples seeking a magical setting with impeccable food, service, and amenities, 40 percent of the clientele is made up of high-level business groups who are attracted by the high-tech conference/meeting facilities and excellent fitness/spa programs.

Accommodations

Seventy-four elegantly decorated and lavishly appointed air-conditioned rooms including six large suites, most of which include private balconies, are located in the original manor house and in the 1970s-vintage east wing. Every accommodation is equipped with a bedside remote control permitting guests to operate the window shutters and awnings, the "do not disturb" indicator, and all bedroom and bathroom lights.

Facilities and amenities include remote control, multi-language cable televisions with special in-house information displays and VCRs, electronic wall safes, fully stocked refrigerator/mini-bars, pant presses, multi-function telephone systems with personally assigned telephone numbers, and marble bathrooms with tubs, showers, hair dryers, magnifying mirrors, heated towel racks, fluffy terry-cloth robes, slippers, and quality toiletries.

The room and bathroom configurations vary. Those in the main manor house tend to be a bit larger and some include separate sitting areas and shower stalls. However, the rooms in the east wing all have balconies and enjoy superb vistas of the lake and Alps, whereas some of the standard rooms in the main building have semi-obstructed views. The Presidential suite and the two one-bedroom suites are sumptuous with Jacuzzi tubs, wet bars, and large living rooms. The junior suites are also magnificent with multiple balconies. They would be designated "one-bedroom" or "full-suites" at other establishments.

As indicated previously, the resort adapts especially well for high-level business meetings. Of the 18 high-tech, state-of-the-art meeting rooms, one can accommodate 120 people theater-style, and another has floor-to-ceiling glass windows with electronic shutters looking out over Lake Geneva. These could be among the best conference facilities in Europe and include chair-side personal computers, connection to the Internet, simultaneous translators, teleconferencing, hi-tech screens, and other equipment. It is possible for a group to reserve the entire east wing for its guests and provide private banquets catered by the main kitchen.

Restaurants, Lounges, and Entertainment

Le Patio is the casual restaurant above the health club next to the pool. When weather permits, the outdoor umbrella-protected tables on the terrace overlooking the lake are particularly pleasant. Breakfast, which is included in the room rates, is served here buffet-style with a selection of à la carte specialty items available at an additional supplement. As an alternative, breakfast can be enjoyed in your room or on your private balcony.

Lunch, dinner, and snacks are also served at Le Patio and special theme dinners are frequently featured.

Le Trianon is the elegant dining room with floor-to-ceiling picture windows, permitting a magnificent view over the lake and surrounding Alps, featuring traditional haute cuisine. The à la carte signature items are amplified by a special "menu of the day" where you can sample several courses exemplifying the versatility of the chef. The restaurant has received one star from Guide Michelin.

Oenophiles will appreciate the choice of 600 international wines from the resort's 7,000-bottle cellar.

A piano player entertains nightly in the panoramic, intimate bar and lounge next to the dining room.

Sport Facilities

A glass-domed indoor swimming pool enjoying the heated rays of the sun and flowing out to the outdoor pool offers guests the simulated sensation of swimming in the clouds above Lake Geneva. The pool has steps leading down to the fitness center and spa facility. The selection of exercise equipment and cardiovascular machines is impressive, as are the men's and women's locker rooms, which include steam rooms, saunas, whirlpools, and showers. Exercise classes and aqua aerobics are offered and guests can arrange for a personal trainer.

The resort boasts one of Europe's finest health spa facilities, Givenchy Spa, featuring 40 different treatments that include body massages, jet spray, aromatherapy, leg and foot reflexology, hydrotherapy, loofah, herbal wraps, aloe body wraps, cellulite firming, color therapy, tanning beds, revitalizing and anti-stress treatments, facials, and an assortment of other services.

A "Golf-Star" simulator is located at the fitness center and a golf pro offers clinics at the resort or will arrange for a tee time at the 18-hole golf course near the hotel, or at any one of the seven other courses along or near the lake. Three super-surface tennis courts are located at the tennis club about a half-mile down the road from the resort and basketball and volleyball courts are located near the spa. Hiking and jogging are possible on the hilly roads and paths surrounding the property; however, you may prefer running along the lake either in nearby Vevey or Lausanne. A funicular railway regularly runs up and down the mountain, terminating near the lake at Vevey. During the winter months, the staff will arrange skiing either on Nordic trails that lace the countryside or on a glacier at Les Diablerets.

The combination of fitness, spa, and conference facilities render Le Mirador Kempinski especially desirable for health-conscious business groups and health/fitness-oriented social groups.

Miscellaneous and Environs

In addition to all of the spa services, there is a hairdresser salon and a small boutique that carries a variety of designer clothes, Le Mirador Kempinski signature items, and sundries. Serious shoppers will prefer to visit nearby Lausanne or Geneva. Boat rides around Lake Geneva (Lac Leman) offer a scenic option for exploring the cities and villages located on the lake. Visitors may also enjoy visiting the medieval town of Gruyeres and Château de Chillon, the castle immortalized in Byron's "Prisoner of Chillon."

To travel to the resort, your best option is to fly into Geneva where you can rent a car. If you prefer, Le Mirador Kempinski will arrange for a private limousine (one to four persons, $200), a minibus (one to eight persons, $330), or its private helicopter ($450 per person). It is possible to take a train from Geneva to Vevey, where arrangements can be made to transport you to the resort by limousine or minibus; or, if you are traveling light, a less expensive option is the funicular railway that transcends the mountain from Vevey to the station, a few minutes' walk from Le Mirador Kempinski. Everything considered, renting a car for transportation to the resort and to explore the area is your most conven-

ient and least expensive choice. The drive from the airport takes approximately 50 minutes.

Commencing in 1999, the resort features tours on Lake Geneva on its private yacht. There is free shuttle service transporting guests to and from Vevey and Montreux.

Le Mirador Kempinski offers a special club membership to locals, which permits them to use the facilities. Thus, you will encounter guests who may not be residing at the hotel. During the main season, July 1 to August 31, more couples and families visit the resort; however, during the remainder of the year, the majority of guests are affiliated with business groups. About half the patrons are European and half from North America.

In early 2006 the resort opened the Centre Medical Mirador offering cutting-edge medical and cosmetic treatments designed to combat the signs of ageing, as well as, the Centre of Esthetique Denistry.

Le Mirador Kempinski is a very special Swiss retreat enjoying a panoramic mountain setting away from the larger cities. The excellent, concerned service, superior cuisine, sumptuous accommodations, exceptional spa and convention facilities, and casual yet elegant environment will appeal to the most discerning resort-traveler.

Le Mirador Kempinski
CH-1801 Mont Pelerin, Lake Geneva
Switzerland
Tel. 41-21-925-1111
Fax 41-21-925-1112
United States: 1 (800) MIRADOR
E-mail: mirador@attglobal.net
Web: www.mirador.ch

SWITZERLAND

PALACE HOTEL, GSTAAD

In the image of a medieval castle set atop a steep hill, the Palace Hotel looks down at its fief – the uniquely charming Swiss village of Gstaad, with its rustic chalets decorated with beautiful flowers, intersected with flowing rivers and streams, surrounded by sloping mountains that are green-clad with enormous towering pines in summer, converting to snow-white ski slopes in the winter. This is the little Swiss town from the storybooks that travelers too often overlook in favor of the more cosmopolitan cities.

The Palace Hotel is an unusual combination of rustic warmth and comfort amidst elegance, taste and conviviality. Sitting on nine acres, the original building was constructed in 1911 and has been renovated frequently. It is owned and managed by the Scherz family. The staff is most congenial and takes an interest in the comfort of their guests. The architecture and decor of the hotel and surrounding village seems to be what others seek to imitate when attempting to portray typical Switzerland.

In addition to its incredible charm and beauty, this is a resort where things are happening. Knowledgeable travelers come from all over the world to enjoy the ambiance, activities, facilities, accommodations, food and service.

Accommodations

The 102 guest rooms vary in size, ranging from comfortable to very large. There are 29 junior, 4 luxury, 2 one-bedroom, 2 two-bedroom and 1 three-bedroom Penthouse suites. All accommodations are done in Swiss Baroque – a style that fits the surroundings. All have new carpeting, beamed ceilings and a cozy rustic feel. In every room, there are sitting areas, large wardrobes, 38-channel televisions with CNN and closed-circuit movies in English, refrigerators and mini-bars, clock radios and comfortable, well-equipped bathrooms with hair dryers, robes, slippers, magnifying mirrors and numerous amenities.

The suites and about two-thirds of the rooms have balconies. The Penthouse Suite is magnificent and possibly the most luxurious ever built in an Alpine resort. Next to the main hotel are 10 chalet-style condominiums built in the 1990s. These 1,700- to 2,300-square-foot palatial apartments come complete with stocked kitchens, dining rooms, two to four bedrooms, private garage space and full hotel service. There are seven meeting rooms, and the largest can seat up to 350 people.

Restaurants, Lounges, and Entertainment

Breakfast is available in the dining room or from room service and is included with the room rate.

Lunch is served in the main dining room and on the Grande Terrace. When weather permits, breakfast and lunch, and often dinner, are also served at the large semi-covered Grande Terrace overlooking the park and mountains. Grilled meats, salads and sandwiches are featured during the summer by the pool on umbrella-covered tables.

For dinner, guests can choose either the large three-section main dining room, the more casual Sans Cravate (where no jacket is required) and the Grill Room. The Grill Room is a very romantic candlelight dining room with pink tablecloths, rustic

decor, music and dancing. The cuisine is superb in all of the dining rooms. The wine list is extensive.

After dinner, you can have drinks in the bar adjoining the Grill Room and dance to a combo or go to the disco. In the winter, an informal fondue restaurant, Le Fromagerie, is also open.

Sport Facilities

During the summer months, guests can take advantage of the four clay tennis courts and the program of tennis instruction, the Olympic-size outdoor pool, the squash court, the summer skiing on Diablerets Glacier, the 18-hole golf course 10 minutes away, the skeet- and trap-shooting range three miles away, the year-round L-shaped indoor pool, the saunas, the steam room, the massages and the exercise equipment. Health and beauty treatments are to be found in the Beautymed Centre within the hotel, provided by the famous "Clinique La Prairie" of Switzerland.

In the winter, there are 60 ski lifts in the area. The Palace Hotel has a bus that – for a small charge – will transport guests to those facilities away from the resort and to the train station in town. Joggers will enjoy running along the narrow river that runs through the town, affording a scenic backdrop.

Miscellaneous and Environs

There are hairdressers, a boutique, a jewelry store and display windows in the hotel. A five-minute walk down the hill will take you into the heart of the town, which runs for about a mile. The town has representative stores from all the major watch manufacturers, boutiques, food shops and numerous bistros and restaurants. As indicated earlier, Gstaad is a "car-free," storybook Swiss town with flowers, chalets, gardens and streams. It is easy to walk around, and whichever direction you walk, you will see lovely mountains and forests.

To travel to Gstaad, you fly into Geneva or Zurich and take a few hours' drive or train ride. The train stops at both airports.

Many families vacation here, and on my last visit there were dozens of teens, preteens and young adults – unusual for European resorts. The activities and facilities lend themselves to families.

Gstaad is one of those rare, exquisitely picturesque, charming little towns that must be seen to be believed, and the Palace, though expensive, is one of those rare, rustic, yet elegant resorts with deluxe accommodations, good sport facilities, excellent cuisine, friendly and efficient service and a wonderful overall ambiance.

Palace Hotel
3780 Gstaad, Switzerland
Tel. (41) 33-748-5000
Fax (41) 33-748-5001
E-mail: palace@gstaad.ch
Web: www.palace.ch

SWITZERLAND

SUVRETTA HOUSE

Majestically nestled in the beautiful mountains of the Ober-Engadine, 6,000 feet above sea level, literally commanding the loftiest location in the Swiss resort town of St. Moritz, the Suvretta House enjoys the privacy of acres of lush green forests, scenic mountain valleys, and private ski slopes. Here, Vic and Helen Jacob manage one of the most impeccably perfect, warm, gracious, aristocratically grand resorts in Europe.

Combining the desired blend of formal and casual, the Suvretta House accomplishes service that is not only impeccable and gracious, but also homey, cuisine that runs the gamut from simple Swiss specialties and irresistible Italian pastas to top-notch Continental and French offerings, spacious accommodations that include most every amenity, sport facilities seldom found in European resorts, elegant evenings in charming surroundings with special entertainment, and just about everything else that will make your stay unparalleled.

A casual atmosphere prevails during the day, with numerous facilities for the entire family, including young children, as well as teens and preteens. In the evening, ties and jackets are required in the lobby and dining rooms, and in the winter formal dinner jackets or dark business suits are suggested. However, families or couples not wishing to dress have numerous options, including the atmospheric, elegantly casual Suvretta Club Bar and Stube immediately below the lobby.

The Suvretta House was built in 1912 by the well-known Swiss hostelers, the Family Bon, who have spent millions of dollars on renovations over the years. Although it retains its original Old World grace and charm, the public areas and accommodations offer almost every modern comfort. The entire staff, right on down from Director Jacob to the concierges, waiters, maids, and busboys, seems totally dedicated to pleasing the guests and fulfilling the motto stated in the Suvretta House brochures, "Our intention is to offer discerning guests a holiday oasis away from the daily hectic world."

Accommodations

The 189 beautifully appointed guest rooms are unusually spacious, elaborately decorated with tasteful period furniture, and afford picturesque views of the surrounding mountains and lakes. The deluxe rooms would be referred to as junior suites at most hotels. Those requiring a separate parlor can purchase two adjoining rooms and one will be converted into a sitting room.

Every double room includes exceptionally generous wardrobe and closet space, a writing desk with lamp and flowers and mirror, a sitting area, twin beds that can be made up as a double, a radio, a television, a private safe, an "e-mail" plug and telephones in the room and in the bathroom, where you will also find double sinks, a heating bar for drying towels and clothes, a scale, terry-cloth robes and a magnifying mirror. The deluxe rooms are larger and contain more furnishings, walk-in closets, and additional wardrobe areas, separate shower stalls and separate shower-bidet compartments. Thirty-five rooms have small balconies. Single rooms are somewhat smaller, with single sinks, but otherwise have a scaled down version of all the amenities. There is no refrigerator or mini-bar; how-

ever 24-hour-a-day room service will be at your door within minutes of your call.

The price structure is somewhat different from other resorts. Prices are quoted per person and not per room, and they include breakfast, plus your choice of lunch or dinner (half-pension). The rates vary depending upon the comparative level of the dollar and Swiss franc. Children under 12 receive reduced rates when residing in the parent's' room.

Although there are numerous conference rooms and ballrooms and possibilities of converting existing public areas to accommodate large gatherings, the resort only hosts large travel groups or conventions during the off season because of management's concern with offending the tranquility and comfort of its regular guests. However, smaller seminars and meetings are accepted during the slow seasons.

Restaurants, Lounges, and Entertainment

Few European hostelries can boast the diversification of restaurants and lounges found at the Suvretta House. Breakfast, which is included, is available in your room, or in The Salon Venise, where you can enjoy an impressive buffet of juices, fruits, meats, cheeses, and cereal, in addition to a large variety of homemade breads and rolls, marmalade, coffee, and tea. The freshly baked homemade breads and rolls are outstanding. During the summer months, breakfast is also served at the Suvretta Stube and on the sundeck.

For lunch, you can choose between the Suvretta Stube, the Sun Terrace by the pool (on warm summer days), the Mountain Restaurants Trutz and Chamanna,(during ski season), accessible only by chair lift up the Engadine Mountains, or the little chalet, Chasellas, located a half-mile up the road.

Traditional tea, accompanied by a pianist, is served in the lobby and main bar from 4:30 p.m. to 6:00 p.m.

In the evenings, gentlemen can don their tuxedos or dark business suits and ladies their formal dresses and dine in the exquisite Grand Restaurant with its artistic wood paneled walls and columns, crystal and brass chandeliers and large picture windows. The menu is Continental, with a diverse range of gourmet offerings, impeccably served.

Before dinner, Anton's Bar is an ideal place for a cocktail. Later in the evening it converts to a cozy club with piano music.

Guests not wishing to dress or preferring a more casual atmosphere can dine at Chasellas or in the Suvretta Stube. The Stube is part of the Suvretta Club, which includes an adjoining cocktail lounge. Although elegant in decor, the mood is casual and the Stube itself is furnished to look like a typical Swiss chalet, but with expensive paneling and comfortable furniture. Guests look out at the grounds of the resort and the mountains. On warm days, meals are served on the adjoining patios. At the Stube, the menu ranges from salads, omelets, pastas, hamburgers, sausages and fondues to superbly prepared seafood, fish and meats. Though described as the more casual restaurant, service is faultless and very concerned.

On the morning I departed from the resort, I had to make a 7:00 a.m. train. I left a wake-up call for 6:00 a.m. and requested breakfast at 6:15 a.m., that my bags be picked up at 6:25 a.m., and a taxi for 6:30 a.m. Service is so perfect that, even this early in the morning, everything went like clockwork. To my surprise, instead of a taxi, the Suvretta House transports its guests in its own limousine.

Sport Facilities

During the winter months, visitors can participate in many sports. Ski lifts and chair lifts transport hotel guests directly into the sunny Suvretta ski area. Cross-country, downhill and snowboard instructors are available on the premises, and there are training slopes behind the hotel for children and beginners. Storage facilities for ski equipment and a ski shop for rental and service are available on the hotel premises, as well as ice skating and curling. The Suvretta snow-sports school is well known throughout Switzerland.

For those not wishing to venture outside, there is a "Suvretta Sports & Pleasure" wellness and fitness club offering two sauna worlds with Finnarium, Caldarium, Sanarium, and Vaporium, a heated swimming pool, an outdoor Jacuzzi, an airy fitness room, looking out to the mountains, with body building and workout machines, massage, solarium and beauty parlor.

During the summer, guests can avail themselves of three clay tennis courts (free of charge) with tennis lessons, a golf putting, pitching and driving range and golf pro on the premises, bocci, volleyball and badminton. Nearby, there is horseback riding, two 18-hole golf courses and fishing and boating on the lake.

Joggers and hikers can choose among the trails near the resort, including a picturesque path overlooking the lake that winds through a forest for 1 ½ miles into town.

All in all, this is an amazing facility for a European resort. It is especially well suited for children. The youngsters can be watched throughout the day by governesses in a large playroom complete with many games and toys. Outside, there is a large playground with swings, slides and the usual equipment. For children ages 3 to 10, hamburgers, cheese sandwiches, pizza, pasta and other acceptable fare are available in the children's own restaurant, the "Teddy Club," and rates for children are very favorable. For the preteens and teens, there is an electronic game room, a special social area, and, of course, all the facilities described earlier.

Miscellaneous and Environs

There are several stores on the premises, including men's and women's boutiques, a perfume-cosmetic store, a beauty shop, a ladies' and men's hairdresser, a kiosk selling souvenirs, magazines, cigarettes and candies, and a ski shop. A complimentary hotel bus transports guests regularly into the center of St. Moritz, which is only a five-minute ride. Here, there are numerous stores, banks, restaurants and hotels to explore.

To reach Suvretta House, you can fly into Zurich or Milan, and then take a three- or four-hour ride by car or train from Zurich, or a scenic bus ride from Milan via Lake Como. The hotel's limousine picks guests up from the St. Moritz railroad station or the nearby airport at Samedan, where smaller craft can fly in from Zurich.

Suvretta House is open from mid-December to the beginning of April, during the ski season, and from the end of June to mid-September, taking advantage of the warmest days of summer. The weather is variable in St. Moritz, and I have seen temperatures in August drop from the high 70s down to the 30s, together with an impressive summer snowfall, so come prepared.

Couples or families with children who are seeking out a charming winter ski resort or a full-facility summer resort in Switzerland will be totally delighted with this gem. Service and attitude here are the best of any resort in the world, and this goes a long way toward guaranteeing a pleasant vacation. This is a resort that is secluded and private, yet accessible in minutes to the excitement of St. Moritz. However, my bet is that once you arrive, ensconce yourself in the sumptuous accommodations, taste the superb cuisine, participate in the many facilities, and become enchanted by the gracious hotel staff, you will not wish to leave.

Suvretta House
Via Chasellas
CH-7500, St. Moritz, Switzerland
Tel. 011-41-81-836-3636
Fax 011-41-81-836-3737
E-mail: info@suvrettahouse.ch
Web: www.suvrettahouse.ch

VICTORIA JUNGFRAU GRAND HOTEL & SPA

The traditional Victoria Jungfrau Grand Hotel and Spa is located in the middle of the town of Interlaken, overlooking the peaks of the Jungfrau and the Bernese Oberland Alps. Built in 1865 by Edouard Ruchti, a member of the Swiss Parliament who wished to establish a palatial hostelry in the country, the hotel is now owned by public Swiss corporations which also own the Palace Lucern. During the 1990s, this regal property underwent extensive refurbishing and renovations to all of the guest accommodations and public areas, including the addition of one of the world's finest health spas and fitness/well-being centers.

The resort is actually two separate buildings, the Victoria and the Jungfrau, that are inter-connected by a newly-constructed, art-deco lobby. The public rooms of the Victoria are decorated in wood, area carpeting and antiques. The Jungfrau is done in colorful marble with expensive period furniture. Together, they are possibly the most elegantly furnished hostelries in Switzerland.

Considered by knowledgeable travelers to be one of the most impeccable establishments in the world, it is internationally acclaimed and it is located in the heart of the internationally renowned resort community of Interlaken, a focal point for skiers, mountain climbers, and travelers seeking winter and summer outdoor activities in the surrounding areas.

Accommodations

The 116 standard rooms, 68 junior suites and 28 duplex, one-bedroom, two-bedroom and magnificent tower suites are among the most expensively and tastefully furnished guest accommodations anywhere.

All the rooms are impeccably designed with unique decors and have radios, televisions offering a variety of programs in all languages, refrigerator, mini-bars, private safes, sitting areas and attractive bathrooms that include magnifying mirrors, hair dryers, terry robes and slippers and numerous amenities. About half of the rooms have balconies looking out to the mountains. Many of the rooms designated as standard and deluxe at this establishment would be considered junior suites at other hotels.

There are 19 conference and banquet rooms and lounges, all equipped with the necessary conference equipment for meetings and seminars. The largest room, the Versailles Ballroom, can accommodate 400 banquet-style.

Restaurants, Lounges, and Entertainment

Breakfast is served in the guest rooms or in La Terass, the bright, elegant dining room that overlooks the town of Interlaken and the Alps.

Gourmet lunches and dinners are served in La Terass. The culinary attraction of the new Jungfräu-Brasserie is a light contemporary cuisine – including specialties of the season – using only natural Swiss products. Adjoining the Jungfräu-Brasserie is the new La Pastateca, specializing in various made-to-order pastas. Cheese specialties are featured at the cozy Carnozet. When weather permits, meals, afternoon tea, coffee and pastries are served on the

open-air Collonades Terrace overlooking the city's promenade and towering mountains.

In the evening, there is quiet dancing to a piano in the Victoria Bar.

Sport Facilities

The Victoria Jungfrau Grand Hotel and Spa is located in a resort town a short distance from all winter and summer sports, including mountain climbing and horseback riding facilities, ski slopes, water sports on the lake and an 18-hole golf course.

The indoor golf and tennis complex in the Jungfrau building is very nice and includes four indoor and three outdoor courts, a pro shop and a snack bar. The exclusive Victoria Jungfrau Spa is composed of a spectacular indoor swimming pool leading out to a large sunning area, whirlpools, saunas, a steam room, solariums, numerous massage wellness and therapy treatments, state-of-the-art exercise equipment and a Clarins beauty treatment center.

Joggers and hikers can run for miles in scenic settings along the tributaries of the lake. More ambitious guests can arrange to hike or climb up famous mountains, such as the Jungfrau, the Eiger and the Wetterhorn.

Miscellaneous and Environs

In addition to its high- and low-season rates, the resort offers attractive spa, excursion and cultural events packages.

In the hotel, there is a hairstylist and a gift shop, and immediately outside the entrance are watch and jewelry stores, boutiques, souvenir and candy shops. You may wish to take a horse-and-buggy ride through the city, a cable-car ride up one of the nearby mountains, a boat ride down the lake, or a hot-air balloon ride in the park across the road from the hotel.

A visit to the Victoria Jungfrau Grand Hotel and Spa is an opportunity to experience the best of Swiss old-world charm, tradition and service in a superbly decorated establishment, while enjoying excellent dining and luxurious accommodations in the world famous resort area of Interlaken, with all of its numerous attractions.

Victoria Jungfrau Grand Hotel & Spa
CH-3800 Interlaken, Switzerland
Tel. 011-41-33-828-2828
Fax 011-41-33-828-2880
E-mail: interlaken@victoria-jungfrau.ch
Web: www.victoria-jungfrau.ch

Hyat Regency Kauai resort & Spa

APPENDIX

RATING THE RESORTS AND PRICE LIST—HIGH SEASON

The following ratings, based upon a five-point scale, are intended to assist the reader in comparing specific criteria. The stars should not be added up because such a total reading could be highly deceptive. If the size, comfort and décor of your accommodations are important, you should never consider a resort with a one-, two- or three-star room rating, no matter how marvelous the food and service or how vast the sports facilities. By the same reasoning, if food and service are important, or if you spend all of your vacation days playing golf, preference must be given to these categories.

Therefore, I must emphasize again that I am not rating the resorts as a whole, but only giving my readers a standard of comparison for accommodations, food, service, major facilities and other considerations.

Explanation of Ratings

Average Standard Room
Evaluation of an average standard (not deluxe) bedroom and bathroom, the decor including condition and tastefulness of furnishings and fabrics, temperature control for comfort, appliances and amenities, and existence or non-existence of balconies or patios, radios, televisions, refrigerators, mini-bars, private safes, robes, slippers and other extra touches.

Public Indoor Areas
Space available, tastefulness of decor and condition of furnishings, existence or non-existence of artwork and special touches, and whether or not the resort accomplishes the feeling it intends to portray.

Service and Attitude
Competence, training and attitude of employees in the restaurant, at reception, maid service and at the special facilities at the resort. Does it work?

Dining Facilities Available
Number of choices for different restaurants at the resort as well as diversity of food offerings, atmosphere and prices charged.

Dining Quality
How good is the resort's top-touted restaurant as to gourmet quality, presentation and atmosphere, as well as the general quality and caliber of the food offered in its other restaurants.

Sport Facilities
The existence, proximity and quality of a full range of sport facilities such as golf, tennis, water sports, bicycling, jogging, horseback riding, aerobics, exercise machines, spa, etc.

Outside Grounds
Size, beauty, lushness and imaginative design of outdoor acreage available to guests.

Swimming Pools
Size, beauty, design and imagination of pool, comfort of surrounding lounge area, and adaptability of pool for serious swimmers.

Beach and Swimming
Quality of sand, lushness of flora and size of beach, as well as clarity, temperature and desirability of water for swimming.

Rating for Singles
Availability of facilities desirable to singles, and actual patronage by singles.

Rating for Children
Availability of facilities, activities, programs and counselors for children, adaptability of other adult facilities for children's needs, and actual patronage by children.

Quick Reerence to the Resorts:
Explanation of Codes

A – A large, full-facility property with expansive grounds offering an impressive variety of sport activities and facilities, as well as dining options.

B – An elegant, refined hostelry offering exceptional service and dining with special appeal to connoisseurs.

C – An especially intimate, romantic resort ideal for honeymooners and other lovers.

D – An ideal resort for families with special facilities and programs for children.

E – A larger property that offers exceptional facilities for business meetings and conventions.

★★★★★ ✦	means nothing better exists
★★★★★	Superb
★★★★	Very good
★★★	Good
★★	Fair
★	Poor

The Breakers, Florida

Price List—High Season

2006-2007 Prices high season—two persons in a room (**non-high season rates can be one-third to one-half less at many resorts). Prices are quoted in dollars or euros.

Because the dollar and euro are constantly changing in value when translated into other currencies, tariffs will vary from time to time.

Codes:

EP	=	European Plan-no meals.
EP+Br	=	breakfast only.
MAP	=	Modified American Plan-breakfast +one meal.
FAP	=	Full American Plan-all meals

$ = U.S. dollars
€ = euros
£ = Pound Sterling

THE CONTINENTAL UNITED STATES

	Code	Page	Average Standard Room (comfort, size, decor)	Public Indoor Areas (appearance, decor)	Service and Attitude	Dining Facilities Available	Dining Quality	Sport Facilities (golf, tennis, and so on)
The Boulders Resort	A, C	26	★★★★+	★★★★	★★★★★	★★★★	★★★★+	★★★★
Fairmont Scottsdale Princess	A, E	30	★★★★★	★★★★★	★★★★★	★★★★+	★★★★+	★★★★★
Four Seasons Resort Scottsdale	A, C	34	★★★★★	★★★★	★★★★★	★★★	★★★★	★★★★★
Hyatt Regency Scottsdale	A, D, E	37	★★★+	★★★★+	★★★★★	★★★★+	★★★★+	★★★★★
The Phoenician Resort	A, E	41	★★★★★	★★★★★	★★★★★	★★★★★	★★★★★/★★★★+ a)	★★★★★
Four Seasons Resort Aviara	A, B, E	45	★★★★★	★★★★★	★★★★★	★★★★	★★★★+	★★★★★
La Costa Resort and Spa	A, E	49	★★★★	★★★★+	★★★★	★★★	★★★★+	★★★★★
The Lodge at Pebble Beach	A, E	53	★★★★★	★★★★	★★★★	★★★★	★★★★	★★★★★
Rancho Valencia	B, C	56	★★★★★	★★★+	★★★★★	★★	★★★★★	★★★
The Ritz-Carlton, Laguna Niguel	A, B, E	60	★★★★+	★★★★★	★★★★★	★★★★★	★★★★★	★★★+
The Broadmoor	A, E	64	★★★★+	★★★★	★★★★	★★★★★	★★★★★	★★★★★
The Peaks Resort & Golden Door Spa	A, E	68	★★★★★	★★★★★	★★★★	★★★	★★★★	★★★★★
The Breakers	A, B, E	72	★★★★+	★★★★★	★★★★★	★★★★★	★★★★	★★★★★
Colony Beach and Tennis Resort	A, D	76	★★★★★	★★★	★★★★	★★★	★★★★★	★★★★★/★★★ b)
Doral Golf Resort and Spa	A, E	80	★★★★★	★★★★★/★★★+ c)	★★★★+	★★★★	★★★★★	★★★★★
Hyatt Grand Cypress	A, D, E	84	★★★★	★★★★★	★★★★★	★★★★★	★★★★	★★★★★+
Villas of Grand Cypress			★★★★★					
The Ritz-Carlton, Naples	A, B, E	89	★★★★★	★★★★★	★★★★★+	★★★★★	★★★★★	★★★★
The Ritz-Carlton Golf Resort								
The Greenbrier	A, E	93	★★★★/★★★★★ d)	★★★★+	★★★★★	★★★★★	★★★+/★★★★	★★★★★

THE CARIBBEAN, BAHAMAS, AND BERMUDA

	Code	Page	Average Standard Room (comfort, size, decor)	Public Indoor Areas (appearance, decor)	Service and Attitude	Dining Facilities Available	Dining Quality	Sport Facilities (golf, tennis, and so on)
Cap Juluca	C	100	★★★★★	★★+	★★★★	★★★★	★★★★	★★★
Malliouhana Hotel	B, C	105	★★★★★	★★★★+	★★★★+	★★★	★★★★★+	★★★★
Curtain Bluff	C	109	★★★★/★★★★+ d)	★★★+	★★★★	★★	★★★★+	★★★★+
One&Only Ocean Club	B, C	113	★★★★★	★★★★	★★★★	★★★	★★★★+	★★★★★
Sandy Lane	A, D, E	117	★★★★★+	★★★★★	★★★★	★★★★	★★★★★	★★★★★
Fairmont Southampton	A, E	121	★★★★/★★★★+ d)	★★★★+	★★★★★	★★★★★	★★★★★	★★★★★
Casa de Campo	A, E	125	★★★★	★★★	★★★+	★★★★★	★★★★	★★★★★+
Four Seasons Resort, Nevis	A, E	130	★★★★★	★★★★★	★★★★	★★★★	★★★★★	★★★★★
El Conquistador Resort	A, D, E	134	★★★+	★★★★+	★★★★	★★★★★	★★★★★	★★★★★
Las Casitas	B	139	★★★★★	★★★	★★★★★	★★★★★	★★★★	★★★★★
La Samanna	B, C	143	★★★+/★★★★ d)	★★★+	★★★★	★★	★★★★	★★★★
Caneel Bay (St. John)	C	146	★★★/★★★+ d)	★★★	★★★+	★★★★	★★★+/★★★★	★★★
Little Dix Bay (Virgin Gorda)	C	150	★★★+	★★	★★★	★★	★★★★	★★★
Peter Island Resort and Spa	C	154	★★★+/★★★★	★★★+	★★★★	★★★	★★★+	★★★
The Ritz-Carlton, St. Thomas	B, D	158	★★★★★	★★★★★	★★★★★	★★★★	★★★★	★★★★+

a) Marie Elaines ★★★★★ / other ★★★★+   b) Tennis ★★★★★ / other ★★★
c) Spa ★★★★★ / Country Club ★★★+/★★★★   d) some / others   e) beach/adjoining public beach

PRICE LIST – HIGH SEASON

Outside Grounds (beauty and size)	Swimming Pools	Beach and Swimming	Rating for Singles	Rating for Children under 12
★★★★★	★★★★	n/a	★	★★
★★★★★	★★★★★	n/a	★★★	★★★★★
★★★★★	★★★✦	n/a	★	★★★★✦
★★★★★	★★★★★	n/a	★★★★★	★★★★★
★★★★★	★★★★★	n/a	★★★	★★★★
★★★★★	★★★★	n/a	★	★★★★
★★★★★	★★★★	n/a	★★	★★★★
★★★★	★★★	★★	★	★★★
★★★★★	★★★	n/a	★	★
★★★★✦	★★★★	★★★	★★★	★★★
★★★★✦	★★★	n/a	★★	★★★★
★★★✦	★★★✦	n/a	★★★★	★★★★★
★★★★	★★★★	★★★	★★★	★★★★★
★★★★	★★★	★★★★★	★	★★★★★
★★★★★	★★★★✦	n/a	★★	★★★★
★★★★★✦	★★★★★✦ / ★★★★✦	n/a	★★★	★★★★★✦
★★★★	★★★★	★★★★	★★★	★★★✦
★★★★✦	★★★★	n/a	★	★★★✦

Price Liste – High Season: Standard Double Rooms	Price Liste – High Season: Suites & Villas
n/a	$ 199 - $ 5.000 (EP)
$ 449 - $ 499	$ 609 - $ 719 (EP)
$ 495 - $ 675	$ 795 - 44.500 (EP)
$ 430 - $ 610	$ 850 - $ 3.240 (EP)
$ 625 - 725	$ 1.650 - $ 3.500 (EP)
$ 355 - $ 465	$ 575 - $ 4.000 (EP)
$ 300 - $ 500	$ 700 - $ 3.000 (EP)
$ 580 - $ 790	$ 975 - $ 2.750 (EP)
n/a	$ 470 - $ 5.000 (EP)
$ 475 - $ 975	$ 875 - $ 4.000 (EP)
$ 330 - $ 495	$ 540 - $ 3.195 (EP)
$ 405 - $ 465	$ 895 - $ 995 (EP)
$ 470 - $ 880	$ 800 - $ 3.980 (EP)
n/a	$ 395 - $ 1.475 (EP)
$ 164 - $ 319	$ 528 - $ 1.007 (EP)
$ 279 - $ 479	$ 695 - $ 5.800 (EP)
n/a	$ 350 - $ 5.800 (EP)
$ 499 - $ 659	$ 1.049 - $ 1.209 (EP)
$ 399 - 549	$ 619 - $ 709 (EP)
$ 389 - $ 524	$ 540 - $ 5.369 (EP)

PRICE LIST – HIGH SEASON

Outside Grounds (beauty and size)	Swimming Pools	Beach and Swimming	Rating for Singles	Rating for Children under 12
★★★★★	★★★	★★★★★✦	★	★★
★★★★★	★★★★	★★★★★	★	★★★★
★★★★★	★★★✦	★★★★✦	★	★
★★★★★	★★★★	★★★★✦	★	★★
★★★★★	★★★★★	★★★★★	★★	★★★★
★★★★✦	★★★✦	★★★★✦/★★★★★✦ c)	★★★	★★★★★
★★★★★	★★★★	★★★★✦	★★★	★★★★
★★★★★	★★★★	★★★★	★★	★★★★★
★★★★	★★★★★	★★★★★	★★★★	★★★★✦
★★★★★	★★★★	★★★★★	★	★
★★★★★	★★★★	★★★★✦	★	★
★★★★★	★★★	★★★★★✦	★	★★★★
★★★★★	n/a	★★★★★✦	★	★
★★★★★	★★★	★★★★★✦	★	★
★★★★★	★★★★✦	★★★★	★	★★

Price Liste – High Season: Standard Double Rooms	Price Liste – High Season: Suites & Villas
n/a	$ 750 - $ 6.450 (EP)
$ 385 - $ 850	$ 1.240 - $ 3.030 (EP)
$ 995	$ 2.095 (FAP)
$ 750 - $ 1.120	$ 805 - $ 7.000 (EP)
$ 2.700 - $ 3.600	$ 3.980 - $ 8.800 (EP)
$ 519 - $ 719	$ 819 - $ 2.849 (EP)
$ 353 - $ 385	$ 664 - $ 1.447 (EP)
$ 645 - $ 955	$ 1.550 - $ 5.400 (EP)
n/a	n/a
n/a	$ 909 - $ 1.519 (EP + Br)
n/a	$ 765 - $ 4.450 (EP)
n/a	$ 450 - $ 1.500 (EP)
$ 650 - $ 875	$ 925 - $ 4.800 (EP)
$ 1.050 - $ 1.425	$ 5.150 - $ 9.700 (FAP)
$ 699 - $ 799	$ 1.500 (EP)

MEXICO

	Code	Page	Average Standard Room (comfort, size, decor)	Public Indoor Areas (appearance, decor)	Service and Attitude	Dining Facilities Available	Dining Quality	Sport Facilities (golf, tennis, and so on)
Fairmont Acapulco Princess	A,D,E	160	★★★★	★★★★★	★★★+	★★★★★	★★★★	★★★★★
Las Brisas	C	164	★★★★	★★★	★★★★	★★★	★★★★	★★
Las Ventanas Al Paraiso	A, C	167	★★★★★	★★★★	★★★★★	★★	★★★★★	★★★★
The Ritz-Carlton, Cancun	B	171	★★★★★	★★★★★	★★★★+	★★★★+	★★★★★/★★★★ a)	★★★
Four Seasons Resort Punta Mita	A,D,E	174	★★★★★	★★★★★	★★★★★	★★★★	★★★★+	★★★★★

HAWAII

	Code	Page	Average Standard Room (comfort, size, decor)	Public Indoor Areas (appearance, decor)	Service and Attitude	Dining Facilities Available	Dining Quality	Sport Facilities (golf, tennis, and so on)
Four Seasons Resort, Hualalai	A,B,D,E	180	★★★★★	★★★★★	★★★★★	★★★★	★★★★+	★★★★★
Hilton Waikoloa Village	A,D,E	184	★★★★+	★★★★★+	★★★★★	★★★★★	★★★★★/★★★★ a)	★★★★★
Mauna Kea Beach Hotel	A, E	189	★★★★	★★★★★	★★★★+	★★★★★	★★★★★+	★★★★★
Hapuna Beach Prince Hotel	A, E	189	★★★★★	★★★★★	★★★★+	★★★★★	★★★★	★★★★★
Mauna Lani Bay Hotel	A,D,E	193	★★★★	★★★★★	★★★★+	★★★★	★★★★★/★★★★ b)	★★★★★
Hyatt Regency Kauai Resort & Spa	A, D, E	196	★★★★	★★★★★	★★★★	★★★★★	★★★★	★★★★★
The Lodge at Koele	A,B,C	200	★★★★	★★★★★	★★★★	★★★★★	★★★★★	★★★★+
Manele Bay Hotel	A,B,C	200	★★★★★	★★★★★	★★★★	★★★★★	★★★★★	★★★★★
Four Seasons Resort Maui at Wailea	A,B,E	205	★★★★★	★★★★★	★★★★★	★★★★	★★★★+	★★★★
JW Marriott Ihilani Resort and Spa	A, B, E	209	★★★★★	★★★★+	★★★★+	★★★★+	★★★★+	★★★★★
Kahala Mandarin Oriental	B, E	212	★★★★★	★★★★★	★★★★★	★★★★	★★★★★	★★★+

a) Donatoni's ★★★★★ / others ★★★★   b) Canoe House ★★★★★ / others ★★★★

PRICE LIST – HIGH SEASON

Outside Grounds (beauty and size)	Swimming Pools	Beach and Swimming	Rating for Singles	Rating for Children under 12	Price Liste – High Season: Standard Double Rooms	Price Liste – High Season: Suites & Villas
★★★★★+	★★★★★+	★★★★	★★★★	★★★★	$ 169 - $ 309	$ 339 - $ 1.599(EP + Br)
★★★★+	★★★★+	★★★	★	★★	$ 350 - $ 547	$ 684 - $ 1.710 (EP + Br)
★★★★★	★★★ ★★	★★ ★★	★	★	n/a	$ 650 - $ 5.000 (EP)
★★★	★★★★	★★★★	★★★	★★★	$ 595 - $ 949	$ 689 - $ 5.500 (EP)
★★★★★	★★★★+	★★★★	★	★★★★	$ 495 - $ 1.025	$ 1.555 - $ 10.570(EP)

PRICE LIST – HIGH SEASON

Outside Grounds (beauty and size)	Swimming Pools	Beach and Swimming	Rating for Singles	Rating for Children under 12	Price Liste – High Season: Standard Double Rooms	Price Liste – High Season: Suites & Villas
★★★★★	★★★★+	★★★	★	★★★	$ 625 - $ 925	$ 1.050 - $ 8.350 (EP)
★★★★★+	★★★★★+	★★★	★★★	★★★★★	$ 199 - $ 639	$ 1.060 - $ 6.150 (EP)
★★★★★	★★★+	★★★★	★	★★★	$ 390 - $ 660	$ 675 - $ 1.650 (EP)
★★★★★	★★★+	★★★★★	★	★★★	$ 370 - $ 650	$ 1.250 - $ 7.000 (EP)
★★★★★	★★★★	★★★★	★★	★★★	$ 430 - $ 920	$ 1.800 - $ 5.900 (EP)
★★★★★	★★★★★+	★★★★	★★	★★★★	$ 465 - $ 805	$ 1.500 - $ 5.000 (EP)
★★★★★	★★★	n/a	★★	★★★★	$ 395 - $ 925	$ 800 - $ 3.800 (EP)
★★★★★+	★★★★	★★★+	★★	★★★★★	$ 395 - $ 925	$ 800 - $ 3.800 (EP)
★★★★★	★★★★	★★★★+	★★	★★★★	$ 395 - $ 890	$ 740 - $ 3.405 (EP)
★★★★	★★★+	★★★★+	★★	★★	$ 425 - $ 585	$ 850 - $ 4.500 (EP)
★★★★+	★★★★	★★★★★	★★	★★	$ 395 - $ 795	$ 1.100 - $ 4.515 (EP)

THE SOUTH SEAS, AUSTRALIA, AND FAR EAST

	Code	Page	Average Standard Room (comfort, size, decor)	Public Indoor Areas (appearance, decor)	Service and Attitude	Dining Facilities Available	Dining Quality	Sport Facilities (golf, tennis, and so on)
Hayman Resort	B,C	218	★★★★/★★★★★ a)	★★★★★	★★★★★	★★★★★	★★★★★	★★★★✦
Westin Denarau Resort	A,E	229	★★★★✦	★★★★	★★★✦	★★★★★	★★★★	★★★★★
Vatulele Island Resort	C	222	★★★★★	★★✦	★★★	★★	★★★✦	★★
The Wakaya Club	C	225	★★★★★	★★★	★★✦	★★	★★★	★★★✦
Amandari, Bali	B,C	223	★★★★★✦	★★★★	★★★★	★★	★★★★	★★
Amankila	B, C	223	★★★★★✦	★★★★	★★★★	★★★	★★★★	★
Amanusa	B, C	224	★★★★★✦	★★★★★	★★★★	★★★	★★★★	★★★✦
Four Seasons Resort Jimbaran, Bali	A, B, C	238	★★★★★✦	★★★★✦	★★★★★	★★★★	★★★★	★★★★
Four Seasons Resort at Sayan, Bali	C	241	★★★★★✦	★★★★✦	★★★★✦	★★★	★★★★✦	★★
The Ritz-Carlton, Bali Resort	A, B, C	245	★★★★★	★★★★★	★★★★★	★★★★	★★★★	★★★★
Shangri-La's Tanjung Aru Resort	A	249	★★★★	★★★★	★★★★	★★★★✦	★★★★	★★★
Shangri-La Hotel, Singapore	A,B,D,E	253	★★★★★✦	★★★★★	★★★★★✦	★★★★★	★★★★★	★★★
Bora Bora Lagoon Resort	C	257	★★★★✦	★★★✦	★★★✦	★★	★★★✦	★★★
Bora Bora Pearl Beach Resort	C	261	★★★★★	★★★✦	★★★★	★★	★★★★✦	★★★
Hotel Bora Bora	C	264	★★★★/★★★★★ a)	★★★	★★★★✦	★★	★★★✦	★★★
Inter-continental Bora Bora	C	267	★★★★✦	★★★	★★★★	★★	★★★★✦	★★
Inter-continental Moorea	C	270	★★★★/★★★★✦ a)	★★★✦	★★★★	★★	★★★✦	★★★
Le Meridien Bora Bora	C	273	★★★★★	★★★★	★★★★	★★	★★★★✦	★★
Amanpuri	C	276	★★★★★	★★★★	★★★★★	★★★	★★★★★	★★★
Banyan Tree Phuket	A, C	280	★★★★★✦	★★★★★	★★★★★	★★★★★	★★★★✦	★★★★★
Mandarin Oriental Dhara Dhevi	A,B,C,D	284	★★★★★	★★★★★	★★★★★	★★★★★	★★★★★	★★★
Mandarin Oriental Bangkok	A, B, E	288	★★★★★	★★★★★	★★★★★	★★★★★	★★★★★	★★★✦
Shangri-La Hotel, Bangkok	A, B, E	292	★★★★★	★★★★★	★★★★✦	★★★★★	★★★★★/★★★★ c)	★★★

AFRICA & INDIAN OCEAN

	Code	Page	Average Standard Room (comfort, size, decor)	Public Indoor Areas (appearance, decor)	Service and Attitude	Dining Facilities Available	Dining Quality	Sport Facilities (golf, tennis, and so on)
Four Seasons Resort, Maldives	C	298	★★★★★	★★★✦	★★★★	★★★★	★★★✦	★★★✦
Island Hideaway at Dhonakuli	C	302	★★★★★	★★★✦	★★★★	★★★★	★★★✦	★★★✦
One&Only Le St. Geran (Mauritius)	A, D, E	306	★★★★/★★★★★ b)	★★★★	★★★★✦	★★★★★	★★★★✦	★★★★★
Prince Maurice (Mauritius)	A, C	309	★★★★✦/★★★★★ a)	★★★★	★★★★	★★★★	★★★★	★★★★

a) some/others b) beach at hotel- ★★★/ beach at outer islands ★★★★★
c) Angelina ★★★★★/ others ★★★★✦ d) beach ★★★★★/ swimming ★★★

PRICE LIST – HIGH SEASON

Outside Grounds (beauty and size)	Swimming Pools	Beach and Swimming	Rating for Singles	Rating for Children under 12	Price Liste – High Season: Standard Double Rooms	Price Liste – High Season: Suites & Villas
★★★★+	★★★★+	★★★★	★★	★★★★	$ 620 - $ 980	$ 2.100 - $ 4.500 (EP)
★★★★★	★★★★	★★★★	★★	★★★★	$ 400 - $ 410	$ 870-960 (EP)
★★★★+	n/a	★★★★★	★	n/a	n/a	$ 1.338 - $ 2.192 (FAP)
★★★★★	★★★	★★★★+	★	n/a	$ 1.900 - $ 2.300	$ 2.800 - $ 7.600 (FAP)
★★★★★	★★★★	n/a	★	★	n/a	$ 650 - $ 3.600 (EP)
★★★★★	★★★★+	★★★★+	★	★	n/a	$ 650 - $ 3.600 (EP)
★★★★★	★★★★+	★★★★	★★	★	n/a	$ 650 - $ 3.600 (EP)
★★★★★	★★★★+	★★★★	★	★★★★	n/a	$ 610 - $ 2.675 (EP)
★★★★★	★★★+	n/a	★	★	n/a	$ 610 - $ 3.025 (EP)
★★★★★	★★★★★	★★★★	★	★★★★+	$ 275 - $ 420	$ 400 - $ 2.400 (EP)
★★★★	★★★★	★★★/★★★★★ b)	★★	★★★★	$ 176 - $ 240	$ 282 - $ 825 (EP + Br)
★★★★	★★★★★	n/a	★★	★★	$ 295 - $ 463	$ 608 - $ 3.315 (EP + Br)
★★★★	★★★★	★★★+	★	★	$ 455 - $ 695	$ 755 - 965 (EP)
★★★★★	★★★★	★★★★★	★	★	n/a	$ 580 - $ 850 (EP)
★★★★★	n/a	★★★★	★	★	n/a	$ 700 - $ 950 (EP)
★★★★+	★★★★	★★★★★	★	★	€ 596 - € 864	€ 829 - € 1.948 (EP)
★★★★★+	★★★★	★★★★+	★	★	€ 331	€ 410 - € 740 (EP)
★★★★★	★★	★★★★★	★	★★	n/a	€ 587 - € 796 (EP)
★★★★★+	★★★★	★★★★★+	★	★★	n/a	$ 650 - $ 7.500 (EP)
★★★★★	★★★★★	★★★★★	★	★★★	n/a	$ 500 - $ 1.100 (EP + Br)
★★★	★★★★	n/a	★★★	★	$ 350 - $ 900	$ 1.100 - $ 6.000 (EP)
★★★★	★★★+	n/a	★★★	★★	$ 350 - $ 480	$ 480 - $ 2.400 (EP)
★★★	★★★★	n/a	★★★	★★	$ 245 - $ 300	$ 390 - $ 2.720 (EP + Br)

PRICE LIST – HIGH SEASON

Outside Grounds (beauty and size)	Swimming Pools	Beach and Swimming	Rating for Singles	Rating for Children under 12	Price Liste – High Season: Standard Double Rooms	Price Liste – High Season: Suites & Villas
★★★★+	★★★★	★★★★★/★★★ d)	★	★★	$ 590 - $ 850	$ 1.900 - $ 2.500 (EP + Br)
★★★★★+	★★★★	★★★★★/★★★ d)	★	★★	€ 600 - € 790	€ 1.015 - € 2.200 (EP + Br)
★★★★★	★★★★	★★★★★	★★	★★★★	n/a	$ 1.166 - $ 7.735 (EP + Br)
★★★★★	★★★★	★★★★★	★★	★★★	$ 1.100	$ 2.200 - $ 7.034 (EP + Br)

EUROPE

	Code	Page	Average Standard Room (comfort, size, decor)	Public Indoor Areas (appearance, decor)	Service and Attitude	Dining Facilities Available	Dining Quality	Sport Facilities (golf, tennis, and so on)
Hotel Schloss Fuschl	B	322	★★★+/★★★★ a)	★★★★	★★★★+	★★★★	★★★★+	★★★★
Auberge des Templiers	B, C	326	★★★★★	★★★★+	★★★★★	★★	★★★★★+	★★
Château d'Artigny	B	329	★★★★/★★★★★ a)	★★★★★	★★★★+	★★	★★★★+	★★
Château du Domaine St. Martin	B, C	335	★★★★★+	★★★★★	★★★★★	★★★	★★★★★	★★
Château d'Esclimont	B	332	★★★★/★★★★★ a)	★★★★+	★★★★★	★★	★★★★★	★★★
Château Les Crayères	B	338	★★★★★	★★★★★	★★★★★	★★★	★★★★★+	★
Domaine des Hauts de Loire	B	341	★★★★/★★★★★ a)	★★★★+	★★★★★+	★★	★★★★★+	★★
Georges Blanc	B	344	★★★★/★★★★★ a)	★★★★	★★★★★+	★★★+	★★★★★+	★★
Hôtel du Cap-Eden Roc	A, B	348	★★★★★	★★★★★	★★★★★	★★★	★★★★★	★★★★
La Côte Saint Jacques	B	351	★★★+/★★★★ a)	★★★★+	★★★★★	★★	★★★★★	★★★
Brenner's Park-Hotel & Spa	A, B	354	★★★★★/★★★★★+ a)	★★★★★	★★★★★	★★★	★★★★★	★★★
Chewton Glenn	B	358	★★★★★	★★★★★	★★★★★	★★	★★★★★	★★★★+
Astir Palace	A	362	★★★+/★★★★	★★★	★★+	★★★★★	★★★★	★★★
Grand Hotel Quisisana	B	366	★★★★★	★★★★★	★★★★★	★★★	★★★★★	★★★
Hotel Cala di Volpe	A	370	★★★★+	★★★★	★★★★	★★★	★★★★	★★★★+
Hotel Cipriani	B	374	★★★★★	★★★★	★★★★★	★★★★	★★★★+	★★+
Hotel Splendido	B, C	378	★★★★/★★★★★ a)	★★★★	★★★★+	★★★	★★★★+	★
Splendido Mare	B, C	378	★★★★/★★★★★ a)	★★★★	★★★★+	★★★	★★★★+	★
San Pietro	B, C	381	★★★★/★★★★★ a)	★★★★★	★★★★★	★★	★★★★★	★★
Santa Caterina	B, C	385	★★★★/★★★★★ a)	★★★★★	★★★★★	★★★	★★★★★	★★
Villa d'Este	A, B	389	★★★★/★★★★★ a)	★★★★★	★★★★★	★★★★	★★★★	★★★★+
The Westin Turnberry Resort	A, B	392	★★★★/★★★★+ a)	★★★★★	★★★★+	★★★★	★★★★+	★★★★+
Barcelo La Bobadilla	A, B	396	★★★★★	★★★★★	★★★★	★★★	★★★★+	★★★★
Byblos Andaluz	A, B	399	★★★★★	★★★★★	★★★★	★★★★	★★★+	★★★★★
Castillo Hotel Son Vida	B, E	402	★★★★/★★★★★ a)	★★★★+	★★★★	★★★+	★★★+	★★★+
Hotel Arts	A, E	405	★★★★★	★★★★★	★★★★★	★★★★★	★★★★	★★★
Hotel Formentor	A	409	★★★★	★★★+	★★★★+	★★★	★★★★+	★★★★
Marbella Club	B	412	★★★★★	★★★+	★★★★★	★★★★	★★★★★	★★★★
Puente Romano	A, B	415	★★★★★	★★★+	★★★+	★★★+	★★★★	★★★★
Badrutt's Palace	B, E	418	★★★★/★★★★★ a)	★★★★+	★★★★★	★★★★★	★★★★★	★★★
Beau Rivage Palace	B, E	421	★★★★★	★★★★★	★★★★★	★★★	★★★★★	★★★
Le Mirador	B, E	424	★★★★/★★★★★ a)	★★★★★	★★★★★	★★★★	★★★★★	★★★★
Palace Hotel (Gstaad)	A, B	428	★★★★★	★★★★★	★★★★★	★★★★★	★★★★★	★★★★
Suvretta House	A, B, E	431	★★★★★	★★★★+	★★★★★	★★★★★	★★★★★	★★★★★
Victoria Jungfrau	B, E	435	★★★★★	★★★★★	★★★★★	★★★	★★★★+	★★★★★

a) some/ others   b) indoor
c) mature ★★★★/ young ★★

PRICE LIST – HIGH SEASON

Outside Grounds (beauty and size)	Swimming Pools	Beach and Swimming	Rating for Singles	Rating for Children under 12	Price Liste – High Season: Standard Double Rooms	Price Liste – High Season: Suites & Villas
★★★★	★★	★★	★★	★★★	€ 471 - € 543	€ 761 - € 978 (EP)
★★★★★	★★★	n/a	★	★	€ 140 - € 260	€ 295 - € 620 (EP)
★★★★★	★★★	n/a	★	★	€ 160 - € 410	€ 570 (EP + Br)
★★★★★	★★★★	n/a	★	★	€ 500 - € 840	€ 1.200 - € 1.600 (EP)
★★★★★	★★	n/a	★	★	€ 140 - € 380	€ 590 - € 890 (EP)
★★★★+	n/a	n/a	★	★	n/a	€ 275 - € 475 (EP)
★★★★★	★★★	n/a	★	★	€ 130 - € 270	€ 320 - € 430 (EP)
★★★	★★	n/a	★	★	€ 180 - € 425	€ 450 - € 655 (EP)
★★★★★	★★★★★	★★	★	★★	€ 450 - € 850	€ 1.050 - € 1.250 (EP)
★★★★★	★★	n/a	★	★	€ 140 - € 360	€ 420 - € 540 (EP)
★★★★	★★★	n/a	★	★	€ 245 - € 545	€ 1.150 - € 1.375 (EP)
★★★★★	★★★★	n/a	★	★★	$ 464 - $ 712	$ 712 - $ 1.312 (EP)
★★★★+	★★★★+	★★★+	★★	★★★	€ 260 - € 280	€ 910 - € 6.000 (EP + Br)
★★★★	★★★★	n/a	★★★★	★★	€ 330 - € 750	ab € 850 (EP + Br)
★★★★	★★★★	★★★★	★★	★★	€ 2.500	€ 4.900 (FAP)
★★★★+	★★★★★	n/a	★	★	€ 815 - € 1.330	€ 1.730 - € 8.330 (EP + Br)
★★★★	★★★+	n/a	★★	★	€ 1.005 - € 1.375	€ 1.634 - $ 4.711 (MAP)
★★★★	★★★+	n/a	★★	★	€ 614 - € 820	€ 1.103 - € 1.945 (EP + Br)
★★★★★	★★+	★★	★	★	€ 460 - € 670	€ 830 - € 990 (EP + Br)
★★★★★	★★	★★	★	★	€ 390 - € 670	€ 800 - € 1.200 (EP + Br)
★★★★★+	★★★★	n/a	★★	★★★+	€ 630 - € 950	€ 1.190 - € 1.850 (EP + Br)
★★★	★★★★b)	★	★★★★	★	£ 395	£ 800 (EP + Br)
★★★★★	★★★★	n/a	★	★★	€ 332 - € 391	€ 574 - € 986 (EP + Br)
★★★★★	★★★★	n/a	★	★★	€ 215 - € 450	€ 535 - € 1.435 (EP + Br)
★★★★★	★★★★	n/a	★★	★★★	€ 466 - € 983	€ 1.380 - € 4.255 (EP + Br)
★★	★★★★	★★★	★★★★	★★	€ 450 - € 675	€ 10.000 (EP)
★★★★★+	★★★+	★★★★	★	★★★★	€ 370 - € 430	€ 665 (EP + Br)
★★★★★	★★★★	★★	★	★	€ 450 - € 645	€ 645 - € 3.750 (EP + Br)
★★★★★	★★★★	★★	★★	★★★	€ 394 - € 690	€ 476-2.400 (EP + Br)
★★★	★★★	n/a	★★★	★★★	$ 375 - $ 1.750	$ 950- $ 10.000 (EP)
★★★★★	★★★	n/a	★★★	★★	€ 315 - € 520	€ 660 - € 2.335 (EP)
★★★	★★★b)	n/a	★	★★	$ 304 - $ 732	$ 800 - $ 8.000 (EP)
★★★★	★★★+b)	n/a	★★	★★★+	n/a	n/a
★★★★	★★★★b)	n/a	★★★★/★★ c)	★★★★★	€ 267 - € 493	€ 1.159 - € 2.080 (MAP)
★★	★★★★b)	n/a	★★★★	★★★	$ 490	$ 640 - $ 1.400 (EP)